What the Bible Says to the Believer

The Believer's Personal Handbook

Leadership Ministries Worldwide
Chattanooga, TN

Published by Leadership Ministries Worldwide · 3755 Pilot Point
Chattanooga, Tennessee 37416

Please address all requests for information or permission to:
Leadership Ministries Worldwide
PO Box 21310
Chattanooga, TN 37424-0310
Ph.# (423) 855-2181 FAX (423) 855-8616
E-Mail info@outlinebible.org
http://www.outlinebible.org

International Standard Book Number

Black	978-1-57407-129-0
Gray	978-1-57407-130-6
Dark Seagreen	978-1-57407-131-3
Camel	978-1-57407-132-0
Blue	978-1-57407-133-7
Paperback	978-1-57407-134-4

Printed in Italy

2 3 4 5 6 13 14 15 16 17

Dedicated

To all the believers of the world
who need and want a closer
walk with the Lord day by day

CHAPTER 1

WHAT HAPPENS WHEN YOU RECEIVE CHRIST

Contents

Chapter 1

What Happens When You Receive Christ

1. *You Are Saved—Set Free from Sin and Death and Given Eternal Life.*

> **Once you were dead because of your disobedience and your many sins. You used to live in sin, just like the rest of the world, obeying the devil—the commander of the powers in the unseen world. He is the spirit at work in the hearts of those who refuse to obey God. All of us used to live that way, following the passionate desires and inclinations of our sinful nature. By our very nature we were subject to God's anger, just like everyone else. But God is so rich in mercy, and he loved us so much, that even though we were dead because of our sins, he gave us life when he raised Christ from the dead. (It is only by God's grace that you have been saved!) (Ep.2:1-5, NLT).**

What was your life like before you received Christ? When God looked down upon you, what did He see?

a. Before conversion, you lived a life that was separated from God, lived as though you were *dead* toward God. Note the words in the above Scripture, "you were dead" (v.1). How can you be living and yet be dead? To answer this question, you need to understand that death, in Biblical terms, means *separation*. It never means extinction, annihilation, non-existence, or inactivity. Death simply means that a person is either separated from his body or from God or from both. Holy Scripture speaks of three deaths:

- *Physical death*: the separation of your spirit from your body. This is what commonly comes to mind when speaking of death. It is when life departs from your body on this earth and you are buried.

> **Just as man is destined to die once, and after that to face judgment (He.9:27, NIV).**

- *Spiritual death*: the separation of your spirit from God while you are still living on earth. This is the *natural state* of people who have not received Christ. People can even be religious and still be *spiritually separated* from God; they are dead toward God.

But she who lives in pleasure is dead while she lives (1 Ti.5:6, NKJV).

➢ *Eternal death*: the separation of a person from God's presence forever. This is the second death, the conscious, eternal separation from God that continues beyond the death of the body.

The Lord Jesus [will be] revealed from heaven in blazing fire with his powerful angels. He will punish those who do not know God and do not obey the gospel of our Lord Jesus. They will be punished with everlasting destruction and shut out from the presence of the Lord and from the majesty of his power (2 Th.1:7-9, NIV).

But the cowardly, the unbelieving, the vile, the murderers, the sexually immoral, those who practice magic arts, the idolaters and all liars—their place will be in the fiery lake of burning sulfur. This is the second death" (Re.21:8, NIV).

b. **Before conversion,** you lived a life in disobedience and sins (Ep.2:1-3). Note that it is disobedience and sins that separate you from God. To disobey means to turn aside or wander away from God and His Holy Word.

To sin means to miss the mark. It is what is meant by coming *short of the glory of God, short of His perfection and righteousness* (Ro.3:23). God is perfect, but you are imperfect. You sin; you miss the mark. You may be respectable, but you are imperfect. You are never all that you should be.

Before conversion, you lived just like the disobedient of the world (v.3). You followed the desires and passions of your flesh, gratified the longings and cravings of your sinful nature. Therefore, you were destined to face the wrath of God, doomed to eternal separation from Him.

c. **When you are converted,** you are redeemed and forgiven your sins through the death of Jesus Christ. To redeem means to deliver, buy back, or set free by paying a ransom. For example, a prisoner of war or a kidnap victim is ransomed or redeemed—saved from the threat of death. In every case, the person is powerless to free himself. He cannot make the payment demanded to liberate himself from his bondage or fate. Someone else has to pay the ransom to redeem him.

When God redeems you, the most wonderful thing happens: your sins are forgiven. The word *forgive* means to pardon, to release, to let go. Your sins are forgiven through the blood of Jesus Christ. How? Jesus died *for you.* He took the penalty of your sins and bore the punishment Himself. Consequently, your sins are removed—washed away, erased—forgiven forever.

d. **Now, you claim** to be converted—saved from sin and death and given life through Jesus Christ. There is no question, if you have truly trusted Christ as your Savior and Lord, God will give you a full and satisfying life, both now and for all eternity. This is His wonderful promise. In light of this, you should always remember *how* God saved you: through the death of His Son:

> **But God demonstrates His own love toward us, in that while we were still sinners, Christ died for us (Ro.5:8, NKJV).**

When Christ died on the cross, He died for you. He was bearing the penalty and punishment of sin for you. He was dying in your place—as your substitute—so that you would never have to face eternal death. Remember...

> **For God so loved the world, that He gave His only begotten Son, that whoever believes in Him shall not perish, but have eternal life (Jn.3:16, NASB).**

What you must do is make sure—absolutely sure—that your faith in Christ is genuine, the right kind of faith. The right kind of faith is known as a saving faith. But how can you know whether or not you have saving faith? One way to measure is to know what saving faith *is not*:

- Saving faith *is not* just believing the fact that Jesus Christ is the Savior of the world.
- Saving faith *is not* just believing history, that Jesus Christ lived upon earth as the Savior just as George Washington lived upon earth as the President of the United States.
- Saving faith *is not* just believing the words and claims of Jesus Christ in the same way that a person would believe the words of George Washington.

- Saving faith *is not* head knowledge, not just a mental conviction or intellectual commitment to Christ.

The right kind of faith, saving faith, is two things. First, saving faith is believing *in* Jesus Christ, believing in who and what He is, that He is truly the Son of God, the Savior and Lord of life. It is believing that Christ died in your place—for your sins—on the cross, and rose again (1 Co.15:3-4). It is fully trusting Him and His sacrificial death as payment for your sins. You must confess or acknowledge Jesus Christ as Savior and Lord and turn your life over to live for Him.

> **That if you confess with your mouth, "Jesus is Lord," and believe in your heart that God raised him from the dead, you will be saved. (Ro.10:9, NIV; see Ac.16:31).**

Second, saving faith is the surrender of your life to Jesus Christ. It is the surrender to live for Christ—to *obey Him* and to *live righteously* as you walk through life day by day. Anything less is not true saving faith. True saving faith is *obedience* to God's Holy Word.

> **And having been perfected, He became the author [source] of eternal salvation to all who obey Him (He.5:9, NKJV).**

As a *professing believer,* you must make absolutely sure that your belief in Christ is genuine and wholehearted, that you have a *true saving faith,* a faith that *obeys* God. If you do not know Christ personally and intimately, you will come up short.

If you sense that you do not have a true saving faith, just call upon the name of the Lord to save you and He will. He cares for you this much. No matter what you have done or how unworthy you feel, if you ask Him to forgive your sins and to save you from eternal death, He will. And the life that He gives you will be both abundant and eternal.

> **For "whoever calls on the name of the Lord shall be saved" (Ro.10:13, NKJV).**

2. *You Are Given a New Life—a New Beginning, a New Start.*

> **Therefore, if anyone *is* in Christ, *he is* a new creation; old things have passed away; behold, all things have become new (2 Co.5:17, NKJV).**

When you sincerely receive Christ as your Savior, you are actually *born again*. God gives you a new nature and makes you a *new creation*, a *new person*. Note the verse above:

a. **What does it mean** to become a new creation? It means that you actually become a new person: your whole being, nature, life, and behavior change.

- ➢ Although you were once dead to God, as a new person you become alive to God.
- ➢ Although you once had no relationship with God, as a new person you are given a special, personal relationship with God.
- ➢ Although you once were living in sin, as a new person you now live in righteousness and holiness.
- ➢ Although you once had to face eternal death, as a new person you have the assurance of eternal life. When the time for death comes, you will be immediately transferred into heaven, into the very presence of God Himself.
- ➢ Although you were once doomed to judgment and eternal separation from God, as a new person you are destined to live eternally in the presence of God.

b. **How do you become** a new creation? Note the words of verse 17: "If anyone is *in Christ*, he is a new person." It is being *in Christ* that makes you a new creature, a new creation. When you *truly believe in Christ*, God counts and credits you as being in Christ. You become identified with Him; that is, you are counted and considered to be *in Christ*.

To be *in Christ* also means that you walk and live in Christ day by day. In other words, you do not "walk after the flesh, but after the Spirit" (Ro.8:1, 4, KJV). It means that "denying ungodliness and worldly lusts, [you] should live soberly, righteously, and godly, in this present world" (Tit.2:12, KJV). It means that you bear the fruit of the Spirit (Ga.5:22-23). It means that you abide *in* Christ, that you become as connected and attached to Christ...

- as parts of the body are connected to each other (1 Co.12:12-27)
- as the branch is attached to the vine (Jn.15:4-7)

From this, it is evident that once you are *in Christ,* you are a new creation, a new person. Christ makes it possible for you to begin life all over again, to get a brand new start, a new beginning (Ep.4:22-24; Col.3:9-10).

3. *You Are Adopted As a Child—a Son or Daughter—of God.*

> **But as many as received him [Christ], to them gave he power to become the sons of God, *even* to them that believe on his name (Jn.1:12, KJV).**
>
> **But when the fullness of the time came, God sent forth His Son, born of a woman, born under the Law, so that He might redeem those who were under the Law, that we might receive the adoption as sons. Because you are sons, God has sent forth the Spirit of His Son into our hearts, crying, "Abba! Father!" (Ga.4:4-6, NASB).**

When you receive Christ into your life as Savior and Lord, Christ gives you the power and the right to become something you were not before: a child of God. You are adopted as a son or daughter into the family of God. The picture of adoption is a beautiful portrayal of what God does for you as a believer. When a child was adopted in the ancient worlds of Greece and Rome, three legal steps were taken:

a. **The adopted child** was adopted permanently. The child could not be adopted today and disinherited tomorrow. Rather, he or she became a son or daughter of the new father *forever.*

   Likewise, your adoption by God establishes a new relationship between you and God forever—that of a father and child (Ro.8:15-16). As a son or daughter of God, you actually have a living relationship with Him, a moment-by-moment access into His very presence (Ro.8:14, 16; Ga.4:6).

b. **The adopted child** immediately gained all the rights of legitimate children in the family. Your adoption by God also gives you all the rights and privileges of a genuine child of God (Ro.8:16-17; 1 Jn.3:1-2).

c. **The adopted child** completely lost all rights in his or her former family. The adopted child was looked upon as a new person—so new that old debts and obligations connected with the former family were cancelled out and abolished as if they never existed.

When you are adopted by God, you become a member of His dear family. You receive a very special relationship with other sons and daughters of God—a family relationship that binds you with other believers in an unparalleled spiritual union (Ac.2:42; Ep.2:11-22; 3:6; 4:4-6, 17-19; 1 Jn.1:3).

In addition, your adoption by God makes you a new person. Once God adopts you, you are taken out from under the authority and power of the world and its sin. You are placed as a son or daughter into the family of God and under His authority. Your old life with its debt of sin, which is death, is cancelled and wiped out (2 Co.5:17; Ga.3:23-27; Ep.4:22-24; 2 Pe.1:4).

Your adoption as a son or daughter of God will be totally fulfilled when Jesus Christ returns to establish God's kingdom on earth (Ro.8:19; Ep.1:14; 1 Th.4:14-17; 1 Jn.3:2). And the joy of your adoption will be shared by all creation on a cosmic scale (Ro.8:21). The day is coming when God will create a new heavens and earth—a perfect universe and environment—for you and the rest of His dear, holy family (2 Pe.3:10-14; Re.21:1-7).

4. *You Receive God's Spirit: Your Body Actually Becomes the Temple of God's Spirit.*

> **And I will ask the Father, and he will give you another Counselor to be with you forever—the Spirit of truth. The world cannot accept him, because it neither sees him nor knows him. But you know him, for he lives with you and will be in you (Jn.14:16-17, NIV).**
>
> **Do you not know that your body is a temple of the Holy Spirit, who is in you, whom you have received from God? You are not your own; you were bought at a price. Therefore honor God with your body (1 Co.6:19-20, NIV).**

When you receive Jesus Christ as your Savior and Lord, God sends the Holy Spirit to live within you. He is your Comforter, Helper, Counselor, and Advocate. As you walk *faithfully* in Christ day by day, the Holy Spirit...

- will fellowship and commune with you, pray & focus your thoughts on the Lord
- will stir you to become more and more conformed to the image of Christ

Note exactly what Scripture says (1 Co.6:19-20): as a true believer, your body actually becomes the temple of the Holy Spirit. The word *body* is singular; each believer is a temple of the Spirit of God. Note three facts:

a. **The Holy Spirit** literally dwells within your body.

> **For we are the temple of the living God. As God has said: "I will live with them and walk among them, and I will be their God, and they will be my people" (2 Co.6:16, NIV).**

b. **The Holy Spirit** is a gift from God. You do not receive the Holy Spirit by working for God. You receive the Spirit of God as a gift from Him.

> **Peter *said* to them, "Repent, and each of you be baptized in the name of Jesus Christ for the forgiveness of your sins; and you will receive the gift of the Holy Spirit (Ac.2:38, NASB).**

c. **God lays claim** to your body. You no longer own your body, not any more. As the Scripture says, Jesus Christ bought your body (1 Co.6:19-20). The idea is that Jesus Christ *bought* you in the marketplace of slavery. He paid the ransom for you. He bought you out of your enslavement to sin, death, and hell.

   Christ's death met all the demands of God's perfect justice. God's justice was completely satisfied when Jesus Christ took your sin upon Himself, died for you, and suffered the hell of separation from God for you. Therefore, you are set free, liberated from sin, death, and hell. You are now free to live righteously and eternally in God's presence—all because Jesus Christ paid the price for you. He paid your ransom. Once you receive Christ as your Savior and Lord, your body belongs to God. For this reason, you are to...

   - glorify God in your body by obeying God's holy commandments—living thoughtfully, righteously, and godly in this present world (Tit.2:11-14).
   - glorify God in your spirit by worshipping Him through prayer and praise as you walk throughout each day (Lu.9:23; 18:1; Jn.4:24; Ep.5:20; 6:18; Ph.4:4; 1 Th.4:16-17; Ps.29:2; 98:1).

5. *You Are Given a Sense of Permanent Peace and Rest.*

> **Peace I leave with you, My peace I give to you; not as the world gives do I give to you. Let not your heart be troubled, neither let it be afraid (Jn.14:27, NKJV).**
>
> **Then Jesus said, "Come to me, all of you who are weary and carry heavy burdens, and I will give you rest. Take my yoke upon you. Let me teach you, because I am humble and gentle at heart, and you will find rest for your souls. For my yoke is easy to bear, and the burden I give you is light" (Mt.11:28-30, NLT).**

To be at peace means to be calm, tranquil, secure, in harmony with others. It is used here to convey that a person is bound, woven, and joined together with God and others in a state of serenity and unity.

The Hebrew word for peace is *shalom*. It means freedom from trouble. Even more, it means experiencing the greatest good, enjoying the very best, possessing all the inner worth possible. It means wholeness and soundness. It means prosperity, in the widest sense, especially the spiritual prosperity of having a soul that blossoms and flourishes.

a. **There is the peace of the world** (Jn.14:27). This is a peace of escapism, of avoiding trouble, of refusing to face facts, or an outright denial of problems. It is a peace that is sought through physical pleasure, self-indulgence, acquiring worldly possessions, positive thinking, or any number of other outlets.

b. **There is the peace of Christ and of God**. This is, first, an inner peace, a peace deep within. It is a tranquility of mind, a composure, a peace that is calm in the face of difficult circumstances and situations. It is more than just a feeling or an attitude of self-control. It is a deep-seated, unwavering consciousness of God's presence and protection.

   Second, God's peace is a conquering peace. It is a peace that is independent of conditions and environment. No sorrow, no danger, no suffering, no experience can take away the conquering peace of God.

> **These things I have spoken to you, that in Me you may have peace. In the world you will have tribulation; but be of good cheer, I have overcome the world" (Jn.16:33, NKJV).**

Third, God's peace is the peace of assurance. It is the peace of unquestionable confidence, the peace with a sure knowledge that one's life is in the hands of God and that all things will work out for good to all who truly love God.

> **And we know that all things work together for good to them that love God, to them who are the called according to his purpose (Ro.8:28, KJV).**

c. **How do you secure** the peace of Christ and of God? Scripture says you must do six things:

- You secure peace by believing in Christ and by being justified—counted righteous—before God.

> **Therefore being justified by faith, we have peace with God through our Lord Jesus Christ (Ro.5:1, KJV).**

- You secure peace by loving God's Word.

> **Those who love Your law have great peace, And nothing causes them to stumble (Ps. 119:165, NASB).**
>
> **These things I have spoken to you, that in Me you may have peace. In the world you will have tribulation; but be of good cheer, I have overcome the world" (Jn.16:33, NKJV).**

- You secure peace by praying about everything.

> **Do not be anxious about anything, but in everything, by prayer and petition, with thanksgiving, present your requests to God. And the peace of God, which transcends all understanding, will guard your hearts and your minds in Christ Jesus (Ph.4:6-7, NIV).**

- You secure peace by being spiritually minded.

> **For to be carnally minded is death; but to be spiritually minded is life and peace (Ro.8:6, KJV).**

- You secure peace by keeping your mind upon God.

> **You will keep *him* in perfect peace, *Whose* mind *is* stayed [kept] *on You,* Because he trusts in You (Is.26:3, NKJV).**

Finally, brethren, whatever things are true, whatever things *are* noble, whatever things *are* just, whatever things *are* pure, whatever things *are* lovely, whatever things *are* of good report, if *there is* any virtue and if *there is* anything praiseworthy—meditate on these things (Ph. 4:8, NKJV).

- You secure peace by keeping God's commandments.

"If only you had paid attention to My commandments! Then your well-being [peace] would have been like a river, And your righteousness like the waves of the sea (Is.48:18, NASB).

The things you have learned and received and heard and seen in me, practice these things, and the God of peace will be with you (Ph.4:9, NASB).

d. **The subject of peace** is often divided into three categories: (1) *peace with God*, which is secured through salvation (Ro.5:1; Ep.2:14-17); (2) the *peace of God*, which is the very peace of God Himself and that points to God as the source of peace (Lu.7:50; Ph.4:6-7); and (3) *peace from God*, the peace that God gives to dwell in your heart as you walk faithfully in Him day by day (Ro.1:7; 1 Co.1:3).

e. **Now, note** a most wonderful fact: in addition to the peace that God gives, Christ also promises to give you a deep sense of *permanent rest*—a rest of soul that passes all understanding (Ph.4:6-7). When you are laboring and weighed down with heavy burdens, exhausted, despairing, and ready to collapse, Christ promises to give you rest of soul.

Rest is available, but you have to come to Christ in order to receive it. Christ's rest is three things:

- It is a *rest of refreshment*: a rest of refreshing your body, mind, and spirit.
- It is a *rest of purpose*: a rest that settles or equips you for life, that infuses you with true purpose, meaning, and significance.
- It is a *rest of encouragement and motivation*: a rest that stirs you to live and undertake your God-given task with enthusiasm, vigor, and endurance.

Return to your rest, O my soul, For the Lord has dealt bountifully with you (Ps.116:7, NASB).

Let us therefore fear, lest, a promise being left *us* of entering into his rest, any of you should seem to come short of it (He.4:1, KJV).

6. *You Are Given the Power to Live Victoriously Over the World Day by Day.*

For everyone born of God overcomes the world. This is the victory that has overcome the world, even our faith. Who is it that overcomes the world? Only he who believes that Jesus is the Son of God (1 Jn.5:4-5, NIV).

These two verses are a great passage of Scripture, verses that should be memorized by every believer. Note that the same point is being made in every statement. A striking emphasis! Thus, the message needs to be both understood and heeded.

- ➢ The person who is *born of God* overcomes the world.
- ➢ The victory gained over the world comes through a person's *faith* in Christ.
- ➢ The person who *believes* that Jesus Christ is the Son of God is the one who wins the battle over the world.

Who is the person truly *born of God*? The person who *believes* that Jesus Christ is the Son of God. The world is overcome by *faith*. Victory is gained over the world by *faith* in Jesus Christ, by believing that Jesus Christ is the Son of God.

The one thing that we all need is victory over the world. The world is full of...

- ➢ suffering
- ➢ disease
- ➢ selfishness
- ➢ arrogance
- ➢ prejudice
- ➢ greed, injustice
- ➢ hate
- ➢ oppression
- ➢ murder
- ➢ war—all kinds of wickedness

Then there is the most fatal blow of all: corruption and death. Without exception, we are all corrupt and we all die. Therefore, the one thing we need above all else is victory over the world's corruption and death.

How, then, can you overcome the world? By *believing* that Jesus Christ is the Son of God. When you believe that Jesus Christ is the Son of God, God gives you a new heart. You are *born of God—spiritually born.* It is your faith, your belief, that overcomes the world. What does this mean? It means that you *trust God*, and when you truly trust Him...

- God will give you victory and enable you to rise above all the trials and temptations of life.

The Lord will rescue me from every evil attack and will bring me safely to his heavenly kingdom. To him be glory for ever and ever. Amen (2 Ti.4:18, NIV; see 1 Co.10:13).

- God will give you victory over all the evil forces and overwhelming obstacles in this life.

Who shall separate us from the love of Christ? *shall* tribulation, or distress, or persecution, or famine, or nakedness, or peril, or sword?...Nay, in all these things we are more than conquerors through him that loved us. For I am persuaded, that neither death, nor life, nor angels, nor principalities, nor powers, nor things present, nor things to come, Nor height, nor depth, nor any other creature, shall be able to separate us from the love of God, which is in Christ Jesus our Lord (Ro.8:35, 37-39, KJV; see Is.41:10).

- God will give you victory over sin.

No temptation has overtaken you that is not common to man. God is faithful, and he will not let you be tempted beyond your ability, but with the temptation he will also provide the way of escape, that you may be able to endure it (1 Co.10:13, ESV).

He himself bore our sins in his body on the tree, that we might die to sin and live to righteousness. By his wounds you have been healed (1 Pe.2:24, ESV).

- God will give you victory over death.

"I tell you the truth, whoever hears my word and believes him who sent me has eternal life and will not be condemned; he has crossed over from death to life (Jn.5:24, NIV).

Because God's children are human beings—made of flesh and blood—the Son also became flesh and blood. For only as a human being could he die, and only by dying could he break

the power of the devil, who had the power of death. Only in this way could he set free all who have lived their lives as slaves to the fear of dying (He.2:14-15, NLT).

- God will give you victory over the coming condemnation and judgment.

But God demonstrates His own love toward us, in that while we were yet sinners, Christ died for us. Much more then, having now been justified by His blood, we shall be saved from the wrath of God through Him. For if while we were enemies we were reconciled to God through the death of His Son, much more, having been reconciled, we shall be saved by His life (Ro.5:8-10, NASB; see Jn.3:16-18).

- God will give you victory over fear and despair and fill you with love, joy, and peace.

But the fruit of the Spirit is love, joy, peace, patience, kindness, goodness, faithfulness, gentleness, self-control; against such things there is no law (Ga.5:22-23, NASB).

- God will give you victory over Satan and all other spiritual forces.

Put on the full armor of God so that you can take your stand against the devil's schemes. For our struggle is not against flesh and blood, but against the rulers, against the authorities, against the powers of this dark world and against the spiritual forces of evil in the heavenly realms. Therefore put on the full armor of God, so that when the day of evil comes, you may be able to stand your ground, and after you have done everything, to stand (Ep.6:11-13, NIV).

7. *You Are Given Wisdom to Know How to Live and What to Do.*

If any of you lacks wisdom, let him ask of God, who gives to all liberally and without reproach, and it will be given to him (Jas.1:5, NKJV).

Sometimes you face difficulties or trials that puzzle you. You simply do not know what to do or how to resolve the problems. You need wisdom, a very special wisdom, to handle the situations.

Once you receive Christ, you are given one of the most amazing resources imaginable: God's very own presence and wisdom. If you lack wisdom—if you do not know what to do or how to handle a difficulty or trial—ask God. You are His child, His son or daughter, and He cares for you. He wants to help you through all the difficult situations that confront you. In fact, God invites you to come to Him to ask for wisdom. And when you sincerely ask, He will fulfill these three wonderful promises:

- He will give you wisdom.
- He will give you a liberal amount, an abundance of wisdom.
- He will not reproach or rebuke you—not scold you—for not knowing how to handle the trial or temptation. The idea is that God will not even question you for lacking wisdom or for not knowing what to do.

God is your Father and He wants to meet your every need. Simply ask Him and He will hear your request and your cry; He will give you the wisdom to conquer the difficulties and problems, the trials and temptations of life.

8. *You Are Given Access—an Open Door—into the Very Presence of God: The Wonderful Privilege of Prayer.*

> **Therefore, having been justified by faith, we have peace with God through our Lord Jesus Christ, through whom also we have access by faith into this grace in which we stand, and rejoice in hope of the glory of God (Ro.5:1-2, NKJV).**
>
> **Let us therefore come boldly to the throne of grace, that we may obtain mercy and find grace to help in time of need (He.4:16, NKJV).**

When you truly accept Jesus Christ as your Savior and Lord, you are immediately given *access* into the presence of God Himself. It is Christ alone who gives you this access. Christ actually brings you to God—introduces and presents you to His Father. And He negotiates peace between you and God. Through His blood on the cross, Christ justifies you. He makes it possible for God to count you righteous and acceptable to Him. As a result, you can approach and talk to God at any time in any place. And whatever you ask of the Father in Jesus' Name, He will give it to you (Jn.16:24). God will answer your prayer either by granting or not granting your request. Sometimes God simply says, "No," and expects you to trust Him. God will always do what is most beneficial for you and others. (See Chapter 5, Section C, pts.1-5, pp.182-192, for more discussion on prayer.)

9. You *Are Given a Spiritual Gift by God.*

> **We have different gifts, according to the grace given us. If a man's gift is prophesying, let him use it in proportion to his faith. If it is serving, let him serve; if it is teaching, let him teach; if it is encouraging, let him encourage; if it is contributing to the needs of others, let him give generously; if it is leadership, let him govern diligently; if it is showing mercy, let him do it cheerfully (Ro.12:6-8, NIV).**

Once you receive Christ, God gives you a very special gift or ability. Note that the gift or ability is from God. You could not attain or secure it by yourself. It is a spiritual gift; that is, it is given by the Spirit of God for spiritual purposes. It is given so that you can fulfill your task on earth. This is part of your *heritage in Christ,* the glorious privilege...

- of being given a very special task on earth
- of being given purpose, meaning, and significance in life
- of being given a special gift or ability to fulfill your task on earth

What are the gifts? Several are singled out in the above passage. But the point is this: identify your gift(s) and abilities and be faithful in using them. (See 1 Co.12:1-31; 13:1-3; Ep.4:7-16 for additional gifts bestowed upon the believer.)

a. **There is the *gift*** *of prophecy.* In the Old Testament, the gift of prophecy was the gift to proclaim and explain the will of God. The proclamation dealt with past, present, and future events. However, in the New Testament, the gift of prophecy changes dramatically. The prophet is seldom seen predicting the future. Instead, he is seen proclaiming what has taken place in the past and what has been *revealed by Christ* concerning future events. The prophet's function is to edify, exhort, and comfort. He or she is the person who proclaims and explains the Word of God...

- the living Word, the Lord Jesus Christ Himself
- the written Word, the Holy Scripture

Having said this, it should be noted that prophecy is the gift of speaking under the anointing of God's Spirit. It includes both prediction and proclamation, and neither one should be minimized, despite the abuse of the gift by some. And there is no question: the gift to predict events has been abused to the point of the ridiculous. However, the abuse of a gift does not eliminate the gift: the Spirit of God does sometimes give believers a glimpse into coming events in order to prepare and strengthen them to face the future.

However, the major function of prophecy is clearly stated by Scripture, and the truth should be learned by all believers:

> **But one who prophesies strengthens others, encourages them, and comforts them (1 Co.14:3, NLT).**

b. **There is the *gift*** *of serving or ministering* to others. This is the very practical ability to help others—to assist them in such a way that they are *built up* and truly strengthened. Most of us know a few people who are always willing to help others when help is needed and who are unusually gifted to do so. All of us can help, and all of us can develop our willingness and ability to help, but there are some believers who are especially skilled in ministering to others.

c. **There is the *gift*** *of teaching*. Teaching is the ability to explain and to ground people in the truth. The Word of God not only needs to be proclaimed by the prophet (preachers, ministers) but also explained by the teacher. People must be rooted in all the truths of God's Word day by day, week by week, and year by year. This is the teacher's task.

d. **There is the *gift*** *of exhortation or encouragement*. This is the very special ability to comfort, warn, and motivate people. The dominant factor would be the motivation and encouragement of people, the ability to stir people to make a decision for Christ and to grow in Him. It is the gift that arouses people to get up and get busy fulfilling their task for the Lord.

e. **There is the *gift*** *of giving*. This simply means the giving of your earthly possessions such as money, clothing, and food. In listing this particular gift, Scripture adds a point: it tells how you are to give. You are to give liberally and generously. The point is this: God gives some persons the special gift to make money in order to have plenty to help others and to spread the gospel around the world (Ep.4:28).

f. **There is the *gift*** *of leadership*. This person is to lead with *diligence*, which means with careful thought, zeal, desire, and concentrated attention. There is no room for laziness, complacency, or irresponsibility. Leaders are the ones who are to blaze the path for other believers, and they are to do it with fervency, hard work, and iron determination.

g. **There is the *gift*** *of mercy* or *kindness*. This is a person who is full of forgiveness and compassion for others. Note that the merciful person is to show mercy with a cheerful or joyful heart. The person with the gift of mercy...

- does not forgive grudgingly
- does not hesitate in forgiving others
- does not show mercy in an annoyed spirit
- does not show mercy in a spirit of criticism or rebuke toward the person who needs help. (This often happens when a person is suffering adversity because of unemployment, lack of education, or some other unfortunate circumstance.)

You, too, must show mercy with a cheerful and joyful heart, doing all you can to lift up a person needing mercy, kindness, or compassion.

10. *You Are Given the Great Hope of Christ's Return to Comfort, Encourage, and Sustain You.*

For the Lord Himself will descend from heaven with a shout, with the voice of an archangel, and with the trumpet of God. And the dead in Christ will rise first. Then we who are alive *and* remain shall be caught up together with them in the clouds to meet the Lord in the air. And thus we shall always be with the Lord. Therefore comfort one another with these words (1 Th.4:16-18, NKJV).

In My Father's house are many mansions; if *it were* not *so,* I would have told you. I go to prepare a place for you. And if I go and prepare a place for you, I will come again and receive you to Myself; that where I am, *there* you may be also (Jn.14:2-3, NKJV).

(See ch.9, pt.2, pp.378-381 for discussion.)

11. *You Become a Citizen of God's Chosen Race and Nation.*

> **But you are a chosen race, A royal priesthood, A holy nation, a people for *God's* own possession, so that you may proclaim the excellencies of Him who has called you out of darkness into His marvelous light (1 Pe.2:9, NASB)**

Once you believe in God's Son, the Lord Jesus Christ, you become very special to God. In fact, you are so special to God that He does four wonderful things for you.

a. You become a citizen of God's *chosen* or *elect race* of people. The idea is that of a *new species* that differs entirely from the other races upon earth. How? How can it be that believers from China, Russia, Asia, Africa, India, Europe, the Americas, the Islands, Canada, and all the other nations of the world form a new race of people? By the Spirit of God.

The Spirit of God is changing people inwardly, not outwardly. He is not changing facial features or skin color. These mean little; they are only superficial differences that change, age, perish, and decay ever so rapidly. God is changing people within their hearts and minds, changing their lives where it really matters. God is implanting His divine nature within believers. When you believe in Jesus Christ, God's divine nature is immediately implanted into your heart and life (2 Pe.1:4).

- You are *born again*.

> **Jesus replied, "I tell you the truth, unless you are born again, you cannot see the Kingdom of God" (Jn.3:3, NLT; see Jn.3:5-6; 1 Pe.1:23; 1 Jn.5:1).**

- You receive a *renewed mind*.

> **And do not be conformed to this world, but be transformed by the renewing of your mind, that you may prove what *is* that good and acceptable and perfect will of God (Ro.12:2, NKJV; see Ro.8:5).**

- You become a *new creature*, a person with a *new nature*.

Therefore if any man *be* in Christ, *he is* a new creature: old things are passed away; behold, all things are become new (2 Co.5:17, KJV; Ep.4:24; Col.3:10).

- You receive a *new spirit.*

However, you are not in the flesh but in the Spirit, if indeed the Spirit of God dwells in you. But if anyone does not have the Spirit of Christ, he does not belong to Him (Ro.8:9, NASB).

b. You become a *royal priest.* To people who have never given their lives to Christ, God seems far away, off in outer space somewhere. In their minds, God does not seem that concerned with human life. They have no personal relationship or fellowship with God. An individual who has a daily relationship with God, who praises God and brings his or her needs to God, knows that God will meet those needs. But all this is missing with people who have never personally committed their lives to Christ. Without Jesus Christ, a person has no access or closeness to God. This is the reason people have often felt the need to have priests who would dedicate their lives professionally to God' and would carry their needs before God for them.

But this is the glorious message of the gospel: when you receive Jesus Christ as your Savior, God makes you a *royal priest.* He gives you open access into His presence forever and ever. You can actually approach God at any time!

Several questions should be asked at this point: Do you actually walk and live in the presence of God like a royal priest? Do you know what it is to have *unbroken communion* with God? To be praying always? If not, may God convict your heart and stir you to recommit your life to prayer and to seeking unbroken communion and fellowship with Him all throughout the day.

Rejoice evermore. Pray without ceasing. In every thing give thanks: for this is the will of God in Christ Jesus concerning you (1 Th.5:16-18, KJV).

Always be joyful. Never stop praying. Be thankful in all circumstances, for this is God's will for you who belong to Christ Jesus (1 Th.5:16-18, NLT).

c. **You become a** citizen of *God's holy nation*. This is a very meaningful title for believers. Just think about it: God is building a *new nation* of people. He is drawing people from all over the world, people from all the nations of the world, and creating a new nation, the *holy nation* of God. Remember: the word *holy* means separated, set apart, and different. God will take any person who is willing to separate from the sin and evil of this world and make that person a citizen of His holy nation. This means that when you trusted Christ as your Savior, you immediately became a citizen of God's holy nation. Now, you are...

- to serve the Sovereign Head of God's nation, God Himself
- to obey the laws of God's nation
- to follow the customs and lifestyle of God's nation
- to defend and speak up for the nation of God

> **And you shall be to Me a kingdom of priests and a holy nation.' These are the words that you shall speak to the sons of Israel" (Ex.19:6, NASB).**

d. **You become God's** very *own possession*. This is a precious thought: that God makes you one of His very own people, a *special possession* of His. Possession has the idea of value, of worth and significance. You are more precious to God than all the priceless gems and treasures of the world. Possession also has the idea of provision, protection, and security. You are God's possession, His very special follower; therefore, He will protect and provide for you and make you secure in every sense of the word.

12. *You Are Given God's Full Provision—Given Everything You Will Ever Need.*

> **But my God shall supply all your need according to his riches in glory by Christ Jesus (Ph.4:19, KJV).**
>
> **He who did not spare His own Son, but delivered Him up for us all, how shall He not with Him also freely give us all things? (Ro.8:32, NKJV).**

God longs to supply all the needs of His dear people (Ph.4:19). This is one of the greatest promises of Scripture.

a. **There is the** great Provider: *God Himself.* No matter what your need is, the need is not greater than God's ability to supply it. God can and will meet your need. But note the pronoun *my*. It is *"my God"* who can provide for your needs. You must make sure that you are a true believer...

   - ➢ that the God you follow is the true and living God, the God who can truly provide for your needs.
   - ➢ that you know God personally—well enough that you can trust and depend upon God to meet your needs.

b. **There is the great** assurance of provision: *"my God shall supply."* God is omnipotent, all powerful; He is able to provide and will supply whatever provision you need.

c. **There is the great** provision itself: *"all your needs."* This promise refers not only to your physical need for food, clothing, and shelter but also to your mental, emotional, social, and spiritual needs. It refers to any need that arises, engulfs, or confronts you. No need will be omitted or overlooked. No need is too big or too small. No need is unimportant to God if you, His child, are experiencing the need.

d. **There is the great** resource: *"according to His riches in glory."* Take all the riches and wealth, the glory and majesty of heaven—it is all available to meet the needs of God's dear people. There is no limit, not even a fraction, to the great resources at God's disposal. God can provide for any need you have.

e. **There is the great** Mediator: *"by Christ Jesus."* This point is most significant, for God does nothing apart from Christ. No person can approach God without coming to Him through Jesus Christ. This is the key to having your needs met: surrendering your life to Christ and asking God to meet your needs because of Christ's great love for you. You must always remember that God has only one child: the Lord Jesus Christ. And God loves His Son so much that He will do anything for the person who honors Christ by living for Him and by sacrificially giving to share the glorious news about Him.

13. *You Are Given God's Guidance As You Walk Day by Day.*

For all who are being led by the Spirit of God, these are sons of God (Ro.8:14, NASB).

Whether you turn to the right or to the left, your ears will hear a voice behind you, saying, "This is the way; walk in it" (Is.30:21, NIV).

Once you accept Jesus Christ as your Savior, God begins to lead and guide you by His Spirit. There are several ideas in the word *lead* or *guide*.

- There is the idea of *carrying and bearing along*. The Spirit leads and carries you through the trials of this life. He bears you up, helping you rise above the corruptions of this world.
- There is the idea of *leading and guiding along*. The Spirit leads and guides you along the way of righteousness and truth. He guides you by moving in advance, going ahead of you. He blazes the path, making sure you know where to walk (see Jn.16:13; Ga.5:18; 2 Pe.1:21).
- There is the idea of *directing on a course and of bringing along to an end*. The Spirit directs you where to go and how to get there, and He brings you to your destined end. The Spirit actually becomes involved in your life, directing you to live righteously and conforming you to the image of Christ. He brings you to your destined end, that is, to heaven, to live eternally in the presence of God Himself.

This is one of the great powers of the Holy Spirit, the power to lead you and to become involved in your life. In fact, one evidence or proof that you are a child of God is just this: Are you being led by the Spirit of God (Ro.8:14)?

Very simply, are you living for God and seeking His guidance through the study of His Holy Word, prayer, and bearing strong witness for Him? If you are truly doing these things, then the Spirit of God will lead and guide you day by day.

CHAPTER 2

WHAT YOUR DAILY RELATIONSHIP WITH GOD SHOULD BE

Contents

CHAPTER 2

WHAT YOUR DAILY RELATIONSHIP WITH GOD SHOULD BE

1. *You Should Set Aside a Quiet Time for Private Worship—Bible Reading and Prayer—Every Day.*

> **Draw near to God [in worship] and He will draw near to you (Jas.4:8a, NASB).**
>
> **In the morning, O LORD, you hear my voice; in the morning I lay my requests before you and wait in expectation (Ps.5:3, NIV; see Ps.55:17).**
>
> **I rise before dawn and cry for help; I have put my hope in your word (Ps.119:147, NIV; see Ps.130:5-6).**
>
> **In the early morning, while it was still dark, Jesus got up, left *the house,* and went away to a secluded place, and was praying there (Mk.1:35, NASB).**
>
> **[Daniel] continued kneeling on his knees three times a day, praying and giving thanks before his God, as he had been doing previously (Da.6:10b, NASB).**

Daily worship—Bible reading and prayer—is an absolute essential in the believer's life. Consider this: when you meet a new person, the only way you can develop a relationship is to spend time with the person. So it is with you and the Lord. When you first placed your faith in the Lord a very special relationship was established between you and God—the relationship of Father and child. Now, you must develop that relationship by spending time with God—a private time every day so you can learn more and more about Him and how He wants you to live.

Always remember this astounding fact: God—the only living and true God, the Creator and Sovereign Majesty of the universe—loves you and wants a close relationship with you. He not only wants to spend a lifetime with you but also to spend every day with you throughout all eternity. Therefore, while you complete your walk here on earth, God wants you to set aside a special time every day just for you and Him—a special time for worship—a time when you...

- ➢ listen to Him by reading His Word
- ➢ praise Him for who He is
- ➢ thank Him for the great salvation He has provided—for you and for the entire universe (Ro.8:18-21; 2 Pe.3:10-13)
- ➢ ask Him to help and guide you and to meet whatever needs you may have

God wants to share all the promises of His Holy Word with you and give you instructions about how to live a full and victorious life. For these and many more reasons, your daily worship time needs to be when your mind is most awake and alert—a time of day when you can focus and concentrate without the distractions and pressures of daily affairs. Here are several practical suggestions that may help:

a. **Get a Bible**, a copy of God's Holy Word, as soon as you can. Begin by reading the New Testament, for it is the New Testament that tells you about Jesus Christ. And it is Christ, the Son of God Himself, who fulfills the teachings and prophecies of the Old Testament. He also establishes God's New Testament (covenant, agreement) with you and all other believers. The New Testament will immediately tell you about Jesus Christ and about how He lived a victorious life despite facing the greatest adversities imaginable.

b. **Before you begin** to read, ask God to show you...
   - ➢ what He is saying in His Word
   - ➢ what lesson He wants you to learn
   - ➢ what He wants to say through you to others

c. **Begin reading** and read to the end of the story or subject. Then, read again—read over and over—until God's Spirit begins to show you the lesson He wants you to learn from that particular passage of Scripture.

d. **Once you see** the lesson God wants you to learn, jot it and the date down in a notebook. By writing it down, you will accumulate all the lessons God teaches you throughout life, and you will have them for review when needed.

e. **After reading** God's Word, pray. And pray as the Lord taught you to pray: pray the *Lord's Prayer*...

> **In this manner, therefore, pray: Our Father in heaven, Hallowed be Your name. Your kingdom come. Your will be done On earth as *it is* in heaven. Give us this day our daily bread. And forgive us our debts, As we forgive our debtors.**

And do not lead us into temptation, But deliver us from the evil one. For Yours is the kingdom and the power and the glory forever. Amen (Mt.6:9-13, NKJV).

Pray *through* the points of the prayer. The *Lord's Prayer* is not to be recited just by memory or as a form prayer, as it so often is.

Note the words "In this manner...pray." Note also Luke's account where the disciples asked Jesus to teach them to pray (Lu.11:1-2). The prayer was given to show believers *how to pray*—how they should go about praying, not the specific *words* they should pray. The very context of what Christ had just taught shows this clearly (Mt.6:5-8).

The *Lord's Prayer* is a model prayer that is to be *prayed through*. It is "in this manner," *in this way, that* you are to pray. Christ was giving words, phrases, thoughts that are to be the points of your prayer. You are to develop the points as you pray. An example would be something like this:

- *" 'Our Father' . . .*: Thank you that you are our Father—that you have adopted me as a son or daughter of yours. Thank you for the wonderful privilege of knowing you personally. Thank you for loving me with a perfect love: '...in that while I was yet a sinner, Christ died for me' (Ro.5:8). Father, you have saved me, made me a part of your dear family. Thank you more than I could ever say." And on and on you are to pray.
- *" ' . . . in heaven' "*: Thank you for heaven—that you are in heaven and that you have given me the hope of being in heaven with you. Thank you that heaven will bring about perfection so that I will be able to worship and serve you perfectly—without flaw, never again failing or coming up short, never again disappointing or hurting you. O' Father, thank you so much for the hope and anticipation of heaven." And on and on you are to pray.

Christ taught us—you and all other believers—to pray in this manner. When you pray through the *Lord's Prayer*, you will find you have covered the scope of what God wants you to pray.

How much pain the Lord's heart must bear because so many of us pray so little! How desperate the hour is! We must learn to pray as Christ taught us to pray—

pray through the *Lord's Prayer*—pray through the points of His prayer. If you are not already doing this, make a commitment this day to pray as Christ taught His followers (disciples) to pray.

f. **When you fail** to have your daily worship time, take these steps. First, if you missed because of a legitimate emergency, God understands. As you are able, offer up a brief prayer throughout the day. Thank God for His love and understanding and continually ask for His help as you deal with the emergency.

Second, if you missed for an unacceptable reason (laziness, lack of priority, living in sin...), ask God to forgive you. He loves you, and He will cleanse you of your sin and failure (1 Jn.1:9).

Third, if you missed or have become inconsistent in your daily worship time, do not become discouraged or defeated. Do not allow feelings of guilt, shame, or unworthiness to overtake you. Do not allow questions such as these to fill your mind:

> *How could God love me and keep on forgiving me when I fail Him so often?*
>
> *Maybe I'm not really saved. If I were, I would be a better Christian and not fail so much.*

Again, do not allow anything to discourage and defeat you—not even your failure. Get up from your fall and begin again. Follow the example of a baby learning to walk. Every time the baby falls, he or she gets up. The baby even gets up smiling, begins again and takes another step. Day after day the baby stumbles about until he or she becomes consistent and is able to walk without falling. You must do the same, for your Father loves you, and He longs for your fellowship and worship (1 Jn.1:3).

Fourth, restart your daily worship time on the very day of your failure, if possible, and if not, then on the very next day. Never think that your worship time is unimportant or that something else is more important. Nothing is further from the truth. Your worship time with the Sovereign Lord—the Lord God of the universe—is an appointment that is far more important than an audience with the president or leader of your nation.

2. *You Should Study God's Word Often—More Than Just Your Brief Daily Bible Reading.*

> **All Scripture *is* given by inspiration of God, and *is* profitable for doctrine, for reproof, for correction, for instruction in righteousness (2 Ti.3:16, NKJV; see Ac.17:11).**
>
> **Like newborn babies, long for the pure milk of the word, so that by it you may grow in respect to salvation, if you have tasted the kindness of the Lord (1 Pe.2:2-3, NASB).**
>
> **"This book of the law shall not depart from your mouth, but you shall meditate on it day and night, so that you may be careful to do according to all that is written in it; for then you will make your way prosperous, and then you will have success" (Jos.1:8, NASB; see Ps.1:2).**

The Bible openly claims to be God's Word: it is *inspired* or *breathed by God* (2 Ti.3:16). God has given you the Bible so that you can know Him and know how to live in this world. You are to study the Bible...

- for *doctrine*: to learn what is true
- for *reproof*: to help you see what is wrong in your life
- for *correction*: to correct you when you do wrong
- for *instruction in righteousness*: to teach you what is right

Really grasp these four things, for they cover the whole scope of life. Within God's Holy Word you will find everything you need to live a triumphant and abundant life that overflows with the very fullness of God Himself. As a follower of God, you should always remember that Scripture alone will mature and equip you to do every good work. You were made for God; therefore, you must live by the Word of God. You are to study and learn exactly how God wants you to live, work, and serve as you walk through life. Therefore, it is not enough just to briefly read a portion of Scripture during your daily worship time. You need far more; you need to study God's Word on a regular basis, both in personal and group Bible study. Then, and only then, will you learn to live as God wants you to live.

3. *You Should Pray and Fellowship with God—Talk and Share with Him—All Day Long.*

> **Devote yourselves to prayer, keeping alert in it with *an attitude of* thanksgiving (Col.4:2, NASB).**
>
> **Pray without ceasing (1 Th.5:17, KJV).**
>
> **What we have seen and heard we proclaim to you also, so that you too may have fellowship with us; and indeed our fellowship is with the Father, and with His Son Jesus Christ (1 Jn.1:3, NASB).**
>
> **Behold, I stand at the door, and knock: if any man hear my voice, and open the door, I will come in to him, and will sup [dine, have fellowship] with him, and he with me (Re.3:20, KJV).**

God's Son, Jesus Christ, came to earth that you might have fellowship with both the Father and His Son as well as with other believers. This is a most wonderful declaration, for it means that God is not far off in outer space somewhere. God is not disinterested and uncaring about what happens to you. God has not left you to fend for yourself as you face trouble on earth. The very opposite is true: God has revealed Himself in the Lord Jesus Christ and has shown that He deeply loves and cares for you. He wants to spend time with you and commune with you every day. Imagine! Jesus Christ, the Son of God, came to earth to show you how to know God personally and how to become close to Him. You can actually fellowship with God...

- develop a relationship with Him, talking and sharing with Him
- learn how to please Him
- cast your problems and needs upon Him
- ask Him for strength to conquer the trials and temptations of life
- know that He will give you a life of love, joy, and peace even in the midst of the trials and sufferings of this life
- know that He will deliver you from sin and death and give you life eternal

You can know both God and His Son personally, just as the above describes. And you can experience fullness of life along with all other believers who truly give their lives to follow Christ. How? By prayer—talking and sharing with God throughout the day. So learn to do what Scripture says: *pray always*. Learn to pray moment by moment—striving to gain an *unbroken consciousness* of the Lord's presence. In fact, note the verses above that deal with prayer. They are commands. God commands you to pray. Prayer—fellowship with God—is one of the primary duties of the believer.

Three important instructions are given in Col.4:2, above, instructions that need to be heeded.

a. **First, *devote yourselves*** *to prayer*. This means to be faithful in prayer, to fellowship and commune with God all through the day. It means to be so committed to prayer that it becomes natural to you. It becomes a priority in your life instead of something you do *when you get a chance* or *if you have the time*.

How is this possible? When you have so many duties and affairs that demand your attention, how can you walk in unbroken prayer and fellowship? What Scripture means is that you...

- develop an attitude *of prayer*.
- walk in a spirit *of prayer*.
- take a mental break from your work and spend a moment *in prayer* as often as your work allows.
- *pray* during the course of the day when your mind is not upon some duty.
- *arise early and pray* before daily activities begin. Spend a private worship time with God in prayer. Make this a continued practice.
- *pray before going to bed*. Spend an extended time whenever possible and make this a continued practice.

In all honesty, the vast majority of us waste minute after minute every hour in useless daydreaming and wandering thoughts—wasting precious time that could be spent in prayer. If you learn to capture these minutes in prayer, you will discover what it is to walk and live in prayer.

Again, this is your duty. It is not something God or anyone else can do for you. You are the one who has to discipline yourself to pray. Only *you* can pray *your* prayers.

Scripture is clear: you are to *devote yourselves to prayer*.

Seek the LORD and his strength, seek his face continually (1 Chr.16:11, KJV; see Ph.4:6-7).

b. **Second, *be alert*** *or watchful in prayer.* To be *alert* means to stay awake, be sleepless, active, on guard. It means to fight against distractions, drowsiness, sluggishness, wandering thoughts, and useless daydreaming. You should strive to discipline your mind and control your thoughts in prayer. Being very honest, this is a problem that afflicts every believer sometimes. Overwork, tiredness, pressure, strain—an innumerable list of things can make it very difficult to concentrate in prayer. This is the very reason God's Word stresses the need to *be alert in prayer.*

Vigilance in prayer is your duty. Again, it is not something that God does for you. You are responsible for watching and concentrating. You are the one who has to learn self-discipline and to rein in your thoughts. For this reason, you should never give up in prayer. You need to...

- struggle against drowsiness and against wandering thoughts
- learn to concentrate—to focus your mind on prayer and keep your thoughts under control
- teach yourself to be alert in prayer

> **And He came to the disciples and found them sleeping, and said to Peter, "So, you *men* could not keep watch with Me for one hour? Keep watching and praying that you may not enter into temptation; the spirit is willing, but the flesh is weak" (Mt.26:40-41, NASB).**

c. **Third, pray** with *thanksgiving.* When someone does something for you, you thank that person. The One who has done more for you than anyone else is God. You need to thank Him. In fact, God's hand is constantly upon your life, looking after and caring for you. So thank Him. Your praise should be lifted up to Him all through the day as you go about your daily affairs. An hour should seldom pass when you have not praised and thanked God several times.

> **In every thing give thanks: for this is the will of God in Christ Jesus concerning you (1 Th.5:18, KJV; see Ep.5:20).**

4. *You Should Love God—Above and Before All Else.*

> **Jesus replied: "'Love the Lord your God with all your heart and with all your soul and with all your mind.' This is the first and greatest commandment (Mt.22:37-38, NIV).**

You must "love the Lord your God." The word *your* indicates a personal relationship, not a distant one. God is not impersonal, distant, and removed. On the contrary, God is personal, ever so close, and you are to be personally involved with God in a daily relationship. *Loving* God is an act that is alive and active, not dead and inactive. You are to maintain a very special and close relationship with God. In fact, you are to love God with all your being, with all your heart, soul, and mind.

Loving God is your chief duty. You are responsible for nurturing a loving relationship with God. Very practically, loving God involves the same factors that loving any person involves.

a. A loving relationship involves *commitment and loyalty*. For example, true love between a husband and wife does not allow lustful behavior with others.

This is significant, for the first commandment deals with *commitment and loyalty*. God strikes at the very core of your carnal and fleshly nature, at your tendency to define love in terms that allow you to satisfy your lustful desires. God says emphatically, "You shall have no other gods" (Ex.20:3). God demands your total commitment and loyalty.

b. A loving relationship involves *trust and respect* for the person loved. You love a person for who he or she is. So it is when you love God. You love God because He is who He is. You love Him because He is...

- ➢ the Creator and Sustainer of life.
- ➢ the Savior and Redeemer of your soul.
- ➢ the Lord and Owner of your life.

c. A loving relationship involves the *giving and surrendering* of yourself. When you truly love someone, there is a drive within your heart to give and surrender yourself to the person, not to take and conquer him or her. You are to so love God, to give and surrender yourself to Him.

d. **A loving relationship** involves *knowing and sharing*. True love desires to know, share, learn, grow, build, work, and serve closely together. Likewise, you are to know and share with God, learning, growing, working, and serving ever so closely with Him.

As you walk throughout the day, you are focused upon one thing after another: self, possessions, the world, the flesh, position, recognition, power, fame, another person. God instructs you to focus your whole being upon Him and to live as He directs you in His Holy Word. Keep in mind that a loving, personal relationship can be maintained only through communication. As you walk about taking care of your affairs, talk to God and allow Him to talk to you through prayer, His Word, and the presence of His Holy Spirit.

5. *You Should Present Your Body to God As a Living and Holy Sacrifice—Every Day.*

> **And so, dear brothers and sisters, I plead with you to give your bodies to God because of all he has done for you. Let them be a living and holy sacrifice—the kind he will find acceptable. This is truly the way to worship him (Ro.12:1, NLT).**
>
> **I eagerly expect and hope that I will in no way be ashamed, but will have sufficient courage so that now as always Christ will be exalted in my body, whether by life or by death (Ph. 1:20, NIV).**

The importance of the human body cannot be overstated. Your body can easily be abused. You can abuse, neglect, and ignore your body...

- ➢ by overeating
- ➢ by becoming inactive or overactive
- ➢ by fighting and killing
- ➢ by partaking of harmful substances
- ➢ by caring for the external and abusing the internal
- ➢ by getting too much or too little rest

Just the mention of these few *sins* clearly strikes the point home to our hearts. We are to present our bodies as *living* sacrifices to God. Note two facts.

a. **God is vitally interested** in your body, not only in your spirit (Ro.12:1). You are to give and dedicate your body *to God*. This dedication...

- ➢ is not to be made to *self*: living as you wish; doing your own thing
- ➢ is not to be made to *others*: living for family, wife, husband, child, parent, companion, or employer
- ➢ is not to be made to *something else*: houses, lands, property, money, cars, possessions, job, profession, recreation, retirement, luxury, power, recognition, fame

Your body is to be offered to God and God alone. In fact, God pleads with you: commit your body to Him because of all He has done for you.

b. **You are to dedicate** your body to God as a *living sacrifice* (Ro.12:1b). The offering of your body is to be *sacrificial*. This is the picture of Old Testament believers offering animals to God as sacrifices. You are to make the same kind of sacrificial offering to God, but note the profound difference: your offering is not to be the sacrifice of an animal's flesh and blood. Your offering is to be your own body: you are to offer your body as a *living sacrifice* to God. A *living sacrifice* means at least four things.

- ➢ A *living sacrifice* means a continuous sacrifice, not just an occasional dedication of your body. You are not to sacrifice your body to God today and then take your body back into your own hands and do as you please tomorrow. A *living sacrifice* means that you dedicate your body *to live for God and to keep on living for God.*
- ➢ A *living sacrifice* means the sacrifice of your body right now, wherever you are. A particular place or time is not needed. You are to give your body to God *right now* while the body is living.
- ➢ A *living sacrifice* means that you sacrifice your own desires in order to do God's will. You are to live a holy, righteous, pure, and moral life for God. You are not to pollute, dirty, nor contaminate yourself with the sins of the world.
- ➢ A *living sacrifice* means that you live for God by serving God. It means that you give up your own physical desires and serve God while upon this earth. You give your body to the work of proclaiming the love of God and to ministering to a

world reeling in desperate need. You present your body to God for His service.

In summary, you are to dedicate your body to God as a *living sacrifice* in the home, church, school, office, plant, field, restaurant, club, plane, car, or bus. No matter where your body is, your body is to be offered to God. Sacrificing to God is not something that is done exclusively in a church nor in any other worship center. Sacrificing to God is carried out in every act of the human body. The world, that is, the whole universe, is the sanctuary of God; and the believer's body is the temple of God (1 Co.6:19-20). Therefore, every act of the believer's body is to be an act of service to God.

> **You were bought at a price. Therefore honor God with your body (1 Co.6:20, NIV).**

6. *You Should Live a Crucified Life in Christ—a Life of Self-Denial and Sacrifice.*

> **Then he said to them all: "If anyone would come after me, he must deny himself and take up his cross daily and follow me (Lu.9:23, NIV).**
>
> **Even so consider yourselves to be dead to sin, but alive to God in Christ Jesus (Ro.6:11, NASB).**
>
> **I have been crucified with Christ and I no longer live, but Christ lives in me. The life I live in the body, I live by faith in the Son of God, who loved me and gave himself for me (Ga.2:20, NIV).**
>
> **And they that are Christ's have crucified the flesh with the affections and lusts (Ga.5:24, KJV).**

You are to count or consider yourself crucified with Christ. What does this mean? When Christ died upon the cross, He denied Himself to the ultimate degree. He sacrificed Himself totally for you. To be crucified with Christ means just this:

- You sacrifice yourself—deny yourself, count yourself as dead—and then you live for Christ (Ga.2:20).
- You treat yourself as though you were dead to sin but alive to God (Ro.6:11).
- You give yourself completely to Christ and His cause in order to follow Him (Lu.9:23).

Note Lu.9:23: the verse tells you what you must do to follow Christ.

a. **You must *deny*** *yourself*. Your nature and tendency is to indulge yourself, to do what you want when you want. But you are not to indulge yourself: you are not to seek the things of this world, its fleshly comforts and pleasures. This does not mean that God does not want you to be comfortable or to prosper in this life. What it means is that those things should not be the focus of your life. You are to deny yourself by discipline and control and prove to be a faithful steward of all God puts into your hands. Use what you have to care for others by helping and serving those in need.

b. **You must *take up*** *your cross*. Taking up the cross does not mean merely bearing a particular hardship in life, such as poor health, abuse, criticism, gossip, opposition, persecution, unemployment, invalid parents or spouse, a wayward child. The cross is also an instrument of death, not just an object to carry or bear. Therefore, to take up the cross means that you die to self daily—die mentally and actively. You let the mind of Christ, the mind of humbling yourself to the point of death, be in you and fill your thoughts every day (Ph.2:5-8; 2 Co.10:3-5). You put your will, your desires, your wants to death. In their stead, you follow Christ and do His will all day long.

   This is not negative or passive behavior. It takes positive, active behavior for you to *will*, to *deny yourself*, to *take up your cross*, to *follow Christ*. You have to act, work, and be diligent, consistent, and enduring in order to die to self.

c. **You must** *follow Jesus*. Human tendency, however, is to follow some*one* else and to give your first allegiance to some*thing* else. Within the world, there are many things available for you to serve and put first, such as...

   - service organizations
   - humanitarian needs
   - social acceptance
   - religion (institutional)
   - profession
   - wealth
   - pleasure
   - family
   - self (fame, honor, power)
   - recreation
   - sports
   - education
   - appearance
   - clothing

However, as a true believer, you must live a crucified life in Christ, a life of self-denial. You are to die to self—your own desires and lusts—as you walk day by day. You are to put Jesus Christ and His kingdom first.

7. *You Should Personally Seek to Know Christ and the Power of His Resurrection—Every Day of Your Life.*

> **That I may know Him and the power of His resurrection and the fellowship of His sufferings, being conformed to His death; in order that I may attain to the resurrection from the dead (Ph.3:10-11, NASB).**

As a believer, you should seek a victorious experience with Christ. Note several very significant points.

a. **You should seek** to know Christ—to know Him personally and to know Him intimately—to know His glorious power over the world and death. As you walk throughout each and every day, your great pursuit in life should be to grow in Christ and to know Him more and more.

b. **You should seek** to know the power of Christ's resurrection. When you face this world's trials, temptations, sin, and death, learn to call upon the power of Christ and He will help you.

c. **You should seek** to know the fellowship of Christ's sufferings: to suffer for the same reasons that Christ suffered as He sought to bring God's salvation, justice, love, and righteousness to earth.

d. **You should undergo** a transformation of your sinful nature by being conformed to Christ's death. Simply subject yourself to God—deny yourself—reject sinful desires. Obey God's Holy commandments and live righteously and godly in this present world.

> **Those who obey God's commandments remain in fellowship with him (1 Jn.3:24[a], NLT).**

8. *You Should Be Inwardly Renewed Day by Day—Changed into the Image of Christ More and More.*

> **That is why we never give up. Though our bodies are dying, our spirits are being renewed**

every day. For our present troubles are small and won't last very long. Yet they produce for us a glory that vastly outweighs them and will last forever! So we don't look at the troubles we can see now; rather, we fix our gaze on things that cannot be seen. For the things we see now will soon be gone, but the things we cannot see will last forever (2 Co.4:16-18, NLT).

So all of us who have had that veil [spiritual blindness] removed can see and reflect the glory of the Lord. And the Lord—who is the Spirit—makes us more and more like him as we are changed into his glorious image (2 Co.3:18, NLT).

Your walk before the Lord is a day-by-day affair. You must submit yourself to God day by day to be inwardly renewed, to be changed more and more into the image of Christ. Five significant points can be gleaned from 2 Co.4:16-18.

a. **You must not** faint or lose heart in your commitment to Christ. Do not give up or quit; do not become discouraged; do not allow anything to defeat you: not people, circumstances, events, exhaustion, persecution, or severe opposition. Nothing, absolutely nothing, should be allowed to drive you away from Christ nor keep you from bearing strong witness for Him.

b. **Your body** is perishing every day. It is in the process of wasting away and dying. As you age, your body will become weaker and weaker, less able to go on. It will ache, slow down, need more rest, and most likely develop some serious problems or diseases. In addition to the normal wear and tear upon the body, people may put enormous demands and pressure upon you and even persecute you. But note the glorious truths of the next three points.

c. **Your spirit** is being renewed day by day. You are renewed when you draw near to God for strength and growth or for relief and deliverance.

   But remember: it is the presence and power of God within your body that renews you. You must seek His presence and power, His renewal day by day. Seeking Him is your duty. When you fulfill your duty—seeking Him—then He renews and conforms you into the image of Christ more and more each day.

d. **Your troubles** or afflictions are light when compared to the glory you will receive in heaven. Note the phrase "a glory that vastly outweighs" all trouble. The picture is that of a set of scales sitting before you. Balance your troubles on one end and the eternal glory you are to receive on the other end. The troubles may be heavy and severe, but when you place the eternal glory you are to receive on the scales, the trouble becomes light.

e. **Your eyes** should not be focused on the physical and temporal, but on the spiritual and eternal. To *gaze* means to focus your eyes and attention on a set goal or end. The goal, of course, is spending eternity with God in the new heavens and earth. You should not focus on the things that are seen (the physical and corruptible), but on the things that are not seen (the spiritual and incorruptible). The reason is strikingly clear: the things that are seen are temporal (brief, temporary, fading, passing, fleeting, and transient); but the things that are not seen are eternal (lasting, enduring, endless, permanent, immortal, and glorious).

The point is this: as you keep your eyes on the spiritual and eternal—on Christ and on the great glory He has planned for you as one of His dear followers—you will be inwardly renewed day by day. You will be changed more and more into the image of Christ. May the Spirit of God help you to focus upon the spiritual and eternal as you live for our wonderful Lord day by day. Amen and Amen!

9. *You Should Forget the Past and Daily Press On for the Heavenly Prize.*

> **No, dear brothers and sisters, I have not achieved it, but I focus on this one thing: Forgetting the past and looking forward to what lies ahead, I press on to reach the end of the race and receive the heavenly prize for which God, through Christ Jesus, is calling us (Ph.3:13-14, NLT).**

Forgetting the past and pressing on is difficult. But as a true follower of Christ you should do so. How? By concentrating and controlling your mind and by reaching forth to those things that are before you. Note the concentration and emphasis of the Scripture: "I focus on this one thing."

In one focused act, you must forget the past and reach forth to those things that are before you. This act involves two steps: both forgetting and reaching forth. The past cannot be forgotten without reaching forth to what lies ahead.

- ➢ You must not sit around defeated—moaning and groaning—when you come short or fail.
- ➢ You must not allow feelings of guilt or regret over the past to consume you.
- ➢ You must not wallow around in self-pity nor allow a sense of unworthiness to grip you.

We are all unworthy, *totally unworthy,* so our failures and shortcomings cannot be used as excuses for giving up and refusing to *press on* in the Christian race of life. God will hold you accountable. When you come short, you are to confess and forsake sin and failure. This is what you and all true followers of God must do. Confess your sin, repent and turn away from the sin, then get up and begin to serve Christ with a renewed commitment. You must not concentrate upon the past. The things of the future are to be the focus of your mind. You are to zero in on the things at hand and on the things that lie ahead. As you do this, you will conquer and overcome in life, and you will receive the heavenly prize that God is preparing for you (1 Pe.1:3-4).

10. *You Should Seek First the Kingdom of God and His Righteousness.*

> **But seek first the kingdom of God and His righteousness, and all these things shall be added to you (Mt.6:33, NKJV; see vv.25-34).**

As you walk through life day by day, you should not be preoccupied with material possessions, not even with the necessities of life such as food, clothing, and housing. Your primary duty is to seek God *first*. In fact, God gives you the greatest promise in the world: your necessities—all of your needs—will be met if you truly seek His kingdom and His righteousness *first* (Mt.6:25-34).

There are two ways you can go about taking care of yourself in this world.

a. **First, working and seeking** in your own strength: depending only upon your own ability and energy; fighting and struggling to make it through one day after another; worrying about succeeding; and fretting about how to keep what you have secured.

b. **Second, working and seeking** in both God's strength and your own: trusting and acknowledging God while doing all you can; putting your hand to the plow and plowing; working diligently and not looking back, and while working, trusting the results to God. God says He will see to it that such a trusting person will always have the necessities of life.

God is your heavenly Father, and He knows your needs. You—His child—are very, very special to Him. If you will do one simple thing, He will take care of you and meet all of your needs: walk in Christ, always seeking first the kingdom of God and His righteousness.

CHAPTER 3

WHAT YOUR RELATIONSHIP WITH OTHERS SHOULD BE

Contents

CHAPTER 3
WHAT YOUR RELATIONSHIP WITH OTHERS SHOULD BE

A. YOU AND YOUR FAMILY

1. *You—the Wife and Husband—Are to Be Filled with God's Spirit and Live Together in a Spirit of Submission and Love.*

> **Be filled with the Spirit....submitting to one another in the fear of God. Wives, submit to your own husbands, as to the Lord. For the husband is head of the wife, as also Christ is head of the church; and He is the Savior of the body. Therefore, just as the church is subject to Christ, so *let* the wives *be* to their own husbands in everything. Husbands, love your wives, just as Christ also loved the church and gave Himself for her, that He might sanctify and cleanse her with the washing of water by the word, that He might present her to Himself a glorious church, not having spot or wrinkle or any such thing, but that she should be holy and without blemish (Ep.5:18b, 21-27, NKJV; see 1 Pe.3:7).**

Human nature reacts against submitting to any*one* or any*thing*. Nevertheless, God commands that every believer, including every husband and wife...

- ➢ be filled with God's Spirit (v.18[b])
- ➢ submit to one another (v.21)

A Spirit-filled person has a submissive and respectful spirit. If you are filled with God's Spirit, you—husband and wife—will not have a spirit of criticism, dissension, envy, divisiveness, or selfishness. You will live in the fear of God; you will submit to each other rather than lose the fullness of God's Spirit. As a genuine believer, walk in a spirit of submission and love with your spouse.

a. You—the wife—must walk in a spirit of submission. First, to submit is God's will; it is a commandment of God. There is to be no equivocation, no argument, not even a question about it. But note the words "as to the

Lord." As a believer, when you do anything, you are to do it *as to the Lord* or as if you were doing it for the Lord. Why? Because you love Him. The Lord has loved and given Himself for you, given Himself that He might save you. This should be the first reason you obey God when He says to do something. You do it *as to Him*, for Him, to please Him.

As a Christian wife, then, do not obey your husband out of resentment or reaction. Submit to your husband because you love both the Lord and your husband.

Second, to submit is God's order for the family (Ep.5:22). There is to be a *partnership* and *order* within the family. This is basic for the family and society to exist. In fact, no organization can survive and exist without a spirit of partnership and order.

God's order for the *family partnership* is for the husband to be the head of the wife and family. The word *head* in Scripture refers to *authority*, not to *person or being*. Neither man nor woman is superior to the other in person or being. Men and women are equal in God's eyes. There is an *essential partnership* between men and women. Neither is independent of the other. Each comes into this world through the natural process that involves both man and woman. And the relationship that exists between them has come from God.

> **In the Lord, however, woman is not independent of man, nor is man independent of woman. For as woman came from man, so also man is born of woman. But everything comes from God (1 Co.11:11-12, NIV).**

In fact, there is neither male nor female in God's eyes. He sees men and women as equals, each as significant as the other.

> **There is neither Jew nor Greek, slave nor free, male nor female, for you are all one in Christ Jesus (Ga.3:28, NIV).**

When God talks about the husband being the head of the woman, He is not talking about ability or worth, competence or value, intelligence or advantage. God is talking about *function and order* within the organization of marriage. As stated, every organization has to have a head for it to be operated in an efficient and orderly manner. There are no greater organizations than God's universe, His church, and the family. Within God's order of things there is a partnership, but every partnership must have a head, and God has ordained that the husband be the head of the marriage partnership.

Third, the great pattern for the wife to follow is that of Christ and the church. Christ is the head of the church. This simply means that Christ has authority over the church. As long as the church lives by this rule, the church experiences love, joy, and peace—order-liness—and it is able to carry out its function and mission on earth to the fullest. So it is with the husband; he is the head of the family, the ultimate authority in the family. You—the wife—are to be submissive to that authority just as the church is to be submissive to Christ. So long as you and the rest of the family live by the rule of submissiveness to one another, your family experiences love, joy, and peace—orderliness—and it fulfills its function and purpose on earth. Of course, this assumes that the husband is fulfilling his role in the family. As in any organization, each member must do his or her part for the partnership to be orderly and to accomplish its purpose.

Fourth, the husband is to be the savior of your body just as Christ is the Savior of the church. Christ is the great Protector and Comforter of the church. So the husband is to be your protector and comforter. By nature, that is, by the constitution and build of the human body, the husband is usually stronger than the wife. Therefore, in God's order of things, your husband is to be your main protector and comforter. These two functions are two of the great benefits that the wife receives from a loving husband who is faithful to the Lord.

b. **You—the husband—**must go beyond submission and love your wife with the very *love of God Himself.* Think about what you just read: you are to love your wife with the very love of God Himself (agape love)! *Agape* love is a thoughtful and unselfish love, a giving and sacrificial love. It is the love of the mind and will as well as of the heart. It is a love of affection and feelings, but it is also a love of *determination and commitment.* It is a love that wills and commits itself to love a person forever. It is the love that always works for the highest good of your wife, that loves her even when she *does not deserve to be loved* or is *utterly unworthy of being loved.*

Imagine what would happen in most marriages if the husband genuinely and wholeheartedly loved his wife, loved her...

- ➢ with a thoughtful and unselfish love?
- ➢ with a giving and sacrificial love?
- ➢ with a love of the will as well as of the heart?
- ➢ with a love of commitment as well as of affection?

One thing that would happen in most marriages would be this: the wife would melt in the husband's arms and willingly accept his authority as the head of the family.

The sacrificial love you, the husband, are to have for your wife involves three things. (Note that the very things said about Christ and the church are to be true of you and your wife.)

First, your love is to be *set apart and cleansed*. The word *sanctify* means to be set apart. When a young man asks a young lady to be his wife, he sets himself apart for her and for her alone. His word and promise of marriage also causes her to set herself apart. Once the man speaks the word and makes the promise of marriage to the woman, he and she both are thereafter set apart for each other and are to keep themselves pure for the other.

Imagine a dirty bride or groom. It is unthinkable! Likewise, a dirty, defiled marriage is totally unacceptable. The one thing above all else that will keep your marriage clean and pure is sacrificial love. If you, the husband, will love your wife to the point that you give yourself sacrificially, your love will not only protect you but will also go a long way toward protecting the sanctity and purity of your wife.

Second, your love is to have no spot or wrinkle or any such thing. Spots are the mistakes that tarnish your life and marriage, mistakes so serious that they are very difficult to wash off your body and out of your mind. They include such things as...

- ➢ mistreatment and abuse
- ➢ loose and immoral behavior
- ➢ withdrawal and avoidance

Wrinkles are things that cause friction, rattle the nerves, and need to be ironed out. They include such things as...

- ➢ an ill temper and a reactionary spirit
- ➢ broken promises and neglect
- ➢ selfishness and rejection

Third, your love is to be holy and without blemish. The word *holy* means to be separate and untainted by evil. Your love—if it is true love—will stir you to remain holy and unblemished and will stir your wife to do the same.

This point is a real revelation. It shows just how dependent the marriage is upon your love as the husband, how much effect your love has upon the marriage. Few wives could reject such genuine love; few wives would refuse to walk hand in hand with their husbands if the husbands truly loved them with an unselfish and sacrificial love.

2. *You—the Wife and Husband—Must Honor Your Marriage Vows and Keep Your Bed Pure: God Will Judge the Adulterer and the Sexually Immoral.*

> **Marriage should be honored by all, and the marriage bed kept pure, for God will judge the adulterer and all the sexually immoral (He.13:4, NIV).**
>
> **Stop depriving one another [of sex], except by agreement for a time, so that you may devote yourselves to prayer, and come together again so that Satan will not tempt you because of your lack of self-control (1 Co.7:5, NASB).**

Marriage is to be honored by all believers. To *honor* a marriage means to highly esteem it; to count it as the most precious and warm bond, one that is to be valued, protected, and treasured.

a. **The marriage bed (sexual relationship) is** to be kept pure (He.13:4). The bed is to be unstained by sin, absolutely free from all moral impurity, uncleanness, and defilement. This is saying at least three things:

- First, you and your spouse are at liberty and are encouraged to be close in bed. Closeness and intimacy are a gift from God; it is even a type of the church (see Ep.5:22f).
- Second, the closeness in bed between you and your spouse will prevent unfaithfulness.
- Third, the bed is to be kept pure. Only you and your spouse are to be close in bed, and only with each other. There is absolutely no place for anyone else in the marriage bed.

The importance of the sexual relationship in your marriage cannot be overemphasized. God's Word says that it is so important that you and your spouse are not to separate for any period of time except for fasting and prayer, and even then separation is not to occur unless it is by mutual consent (1 Co.7:5).

> **Do not deprive each other of sexual relations, unless you both agree to refrain from sexual intimacy for a limited time so you can give yourselves more completely to prayer. Afterward, you should come together again so that Satan won't be able to tempt you because of your lack of self-control (1 Co.7:5, NLT).**

b. The adulterer and the sexually immoral (fornicators) will be judged by God (He.13:4). These two classifications include all forms of sexual vice: premarital sex, adultery, homosexuality, and all abnormal sex. Note two stated facts. First, God knows who commits these vices. He knows every single person who is immoral. He sees every immoral act, exactly what is done. No one—not a single immoral person—can hide from God. There is not a closed door anyplace that blocks His sight. God knows.

Second, God calls every sexual vice by its proper name. People may call *forbidden sex* a loving, caring, exciting, and stimulating experience. They may consider it a sexual conquest over a desirable individual—a real ego-booster. But not God. God calls it by its real name: adultery and sexual immorality. God knows what immorality causes:

- loss of innocence
- broken homes
- damaged minds
- destroyed lives
- disease
- unwanted pregnancies
- abortion (murder)
- guilt

Such devastation of life and emotions is the reason God does not deal lightly with sexual vice. Sexual sin is one of the most destructive vices on earth, no matter what people may say. God made human nature with a strong desire for love—the love of a spouse and a family. Any refusal to fulfill this desire or to distort or abuse it by immoral behavior can only damage you and your spouse.

In fact, the great tragedy with sexual vice is this: it always involves others, not only the illicit partner but also parents, children, brothers and sisters, grandparents, other relatives, friends, neighbors, and coworkers. Many are affected and some totally crushed by the immoral behavior.

The point is this: the adulterer and the sexually immoral will be judged by God. There will be no escape.

> **Now the deeds of the flesh are evident, which are: immorality, impurity, sensuality....envying, drunkenness, carousing, and things like these, of which I forewarn you, just as I have forewarned you, that those who practice such things will not inherit the kingdom of God (Ga.5:19, 21, NASB).**

3. *You—the Wife and Husband—Must Understand That God Forbids Divorce Except for Adultery.*

> **"Furthermore it has been said, 'Whoever divorces his wife, let him give her a certificate of divorce.' But I say to you that whoever divorces his wife for any reason except sexual immorality causes her to commit adultery; and whoever marries a woman who is divorced commits adultery (Mt.5:31-32, NKJV).**
>
> **But to the married I give instructions, not I, but the Lord, that the wife should not leave her husband (but if she does leave, she must remain unmarried, or else be reconciled to her husband), and that the husband should not divorce his wife (1 Co.7:10-11, NASB).**

When God created the first man and woman, He formed the institution of marriage and the family. God created man and woman to live together as husband and wife and to bear children through the most precious and intimate bond of love and sex. God never intended for any husband and wife to rip themselves and their children apart through the agonizing pain of divorce.

a. **Divorce is disallowed.** Notice the enormous protection given in God's pronouncement. There is protection of the family, including the wife, husband, and children. There is emotional, physical, mental, and spiritual protection—protection against a family's being ripped apart and having to undergo all the strain and disruption that follows. Divorce is one of the most traumatic experiences of human life, for it tragically disrupts and devastates the lives of so many. It can paralyze husbands, wives, children, parents, friends, the church, co-workers, and any other relationships.

Because divorce affects so many lives, it is of critical concern to Christ. When anyone hurts, Christ hurts. And because divorce hurts so much and disturbs so many, Christ sets out to correct the world's corrupt concept of marriage and easy divorce. There are at least four attitudes toward marriage, three of which are *loose attitudes* that often lead to divorce.

- *A back-door or trial marriage*: "If it works, OK; if it doesn't work, OK."
- *A cheap, sensual marriage*: "If it feels good, do it." Such a marriage is based upon some attraction other than love, such as sex, appearance, status, or finances.
- *An adventuresome marriage*: the marriage is entered into for the experience and the adventure of being married. "It's the thing to do." "All my friends are doing it."
- *A marriage of commitment*: the full conviction of both spouses that they should fulfill the solemn vows taken—a conviction before God.

There is only one basis for marriage that can absolutely prevent divorce: a true commitment before God to both a spiritual and physical union (see point 1 above, pp.49-53).

b. **The one exception** for divorce is the sin of adultery by one of the spouses. In such cases, God does not command divorce, but He allows the innocent party to divorce the immoral spouse. However, it should always be remembered that adultery is not the only sin that can break the close bond and spiritual union of a marriage. A spouse's *selfish, mean,* or *uncompromising* spirit can also destroy the love, trust, and hopes of a marriage as well as the lives of other family members.

4. *You—the Father and Mother—Are Not to Provoke Your Children but to Discipline and Instruct Them in the Lord.*

> **Fathers, do not provoke [exasperate] your children to anger, but bring them up in the discipline and instruction of the Lord (Ep.6:4, NASB).**

As a parent, you are bound to upset and irritate your children sometimes. Your discipline and correction of them are seldom enjoyable experiences. The very nature of reproof is that of disturbance and irritation. But that is not what this instruction is referring to. The word *provoke* means to arouse to wrath or anger, to provoke to the point of utter exasperation and resentment.

a. **You provoke** a child by refusing to accept that things do change. Time and generations change. This does not mean that your child should participate in or be allowed to do everything that his or her peers do, but it does mean that you need to be alert to the differences between your and your child's environment and trends. You should allow your child to be a part of his or her own generation. You should not try to conform your child to your childhood traditions. Your childhood generation does not exist now nor will it ever exist again.

   The point is this: you must not resist normal and natural changes that take place between generations. If you resist and forbid your child to be a part of his or her own age group, you will cause resentment, and most likely, your child will be provoked to anger.

b. **You provoke** a child by overcontrolling him or her. Overcontrol ranges all the way from stern restriction and discipline to child abuse. Disciplining and restricting your child *too much* will either stifle the growth of your child or stir him or her to rebel. You will cause your child either to withdraw or to flee from you.

   How much should your child be restricted? Should you allow your child to do everything he or she wants? No! There must be a limit placed upon the child and discipline must be exercised when the limit is crossed. What you as a Christian parent need to remember is this: *some parents allow their children* to participate in every function and activity offered to the child. Sadly, these children are usually the ones who get into trouble, rebel against authority, and cause serious strife within the family.

   There must be a balance between family life and your child's social life. Your child should be allowed to do his or her own thing sometimes and should be required to share with the family at other times. As your child grows older, he or she should, of course, be allowed to break away from the family more and more in order to be prepared to step out into the world. Your child needs free time away from the family as well as some family time in order to grow into a healthy person.

c. **You provoke** a child by undercontrolling him or her. This is one of the most prevalent problems in society. There is a tendency for some—those who are wealthy or who had little growing up—to pamper, indulge, and give their children everything imaginable, well beyond what children need or what is best for them. Parents overindulge children for five reasons.

- Parents indulge and pamper their children in order to escape responsibility for them: to keep them from interrupting their time or schedules; to get the children out from under their feet. Parents need some free time, but too many parents live selfishly. They want nothing to interfere with their own desires and needs. Too many parents push their children away and allow their children to run around unrestricted. Too few sacrifice their own time and interests to look after their children as much as they should.
- Parents indulge and pamper their children in order to gain social standing or to relive their own childhood. Some parents never had much when they were growing up and were not allowed to do what they wanted to do as children. So they see to it that their children have everything they want and do everything that everyone else does. They are determined that their children will have all the things they never had, no matter what it costs.
- Parents indulge and pamper their children because they have a false understanding or philosophy of child rearing, believing it is a child's right to have whatever he or she wants.
- Parents indulge and pamper their children because of misguided devotion and love. They give in to ill behavior, whining, pouting, and temper-tantrums just to secure peace and quiet and to keep from losing the favor and affection of their children.
- Parents who are insecure and lonely sometimes pamper their children. They cling to them as long as possible, dreading the day when they must grow up and leave—if ever. The children essentially fill the parent's needs for security and friendship.

d. **You provoke** a child by living an inconsistent life before him or her. Parents who tell a child one thing and then turn around and do the opposite are full of hypocrisy. Yet, how common! How many children are doing things secretly because they see their parents do them?

- drinking alcohol or taking drugs
- watching inappropriate television programs or movies
- reading immoral stories or looking at pornography
- eating too much
- wasting time or being lazy
- dressing inappropriately or immodestly; wearing clothes that are too tight or that expose too much of the body

- attending social functions that are slack regarding alcohol or drug abuse, morality, profanity, and marital fidelity

Seeing you live an inconsistent life can seriously provoke your children and turn them against you.

e. **You must bring up** your child in the ways of the Lord. Do not rear your child after your own ideas and notions of what is best but rather in the discipline and instructions *of the Lord*. God's Word is to be the guide for Christian parents in rearing their children. The benefits of bringing up your children in the Lord are innumerable. A few are as follows:

- They learn about love: that they are loved by God and by all who trust God, and that they are to love others.
- They learn about a victorious power and triumphant life: that God will help His followers through all; that there is a supernatural power available, a power to help them when loved ones have done all they can.
- They learn about hope and faith: that whatever happens, no matter how great a trial, they can still trust God and hope in Him. He has provided a very special strength to carry them through the trials of life, no matter how painful. They will know that God has provided a special place called heaven where He will carry them and their loved ones when they face death.
- They learn the truth about life and service: that God has given them the privilege of life and of living in a beautiful world and universe; that the bad that exists in the world is caused by evil people; that despite such evil, they are to serve in appreciation for life and for all of God's blessings. They are to work, and work diligently, making the greatest contribution they can to society.
- They learn about trust and endurance: that life is full of temptations and pitfalls that can easily rob them of joy and destroy their lives; that the way to escape the temptations and pitfalls is to follow Christ and endure to the end.
- They learn about peace: that there is an inner peace that only God can give, a sustaining peace that will carry them through everything they encounter.

As stated, the benefits of rearing your children in the Lord are innumerable, so teach them the Word of God. Do not provoke or exasperate them, but rear and discipline them as God instructs.

5. *You—the Parent and Every Other Adult—Are Strongly Warned: You Must Never Abuse or Lead a Child Astray.*

> **"But whoever causes one of these little ones who believe in Me to sin, it would be better for him if a millstone were hung around his neck, and he were drowned in the depth of the sea (Mt.18:6, NKJV).**

Leading a child astray is the worst conceivable sin. In fact, Jesus said it would be better to drown yourself than to lead a child astray. This sounds very severe. But as always, Christ meant exactly what He said and said exactly what He meant. There are several ways you cause children to sin.

- By leading them to do wrong and teaching them to sin. Picture sexual abuse as well as encouraging acts of disobedience and lawlessness.
- By example, by the things you do. Often, you may not be aware that children see and are observing you. Nevertheless, they are, and they learn from what you do. Children think, "If it's all right for dad and mom, then it is bound to be all right for me." "If they can do it and still get by as well as they do, then I can too."
- By overlooking or dismissing wrong; by excusing or downplaying evil behavior; by claiming some sins are trivial by suggesting: "Oh, that's all right. There's not that much to it." "It isn't going to hurt anyone." "Don't pay any attention to it. Just forget it."
- By ridiculing and poking fun at, or joking and sneering at a child or young person's attempt to do right: "Don't be so narrow-minded. You're acting like a fanatic. You and your religion."
- By looking, touching, and tasting things that are socially acceptable but sinful to God. They are harmful, habit-forming, and physically stimulating. For this reason, they should be left alone and never encouraged by statements such as, "Just try it once. No one will know." "How can it be wrong when it tastes (looks, feels) so good?"

- By threatening or abusing a child. The threat can range all the way from loss of friendship or acceptance to rejection, abuse, or severe punishment.

Christ issues a severe warning to you and all other adults: you will suffer the most severe punishment—a punishment beyond imagination—if you abuse or lead a child astray.

6. *You—the Child—Are to Obey Your Parents.*

> **Children, obey your parents in the Lord, for this is right. Honor your father and mother (which is the first commandment with a promise), So that it may be well with you, and that you may live long on the earth (Ep.6:1-3, NASB).**

To *obey* means to follow the directions or guidance of an instruction. When a parent instructs a child, the child is to obey the parent. But what about the repulsive problems so evident in society: the problems of parental abuse—physical, sexual, and mental abuse? Is a child to obey a parent when the parent is so devilishly wrong? No! A thousand times, no! Two points stand out:

a. **First, to obey** your parents means to obey them *in the Lord*. Note the command again: "Children, obey your parents *in the Lord*." The phrase "in the Lord" means at least two things. There is a limit to the child's obedience. When a parent is not acting *in the Lord*, the parent is not to be obeyed. The Lord has nothing whatsoever to do with the filth of unrighteousness and abuse of precious children. If a child can break away and be free from such parental corruption, he or she has every right to do so. The Lord came to set us free from the abuse and the filth of sin, not to enslave people to it, especially not children.

One of the most severe warnings ever issued in all of history was issued by the Lord Jesus to adults who abuse children (see pt.13, p.73). Note again what Jesus said:

> **"But whoever causes one of these little ones who believe in Me to stumble, it would be better for him if a millstone were hung around his neck, and he were thrown into the sea. If your hand causes you to sin, cut it off. It is better for you to enter into life maimed, rather than**

having two hands, to go to hell, into the fire that shall never be quenched (Mk.9:42-43, NKJV).

The abusing parent had better heed, for one thing God absolutely will not tolerate is the abuse of a child. As believers, we must teach the Word of God: children are to obey their parents, but they are to obey only if the parents' instructions are *in the Lord*. If a parent is abusing a child, *beyond mild spanking* (appropriate Scriptural spanking), the child should go to some other adult he or she feels close to or someone in authority to ask for help.

The phrase *"in the Lord"* also tells you why you are to obey your parents. Obeying your parents is right; it is of the Lord; it pleases the Lord.

Note the emphasis: you are not told to obey because it pleases your mother or father but because it pleases the Lord. Pleasing your parents is, of course, a reason for obeying them; but the *first* reason for obeying your parents is that it pleases the Lord. You are to walk so closely to the Lord that your desire is to please Him at all times. And when you do so, then obeying your parents will become an automatic response.

b. **Second, to obey** your parents means to honor them. It means to respect, esteem, and value your father and mother; to be kind and obedient to them. Scripture is not speaking to any certain age child. It is speaking to all who have parents still living. You are to honor your father and mother and *to esteem and value them as precious*—to respect and reverence them. Tragically, this is a dwindling trait today. Too often a child's response to parents is that of...

- speaking disrespectfully
- grumbling
- not listening
- acting like a know-it-all
- disregarding instructions
- calling parents cute but disrespectful names

In addition to these, there is the dishonor of delinquency, crime, drugs, alcohol, immorality, the abuse of property, and so on. And when it comes to adult children with aged parents, there is the dishonor of neglect or abuse, ignoring a parent's needs and shuffling a parent to the side, failing to adequately care for him or her. Too many of us forget how much our parents have done for us. They gave us life and took care of us for years. Too many of us forget the rich experience and knowledge that our parents have gained through the years. We could put their wisdom to great use in meeting community and world needs. And even if our parents failed to be and to do all they should have, we as believing Christians are instructed to honor them. We are to honor them because we are true followers of the Lord Jesus Christ.

There are two promises made to children who honor their parents.

- Things will go well for the child. Does this mean that you will never have problems or have to suffer? No. This is not what Scripture means. God means that He will be with you, strengthen and take care of you so that you can *walk through* the trials of life victoriously. You will be made strong *where it counts—in the inner person*. You will be enabled to conquer and be victorious over whatever confronts you as you journey through life.
- The child is assured of living a long life on earth. There are exceptions to this, but in most cases, children will live longer if they honor their parents *in the Lord.* An obedient and righteous child is not as exposed to wickedness as much as disobedient children are. The disobedient experience far more tension in the home, troubled relationships, immorality, disease, drug addiction, lawlessness, violence, accidents, and a host of other problems that cause premature death. Therefore, if you as a child will obey your parents in the Lord, you are more likely to live a long life. This is the promise of God.

  In some cases, however, babies, children, and adult believers are taken on to heaven before the normal life span. Does this violate God's promise? Certainly not. God always knows what is best. For some reason, God wants the precious child or adult believer with Him sooner than He wants most. He longs for their presence and love and wants to bless them with the perfection and glory of heaven sooner than others.

7. *You—the Young Person—Are to Be an Example Both to Your Family and to Others.*

Don't let anyone look down on you because you are young, but set an example for the

> **believers in speech, in life, in love, in faith and in purity (1 Ti.4:12, NIV).**
>
> **Even a child is known by his deeds, Whether what he does *is* pure and right (Pr.20:11, NKJV).**

As a Christian young person, you should use your enormous energy to grow in Christ and to grow quickly. You should strive to be as mature in Christ as possible for your years.

a. **You should be** an example in your speech, both in what you say and in the way you say it. Control your conversation and tongue at all times—never using profanity nor speaking immorally or angrily—no matter what happens or who you are with.

> **"But I tell you that every careless word that people speak, they shall give an accounting for it in the day of judgment. "For by your words you will be justified, and by your words you will be condemned" (Mt.12:36-37, NASB).**

b. **You should be** an example in your conduct or behavior. Be disciplined and controlled. Wherever you go, always demonstrate that you are a true follower of the Lord, that you are living for the Lord in all godliness and righteousness.

c. **You should be** an example by your love. Excel in and overflow with love. The love you are to have is the love that *reaches out* to everyone. This means...

    - the unattractive
    - the handicapped
    - the fatherless
    - the shy
    - the rejected
    - the poor
    - the sick
    - the sinner
    - the spiteful
    - the oppressor

    How in the world can you love some of these people? How is it possible to love those who do evil and treat you as an enemy? Is it even practical or humanly possible? Not at all. It is not possible for you to love those who dislike, hate, or persecute you—not humanly possible. But there is a way: the Lord can empower you to love *all people.* Therefore, as a young person, you need to ask God to give you the strength to love everyone—even your enemies.

d. **You should be** an example in faith, that is, in faithfulness. Be loyal to the Lord Jesus and the church regardless of the demands, hardships, temptations, trials, or opposition. No matter what the circumstances, as a young person, you are to strive to be faithful and loyal.

> **And he said to *them* all, If any *man* will come after me, let him deny himself, and take up his cross daily, and follow me (Lu.9:23, KJV).**

e. **You should be** an example in purity. Live a moral, clean, honest, and just life. Keep yourself completely free of covetousness, lustful thoughts, worldliness, pride, immorality, and all other known sins. Live a life of purity that far exceeds the standards of the world, a life as pure as humanly possible.

> **Blessed *are* the pure in heart: for they shall see God (Mt.5:8, KJV).**

8. *You—the Adult Son or Daughter—Are to Take Care of Your Elderly Parents and Grandparents.*

> **But if a widow has children or grandchildren, these should learn first of all to put their religion into practice by caring for their own family and so repaying their parents and grandparents, for this is pleasing to God (1 Ti.5:4, NIV).**
>
> **If anyone does not provide for his relatives, and especially for his immediate family, he has denied the faith and is worse than an unbeliever (1 Ti.5:8, NIV).**

This is a strong statement. In fact, your very first duty as an adult child is to put your religion to work in the home, that is...

- to live for Christ in the home
- to be responsible in caring for your own family

A true believer must be a testimony at home before he or she is a testimony anyplace else. Your first duty as a Christian is to love and care for your own family, and this includes your parents and grandparents. In most cases, your parents and grandparents loved and took care of you when you were a child. It is fitting, then, for you to return the love and care when they are no longer able to take care of themselves.

Scripture declares that this is *"pleasing to God."* As a follower of Christ, you must love and take care of your immediate family or else you receive the disapproval of God (see 1 Ti.5:8).

9. *You—the Young Married Woman—Are to Live Wisely: Be Pure and Committed to Your Husband and Children.*

> **The younger women [are] to love their husbands and children, to be self-controlled and pure, to be busy at home, to be kind, and to be subject to their husbands, so that no one will malign the word of God (Tit.2:4-5, NIV).**

As a young married woman, how are you to behave as you walk in the world day by day? God's Holy Word spells out seven traits:

a. **You are to love** your husband (v.4). The only way a young married couple can be bound together and have the kind of life they desire is by loving each other.

   The word used here for *love* actually stresses affection, care, tenderness, warmth, and feelings. You are to have *affection* for your husband. Keep in mind that you may live in a mansion, be a beautiful woman, have the finest furnishings, have the very best wardrobe, and have a husband who loves you dearly, but if you do not love your husband in return, you will both be unhappy and probably miserable. To prevent the doom of your marriage, learn to love your husband. Christ can help and teach you to love him.

b. **You are to love** your children (v.4). There is no greater call or task on earth than that of being a mother. Yet, despite the great call and privilege of motherhood, there are two problems concerning this command that need to be covered—the problems of child abuse and of putting career before children. In today's society, where two parents often have to work, parents have to make a very special effort to guard against both of these problems. Oliver Greene states it well:

> *This verse* [Tit.2:4] *seems unnecessary—and yet it is very important. Most animals will fight and die to protect their young, but some men and women are so totally depraved that they lose all respect and love for their own flesh and blood—their children [consider child abuse]. The aged saints are to teach the younger women to love their children. Any precious mother with a baby in the*

home has a full time job twenty-four hours a day, seven days a week. [But] *no other person will ever love your child as you love* [him or her, not] *if you are a true mother. No other person can train and discipline* [your] *child as you will if you are a true mother. No person can take the place of a mother; therefore, mothers should love their children above fame, fortune, beauty, houses, or social prestige. Children should come first in the heart of a mother; and she should forsake all except her husband to give her love, time, and attention to her children. The best friend any child will ever have on the face of this earth is a godly, consecrated mother who loves him* [or her].[1]

Matthew Henry says the following:

[Young mothers are] "to love their children, not with a natural affection only, but a spiritual, a love springing from a holy sanctified heart and regulated by the word; not a fond foolish love, indulging them in evil, neglecting due reproof and correction where necessary, but a regular Christian love, showing itself in their pious education, forming their life and manners [properly], *taking care of their souls as well as of their bodies.*[2]

c. **As a young** married woman, you are to be self-controlled (v.5). Simply stated, you are not to live a life of license within the home nor out in public: partying, drinking, overeating, or indulging in any sense of the word. Curb your sinful desires and emotions.

d. **As a young** married woman, you are to be pure (v.5). Be pure morally and sexually, pure in thought and deed.

But I say, anyone who even looks at a woman [or man] with lust has already committed adultery with her in his heart (Mt.5:28, NLT).

e. **As a young** married woman, you are to be busy *at home, to be a* homemaker (v.5). No better exposition of this command could be given than that written by Oliver Greene:

This does not mean that the wife is never to go out of the home, never to take part in any outside interests; but she is not to neglect the duties of the home in order

1 Oliver Greene. *The Epistles of Paul the Apostle to Timothy and Titus.* (Greenville, SC: The Gospel Hour, 1964), p. 442f.

2 Matthew Henry. *Matthew Henry's Commentary*, Vol.6. (Old Tappan, NJ: Fleming H. Revell, Col, n.d.), p.863.

> *to participate in things outside the home....She is to be diligent at home—not lazy or slothful, not unconcerned about the home and the things pertaining thereto—but to give her best to the home, seeing that things are in order and that the home is kept as becomes a Christian....Christianity puts the right kind of pride in the heart—and a woman who is a believer should take pride in her home, which is her castle. She should keep that home clean, neat, and presentable.*[3]

f. **As a young** married woman, you are to be *kind* and *good*: of the highest quality and character, virtuous through and through, good-natured, and caring. There is to be no vice, no dirt, and no pollution in your life. Be pure and clean, of the highest integrity. Do not be an idle person, a gossip, or a busybody. Be purposeful, serving people and doing good, showing care and kindness, helping wherever you can (see 1 Ti. 5:13).

g. **As a young** married woman, you are to be subject *to your own husband* (v.5). There is to be a *partnership* and *order* between you and your husband (see point 1 above for discussion, pp.49-53).

Note why you must live and behave as God says: that the Word of God will not be maligned, that is, dishonored, reproached, or slandered. If you profess Christ but do not live for Him, you bring reproach upon God's Word. How? It stirs unbelievers to think:

> *There must be no power in the Word of God, no power to change lives—no power to give love, joy, peace, or hope. There must be no advantage to believing Christ and to trusting the promises of God's Word. The promises must be meaningless and powerless. They have made no difference in this young wife's life.*

Regardless what some may say or think, the Word of God is alive and powerful; it does change lives (He.4:12). The problem with some wives is simply this: they...

- ➢ do not spend time in a genuine study of God's Word, learning how to live.
- ➢ do not spend time in genuine prayer, asking God to help them live victoriously over the temptations and trials of this life.
- ➢ do not discipline their lives nor control their tongues as the Word of God demands.

---

[3] Oliver Greene. *The Epistles of Paul the Apostle to Timothy and Titus,* p. 444f.

The result, of course, is the charge of hypocrisy, and the Word of God is reproached and slandered. What an indictment against a young lady: being a hypocrite and being the cause for the Word of God being blasphemed!

10. *You—the Young Married Man—Are to Be Self-Controlled.*

> **Similarly, encourage the young men to be self-controlled (Tit.2:6, NIV).**

Self-control is the only command given to you as a young married man because it covers all the other commands of God. A self-controlled man obeys all of God's commandments, including the commandment to love his wife and children. Self-control means that you are disciplined and restrained and that you curb emotions, passions, and desires. It means that you have a mind that is sound and focused upon pure and clean thoughts and meaningful things. It means that you control your life and stay focused upon the purpose, meaning, and significance of life. This is a critical charge for young men. Four reasons are readily apparent.

a. **As a young married man,** you have strong sexual desires. If you are not careful, you will be aroused to pay attention to the opposite sex. This is normal and natural; it is the way God has chosen to cause young men and women to become attracted to each other and to marry and carry on the human race. But remember, this is the very reason for God's clear exhortation. As a young married man, you need to control yourself. Be noble and honorable, disciplined and restrained, keeping yourself pure for the sake of your family and Christ. Passion can engulf and drown you and your family.

b. **As a young married man,** you must control your relationship with your wife—control your emotions, responses, temper, and words. If you speak or act harshly or abusively, you can do irreparable damage to the delicate spirit of your young wife. You can cause damage that will affect your marriage for many years to come (1 Pe.3:7).

c. **As a young married man,** you are discovering yourself, searching for and finding your place in society.

Three of life's biggest decisions must be made while you are young:

- the decision regarding *leaving home*: when to leave home and take on the total responsibility for yourself and perhaps a family.
- the decision regarding *marriage*: who and when to marry and to begin a family.
- the decision regarding *employment or profession*: what path of work to pursue in life.

The years of youth up until middle age are usually an unsure time for young men. This is a time when you have to struggle to secure your place in the world. This is the reason for this direct charge: you—as a young man—must control yourself.

- Control the urge to attack, react, trample, bypass, neglect, ignore, or abuse people in order to move ahead.
- Control the urge to back off, go along, or compromise. Never lose your vitality or energy, your ambition or dreams. Rather, seek to move ahead and to make the greatest contribution you can for society and for Christ.

d. **As a young married man,** you are full of visions and dreams and expectations. Because of your excitement, you could get reckless and make mistakes. Hence the reason for this charge: you should be adventuresome and pursue your dreams with all the energy you have, but you must also be self-controlled and disciplined as you move forward in life.

11. *You—the Believer—and Your Unbelieving Spouse Are to Stay Together If Your Spouse Is Willing: You Are Not to Divorce.*

But to the rest I say, not the Lord, that if any brother has a wife who is an unbeliever, and she consents to live with him, he must not divorce her. And a woman who has an unbelieving husband, and he consents to live with her, she must not send her husband away. For the unbelieving husband is sanctified [exposed to a holy life] through his wife, and the unbelieving wife is sanctified through her believing husband; for otherwise your children are unclean, [do not have a godly influence] but now they are holy.

> **Yet if the unbelieving one leaves, let him leave; the brother or the sister is not under bondage in such *cases*, but God has called us to peace. For how do you know, O wife, whether you will save [convert] your husband? Or how do you know, O husband, whether you will save your wife? (1 Co.7:12-16, NASB)**

This issue arose in the Corinthian church when one partner in a marriage became a believer. Paul says that the issue was never discussed by the Lord. Given this fact, you must follow the instructions of other Scriptures: be faithful to your unbelieving spouse and honor your marriage vows. If you are married to an unbeliever, Scripture gives three instructions:

a. **First, stay** together (vv.12-13). The believing spouse should stay, if the unbelieving spouse is willing. The reasons are clearly seen.

   ➢ As the believer, you will influence your spouse for Christ. You will expose him or her to God's forgiveness and salvation and to His promise of eternal life. If your unbelieving spouse *is willing* to remain with you, the marriage is not to be dissolved. Simply stated, God accepts the marriage of such a couple if the unbelieving spouse is willing to accept the fact that his wife or her husband is a Christian *who lives for the Lord*. The unbeliever must support the spouse in his or her loyalty to Christ and His church.

   ➢ As the believer, you will influence your children for Christ (v.14). Your presence as a believer in the family will touch the whole family for God, as long as your spouse supports you. Your whole family is accepted by God as a sanctified family (exposed to holy behavior), set apart for Him and His cause.

b. **Second, separate** if your unbelieving spouse desires (v.15). If your unbelieving spouse leaves, you are to let him or her leave. The bond of marriage is broken.

   The point is that God has called you to *peace*. Peace is certainly the purpose of God in the believer's life: peace with God and peace with each other. If your unbelieving spouse will not live in peace and allow you to carry the gospel of peace to the world, you are to continue living for God even if it means divorce. You must obey God and His Holy Word rather than follow the worldly behavior of society (Ac.5:29).

c. **Third, the reason** you are to cooperate with your unbelieving spouse is clear. Your unbelieving spouse may be won to Christ by your righteous life (v.16).

12. *You—the Widow or Widower—Are to Live Above Reproach.*

> **The widow who is really in need and left all alone puts her hope in God and continues night and day to pray and to ask God for help. But the widow who lives for pleasure is dead even while she lives (1 Ti.5:5-6, NIV).**

You may be a believer who is all alone—without husband, wife, children, or close relatives. God gives you a word of strong encouragement: "Your widows, too, can depend on me for help" (Je.49:11, NLT). Do as the Scripture says...

- trust and put your hope in God
- continue to pray and ask God for help night and day
- focus your life upon Christ and His church

Whatever you do, guard against what some widows and widowers do: live for pleasure. They give themselves over to the flesh and the world. They party, get drunk, and live immoral lives. You are not to indulge and give license to worldliness and sin. Such a person is *dead while he or she lives—dead* to God and to the things of God. Their minds are upon their clubs and parties, the world and the flesh, not upon the Lord and His church and the desperate needs of a dying world. As a true believer, you must live above reproach. And, if you choose to remarry, you are to marry a believer (1 Co.7:39).

13. *You—Adult and Child—Should Be Aware That God Has Assigned a Guardian Angel to Watch Over You.*

> **"See that you do not look down on one of these little ones [little children]. For I tell you that their angels in heaven always see the face of my Father in heaven (Mt.18:10, NIV).**
>
> **Are not all angels ministering spirits sent to serve [care for] those who will inherit salvation? (He.1:14, NIV).**

You must always remember that Christ came from the spiritual world or dimension to reveal heaven to us. One truth He taught was the reality of angels, that is, heavenly messengers. Here He teaches that children have *guardian angels* who have direct access to God. This fact is a warning to the offender: every sin and stumbling block placed before children is brought before Him, so no offense will go unpunished. It is also an encouragement to every child of His: children have a most favored position with the Lord because their guardian angels are always *before the face of God*. There could be no greater privilege than that given to angels, to be before God always *beholding His face*. They are a magnificent order of beings who have been created by God to be His messengers and servants. They have the glorious privilege of living in God's presence and of serving Him day and night.

Angels have a very important function in God's dealings with children and with believers: they are all *ministering spirits sent forth* to help all true believers (He.1:14). God uses angels in your life to guide, protect, and encourage you.

a. **They protect** and deliver you and your children—either *through* or *from* trials (Ps.34:7; Ps.91:11; Is.63:9; Da.3:28; 6:22; Ac.12:7-11).

b. **They guide** and lead you in your service for God (1 K.19:5; Mt.2:13, 19-20; Ac.5:19; 8:26).

c. **They encourage** you (Ac.27:23-25). This assistance begins at childhood and continues on throughout life (He.1:14; see Mt.18:10; Ps.91:11).

d. **They escort** you and all other believers into heaven (Lu.16:22).

Guardian angels have been assigned both to you and your children. Furthermore, they have direct access to God, which means they are able to help you and your dear children as you walk day by day, trusting and following the LORD.

B. YOU AND YOUR NEIGHBOR

1. *You Are to Love Your Neighbor As Yourself.*

> **"The second [most important commandment] is this, 'You shall love your neighbor as yourself.' There is no other commandment greater than these" (Mk.12:31, NASB).**

To love your neighbor is a command, not an option. If the commandment is not obeyed, God is displeased, and you stand guilty before Him.

A question naturally arises, then: Who is your neighbor? Jesus answered the question Himself in the *Parable of the Good Samaritan*. A neighbor is any person and every person, even if the person is socially despised (Lu.10:25-37, esp. 36-37). Your neighbor is everyone in the world, no matter his or her status, condition, or circumstance. Every individual should be highly esteemed and helped, and no individual should be mistreated or wronged. Scripture goes even further to say that you should esteem every person better than yourself (Ph.2:3). In fact, loving your neighbor as yourself involves treating others as you want them to treat you. A very practical list of ways showing how you are to live out your love for others is given by Scripture (1 Co.13:4-7; see Section C, pt.2, pp. 84-86 for a discussion of the fifteen acts of love).

2. *You Should Owe No Debt to Any Person Except the Debt of Love.*

> **Let no debt remain outstanding, except the continuing debt to love one another, for he who loves his fellowman has fulfilled the law. The commandments, "Do not commit adultery," "Do not murder," "Do not steal," "Do not covet," and whatever other commandment there may be, are summed up in this one rule: "Love your neighbor as yourself." Love does no harm to its neighbor. Therefore love is the fulfillment of the law (Ro.13:8-10, NIV).**

God's Word could not be any more *straightforward*: as a believer, you should always pay your debts and fulfill your obligations, and you should do so on time. Being irresponsible in financial matters will damage the name of Christ and push people further away from the Kingdom of God. Hence, God is very clear about living above reproach. One of the most significant ways to do so is to pay your debts and fulfill your obligations on time. The *only* thing you should ever owe another person is the debt of love.

a. **You are to love** your neighbors, not commit adultery (or any other illicit sexual act) against them. If you truly love others, you will not hurt or harm them. You will not bring pain into their lives (and yours) by committing adultery.

b. **You are to love** your neighbors, not murder them. Remember, though, that God's Holy Word says anger and hate are equal to murder. This additional element makes the command more difficult to obey. In order to love your neighbor, you have to learn to control your anger and conquer the urge to hate.

> **Everyone who hates his brother is a murderer; and you know that no murderer has eternal life abiding in him (1 Jn.3:15, NASB).**

c. **You are to love** your neighbors, not steal from them—neither legally nor illegally. Keep in mind that...

- ➢ you can sometimes use the law to steal.
- ➢ you can take from others without ever breaking a law.
- ➢ you can acquire too much of something, well beyond what you need, something that rightfully belongs to others. You can hoard and misuse it, refusing to help those who are in desperate need.

The Bible teaches that stealing is the taking of anything (including money) that rightfully belongs to others. If you truly love your neighbor, you will not steal what is rightfully his or hers.

d. **You are to love** your neighbors, not bear false witness against them. *Bearing false witness* means far more than just lying about someone in court. It includes any kind of lying, and there are several kinds that need to be guarded against in particular:

- ➢ There are rumors, gossip, and tale-bearing.

> **" 'Do not go about spreading slander among your people. "'Do not do anything that endangers your neighbor's life. I am the LORD (Le.19:16, NIV).**

- There are subtle and suggestive hints that create a bad impression about someone.

> **"You shall not bear a false report; do not join your hand with a wicked man to be a malicious witness (Ex.23:1, NASB).**

- There is deception.

> **Do not be a witness against your neighbor without cause, And do not deceive with your lips (Pr.24:28, NASB).**

- There are accusations and criticisms about a person that condemn the individual in the minds of others, things that should be discussed with the individual face-to-face.

> **"Blessed are you when *people* insult you and persecute you, and falsely say all kinds of evil against you because of Me (Mt.5:11, NASB).**

- There is exaggeration or flattery that stretches the truth about a person, whether praising or criticizing the individual.

> **A lying tongue hates those it crushes, And a flattering mouth works ruin (Pr.26:28, NASB).**

When sin, failure, or bad news is discovered about a person, God expects you to love and comfort that individual, not tear him or her down through your false witness.

> **Help, Lord, for the godly man ceases to be, For the faithful disappear from among the sons of men. They speak falsehood to one another; With flattering lips and with a double heart they speak (Ps.12:1-2, NASB).**
>
> **I will not tolerate people who slander their neighbors. I will not endure conceit and pride (Ps.101:5, NLT).**

e. You are to love your neighbors, not covet what they have. Instead of desiring their possessions, you ought to be focusing on being a blessing to them and building them up. You need to encourage them to know the Lord and to surrender their lives to the great task of meeting the needs of a lost and dying world. (See

Chapter 4, Section A, pt.10, pp.123-126 for more discussion).

> **"You shall not covet your neighbor's house; you shall not covet your neighbor's wife or his male servant or his female servant or his ox or his donkey or anything that belongs to your neighbor" (Ex.20:17, NASB).**

3. *You Must Not Be Prejudiced or Discriminate Against Anyone—Not Show Partiality or Favoritism.*

> **My brothers, as believers in our glorious Lord Jesus Christ, don't show favoritism. Suppose a man comes into your meeting wearing a gold ring and fine clothes, and a poor man in shabby clothes also comes in. If you show special attention to the man wearing fine clothes and say, "Here's a good seat for you," but say to the poor man, "You stand there" or "Sit on the floor by my feet," have you not discriminated among yourselves and become judges with evil thoughts? (Jas.2:1-4, NIV)**

You should never reject or favor people because of their race, color, nationality, social standing, financial status, title, appearance, or any other criteria. The charge is clear: if you truly believe in the Lord Jesus Christ—the Lord of glory—you are not to hold prejudice in your heart against anyone. You should show no hint of partiality or favoritism. It is both evil and judgmental and it is strictly forbidden.

Scripture paints a very clear picture of partiality. Two people visit a church. One is wearing fine clothing and expensive jewelry and gives the immediate impression of being somewhat wealthy. The other individual is shabbily dressed and instantly comes across as being poor.

What happens when these two visitors enter the church? The rich person is warmly welcomed and escorted to a good seat. But the poor individual is guided to a seat in the back or told to stand or be seated away from everyone else. The poor individual is treated as though he or she were less important than the others.

If there is to be no distinction within the Lord's church, there is certainly to be no prejudice, discrimination, or favoritism among us—not at work, play, school, social events, or anywhere else. At least two things are wrong with showing prejudice and partiality.

a. **First, showing partiality** sets you up as the judge of other people (v.4). It makes you as God; it says who is of value and acceptable within society and who is not. Your prejudice or partiality sets you up as being better and more acceptable than others. It exalts you and demeans others. Discrimination exposes an attitude of arrogance, a spirit of self-exaltation. God wants everyone—the poor as well as the rich—to become acceptable to Him. As a true follower of Christ, you are never to show prejudice or discrimination. Rather, accept and help everyone.

b. **Second, showing partiality** exposes your evil thoughts (v.4). It shows that you focus upon mundane and changeable things, things such as appearance, clothes, cars, houses, and all the other outward things that change, waste away, rot, and decay ever so rapidly. Such thoughts are corrupt and evil because they focus upon corruptible things and neglect the inner person entirely. It says that color, race, religion, and material things are more important than people's souls. This, of course, is foolishness. Yet, it is exactly how so many people behave because, in reality, most people in the world do show prejudice.

   Make it your goal never to show partiality, not to a single soul. Look at people only as fellow human beings. What matters is the life and health, the soul and spirit of every man and woman, boy and girl. What matters is that they be saved and come to know the love, joy, and peace that only Christ can bring. However, the only way people can ever come to Christ is for people, especially believers, to stop discriminating against them and begin to love them and win them to Christ.

4. *You Are to Do All You Can to Live at Peace with Everyone.*

> **Pursue peace with all *people,* and holiness (He.12:14a, NKJV)**

To *pursue* means to chase or go after, to stick to it. In this verse, it has the idea of swiftness and endurance, of diligently working for peace. Sadly, we live in a world that is full of selfish and evil people who could care less about peace, as long as they get what they want. While peace is not always possible, you must not give up in your pursuit of peace. Four significant factors need to be carefully considered:

a. **Some people are** self-centered. They are trouble-makers, complainers, dissenters, fighters, image-seekers, warmongers, or some other unpleasant character. Many have no interest in living in peace with you or anyone else, especially if you are a true believer.

b. **You need to work** for as much peace as possible, whether it is in your family, workplace, church, community, or nation. Some level of harmony can usually be achieved—at least part of the time. Never give up as long as there is a glimmer of hope. Strive to achieve as much peace as possible, but remember, peace is not always possible—not with everyone.

c. **The cause of conflict** must not arise from within you, not as a believer. Always try everything possible to bring about peace and to keep peace (Ro.12:20; see Mt.5:39-41). But, as stated above, this may not be possible because of the wickedness of others or because the control of peace is not within your hands. It is possible that some will not live peaceably. Just make sure you are not the cause of the conflict, that you do not bring reproach upon the name of Christ.

d. **You must face** each situation objectively—not emotionally—and determine whether you are to turn the other cheek or defend yourself. Jesus spent His life combating evil and wrong, and He did not always turn the other cheek (Jn.18:22-23); neither did Paul (Ac.23:2-3). Scripture encourages the believer not to give license to anyone, and the command is strong. For example, if a person does not work because of laziness, the person should not eat (2 Th.3:7, 10).

As a believer, the governing principle you are to follow is clear: "Do not be overcome by evil, but overcome evil with good" (Ro.12:21, NKJV). There are times when an attacker, if allowed to continue, is encouraged in his or her evil nature of indulgence and license. If allowed to continue, the person's evil might overcome you—either *within,* through bitterness and revenge, or *without,* through domination. Thus, you are not to sacrifice truth in order to preserve peace, not within your family, community, or any other place. Evil is not to be allowed to overcome truth. Always take a stand against evil, never giving in to its corrupting and destructive influence.

5. *You Are to Treat People the Same Way You Want Them to Treat You.*

> **Therefore, whatever you want men to do to you, do also to them, for this is the Law and the Prophets (Mt.7:12, NKJV).**

The golden rule is probably the most well-known thing Jesus ever said. It is the summit of ethics, behavior, righteousness, and godliness. It is a very practical statement that shows exactly how God wants you to live and act. There are three significant facts that set the golden rule apart from all other teachings and make it the summit of human behavior.

a. **The golden rule** demands *true* justice. Note the wording: it is not negative and passive, yet it tells you *how not to behave*. If you truly practice the golden rule, it puts restraints upon you. For example, the golden rule teaches you not to lie, steal, cheat, or injure people. And it teaches you much more.
b. **The golden rule** is concerned with true love and with positive, active behavior.
   - It is more than not doing wrong (lying, stealing, cheating).
   - It is more than just doing good (helping, caring, giving).

   The golden rule teaches you to search and seek for ways to do the good that you want others to do to you. It is seeking ways to treat others just as you want them to treat you.
c. **The golden rule** teaches the whole law. The whole law is contained in the words: "You shall love your neighbor as yourself" (Mk.12:31, NASB). All human beings want others to treat them as they should: to love and care for them and to demonstrate that love and care in their daily lives. Likewise, you are to love and care for others while on earth. You are to give earth a taste of heaven before all things end. When you treat people so favorably and they get a taste of heaven, they are more likely to turn to God and live righteously. They are more likely to help erase lawlessness, injustice, and evil from the face of the earth.

6. *You Must Not Hate Any Person: In the Eyes of God, Hate Is Equal to Murder.*

> **If anyone claims, "I am living in the light," but hates a Christian brother or sister, that person is still living in darkness. Anyone who loves another brother or sister is living in the light and does not cause others to stumble (1 Jn.2:9-10, NLT).**
>
> **Anyone who hates another brother or sister is really a murderer at heart. And you know that murderers don't have eternal life within them (1 Jn.3:15, NLT; see 1 Jn.2:9-10).**

Many people have always felt free to mistreat others, especially those who have been mistreated themselves. But Jesus Christ has shown that we are not to mistreat people *no matter what they have done*, that we must love everyone no matter who they are. Therefore, if you are a true follower of God, you are to love your neighbors, even those who are your enemies.

Scripture is clear: if you hate your neighbors—neglect, dislike, criticize, backbite, or mistreat them—you are not living in the light, not living *in Christ*. You are making a false profession. You do not know God, not really, no matter what you may claim. You are living in the darkness of this world, living as so many people in the world do, hating someone.

But look closely at what this verse says: if you hate your brother (or sister) you are a murderer (1 Jn.3:15). Hate is equal to murder and, in God's eyes, hate is the very same thing as murder.

Anger, bitterness, and contempt are just as serious in God's eyes as murder. Why? Because the person who hates has the very same feelings and spirit that the murderer does—a spirit of anger, bitterness, and contempt. The murderer reacts differently, more violently, but the hearts of both the hater and the murderer are the same. And God looks and judges by the heart. Some persons can camouflage what is in their hearts, but they cannot hide it from God. God knows their heart.

Note that murderers do not have eternal life within them. The implication is that neither does any person who hates his brother or sister. If you do not love, if you have negative feelings swirling within your heart, if you have allowed your heart to become hardened against your brother or sister—God says you do not have eternal life dwelling within you. You have death, separation, alienation, division. You have *cut off* fellowship with another human being; you have *put to death* the relationship that exists between you and your brother or sister. This is clear evidence that you have not truly trusted Christ as your Savior and Lord. A true believer—one who has eternal life dwelling within—will not continue to live with a spirit of hatred.

> **If someone says, "I love God," and hates his brother, he is a liar; for he who does not love his brother whom he has seen, how can he love God whom he has not seen? And this commandment we have from Him: that he who loves God *must* love his brother also (1 Jn.4:20-21, NKJV).**

C. You and Other Believers

1. *You Are to Love Other Believers with a Fervent Love—a Godly and Brotherly Love.*

> **"A new commandment I give to you, that you love one another, even as I have loved you, that you also love one another. "By this all men will know that you are My disciples, if you have love for one another" (Jn.13:34-35, NASB; see 1 Th.4:9).**

a. **Christ gave** you a new commandment: you are to love other believers with a *godly love*. God's love is what is known as *agape* love, which means a selfless and sacrificial love. It is God's love that drove Christ to die for you when you rejected God and stood as an enemy of God (see Ro.5:6-10).

For this reason, you are to love all believers with the very same love God has showered upon you. No matter how hostile or hurtful others have been or how undeserving or unworthy you feel they are, you are to love all believers with the very love of God Himself. This is the new commandment Christ has given you as a follower of His.

b. **God also commands** you to love other believers with a brotherly or sisterly love (1 Th.4:9). This is the very special love that exists between the brothers and sisters within a loving family, brothers and sisters who truly cherish each other. It is the kind of love...

- ➢ that holds deep affection for each other
- ➢ that nurtures each other
- ➢ that shows concern and looks after the welfare of each other
- ➢ that joins hands with each other in a common purpose *under one father*

There are three reasons why you must love other believers with a brotherly and sisterly love. First, you and other believers need each other in order to make it through life. Living for Christ is not easy in a corrupt world that offers the bright lights of pleasure but ends up in suffering death. We all face one temptation after another and seemingly endless trials. Some of us give in to the temptations and others of us react against the trials. Thus, we need God's love to accept, forgive, encourage, and restore one another.

Second, you and other believers will face differences. When differences arise, there is always the danger of becoming upset, angry, judgmental, or divisive. At such times, only a deep love will keep you from reacting.

Third, the greatest threat to your church and to the body of believers within your community is internal strife and divisiveness. Nothing destroys a church or body of believers any quicker than conflict, criticism, bickering, gossip, selfishness, cliques, and the ambition to have one's own way or to secure a certain position.

Therefore, you and other believers are to love one another with God's love. You are to love one another as *brothers and sisters* who belong to the family of God.

2. *You Are to Demonstrate Your Love—Act It Out, Show It—Every Moment of Every Day.*

> **Love is patient, love is kind. It does not envy, it does not boast, it is not proud. It is not rude, it is not self-seeking, it is not easily angered, it keeps no record of wrongs. Love does not delight in evil but rejoices with the truth. It always protects, always trusts, always hopes, always perseveres (1 Co.13:4-7, NIV).**

God actually tells you how you are to love others. He gives you a list of fifteen acts—the very behaviors you are to practice as you walk throughout life. The list reveals exactly how you are to live day by day, how you are to demonstrate that you truly love others. (A suggestion: each week, focus on two of these behaviors, looking for opportunities to practice the two. For example, begin this very day to practice patience and kindness every chance you can. Before long, the acts of love will be a part of your very nature. You will discover that you are demonstrating true love for people. And your family, friends, church, and world will be a far better place—all because you deliberately chose to obey God and to become a far more loving person.)

a. **Love is patient.** It suffers a long, long time no matter the evil or injury done by a person against you and no matter the neglect by a loved one.

   Love refuses to be resentful or to react and retaliate against people. Love always controls itself in order to seek reconciliation and good relations.

b. **Love is kind.** It is courteous, helpful, and giving. Love does not revel in hurting and neglecting others. Love reaches out in kindness by being helpful, giving, and showering favor upon the person who neglects or hurts you.

c. **Love does not envy**. It is not jealous. It does not hold feelings against others because of what they have, such as position, friends, recognition, possessions, popularity, abilities. Love does not begrudge, attack, or downplay the abilities and success of others.

d. **Love does not boast**. It does not brag or seek recognition, honor, or applause from others. On the contrary, love seeks to recognize, honor, and applaud other people.

e. **Love is not prideful**. It is not puffed up, arrogant, or conceited. If you truly love, you do not think or act as though you are better or above others. Love is modest and humble; it recognizes and honors others.

f. **Love is not rude**. It does not act indecently, unmannerly, or disgracefully. If you truly love, you do nothing to shame yourself or others. Love is orderly and controlled; it behaves and treats all individuals with respect and honor.

g. **Love is not self-seeking**. It does not insist upon its own rights; it is not focused upon who you are nor upon what you have done. Love seeks to serve, not have others serve you. Love is acknowledging others, not insisting that others acknowledge you; it is giving to others, not insisting that others give to you.

h. **Love is not easily angered**. It is not ready to take offence, not quick tempered, not *touchy,* does not become exasperated. If you truly love, you control your emotions and never become angry without a cause (Ro.12:18).

i. **Love does not keep a record of wrong** done against you. Love stirs you to suffer the evil done to you and to forget it.

j. **Love does not delight in evil**. Love never takes pleasure in unrighteousness or sin. If you truly love, you do not dwell upon sin and wrong, nor pass along the reports of sin and wrong.

k. **Love rejoices in the truth**. It rejoices when the truth is known and when it prevails. Love never covers or hides the truth; love is courageous in that it faces the truth.

l. **Love always protects**. The Greek word means both to cover all things and to bear up under all things. Love does both: it stands up under the weight and onslaught of all things and it covers up the faults of others. It has no pleasure in exposing the wrong or weaknesses of others. Love bears up under any neglect, abuse, ridicule—anything that is thrown against it.

m. **Love is completely trusting**. It is always eager to believe the best. Love sees and understands the circumstances, and forgives and believes the very best about a person.

n. **Love never ceases to hope**. Love refuses to accept failure; it always hopes for the best and for the ultimate triumph of the good. No matter how difficult gaining the victory may seem, love always hopes for a triumphant restoration and conquest.

o. **Love always perseveres**. The word is a military term meaning to stand against the attack of an enemy. Love actively fights and perseveres against all attacks. Love is strong, and it struggles against every assault to be unloving. If you truly love, you endure all things. No matter what attacks you, your love endures the attack and continues to love.

3. *You Are to Seek Peace with Other Believers—Always Seek to Live in Harmony with Everyone.*

> **Finally, all *of you be* of one mind, having compassion for one another; love as brothers, *be* tenderhearted, *be* courteous (1 Pe.3:8, NKJV).**

When the world looks at you, what do they see? A person who is filled with prejudice and discrimination, giving preference to some people and degrading others? In your day-to-day behavior, are you seen as...

- combative?
- argumentative?
- divisive?
- a bickerer?
- a brawler?
- a complainer?

Hopefully, the world does not see you like this, for you are important to God and to the building up of His kingdom. When you first approached God through Jesus Christ, God adopted you into His dear family and you became His son or daughter—a brother or sister to all the other children of God. Furthermore, God's Spirit entered your life just as He does the life of every believer. Simply stated, God's Spirit, who lives within all believers, bound you and all other believers together. There is a spiritual bond of peace that God's Spirit works out between you and other believers; therefore, you are to...

- ➢ set aside all divisiveness, differences, and prejudices
- ➢ stir up love, peace, and unity

How can you and all other believers live in peace and demonstrate a spirit of unity among yourselves? How can believers from all over the world, who have such diverse personalities and cultures, be closer than earthly brothers and sisters? Scripture spells out how in six points:

a. **You need to be** of one mind with other believers. Focus your mind on Jesus Christ, on becoming like Him and being conformed to the very image of Christ. Keep your mind upon living a holy, righteous, and pure life and upon carrying out the mission of Christ to reach the whole world with the glorious gospel.

b. **You need to be** compassionate toward other believers, always showing sympathy for them:

   - ➢ Suffer with those who suffer.
   - ➢ Weep with those who weep.
   - ➢ Rejoice when others are honored.
   - ➢ Be supportive of leaders under great pressure in difficult times.
   - ➢ Hurt with those who are criticized and attacked.
   - ➢ Grieve over the sorrows of others.

   Unity cannot exist unless you and other believers feel compassion and kindness for one another. You cannot be selfish and aloof, nor seeking attention and your own way if you are to be unified. Unity demands sympathy—that you feel for one another—that you feel so deeply that you actually experience what other believers are experiencing: pain, hurt, abuse, suffering, joy, and rejoicing.

c. **You need to have** brotherly love for other believers. Treat every believer as though he or she is a member of your family, for each one is as much a member of God's family as you are.

d. **You need to be** tenderhearted toward other believers—be sensitive and considerate toward the needs of others.

e. **You need to be** courteous and humble. You may occupy a high position or have power, wealth, fame, and much more; but you are *to live* in a spirit of submissiveness and lowliness, not to act proud, arrogant, or assertive. Humility is to be developed. Scripture tells you how:

> **Don't be selfish; don't try to impress others. Be humble, thinking of others as better than yourselves. Don't look out only for your own interests, but take an interest in others, too (Ph.2:3-4, NLT).**

4. *You Should Motivate Other Believers to Love One Another and to Do Good Works.*

> **And let us consider one another in order to stir up love and good works (He.10:24, NKJV).**

To *consider* means to fix your attention upon and to be concerned about—to watch over. What an exhortation to you and all other believers!

How different the world would be—how much stronger the church would be—if you and other believers heeded this exhortation! You should stir up one another and make sure you are living for Christ, that you are loving one another and doing good works. This simply means...

- to be considerate of one another
- to show concern for one another
- to meet one another's needs
- to strengthen one another's weaknesses
- to help one another through the trials and temptations of life

It means that you love by actions and not just in your words—that you...

- feed the poor
- visit the sick and shut-ins
- look after the orphans and the children of broken homes and single parents
- become a friend to the lonely
- give direction to the empty and those without purpose
- bear strong witness to unbelievers and restore backsliders

Again, believers are being exhorted to give attention to other believers. Why? To make sure none are being negligent or careless in their service, to stir one another to love and to do good works. This is your duty, the duty of every true believer. Your faith in Christ is not to be a *dead* faith but a *living* faith, a faith that stirs you to action. You should motivate other believers to love one another and to do good works for the sake of a sick and needful world.

D. YOU AND YOUR ENEMIES: THOSE WHO OPPOSE AND PERSECUTE YOU

1. *You Are to Love and Pray for Your Enemies and All Who Curse, Hate, and Mistreat You.*

> **"But I say to you who hear, love your enemies, do good to those who hate you, bless those who curse you, pray for those who mistreat you (Lu.6:27-28, NASB).**

God's law says, "You should love your neighbor as yourself" (Le.19:18). People make two serious mistakes in interpreting this law:

- Some people say *neighbor* refers only to people of their own community, religion, and nation. They do not include anyone else. In fact, they shut out and cut off everyone else.
- Other people rationalize that they are to *hate their enemies.* If God says, "Love your neighbor," they reason and add, "Hate your enemy" (those *not* their neighbors).

There is no question, human reasoning actually leads you to think you should oppose your enemy. But such thinking is not of God, and it is not what God knows to be best for the world: love, joy, peace... (Ga.5:22-23). The real meaning of the law *to love* involves four very practical acts (see 1 Co.13:4-7).

a. "Love your enemies" (v.27). The word for *love* is *agape* love. This is the love of the mind, reason, and choice. It is a sacrificial love, that is, a love that cares, gives, and works for another person's good no matter how the person may respond to or treat you. You are to deliberately choose to love a world of antagonistic people for their own good (their salvation and hope of eternity).

However, your love is not to be complacent acceptance of wickedness and license. You are not to sit back and allow a person to do as he or she pleases if the behavior is hurtful. Agape love is putting a stop to sin and license as much as possible. It is restraint, control, discipline, and even punishment when it protects the offender from him- or herself and protects those whom the individual hurts. Very simply, it is like a parent controlling a child for his own good and for the good of those who love him.

b. "Do good to those who hate you" (v.27). Imagine the impact of these words to the people of Jesus' day. They were an enslaved people, conquered and hated by the Romans, yet Jesus was saying, "Do good to them."

Note that *doing good* goes beyond words; it actually does *good* for those who hate you. It means that you reach out to them through their families, friends, and other known associations. It searches for ways to do good to them, realizing that they need to be reached for Christ. If no immediate way is found, then you continue to bless them, ever waiting for the day when they will face one of the crises that comes to every human being. And then you go and do good, ministering as Christ Himself ministered.

c. "Bless those who curse you" (v.28). People do curse other people. When someone curses you, bless the curser. Do not rail back. Speak softly; use kind and reconciling words.

d. "Pray for those who mistreat you" (v.28). This refers to those who attempt to shame and hurt you. People may mistreat, abuse, attack, and persecute you. What are you to do? Christ says, "Pray for them." Pray for God to forgive the persecutor. Pray for peace between yourself and the persecutor. Pray for the persecutor's salvation and correction.

Praying for the persecutor will greatly benefit you. It will keep you from becoming bitter, hostile, and reactionary.

2. *You Are Not to Retaliate nor Seek Revenge Against Those Who Hurt or Harm You.*

> **"You have heard that it was said, 'An eye for an eye , and a tooth for a tooth .' "But I say to you, do not resist an evil person; but whoever slaps you on your right cheek, turn the other to him also (Mt.5:38-39, NASB).**
>
> **Never take your own revenge, beloved, but leave room for the wrath *of God,* for it is written, "Vengeance is Mine , I will repay," says the Lord. "But if your enemy is hungry , feed him, and if he is thirsty , give him a drink ; for in so doing you will heap burning coals on his head." Do not be overcome by evil, but overcome evil with good (Ro.12:19-21, NASB).**

a. This law—"an eye for an eye, and a tooth for a tooth"—has been greatly abused down through the centuries. It is often thought to be justification for retaliation. But God's purpose for the law was to *show mercy* and to *limit vengeance*. Christ clarifies the law, saying that a person is not to retaliate. You are not to seek evil for evil; that is, do not bear a grudge or resent those who have mistreated you. Do not seek revenge or look for a chance to retaliate. Instead, forgive; go out of your way to help those who do evil against you. Such an attitude is the only way to ever reach them for the Kingdom of Heaven (Mt.4:17; 5:3, 10, 19, 21-22).

However, Christ is not saying you are never to resist evil. Jesus followed the new law in that He observed the spirit of the law, but He was not enslaved by it. There are times when a person needs to take a stand against evil. (See ch.5, section Q, pt.2, pp.257-258 for more discussion.)

b. **Christ teaches you** how to treat those who do wrong against you. You are to accept physical injury: turn the other cheek. Turning the other cheek is difficult. It means that you do not retaliate against the most terrible insults or bitter contempt—not even against threats of bodily harm. You are not to challenge, resent, retaliate, or enter a legal action against an attacker; rather, you prepare for another slap and bear it patiently. You let it pass and accept it. You forgive and entrust the matter to God. There is the knowledge that God will work all things out for good as you go about your life and service for God. If you endure shameful treatment, you will reap eternal glory (Ro.8:16-17).

c. **You must** never give any place to revenge (Ro.12:19). Vengeance belongs to God. Note the word *beloved*. The exhortation is definitely directed to believers. It would be a wonderful thing if everyone practiced and lived by this rule, but the world never has and never will live free of vengeance. However, you, the *beloved* of God, are given no choice. If you are a sincere follower of God, leave vengeance up to God. Vengeance belongs to God, not to you.

Scripture is clear: God will repay; God will execute vengeance. The day of His wrath is coming upon all the wicked mockers and persecutors of His people, all who hurt and harm His people, and it will be inescapable.

d. **You must treat** an enemy with kindness. By doing good, you heap "coals of fire" on your enemy's head. Your kindness will shame and cause anguish for the individual. In lonely moments, an enemy's thoughts will focus upon his or her evil treatment of you and other believers. God's Spirit will stir that person to think and wonder about God. There is some chance your enemy might repent and be converted.

e. **Vengeance makes** evil victorious. If you take vengeance, then you allow evil to conquer you, and this you should never do. As you go forth day by day, conquer evil by doing good. Overcome evil by doing what you should do, in particular, by doing good toward those who mistreat and abuse you.

> **"But I say to you, love your enemies and pray for those who persecute you" (Mt.5:44, NASB).**

CHAPTER 4

WHAT YOUR DAILY BEHAVIOR SHOULD BE

Contents

CHAPTER 4

WHAT YOUR DAILY BEHAVIOR SHOULD BE

A. YOU AND GOD'S AGELESS COMMANDMENTS

1. You Are Not to Believe in False Gods.

"You shall have no other gods before Me (Ex.20:3, NASB).

God exists. There is a Creator of the universe: the one true and living God. He is the LORD God of the universe, the Father of the Lord Jesus Christ. He created all that is, including the laws that govern the universe and that sustain the human race. The fact that God created you means that God cares for you. He cares about your welfare, what happens to you as you walk through life day by day. God cares about something else as well; He cares about what you think of Him. In fact, what you think about God determines your eternal fate.

Considering its importance, you need to understand specifically how this commandment is broken or violated. But first, one very important truth needs to be addressed:

a. **This commandment** declares that God alone is the *Supreme Being*, the absolute authority of the universe. There is no other *supreme being*, no other god who created or who rules over the universe. He alone is the LORD, the only living and true God.

As such, you *must acknowledge* the only true and living God, that the LORD Himself exists. God has declared that people who think there is no God are wrong. *Atheists* may deny God, and *agnostics* may question if God really exists, but God is forceful in His declaration: "I AM—I AM the LORD Your God" (Ex.20:2, KJV).

"The fool [has] said in his heart, There is no God" (Ps.14:1, KJV).

"I am the Lord: that is my name: and my glory will I not give to another, neither my praise to graven images" (Is.42:8, KJV).

b. **This commandment requires** that you have *no other gods, none whatsoever* (v.3). It is not enough just to acknowledge that God is, that He *exists.* In addition, you must not set up anything else as a god. You must not believe that any other being in the world is the ultimate source of the universe. No spirit or combination of spirits and no impersonal mass, energy, or gas is *the force* behind all things in the universe.

   This first commandment is also saying that you are not to look to other beings, animals, or material things as God. You are not to look in the sky above or in the earth below or in the depths of the sea and declare that anything therein is God.

   There are not many gods (polytheism). There is only one living and true God, only one true Creator, only one LORD and Majesty of the universe (monotheism). All other so-called gods are nothing more than...

   - people's ideas and imaginations
   - lifeless and powerless objects
   - images made from substances such as metal, wood, stone, chemicals, or dirt—all elements God Himself created

c. **This commandment requires** that you put no other gods *"before Me* [the only living and true God]*"* (Ex.20:3). The words *before Me* literally mean *before My face, against My face, in hostility toward Me, in My presence, in My sight.*

   If you set up anything in your heart or mind that absorbs the love and service that belong only to the true God, then that thing becomes a rival interest, another god. Whatever your heart clings to, that becomes your god. Consequently...

   - the proud person who idolizes self makes self a god
   - the ambitious person who does whatever is necessary to climb to the top makes a god out of his or her ambition.
   - the covetous person who craves more and more worldly possessions makes a god out of this world's goods
   - the immoral person who craves sex makes a god out of sex
   - the glutton who craves food makes food a god
   - the adoring companion—whether husband, wife, parent, friend, boyfriend, or girlfriend—who sets his or her *first affection* on the person loved instead of upon God makes that person a god

Without knowing it, you can make a god out of anything that you esteem, love, fear, or serve more than God. It does not even need to be a person to be elevated to that position. You can make a god out of...

- heavenly bodies
- science
- animals
- career
- family
- sex
- food
- money and property
- position and power
- recognition and fame
- celebrities and sports stars
- sports and recreation
- television or movies
- partying and dancing

A false god can be any *thing* or any *person* that takes precedence in your life over the living and true God. Your first allegiance—the most important thing in your life—is to be the LORD God. He is to be enthroned in your heart. You should strive, even struggle, to be sure God is always given His rightful place in your life, for there is only one true God.

2. *You Are Not to Make or Worship False Gods.*

> **"You must not make for yourself an idol of any kind or an image of anything in the heavens or on the earth or in the sea. You must not bow down to them or worship them, for I, the Lord your God, am a jealous God who will not tolerate your affection for any other gods. I lay the sins of the parents upon their children; the entire family is affected—even children in the third and fourth generations of those who reject me. But I lavish unfailing love for a thousand generations on those who love me and obey my commands" (Ex.20:4-6, NLT).**

Every person on earth worships something. The great tragedy is that many people worship something other than the only true and living God.

In fact, the number of false gods people worship is endless. Every person has an image of what the *supreme* authority of the universe is, an image of what people should acknowledge or worship. Yet, the unmistakable emphasis of this commandment is that you must give your life to the only true and living God, that you must worship Him and Him alone. Note four significant points:

a. **This commandment prohibits** the *making* of any idol or any image for the purpose of worship (v.4). Verse four is very explicit: nothing in the universe is to be made into an idol, held up as an object of worship...

- not heavenly creatures such as angels, demons, or some imaginary god
- not heavenly bodies such as the sun, moon, or stars
- not earthly creatures such as cows, elephants, or people
- not water creatures such as fish, crocodiles, or sea animals

A question needs to be asked at this point: What about images such as pictures, crucifixes, statues, and other symbols that are used to stir and remind us to pray and worship? Is this commandment speaking against such images? Reason and honesty demand that we acknowledge the following fact: there is a tendency within human nature to focus on the object (the picture, crucifix, statue) instead of upon God. With that in mind, if we use visible objects to arouse us to pray and worship, there is great danger...

- that a pure and spiritual worship of God will fade and be degraded
- that the physical object will become more valued and receive more of our attention than God. Why? Because God is a spiritual being and is unseen, and the physical object is seen.

William Barclay has an excellent statement on idolatry. Consider carefully what he says:

> *[Idolatry] began because men found it difficult to worship a god they could not see. So they said to themselves, "We will make something which will represent the god and that will make it easier to think of the god." In the first instance the idol was never meant to be the god; it was meant only to stand for the god...*
>
> *The trouble was that men began to worship the idol instead of the god it stood for; men began to worship the symbol instead of the reality it was supposed to represent. It is not really difficult to see how idolatry began, and it is not really so silly as it looks. For all that, we may well be saying, "I am not likely to do a thing like that." But perhaps we are more likely to do it than we think.*
>
> *Take a very small thing first of all. Quite a lot of people carry some kind of lucky mascot, some kind of charm. Some carry a lucky penny or a lucky sign of the zodiac, or, for instance, if they go on a journey, they take a St. Christopher sign to avoid accidents. That is really idolatry, for it is believing that in some way the carrying*

of a little bit of metal or plastic can have an effect on their lives.

But there is something much more serious than that. The real essence of idolatry is that a man worships a thing instead of God.

There is no doubt at all that there is a great deal of that today. People assess their success in life by the number of things which they possess....

This is obviously wrong.[1]

Having said this, the commandment does not forbid artistic talent, that is, the making of sculptures, pictures, statues, and crucifixes for their artistic beauty and appreciation. The commandment strikes against making and using images and idols...

- for the purpose of worship
- for the purpose of giving us guidance in our lives and looking after us

This steals our hearts away from the only living and true God. Adrian Rogers, an excellent expositor of God's Word, makes a statement on idolatry that is well worth your attention.

Idolatry is wrong because it gives a distorted or false picture of God. An idol is a material thing, and no idol can represent the invisible, spiritual God. Jesus said in John 4:24, 'God is a Spirit.'... That is, spirit is His very essence.

No wonder, then, that Jesus went on to say, 'They that worship him must worship him in spirit and in truth.' What material thing could possibly represent spirit?...There is nowhere where God is not, and no material thing can represent Him.

There's nothing you can compare God to or with. There's nothing that says, "This is what God is totally like." God Himself asked, "To whom then will ye liken me, or shall I be equal?" (Isaiah 40:25). We can say one man is like another man, one chair is like another chair, one piano like another piano, and so on. But there's only one God. You can't compare Him to anything or anyone....

Suppose a woman walks into a room and finds her husband embracing another woman. He sees his wife out of the corner of his eye and says, "Now wait a minute, honey. Don't get the wrong idea here. Let me tell you what I was doing. This woman is so beautiful, she

1 William Barclay. *The Old Law and the New Law.* (Edinburgh, Scotland: The Saint Andrew Press, 1972), pp.11-13.

reminded me of you. I was really just thinking of you when I was embracing her."

There's not a woman in America who would buy that, including my wife, Joyce! And God doesn't buy it either when we worship something else and say, "Now, Lord, wait a minute. Don't get the wrong idea here. I was only worshiping this thing because it reminds me of You. I'm really worshiping You."

No, you really aren't. That's what the Second Commandment is all about.[2]

b. **This commandment prohibits** the *worship* of any false god whatsoever, prohibits the worship of anything other than God Himself (v.5). This strikes a death blow against one of the most common beliefs and claims of people: that all religions worship the same god, that no matter what we may call god and no matter what religion we follow, we all worship the same *supreme being*.

Remember the first commandment: there are no other gods; there is only one true and living God (v.3). Therefore, if you create a god within your mind and if you worship some other so-called god, you misrepresent the truth. Your idea of God is inaccurate, incomplete, and false. Understandably, false worship is a gross insult to the *only* living and true God, to the *only* Sovereign LORD and Majesty of the universe.

Simply stated, it is wrong to worship the image of God created by your or anyone else's imagination. God has revealed Himself, exactly who He is and what He is like, in the Lord Jesus Christ and in the Holy Bible. It is the God revealed by Jesus Christ and the Holy Bible that you are to keep in your mind and worship. He alone is the *LORD God of revelation*.

c. **God prohibits** the worship of idols because He is a jealous God (v.5). The Hebrew word for *jealous* means to be red in the face. God loves and cares for you. He does not want you or anyone else living in error and following false gods, because they can do absolutely nothing to meet the deep needs of your heart or to empower you to live forever. So the LORD is jealous of anything or anyone that turns you and others away from the truth and from God Himself.

If you give your primary attention, honor, time, or money to any *thing* or any *one* other than God Himself, you are committing *spiritual adultery* against God

---

2 Adrian Rogers. *Ten Secrets for a Successful Family*. (Wheaton, IL: Crossway Books, 1996), pp.44-45.

(Mt.12:39; Js.4:4). You are turning away from God to something else. The result: God becomes jealous because you are being unfaithful to Him. You must never forget: God does not tolerate unfaithfulness. He will never allow a rival to replace Him. God's jealousy will not allow His glory and honor to be transferred to another object or person.

d. God prohibits the worship of idols because the influence of idolatry is passed down from the parents to their children (vv.5-6). If you worship false gods, put other things or people before God, then you will most likely lead your children and grandchildren into idolatry. What you do greatly influences and affects your family.

If you worship idols, your children will most likely worship idols also. And all idolaters will be judged by God. Therefore, the sin of idolatry and the judgment upon idolatry are passed down from generation to generation. Terrible consequences! All due to the *sins of the fathers and mothers*, especially the evil sin of idolatry.

This is what is known as the *judicial judgment of God*, a judgment that is justly deserved. If parents sow the seed of idolatry, they are usually going to bear children who will be greatly influenced by their behavior. The children will deny God and worship the idols of this world. This does not mean that God holds a child guilty for the sins of his parents. God is not talking about the guilt of sin. He is talking about the results, the consequences of sin. Each person will bear the judgment for his or her own sin. No person will ever be judged and punished for the sins of others.

Quite the opposite is true for the children of loving and obedient parents. God says He will actually lavish His love on them for a thousand generations (v.6)! Note that the sin and punishment of idolatry are passed down for three or four generations, but the love of God is lavished on the children of loving, obedient parents for *thousands of generations*.

This demonstrates the awesome influence of parents upon their children and the absolute necessity for them to set a godly example before them.

3. *You Are Not to Misuse God's Name or Use Any Profane or Vulgar Language.*

> **"You must not misuse the name of the Lord your God. The Lord will not let you go unpunished if you misuse his name" (Ex.20:7, NLT).**

How is this commandment broken or violated? There are at least four ways that you can misuse God's name or take His name in vain.

a. **You misuse** God's name through *profanity and vulgarity. Profanity* is the irreverent or contemptuous use of God's name. Vulgarity is using crude, distasteful, or offensive language. No one has the right to profane or curse God or anything else in His creation, including other persons.

b. **You misuse** God's name by *swearing falsely*. Perjury, lying under oath, is wrong. Swearing falsely may take place before a neighbor or business partner, a wife or husband, a judge or jury—anyone. Far too often, when we are called upon to swear or take an oath to verify that we are telling the truth, we lie; we swear falsely.

> **"Simply let your 'Yes' be 'Yes,' and your 'No,' 'No'; anything beyond this comes from the evil one" (Mt.5:37, NIV).**

c. **You misuse** God's name by speaking it in an *irreverent way*, in a frivolous, dishonoring, or flippant way. *Reverence* is the key word. When God's name is spoken, it is always to be with *reverence*. For example, all the little expletives or exclamatory statements that use God's name in a trivial or careless way are wrong:

- God Almighty
- Sweet Jesus
- Lord have mercy
- Oh, my God
- God or Christ (when spoken carelessly)
- The Man upstairs
- Somebody up there

Any use of God's name that is not reverent—that is not in prayer, praise, witness, worship, or a respectful conversation—is wrong. This means that all the flippant joking about God, the humorous stories that use God's name playfully are wrong. It also means that the superficial prayers said using God's name carelessly, repeatedly, and thoughtlessly are wrong: "Lord do this; Lord do that," "Lord bless," "Lord help."

God's name is sacred: it is holy, righteous, and pure. God's name encompasses all that He is—His omnipotence, omnipresence, and omniscience. God's name is always to be worshipped, praised, reverenced, never dishonored, misused, or taken in vain.

d. **You misuse** God's name through *hypocrisy,* through claiming the name of the Lord in an insincere or dishonest way. A hypocrite....

- is a person who professes the name of God, that is, to know God, but who lives for self and the world
- is a person who uses God's name to manipulate people (to get what he or she wants)
- is a person who uses God's name to secure support for causes that are not necessarily God's will (for example, politicians or religious leaders)
- is a person who uses God's name to secure followers or to deceive people

> **"Not everyone who says to me, 'Lord, Lord,' will enter the kingdom of heaven, but only he who does the will of my Father who is in heaven. Many will say to me on that day, 'Lord, Lord, did we not prophesy in your name, and in your name drive out demons and perform many miracles?' Then I will tell them plainly, 'I never knew you. Away from me, you evildoers!' " (Mt.7:21-23, NIV).**

God's message is clear. You must not misuse His name for one terrifying reason: the Lord holds you accountable; you will be punished. You may abuse God's name and think you have escaped correction or punishment, but God knows. And Scripture declares that God will take vengeance upon the person who insults His holy and glorious name. For this reason, carefully guard your heart and your tongue so that you never misuse God's holy name.

4. *You Are to Observe the Sabbath Day by Keeping It Holy.*

> **"Remember the sabbath day, to keep it holy" (Ex.20:8, KJV).**

Work, rest, and worship—these are three of the basic essentials of human life. You need all three because God made you this way. This is what the Sabbath is all about. God Himself divided time into seven days, for He created the universe in six days, then rested on the seventh day (Ge.2:1-3). Likewise, God says that you are to work for six days, then rest and worship on the seventh. God Himself set the day aside for you because He loves and cares for you; He knows what you need. You need a full day every week for rest, relaxation, and worship—so much so that God made it one of the ten great laws that are to govern human life.

a. The Hebrew word *Sabbath* does not mean the seventh day (Saturday) as so many people think. The word *Sabbath* means a time of rest. Thus, the Sabbath day is a day to cease from work, to rest from work. This is significant, for God is charging us to *keep* the Sabbath. He is not specifying a particular day of the week when you are to worship and rest. God simply says, work six days, then rest on the seventh day.

This fact is important for industrialized and technological societies. Why? Because so many people *have* to work on Saturday or Sunday, on the day set aside by their religion as the day of worship and rest. In many cases, factories cannot shut down their huge furnaces, boilers, or machines without damaging them mechanically. They have to be operated continually, requiring thousands upon thousands of people to work on Saturday and Sunday. The same is true with many service industries and other businesses.

When businesses have to operate seven days a week, what are the employees of these businesses to do about worship and rest? Three very practical things need to be done:

- ➢ The church needs to provide other services during the week so people who have to work on Saturday or Sunday can worship together at other times.
- ➢ People who work on the regular day of worship still need to rest and make every effort to worship God at the alternate services scheduled by the church.
- ➢ When alternate services are not available, people still need to set aside a very special time of prayer and devotion on their day off, their day of rest.

When God gave this law to Moses, the Jews set aside the seventh day, Saturday, as their day of worship and rest. Today, others follow their practice. But the largest body of Christian believers have switched their day of worship and rest from the last day of the week to the first day of the week, Sunday. Why?

- ➢ Because Jesus Christ burst loose from the bonds of death on the first day of the week. Believers wish to celebrate His glorious resurrection and the great hope of their salvation on the very day He arose.
- ➢ Because the first day of the week is called *"the Lord's day"* (Re.1:10). Believers want to worship on the Lord's day.

- Because the early followers of Christ switched their day of worship and rest to the first day of the week. The tradition has continued down through the centuries.

> **"And upon the first day of the week, when the disciples came together to break bread, Paul preached unto them, ready to depart on the morrow; and continued his speech until midnight" (Ac.20:7, KJV).**
>
> **"On the first day of every week each one of you is to put aside and save, as he may prosper, so that no collections be made when I come" (1 Co.16:2, NASB).**

b. The Sabbath, the day of rest and worship, is to be kept *holy.* To be holy means to be sanctified, set apart, dedicated to God. Thus, the Sabbath, the day of worship and rest...

- is to be a day set apart and devoted to God for worship and rest
- is to be a day that is honored and made sacred in obedience to God and His command
- is to be a day that focuses our minds upon living pure and clean lives, lives free from all defilement, sin, and evil
- is to be a day that is different and distinct from all other days of the week and people's busy schedules

> **"Exalt the Lord our God, and worship at his holy hill; for the Lord our God is holy" (Ps.99:9, KJV).**

God gave the fourth commandment for our good. Without the Sabbath rest, we would soon break down our bodies and be constantly exhausted, physically drained. Productivity would soon decline. This has been proven time and again in dictatorial nations and in slave markets that demand almost continuous work with no rest for its labor force. Productivity—as well as health, physical strength, mental alertness, and ability—declined sharply.

Resting one day a week is absolutely essential for the human body. Business and labor leaders, government officials and individuals—we all must protect our bodies and the productivity of our society and economies. How? By obeying God's fourth commandment: Remember the Sabbath day; keep it holy.

5. *You Are to Honor Your Father and Your Mother.*

"Honor your father and mother. Then you will live a long, full life in the land the Lord your God is giving you" (Ex.20:12, NLT).

The family is of vital importance, for the family was the first institution formed upon earth. God created the first man and woman, Adam and Eve, and they became man and wife; then Eve bore a son. Thereby, the first family was formed, created as the most important institution on earth, as the foundation of all human life and development that was to follow. It is the family unit that forms communities, societies, and nations. Consequently, as goes the family, so goes life on earth.

This truth has very serious implications for every generation: we must give attention to the family and strengthen it if the human race is to survive. The very survival of society and civilization depends upon strong families—fathers, mothers, and children—who honor and respect one another. For this reason, you, regardless of your age, must give attention to and fight against the evils that break down and destroy the family...

- selfishness
- disrespect
- withdrawal
- adultery
- divorce
- abuse
- hatred
- disobedience
- sexual deviancy
- indulgence
- license
- gambling
- alcohol, drugs
- pornography
- greed
- lawlessness
- unbelief
- ungodliness

God established the primacy—the preeminent status—of the family forever when He created the first man and the first woman. He reinforces the importance of the family with this great commandment: Honor your father and your mother.

The first four commandments covered your duty to God. But your very next duty is to honor your parents. The divine order is exactly this: God first, then your parents. (See Chapter 4, Section A, pt.6, pp. 61-63 for discussion of this commandment.)

6. *You Are to Value Human Life and Not Commit Murder.*

"You must not murder" (Ex.20:13, NLT).

Lawlessness, violence, and murder are sweeping over the earth. Untold numbers of people are being murdered and slaughtered every year. In some societies, the value of human life is almost worthless. In general, people have become desensitized and hardened to brutality and bloodshed.

- The headlines of news and media reports are usually filled with terrible crimes. Only the names and locations change.
- The entertainment industry (television, movies, video games, music, books, and other outlets) often focuses upon lawlessness, violence, and murder. Tragically, life is pictured as cheap, and our minds—especially young minds—are bombarded by endless acts of savagery and slaughter.
- The rich, powerful, and lawless sometimes enslave, assault, and even murder others in order to enrich themselves. They consider certain human beings, even young children, to be nothing more than chattel property.

The subject of this commandment can never be overemphasized: You must not murder. Six significant points need to be thought through when dealing with this commandment.

a. **The purpose** for this commandment is to preserve life, to teach you the *sanctity of all human life.* You are to honor and hold human life in the highest regard. You are created in the image and likeness of God; therefore, your life is of infinite value to God (Ge.1:26-27). In fact, your life is valued above all the wealth in the world (Mt.16:26; Mk.8:36). Hence, the sanctity of human life is to be honored above all else.

> **"For what will it profit a man if he gains the whole world, and loses his own soul?" (Mk. 8:36; see Mt.16:26, NKJV).**

b. **What is forbidden** by this commandment? The Hebrew word for *murder* refers to the premeditated and unauthorized taking of life. This commandment is broken either by a planned murderous attack upon a person(s) or by a rash, reckless attack. But there are also other forms of murder that are just as wrong as lifting one's hand to kill another person. All over the world, there are individuals who commit murder...

- by forcing people to work in harsh and dangerous conditions that will injure or eventually kill them, that lead to their premature death

- by forcing people to live in appalling conditions, so horrible that the environment or lack of basic necessities eventually kills them
- by selling people drugs that eventually enslave and sometimes kill them

We must control and punish the lawless, the violent, and the murderers who roam the streets and, in many cases, sit in the plush offices of authority and rule. Evil individuals, groups, gangs, and organizations need to be stopped and taught to obey this commandment or else a *free and just* civilization can never survive. The only conceivable way we can have safe streets and parks, unlocked doors, and the freedom to move about is to do our best to stamp out lawlessness, violence, and murder.

c. **This sixth commandment** is not a blanket law against all killing. God's Word clearly says that some taking of life is justified, understandable, and allowed...

- as capital punishment (Ge.9:6)
- in a justified war (De.13:15; 1 S.15:3; 2 S.10:1f)
- in the defense of ourselves, for example, if a thief breaks into our home (Ex.22:2)
- in accidental killing (De.19:5)
- in killing animals for food (Ge.9:3)

d. **The judgment of God** upon the murderer is death: spiritual and eternal death.

> **"But for the cowardly and unbelieving and abominable and murderers and immoral persons and sorcerers and idolaters and all liars, their part *will be* in the lake that burns with fire and brimstone, which is the second death" (Re.21:8, NASB).**

e. **Can a murderer be** saved and forgiven for taking someone's life? Scripture says a resounding "Yes!" Although, if you are a murderer, you must confess your sin, repent, and turn away from your life of sin. You need to genuinely give your heart and life to Jesus Christ and live for Him.

> **"Let the wicked forsake his way, and the unrighteous man his thoughts: and let him return [to] the LORD, and he will have mercy upon him; and to our God, for he will abundantly pardon" (Is.55:7, KJV).**

> **"For the wages of sin is death; but the gift of God is eternal life through Jesus Christ our Lord" (Ro.6:23, KJV).**

f. **Jesus Christ taught** that this commandment means far more than just prohibiting the killing of people. He enlarged the meaning to include both the anger that is aroused within the heart and the lawless motives that drive a person to kill someone else.

> **"You have heard that our ancestors were told, 'You must not murder. If you commit murder, you are subject to judgment.' But I say, if you are even angry with someone, you are subject to judgment! If you call someone an idiot, you are in danger of being brought before the court. And if you curse someone, you are in danger of the fires of hell" (Mt.5:21-22, NLT).**

Christ is saying that the human race misreads or diminishes God's law. We interpret God's law to say what we wish it to say. We apply it only to the outward act, in this case, to the act of murder. We fail to look within ourselves to the *cause* of the act.

Murder goes deeper than just the outward act. It is an act born from within: an act of anger, bitterness, enmity. Murder arises from an uncontrolled spirit, from an inner anger. Anger itself is the root sin, the sin that first breaks the law of God. And the growth of anger is dangerous. Unresolved anger will fester and can quickly get out of control, even giving birth to murder.

As a believer, you are to control your anger and never take the life of another. But always remember, there is justified anger. In fact, as a believer, you should be angry with those who sin and do wrong, who are unjust and selfish in their behavior. However, justified anger is always disciplined and controlled; it is always limited to those who do wrong either against God or against others. The distinguishing mark between justified and unjustified anger is that justified anger is never selfish; it is never merely a reaction to what has happened to you. It is anger that is purposeful. Justified anger seeks to correct a wicked or irresponsible situation in the most peaceful way possible.

> **"Be angry, and *yet* do not sin; do not let the sun go down on your anger" (Ep.4:26, NASB).**

> **"If possible, so far as it depends on you, be at peace with all men" (Ro.12:18, NASB).**

Too often, hurt feelings exist between those who are supposed to be the closest (husband and wife, parent and child, close friends, and a number of other relationships). The LORD is clear about the matter: you must never allow anger to take hold of your heart without just cause, and you must never commit murder.

7. *You Are Not to Commit Adultery or Any Other Act of Immorality.*

> **"You shall not commit adultery" (Ex.20:14, NASB).**

There is, without question, a cesspool of immorality in society today. Yet, most honest and thinking observers of history would say that immorality is, and has been, a very serious problem in every generation of human history. Why is it such a problem? Because immorality threatens the family, the very foundation of society and civilization. The family is the primary place where trust, loyalty, and love are to be taught and demonstrated. If we will not be faithful and loyal to our families, whom we can see, how can we be trusted to be faithful and loyal to our nation, society, and civilization, which are intangible ideals?

God gave us this commandment—you must not commit adultery—to preserve the great qualities that bring peace, love, and trust to our lives, qualities that build healthy minds and hearts. With this in mind, it is critical to grasp the broad scale of this important commandment concerning morality.

a. **What God says** is simple and binding. It is not open to interpretation. "You shall not commit adultery." You are not to debase or corrupt yourself nor to have sex outside of marriage. Scripture teaches that you become sexually impure in at least three ways:

   - You have sex with someone other than your spouse. This is what is commonly called *adultery*.
   - You have sex before marriage. This is known as *fornication*. Fornication refers to any sexual immorality, either before marriage or during marriage.
   - You fantasize about and lust after a person other than your spouse, allowing your thoughts to wander and to dwell upon another person (Mt.5:27-30).

The sin of adultery also embraces all that leads up to the act of sex, not just the sexual act itself. Adultery is far more than just being sexually unfaithful in marriage. This commandment, which applies equally to men and women, forbids any *thought or act...*

- that corrupts or makes you impure for marriage
- that spots or defiles your marriage
- that causes you to lose your virginity
- that keeps you from being able to offer yourself as a pure virgin when married

When dealing with adultery, a person's thought-life is key, for adultery is committed in the heart long before the sexual act is committed. Always keep in mind that God's law is spiritual. It deals with what is in the heart and mind. This commandment forbids committing adultery in the heart and, by implication, the act of adultery itself. You are...

- not to prostitute your thoughts and imagination
- not to allow impure, lustful thoughts
- not to indulge in illicit fantasies

> **"You have heard the commandment that says, 'You must not commit adultery.' But I say, anyone who even looks at a woman with lust has already committed adultery with her in his heart. So if your eye—even your good eye—causes you to lust, gouge it out and throw it away. It is better for you to lose one part of your body than for your whole body to be thrown into hell. And if your hand—even your stronger hand—causes you to sin [through touching], cut it off and throw it away. It is better for you to lose one part of your body than for your whole body to be thrown into hell" (Mt.5:27-30, NLT).**

b. What causes adultery and immorality? The explanations are many and varied, but perhaps they can all be summarized under the following five categories.

First, immorality can be caused by corrupt moral standards or a lack of moral standards. Some people have never been taught, nor are they aware, that sex outside of marriage is wrong in the sight of God. In some cases, society has become so corrupt through the years that belief in the sanctity of sex and marriage has been lost, as well as a belief in the true and living God.

Second, immorality can be caused by lax or liberal moral standards or by selfish, worldly living. Some people either ignore or deny God's commandment or they *redefine* it to mean what they want so they can live as they wish.

Third, immorality can be caused by the need for companionship, attention, or love, or by the need for appreciation and fulfillment. Many people reach out to others because of these very basic needs. This is especially true during marriage when a husband or wife fails to meet these needs in his or her spouse.

Fourth, immorality can be caused by anger, hostility, or a desire for revenge. A host of behaviors such as coldness, indifference, neglect, a biting tongue, harshness, or selfishness can anger spouses and cause them to turn elsewhere out of spite. But what may start out as a simple means to hurt a spouse can quickly lead to lustful thoughts and temptations and end up in adultery.

Fifth, immorality can be caused either by poor ego strength or by an inflated ego, either by a lack of self-esteem or by an exaggerated sense of self-worth. The need to display one's power and importance through the challenge and conquest of an affair can also cause immoral behavior. Since the most intimate thing a person can give to another person is his or her body, the sexual act becomes a challenge for many people; it is an ego booster, an act that can build a person's feelings of worth or add to his or her trophy case of conquests.

Bear in mind that sex is a very normal, natural act, a most precious and cherished act given by God. God has built the desire for sex into the very nature of human beings. In fact, sex is the most intimate experience God has chosen for us to nourish the great virtues of life and to carry on the human race. But our depraved, sinful hearts have corrupted sex, so much so that we have developed a sex-crazed society. In very practical terms, immorality can be caused...

- by ignoring or denying God and His Holy Word
- by ignoring right vs. wrong
- by a lack of teaching and training
- by unsatisfying or inadequate sexual relations with a spouse
- by the coldness or alienation of a husband or wife
- by living in a dream or fantasy world due to such things as pornography or suggestive music, films, or books
- by not guarding the marital relationship, getting too close and becoming attracted to or tempted by another person

c. **Why does God** forbid adultery, prohibit immorality? Remember what is stated above: God has so intertwined sex within our nature that we instinctively desire it. God not only approves of sex but He also created the experience of sex. At the same time, though, He put boundaries and limits around sex. Sex was created for marriage and for the home and *only* for marriage and the home. This leads us to the purposes for sex, the reasons God gave this seventh commandment.

God gave the seventh commandment to preserve and safeguard our value as individuals, the sanctity of our bodies and spirits. When a man and woman lie together, they are never more vulnerable. Lying together, their bodies and spirits are more exposed than at any other time. God intended the act of sex to be one of the most intimate, warm, and precious experiences of human life. Sex was created so that two people could grow together and nourish each other in...

- love
- joy
- peace
- trust
- loyalty
- perseverance
- devotion
- comfort
- care
- security
- self-esteem
- a sense of fulfillment

On and on the list could go, but note all the wonderful and strong qualities that the sexual union is supposed to develop between two people. These things are so important for a healthy personality that God devised a perfect plan. He ordained that one man and one woman were to give their lives to each other, that they were to focus upon sharing and developing the wonderful qualities of life in the other. For this reason, God ordained marriage. But, sex outside of marriage rarely develops these qualities. Illicit sex causes problems such as...

- shame
- guilt
- jealousy
- a sense of being used
- selfishness
- broken marriages
- financial problems
- insecurity
- disloyalty
- unhappiness
- disease
- a cheapening of sex
- broken trust
- unwanted pregnancies
- loss of self-esteem
- loss of respect for others
- loss of respect by others
- dissolution of the family
- problem children
- insecure children
- emotional problems
- a lack of fulfillment
- loss of affection
- ruined relationships

God also gave the seventh commandment to preserve the family and the human race—society itself. The family is the basic unit of any society; therefore, the family has to be protected and preserved for society to survive. When husbands and wives are living in love and are faithful to each other, the great qualities of life are learned and taught. These qualities—loyalty, trust, commitment, love, joy, and peace—are the very qualities that grow and develop fruitful lives, families, and nations. No family, society, or nation can survive without these great qualities.

God demands the *sanctity of marriage*. He demands that husbands and wives be pure and faithful to each other, that they love each other and never commit adultery:

> **"You shall not commit adultery" (Ex.20:14, NKJV).**
>
> **"Abstain from fornication" (1 Th.4:3, KJV).**
>
> **"Abstain from fleshly lusts, which war against the soul" (1 Pe.2:11, KJV).**

d. How can you guard yourself and keep from committing sexual sin in a sex-crazed society—a society that uses sexual appeal to sell products, provide entertainment, pleasure, recreation, and clothing for every occasion? Scripture says the following:

- Never take a second look. And if you can prevent the first look, *never* look. As someone has said, you cannot keep the birds from flying over your head, but you can prevent them from roosting there.

> **"But I say, anyone who even looks at a woman with lust has already committed adultery with her in his heart" (Mt.5:28, NLT).**

- Flee temptation; flee the very appearance of evil. You need to flee at the very first offer, the very first sight, the very first thought, the very first urge (desire).

> **"Abstain from all appearance of evil" (1 Th.5:22, KJV).**
>
> **"Flee fornication [all forms of illicit sex]" (1 Co.6:18, KJV).**
>
> **"It is God's will that you should be sanctified: that you should avoid sexual immorality; that each of you should learn to control his own body in a way that is holy and honorable, not in**

passionate lust like the heathen, who do not know God" (1 Th.4:3-5, NIV).

- Never participate in suggestive, immoral talk, not even once. Neither should you stand by idly if such talk is taking place. You should either voice your objection to the offensive language or leave the scene as soon as possible...or both. Your actions, one way or the other, will strengthen or weaken your testimony for Christ.

"But among you there must not be even a hint of sexual immorality, or of any kind of impurity, or of greed, because these are improper for God's holy people. Nor should there be obscenity, foolish talk or coarse joking, which are out of place, but rather thanksgiving" (Ep.5:3-4, NIV).

8. *You Are to Respect People's Property, Not Steal It.*

"You must not steal" (Ex.20:15, NLT).

We live in a world where people have little respect for the property of others. Even when devastating tragedies (such as hurricanes or earthquakes) strike, people race to see how much they can steal before the authorities restore order.

Such behavior is absolutely despicable and tends to represent the worst in society. Although most thefts are not so dramatic or public as this, unfortunately, so many people in society steal that the act has become a very common crime. And if a thief does not assault or kill the victim, he or she is simply called a *common thief*. Thievery, robbery, and swindling have become epidemic, contributing to the lawlessness within society. Furthermore, stealing can become so widespread that it threatens the very foundation of a nation's economy and society. Just think of...

- government leaders who steal and misuse funds
- bankers, business leaders, managers, and stock brokers who manipulate markets and steal from public investors and retirees
- organizations and programs that fleece their customers or the public at large
- employees who steal from their employer

- ➢ employers who steal through unfair prices and wages
- ➢ the rich and famous who steal by living extravagant and indulgent lifestyles, hoarding and banking when so many are in such desperate need throughout the world
- ➢ individuals and companies that steal by taking or abusing so much of the earth's wealth and resources
- ➢ friends, neighbors, acquaintances, and strangers who steal or are dishonest in any number of ways

Stealing shows a disrespect for property and for human life. It leads to more and more lawlessness, and sometimes even assault, murder, and suicide. Stealing can create a great deal of havoc and can cause total devastation by bankrupting families, companies, communities, and even nations. Interestingly, stealing causes loss not only for the victim but also for the thief. The victim, of course, loses whatever object (physical or otherwise) is stolen; in addition, the loss can be very painful and sometimes irreplaceable. The thief, though often undetected, can lose his or her reputation and integrity. The thief also lacks the inner sense of accomplishment and fulfillment that result from a job well done and that build strong self-esteem. And, eventually, unless the thief repents and turns to God, he or she faces the judgment of God.

a. **Stealing is** taking and keeping something that belongs to another. Always remember that God has made you to work and has put within you a desire to move ahead, a drive to produce, accomplish, and possess. This is the reason you desire things you do not have. The desire is normal and natural; it is God-given. But the legitimate way to fulfill that desire is to work for what you want and can achieve in life. The illegitimate way to fulfill the desire is to steal. When you act out your desire and take something that does not belong to you—either secretly or by force—it is stealing.

b. **Stealing is** a problem of the heart. It begins with a lust, an urge, a coveting within the heart. When the desire is planted and you allow it to take root—when you nurture and develop the unregulated urge—it will eventually conceive and you will steal. This is exactly what God says:

> **"But each one is tempted when he is carried away and enticed by his own lust. Then when lust has conceived, it gives birth to sin; and**

when sin is accomplished, it brings forth death" (Jas.1:14-15, NASB).

c. **God's purpose** for commanding you not to steal can be simply stated: it is to protect people's property and their right to own property, to preserve peace among neighbors and within society. Stealing causes loss, sometimes devastating loss, to the victim. Stealing can also lead to hard feelings, broken relationships, loss of employment, imprisonment, and even revenge. This commandment protects your right...

- to feed, house, clothe, and provide for yourself and your family
- to own property
- to reap and keep the property and rewards of your labor
- to secure enough goods and money to help meet the desperate needs of the poor, the suffering, and the lost of this world

> **"He who steals must steal no longer; but rather he must labor, performing with his own hands what is good, so that he will have *something* to share with one who has need" (Ep.4:28, NASB).**

d. **This commandment** can be broken and violated in many ways. In fact, stealing is so common and so costly to society that the ways people go about stealing need to be studied. Besides being a sin against society and the victims, stealing is a sin against God. And unless the thief repents and turns to God, stealing condemns him or her to death, eternal death. For this reason, the various forms of stealing need to be looked at in some detail. You break God's commandment when you steal...

- by robbing a person, store, company, organization or bank
- by shoplifting
- by not paying bills
- by keeping something borrowed
- by failing to pay debts
- by not paying due taxes
- by taking away the good reputation and character of another through lies, gossip, or rumor
- by cheating on a test or passing off someone else's work as your own
- by taking away a person's right to justice (Is.10:1-3)

- by false or deceptive advertising
- by keeping an overpayment, an excessive refund check, or an over-shipment of goods
- by overcharging or price-gouging: charging unfair prices
- by kidnapping or enslaving people for work and profit
- by breaking the rules or cheating to win something, a game or a prize
- by taking things from your employer
- by making unauthorized phone calls
- by padding expense reports
- by unjustly extending business trips at company expense
- by manipulating information or stocks for personal gain
- by abusing sick days
- by loafing on the job or not giving a full day's work: arriving at work late or leaving work early without permission

All acts of stealing are wrong. Be alert and reject any and all temptations to steal.

e. **What are the** consequences of breaking this commandment not to steal? God's Word is clear:

> **"Do you not know that the wicked will not inherit the kingdom of God? Do not be deceived: Neither the sexually immoral nor idolaters nor adulterers nor male prostitutes nor homosexual offenders nor thieves [note this] nor the greedy nor drunkards nor slanderers nor swindlers will inherit the kingdom of God" (1 Co.6:9-10, NIV).**

God hates the sin of stealing because of the *direct association* with the greatest thief of all, Satan himself. Scripture exposes Satan for what he is: a thief.

> **"The thief [Satan] comes only to steal and kill and destroy; I came that they may have life, and have *it* abundantly" (Jn.10:10, NASB).**

God has spared no judgment for the thief of all thieves. Likewise, God will give every thief his or her due justice. Anyone who breaks this holy commandment will suffer serious consequences. A thief would do well to heed God's strong warning!

9. *You Are Not to Lie or Give False Testimony About Anyone.*

"You shall not bear false witness against your neighbor" (Ex.20:16, NKJV).

Lying—bearing false testimony—is common to all of us. We have all lied sometime in the past. We have...

- told little white lies
- twisted the truth or told a half-truth
- stretched the truth to justify an action
- gossiped, not knowing the truth
- discredited or slandered someone
- sought to escape blame by skirting around the truth
- tried to place blame elsewhere
- hinted at or suggested an untruth about someone
- exaggerated the truth in order to boost ourselves
- raised an eyebrow, shrugged a shoulder, or made a gesture to avoid disclosing the truth or to imply agreement with an untruth

Scripture emphatically declares: "All men are liars" (Ps.116:11). Lying is so common that it is frequently condoned, accepted, and even expected by many people. But lying is never justified. Sometimes silence is, but not lying, not answering dishonestly. Leaders, both business and political, can say almost anything and people either accept or overlook their twisting of the truth. A person's character, word, and integrity seem to matter little. Making false claims and promises has become a way of life. There is a sense that people simply cannot survive or get ahead unless they twist the truth to enhance their image. Telling the truth and being honest have fallen by the wayside.

Yet, lying threatens the very foundation of society. Nothing can survive when it is filled with lies, not for long. Any organization or group will collapse in the wake of broken promises, mistrust, and severed relationships.

This is the great concern of the ninth commandment, the concern for truth, that you build your life upon truth. Within society, families, friendships, businesses, social organizations, schools, churches, communities, and governments must be built upon truth. Note several important points:

a. **This commandment governs** a person who gives evidence in court, but the commandment is much broader than that. It covers far more than just legal testimony. God is stating that you are never to lie about a neighbor, not on any occasion. You are never to bear false witness *against* a neighbor, and you are never to bear false witness *to* a neighbor. You should always tell the truth, the whole truth, and nothing but the truth.

> **"So stop telling lies. Let us tell our neighbors the truth, for we are all parts of the same body" (Ep.4:25, NLT).**
>
> **"Don't lie to each other, for you have stripped off your old sinful nature and all its wicked deeds" (Col.3:9, NLT).**
>
> **"Do not spread false reports. Do not help a wicked man by being a malicious witness" (Ex.23:1, NIV).**

b. **A lie has** at least four harmful effects upon people. First, lying *misrepresents the truth.* It camouflages and hides the truth. The person lied to does not know the truth; therefore, he or she has to act or live upon a lie. If the lie is serious, it can be very damaging:

- ➢ A lie about a business deal can cost money and cause terrible loss.
- ➢ A lie about loving someone can stir emotions that lead to destruction.
- ➢ A lie about the salvation of the gospel can cost a person the hope of eternal life.

Second, lying *deceives a person.* It leads a person astray, and eventually causes misunderstanding, disappointment, bewilderment, helplessness, emotional upheaval, loss, and at times leads to immorality and destruction.

Third, lying *establishes an insincere relationship*, a relationship built on sinking sand. Two people cannot possibly be friends or live together if the relationship is based upon lies. Lying destroys confidence, security, love, trust, and hope.

Fourth, lying always *hurts someone.* If a person is being talked about, that individual has feelings just like you do, feelings that are subject to being hurt and suffering pain. So, when you spread lies, rumors, or even suspicions about someone, you are eventually going to cause pain—sometimes a great deal of pain—for the victim and his or her loved ones. (Imagine how God feels about this!)

c. **When you lie or bear** false witness against someone, it is usually your loved ones or good friends whom you talk to, people you feel you can trust. However, what is overlooked is that your loved ones and friends also have good friends whom they feel they can trust. And so the false report or gossip is spread further and further afield; subsequently, more damage and hurt are done to people and to the cause of Christ. This is the reason God forbids you and all other believers to speak negatively about another person, whether true or untrue, except in dealing with the actual individual involved with the issue.

> **"A man who bears false witness against his neighbor *Is like* a club [hammer], a sword, and a sharp arrow" (Pr.25:18, NKJV).**

d. **If you truly love the Lord,** you will not bear false witness about anyone. If there is a problem or a questionable report, you should deal with the person face-to-face, seeking to restore him or her to the faith. And, remember, love does not deal with a person in harshness, but in love and tenderness, being guided by the Holy Spirit of God.

> **"Dear brothers and sisters, if another believer is overcome by some sin, you who are godly should gently and humbly help that person back onto the right path. And be careful not to fall into the same temptation yourself. Share each other's burdens, and in this way obey the law of Christ" (Ga.6:1-2, NLT).**

e. **What is the decision** required by this commandment? Obedience! Telling the truth is not optional. You must conquer and overcome any habit of lying, any kind of lying. On a daily basis, you should make every effort to guard, prevent, and keep yourself from lying. Obedience to God's holy commandment requires it.

10. *You Are Not to Covet.*

> **"You must not covet your neighbor's house. You must not covet your neighbor's wife, male or female servant, ox or donkey, or anything else that belongs to your neighbor" (Ex.20:17, NLT).**
>
> **Then he said, "Beware! Guard against every kind of greed. Life is not measured by how much you own." Then he told them a story: "A rich man had a fertile farm that produced fine**

> **crops. He said to himself, 'What should I do? I don't have room for all my crops.' Then he said, 'I know! I'll tear down my barns and build bigger ones. Then I'll have room enough to store all my wheat and other goods. And I'll sit back and say to myself, "My friend, you have enough stored away for years to come. Now take it easy! Eat, drink, and be merry!"' "But God said to him, 'You fool! You will die this very night. Then who will get everything you worked for?' "Yes, a person is a fool to store up earthly wealth but not have a rich relationship with God" (Lu.12:15-21, NLT).**

This commandment forbids coveting anything that belongs to your neighbor: his or her home, possessions, profession, or anything else. People should be able to live in peace and feel secure. They should not have to worry about anyone coveting or stealing what they have. God wants you and everyone else to feel secure and protected. God wants you to know that your family members, property, possessions, livelihood, joy, and all else are safeguarded from covetousness and theft by others.

Covetousness is an inward sin, a sin of the heart and mind. It is an unhealthy *desire* within that can lead to outward sin.

Before a person ever lies, steals, or kills, the desire or thought to take such action arises in his or her heart. The desire to do something always precedes the actual act. You commit immorality either because you desire a particular person or you crave sex. You steal either because you crave the thing stolen or yearn for the excitement of stealing. Covetousness is, first of all, aroused in the heart and mind; so coveting is basically a heart problem.

The charge of Jesus in Luke 12 above is strong. He gives a double warning: *"Beware! Guard against"* (Lu.12:15). The word *beware* means to guard oneself from an enemy. The enemy in this case is covetousness, the desire for more and more of this world's wealth and possessions. It is this excessive desire (lust) that causes so much lawlessness, crime, immorality, and violence in the world. This is the reason Christ issues such a strong warning against covetousness or greed. What we so often fail to understand is that our true joy and comfort, our souls and bodies, do not depend on what we possess. *Many poor people* are happy and comfortable with healthy souls and bodies. Life does not consist of possessions—a beautiful home, the latest clothes, a new car, property, wealth.

To help us grasp this fact, Christ shared a parable about a man who was wealthy and profoundly *self-centered*. In just three short verses describing his thoughts, the rich man said "I" six times and "my" four times. His attention was solely upon himself. The parable is straightforward:

- The man was blessed materially, tremendously so, but he did not *thank God* for his blessing.
- The man called the fruits of the ground and the possessions he had *"my fruit"* and *"my goods"* (vv.17-18).
- The man gave no indication that he had given his soul to God.
- The man became *puffed up*, prideful with what he had done. He began to think only in terms of what he could do to further build up what he had, but only for his own sake.

The big mistake of the rich man was *selfishness.* His sole purpose was to be at ease, to have plenty to eat and drink, and to enjoy life as he wished. He thought only of himself. He gave no thought to helping others. He forgot or was totally unaware that he lived in a needy world that was lost and dying without Christ and His glorious salvation.

Sadly, this rich man planned to put off living and enjoying life until he got his barns built. The idea is that he was a *workaholic* consumed with a passion to get what he wanted. (How like so many in this materialistic society!)

Still, the most shocking fact is this: the rich man was never able to do these things. He died that very night, the same day he made the decision to increase his estate.

Christ wants you to learn at least two lessons from this parable.

a. **First, you need to prepare,** because you may die this very day. God knew the greed and covetousness of the rich man's heart, and He knows your heart. God knew the man's thoughts and the fact that he was to die that very night. The man did not know it, nor did anyone else. But God knew.

   You must never forget that you also have a night (a day) to die. And on that exact day your soul will be required, even as the rich man's was. God requires and demands that every soul die and face Him. In the case of the rich man, God called him a *fool.* Why? Because he was going to store up his wealth, far more than he would ever need. He was going to hoard his wealth and never use it for good—never use it to help the needy or to carry the message of God's salvation to the world. The rich man had refused to think about the uncertainty of life, about the possibility that he might not live as long as he wished to live. But he never considered this fact. Take heed! You need to be prepared, always aware that God may require your soul on this very day.

> **And as it is appointed for men to die once, but after this the judgment (He.9:27, NKJV).**

Bear in mind that the rich man was not going to cease existing. Rather, he was to exist in another world, the spiritual world, totally separated from God. All because he did not have a relationship with God here on earth.

b. Second, you need to realize that your wealth is not a permanent possession; someone else will get it when you die. The rich, covetous man left every penny and possession behind. He took nothing with him.

The very same thing will happen to you when your soul is demanded by God. You will leave all your money and possessions behind. Someone else will get everything. What God wants while you are living is for you to seek Him first and to develop a rich relationship with Him. Then, He wants you to put your money to work by helping the needy and reaching the world with the glorious gospel of salvation. Common sense also tells you that when you die, God would want the bulk of what you leave behind to continue to do the work of God, not to be given away to those who would spend it on foolish living.

> **"For we brought nothing into this world, and it is certain we can carry nothing out" (1 Ti.6:7, KJV).**

B. You and Your Daily Walk

1. *If You Claim to Know God, You Need to Walk As Jesus Did and Imitate God.*

> **"Whoever claims to live in him must walk as Jesus did" (1 Jn.2:6, NIV).**

a. **If you say** that you know God, that you belong to Him, then you have a responsibility to *walk* as Jesus Christ walked (also see ch.3, pt.7). In fact, Scripture says that you *must* walk as Jesus did. This means that you have a debt, a constraint, an obligation to do so. Observe closely *how* Christ walked while He was on earth. He walked...

- ➢ believing and trusting God
- ➢ praying and fellowshipping with God
- ➢ honoring and obeying all of God's commandments
- ➢ teaching and telling others about God
- ➢ loving and caring for others
- ➢ giving and sacrificing all He was and had to God

b. **If you are** truly a child of God, you need to follow and imitate Him.

> **"Be imitators of God, therefore, as dearly loved children" (Ep.5:1, NIV).**

The true believer follows God and holds God up as the perfect pattern to follow. Just as children learn by imitating their parents, so you are to learn by imitating God. But before you can imitate God, you have to commit and attach yourself to Him. You have to surrender and devote your life to God and then begin to follow Him. Scripture says that you are actually to imitate or model yourself after *God*.

- ➢ Christ said: "Therefore you are to be perfect, as your heavenly Father is perfect" (Mt.5:48, NASB).
- ➢ God demands: "You shall be holy, for I the LORD your God am holy" (Le.19:2, NASB).
- ➢ The apostle Paul declared: "But we all...are being transformed into the same image [of Christ] from glory to glory" (2 Co.3:18, NASB).
- ➢ The apostle Peter charged: "But just as he who called you is holy, so be holy in all you do; for it is written: "Be holy, because I am holy" (1 Pe.1:15-16, NIV).

2. *If You Are Truly a Follower of God, You Need to Walk Carefully—Not As a Fool, but As a Wise Person.*

> **"Therefore be careful how you walk, not as unwise men but as wise" (Ep.5:15, NASB).**

Life is a walk, a path that you trod every day. When you arise in the morning, you begin to walk around and take care of your daily affairs. As a follower of God, He expects you to walk carefully and deliberately, just as you should. According to this verse, there are two kinds of people walking through life:

a. **There is the fool** or unwise person: this person is worldly-minded. The unwise simply arise and go about their daily routine with little thought about God or what happens beyond this life. If they make a mistake here and there, it does not matter that much to them. Making mistakes is just the way of human life. They think they will be acceptable to whatever god there is, if there is one, as long as they live a life...

   - that is fairly decent, honorable, and useful
   - that pays its dues to God here and there

   The unwise are not concerned about watching every step or about being alert to the temptations and pitfalls in life. Living a guarded and godly life is not that important to them.

b. **There is the wise** person: this person is spiritually-minded. As a believer, you must be wise, for you are a person who has been chosen by God for a very specific mission. You know God personally and know that you are on earth to live a righteous and godly life and to bear testimony to the Lord Jesus Christ. Therefore, when you arise in the morning and go about your daily affairs, walk in the presence of God and praise Him all day long. Do all you can to avoid the corrupt influences of this world:

   - profanity
   - off-colored jokes
   - suggestive language
   - pornography
   - indecent clothing
   - immoral behavior
   - drugs and alcohol
   - offensive music, books, and movies
   - over-indulgence
   - discrimination
   - selfishness and pride

As a wise person, be concerned about every step you take in life, making sure your walk is purposeful, disciplined, and focused. Constantly keep in mind that the only answer to the evil and the problems in life is Jesus Christ and His righteousness. Walk carefully, not as a fool, but as a wise person.

C. YOU AND THE WORLD

1. *You Are to Live As an Alien and Stranger on Earth, Abstaining from Fleshly Lusts.*

> **"Beloved, I urge you as aliens and strangers to abstain from fleshly lusts which wage war against the soul" (1 Pe.2:11, NASB).**

We live in a day when the flesh is exalted and flaunted and the lusts of the flesh are constantly stimulated, encouraged, promoted, and endorsed. People's self-esteem and image in the eyes of others are often determined...

- by how much money, land, or goods they possess
- by how much power and authority they have
- by how much recreation and pleasure they are able to enjoy
- by how famous they become
- by how many people they influence, manage, or control
- by how many people they conquer and enjoy sexually

Scripture is clear, though: we are to abstain from fleshly lusts.

a. **First, you are to abstain** from fleshly lusts because you are an alien and stranger on earth. A believer is an alien in the sense that he or she belongs and owes allegiance to another world. The believer is a citizen of heaven and subject to the laws of God.

As a believer, you are only a temporary resident on earth. You now belong to God and to heaven; therefore, your true legal status is in heaven. You are no longer to follow the standards and ways of the world but the standards and ways of God and His Holy Word. In fact, the standards of the world are far lower than God's standards. You are to live as one whose mind is upon a far greater home and world where *perfection* is the rule and standard. Never forget that you are only passing through this world on your way home to heaven.

What impact should this truth have upon you as you walk day by day in this world? Very simply, you are not to become entangled with the world and its affairs, with its customs and lifestyles, but rather with the things of heaven.

But our citizenship is in heaven. And we eagerly await a Savior from there, the Lord Jesus Christ (Ph.3:20, NIV).

b. You are to abstain from evil desires and fleshly lusts because they war against your soul. The flesh is strong and difficult to control, and it never lets up its assault against your will.

What are the lusts of the flesh? What kinds of sins are being referred to by Scripture? They are far more than the sexual sins usually thought about when the lusts of the flesh are mentioned. Fleshly lusts are the passions and desires of the old, sinful nature. They paint a picture of human nature seen or experienced by most of us every day. Galatians 5:19-21 gives a list of examples, and we list them here in outline form for simplicity:

"The acts of the sinful nature are obvious:

- **sexual immorality**
- **impurity**
- **debauchery**
- **idolatry**
- **witchcraft**
- **hatred**
- **discord**
- **jealousy**
- **fits of rage**
- **selfish ambition**
- **dissensions**
- **factions**
- **envy**
- **drunkenness**
- **orgies**
- **and the like.**

I warn you, as I did before, that those who live like this will not inherit the kingdom of God" (Ga.5:19-21, NIV).

The lusts of your flesh, with its unregulated urges and passions, wage war against your soul. You frequently sense an urge to do what you want, to lift the restraints and to follow your own desires. You know you should not, but the desires tug at you and struggle against your soul. Think how often you have experienced the power of the flesh, caved in, and done something that you did not intend to do. You fought against doing it and knew it was harmful, yet you could not resist the temptation. You gave in to the power of the flesh and acted on it. You...

- ➢ overate
- ➢ reacted in anger
- ➢ indulged
- ➢ got drunk
- ➢ started smoking
- ➢ lusted
- ➢ coveted
- ➢ spent too much money
- ➢ were prideful
- ➢ used profanity
- ➢ acted selfishly
- ➢ acted immorally
- ➢ cheated, lied, or stole
- ➢ looked at pornography or other inappropriate material

The flesh is so strong that at times it keeps you from doing what you should. And the more you follow the lusts of your flesh, the more freedom and liberty you lose. You become a slave to whatever fleshly lusts you set your heart on. On top of that, you will find it increasingly difficult to break away from them. The only hope of ever controlling the flesh is to walk in the Spirit of God—in His presence and power day by day.

2. *You Are to Separate Yourself from the Unbelievers of the World.*

> **Therefore, come out from among unbelievers, and separate yourselves from them, says the Lord. Don't touch their filthy things, and I will welcome you. And I will be your Father, and you will be my sons and daughters, says the Lord Almighty" (2 Co.6:17-18, NLT).**

These two verses refer back to the Old Testament, when God led Israel out of the Babylonian captivity. He told them to leave everything behind (Is.52:11-12). They were to take nothing out of the defiled land because they were to begin a totally new life under His leadership. Two key points stand out here:

a. **First, you are** to come out from among unbelievers and be separate. What does this mean? Of course, it *does not* mean that you are to leave the cities, communities, and work places of the world. You are not to isolate yourself from unbelievers. It *does not* mean that you are to have nothing to do with unbelievers—never talking to or associating with them. Both believers and unbelievers inhabit the world; thus, we have to share the world. What God means is at least three things:

   1) Your lifestyle as a believer should differ from that of unbelievers and should differ radically:

      - You should not be *unequally yoked* or intimately involved with unbelievers.
      - You should not be in *fellowship* with unbelievers, not share or participate in the worldly, ungodly functions and events of unbelievers. This is not to say that you cannot be present at the same function as an unbeliever, say a wedding or funeral or sporting event. However, you should not be attending ungodly events or acting in an ungodly manner at any event.

- You should not be in *communion* with unbelievers, not so closely bound in partnership that there is an expectation that you will be a part of their ungodly activities and behavior.
- You should not be *associated, affiliated,* or *identified* with the infidel, a person who has rejected Jesus Christ.
- You should not *worship* with unbelievers nor participate in their worship of the idols and false gods of this world.

2) You should not touch any unclean thing (v.17). No longer should you live like an unbeliever or sinner who is influenced by the world. You should not participate in the sins of unbelievers.
3) You need to live a life of separation from the wicked unbelievers of the world (v.17). This is a command, and there is to be no questioning or ignoring of the command. God demands separation. In fact, separation is so important to God that it is essential in order to be *received by God* (see point b. below).

Simply stated, even though you are *in* the world, you are not to be *of* the world. You are not to take part in the sins of the world nor live a worldly life.

b. Second, the results of separation are phenomenal. If you separate yourself from unbelievers and dedicate your life to God, God Himself receives and welcomes you! God cannot receive a person who lives in sin and shame, in worldliness and immorality, in covetousness and idolatry. But if you come out from the world and separate yourself, God will receive you and treat you just as a father does his sons and daughters. God will stay close to you and maintain fellowship with you, look after and take care of you. As your Father, God will *favor and nurture you* with...

- love
- joy
- peace
- provision
- guidance
- protection
- discipline
- growth
- reward

3. *You Are Not to Love the World nor Anything in the World.*

> **"Do not love the world nor the things in the world. If anyone loves the world, the love of the Father is not in him. For all that is in the world, the lust of the flesh and the lust of the eyes and the boastful pride of life, is not from the Father, but is from the world" (1 Jn.2:15-16, NASB).**

Does this mean that we are not to appreciate the beauty, splendor, and resources of the earth and the stars of the sky? No! God has given us the earth and the universe to appreciate and enjoy and to provide for our needs. What, then, does Scripture mean by *not loving the world*?

- The *world* represents the earth and the universe that are passing away. The world is corruptible and deteriorating and will eventually be destroyed. Therefore, you should not become attached to the world; instead, you need to love and be attached to God and to heaven. You need to guard against loving the world so much that you desire to stay here more than you desire to be with God in heaven.
- The *world* represents a system of man-made governments and societies, some good and some bad, but none perfect. As a law-abiding citizen, you should respect and be loyal to the good on earth, but reject and stand against the bad. As a believer, though, you should not love any of the systems of man's organizations, not to the point that you are more attached to them than you are to God and heaven—His coming kingdom.
- The *world* represents a system of evil and rebellion against God. The world is full of sinful people, people who are wicked and rebellious, who take a stand against God Himself. When it comes to the values of this world, you need to maintain a proper perspective: you should not love this sinful system of the world.

In light of this definition of the world, God is declaring that you are not to love the attachments, the man-made systems, or the sinful possessions and pleasures of this world. Instead, you need to exercise control.

a. **First, you need to** *control your flesh*. The *flesh* is the seat of desires and urges. You have desires and urges in order to live a healthy and normal life. But they have to be controlled. If they are not controlled, then the flesh goes beyond desire and begins to lust. And you must always guard against lust (see pt.1, pp.130-132 for more discussion).

b. **Second, you need to** control *your eyes*. The eyes have to do with seeing and wanting what you see. Again, there is nothing wrong with desiring what you see if the desire is controlled. But the desire becomes wrong when you see and desire what is directly forbidden by God. What are the sins of the eyes? Scripture says the following:

- There is the lust of the eyes for sex.

> **"But I say, anyone who even looks at a woman with lust has already committed adultery with her in his heart" (Mt.5:28, NLT).**

- There is the lust of the eyes for all kinds of evil.

> **"But when your eye is bad, your whole body is filled with darkness. And if the light you think you have is actually darkness, how deep that darkness is!" (Mt.6:23, NLT).**

- There is the lust of the eyes for the things of others.

> **And He said to them, "Take heed and beware of covetousness, for one's life does not consist in the abundance of the things he possesses" (Lu.12:15, NKJV).**

- There is the lust of the eyes for the pleasures and possessions of the world.

> **"Whatever my eyes desired I did not keep from them. I did not withhold my heart from any pleasure" (Ec.2:10, NKJV).**

- There is the lust of the eyes for wine, drugs, and alcoholic drinks.

> **"Who has woe? Who has sorrow? Who has contentions? Who has complaints? Who has wounds without cause? Who has redness of eyes? Those who linger long at the wine, Those who go in search of mixed wine. Do not look on the wine when it is red, When it sparkles in the cup, *When* it swirls around smoothly" (Pr.23:29-31, NKJV).**

- There is the lust of the eyes for other gods.

> **"You shall not make idols for yourselves; neither a carved image nor a *sacred* pillar shall you rear up for yourselves [to look upon]" (Le.26:1, NKJV).**

c. **Third, you need to** *control pride*. You should have pride in yourself, a strong self-image and a sense of worth. But pride is sinful when you become focused upon yourself to the neglect of others (spouse, family, and all the needy of the world).

Pride is also sinful when you begin to feel self-sufficient, completely capable of handling life yourself, apart from God. Sadly, the prideful often feel that strong self-image, ego, and personal strength are the basis of life, that there is little need for God, if any. They feel they can plow through life by themselves and conquer whatever problems and circumstances confront them. The prideful feel superior to others in some way, whether it be in looks, ability, position, education, wealth, fame, or any number of areas. They are often arrogant and boastful, believing they deserve and have a right to all the comfort, pleasure, luxury, and honor available to people.

Yet, Scripture is clear: you must not love the world nor anything in the world. If you love the world, the love of God the Father is not in you.

4. *You Are Not to Be Conformed to the Behavior and Values of This World but Be Transformed by Renewing Your Mind.*

> **"And do not be conformed to this world, but be transformed by the renewing of your mind, that you may prove what *is* that good and acceptable and perfect will of God" (Ro.12:2, NKJV).**

First, you are not to be conformed to this world. The word *conformed* comes from the root word *schema,* which means fashion, the outward form, the appearance of something. It is the appearance that changes from day to day and year to year.

The world, the very fashion and appearance of it, changes. But the world is not what it seems to be. The world...

- seems to be lasting, permanent, ever evolving
- seems to offer the very best of everything: pleasure, wealth, recognition, honor, fame, happiness

However, the *fashion or appearance* of the world is deceptive. The world and the things of the world do not last. They are not permanent and unending. Even the very *spirit of the world* has within it the seed of corruption. The seed of corruption is seen in the acts of the world and its nature, in the terrible spirit of...

- selfishness
- greed
- hatred
- ungodliness
- pride
- division
- war
- suffering
- disease
- death
- disorder
- decay

As a believer, you must not be conformed to this world because the world and everything in it is passing away.

> **And those who use this world as not misusing *it.* For the form of this world is passing away (1 Co.7:31, NKJV).**
>
> **And the world is passing away, and the lust of it; but he who does the will of God abides forever (1 Jn.2:17, NKJV).**

Second, you need to be *transformed* by the renewing of your mind. The *mind* refers to your inner being—your very nature and essence, who you are as a person.

The Bible clearly says that you must undergo a radical change within your inner being in order to escape the world and its destiny. You have to be transformed and changed inwardly. Your very nature—your heart and mind—have to be changed.

How can you be transformed within? As simply as can be stated, "by the renewing of your mind." Your mind needs to be made new, converted, changed, turned around, regenerated. Remember, your mind has been affected by sin. Therefore, it desperately needs to be renewed. Your mind is far from perfect. It is *basically worldly*, that is, selfish, self-focused, self-seeking. It is centered on this world, its possessions and fleshly lusts. Consequently, your mind must be continually renewed by the *presence and the image* of Christ in your life. When you receive Jesus Christ as your Lord, you are *spiritually*...

- born again (Jn.3:3-8; 1 Pe.1:23)
- made into a new person (Ep.4:24; Col.3:10)
- made into a new creature (2 Co.5:17)
- given the mind of Christ (1 Co.2:16; see vv.9-15)
- changed into the image of Christ (2 Co.3:18; see Ro.8:29; 1 Co.15:49; Col.3:10; 1 Jn.3:2)

This means a most wonderful truth: when you receive Jesus Christ into your life, Christ changes your mind to focus upon God. In addition, He stamps His image upon you. Whereas your mind and image used to be centered on the world, they are now *transformed* and centered on spiritual matters. Your mind and image are renewed, changed, turned around to focus upon God.

Once you receive Christ as your Savior, you should be living a *transformed life*. You should be walking day by day in Christ, focusing your mind more and more on God and spiritual things.

> **"For those who live according to the flesh set their minds on the things of the flesh, but those *who live* according to the Spirit, the things of the Spirit. For to be carnally minded *is* death, but to be spiritually minded *is* life and peace" (Ro.8:5-6, NKJV; see 2 Co.10:5).**

Third, you need to *prove*—to *learn* and *follow*—the will of God. This is certainly understandable. If your mind is not renewed and focused upon God, how can you ever learn the will of God? How can you ever follow the will of God? The only conceivable way you can *learn* God's will is to focus and keep your mind on God and on the things of God. God's will is...

- *good*: beneficial and helpful
- *acceptable*: pleasing and satisfying
- *perfect* (teleion): without error or mistake, setting you free from any need, completely fulfilling your life

In summary, you gain victory over the world by obeying the charge in this verse: you are not to be conformed to this world, but be transformed by the renewing of your mind. You should strive to focus your mind upon God and the things of God day by day.

5. *You Are to Dress and Behave Modestly.*

> **And I want women to be modest in their appearance. They should wear decent and appropriate clothing and not draw attention to themselves by the way they fix their hair or by wearing gold or pearls or expensive clothes. For women who claim to be devoted to God should make themselves attractive by the good things they do (1 Ti.2:9-10, NLT).**
>
> **Don't be concerned about the outward beauty of fancy hairstyles, expensive jewelry, or beautiful clothes. You should clothe yourselves instead with the beauty that comes from within, the unfading beauty of a gentle and quiet spirit, which is so precious to God. This is how the holy women of old made themselves beautiful. (1 Pe.3:3-5a, NLT).**

These two passages are addressed to women but can be applied to men as well, especially in today's society. All believers are to be modest in their appearance. As a believer, you should wear or adorn yourself with proper clothing. The word *adorn* is really a better translation of what Scripture means than *wear* or *clothe yourself.* It refers to the ornaments, the clothing, and the arrangement of clothing on your body; but it also refers to your behavior and demeanor, that is, the way you carry yourself, walk, move, and behave in public. Keep in mind that this passage is being written to genuine believers, women and men who truly believe in the Lord and wish to honor the Lord by having a strong testimony for Him. As a true believer, you certainly need to be modest in your dress and behavior. And you need to build a strong testimony—a testimony that you love the Lord and have committed your life...

- to help people, not to seduce them
- to point people to Jesus, not to attract them to yourself
- to teach people righteous behavior, not fleshly and worldly behavior
- to serve people, not to destroy them

How you dress shows whether you live in close communion with God and have a desire to please Him, or have a deep desire for the things of the world and for the gaping, lustful attention of others.

God's Holy Word is clear: as a true believer, you are to dress and adorn yourself with good works. You are to demonstrate a godly lifestyle. Your mind is to be upon helping, saving, and teaching people, not upon attracting, seducing, and destroying them through immoral dress and behavior.

Think about a significant fact that is often ignored or in some cases simply not known: true beauty is inward, not outward. Picture a woman who is focused upon Christ and good works: she is at peace with herself. She is filled with assurance and has strong self-esteem. She has purpose and meaning in life and knows that she is perfectly secure and looked after by Christ.

- Picture her smile that arises from a deep-seated, inner joy.
- Picture her walk that is steady, determined, and optimistic.
- Picture her dignity, calmness, confidence, and purposefulness.

Now, picture her beauty. No matter what she looks like, no matter how modest her clothing is, she is beautiful. Just how true this is can easily be seen by looking at her opposite. Picture the woman who focuses upon the world, who is primarily concerned with her looks, her clothing, and how she appears to others:

- Picture her smile—that sometimes arises from an emptiness within and the need to be accepted and approved.
- Picture her walk and movements—that reveal the need to attract attention and, by such, to have her ego boosted. Her walk and movement also reveal an insecurity and a fear of not being accepted for who she is within.
- Picture her behavior of looseness and restlessness, showing her lack of genuine purpose, meaning, and significance in life.

Now, picture this woman's behavior. Every thinking and honest man knows that no matter how attractive her facial and body features may be, this woman lacks true inner beauty. In the eyes of so many in the world, she is good for only one thing: to be used to satisfy men's lust for sexual pleasure or to be used to gratify their greed for money through exploitation.

As stated, true beauty is not in looks; true beauty is from within. If you are beautiful within—if you are really devoted to God and given over to good works—God will flood you with a beauty that far surpasses any beauty of the flesh or outward appearance (read Pr.31:10-31).

D. You and Questionable Functions and Behavior

1. *You Should Consider Five Questions About Every Questionable Function and Behavior.*

> **"Everything is permissible"—but not everything is beneficial. "Everything is permissible"—but not everything is constructive. Nobody should seek his own good, but the good of others. Eat anything sold in the meat market without raising questions of conscience, for, "The earth is the Lord's, and everything in it." If some unbeliever invites you to a meal and you want to go, eat whatever is put before you without raising questions of conscience. But if anyone says to you, "This has been offered in sacrifice [to idols]," then do not eat it, both for the sake of the man who told you and for conscience' sake (1 Co.10:23-28, NIV).**

The subject of this passage deals with the limits of *Christian liberty*. The Corinthian believers were concerned about participating in certain social functions with their neighbors and fellow employees, concerned about their testimony before others (Ro.14:1-23; 1 Co. 8:1-13). Likewise, when you participate in a function or go along with a certain behavior, you need to consider your Christian testimony before others, lest you become identified with that function or behavior. Does this mean that you can never attend a social or fellowship held by an unbeliever? And what about more specific questions: What activities and functions can you as a believer participate in? What can you buy and eat and drink (1 Co. 10:31; see 1 Co.8:8; Ro.14:21)? In these verses, Scripture suggests five questions that you should always ask when faced with a questionable activity or behavior.

a. **Question 1:** Is the function or behavior beneficial and edifying (v.23)? It may be lawful, legitimate, and allowed, but...

   - Is it worthwhile, useful, constructive?
   - Is it edifying? Does it build you and others up and mature your faith in Christ, or does it bring you down and call your faith into question?

b. **Question 2:** Does the function or behavior seek the good of others (v.24)? You should never seek only to please yourself but also consider what is best for others.

c. **Question 3:** Does the function or behavior violate your conscience (vv.25-26)? This passage deals specifically with the Corinthian problem. It was a common practice for the temple priests to take the meat from animal sacrifices to the markets for retail sale. Some believers were bothered by the fact that they might be purchasing meat that had been offered to idols. Very simply, Paul told them to buy the meat and ask no questions about its source, for the earth, with all its creatures and provisions, is the Lord's. The animal was created by God for food; so, if there was a wrong, it was committed by the idol worshippers, not by the believer who used the animal as God purposed.

   While you should not do anything that violates your conscience, you should also guard against asking needless questions and making a fuss over trivial matters. Personal opinions, misgivings, rules, and regulations that disturb conscience are *not to be pressed and made into an issue*. When dealing with questionable functions and behavior, make sure you never do anything that violates your conscience.

d. **Question 4:** Are you being courteous and kind by participating in the function or engaging in the behavior (v.27)? If an unbeliever invites you to a social function and you are inclined to go, then you should go out of courtesy and kindness. Even so, you must never forget that a clear conscience before God is much more important than any social function. This principle applies to the specific activities at social functions as well. You should never participate in an activity...

   - that would violate your conscience (vv.25, 27, 28)
   - that would mark or identify you as a worldly person (1 Co. 10:16-18)

e. **Question 5:** Does your participation hurt the conscience of another person (v.28)? The verse is clear: if partaking of any meat or drink or participating in a function or activity offends a fellow believer, then you should not partake or participate. A fellow believer's conscience and spiritual growth are far more important than any food or drink or social event. This is the test that controls all the others. Even if your own conscience is not bothered, you are to act for the sake of others. You should not do things if they offend the conscience of others—no matter how lawful, legitimate, and acceptable they are. You should never damage your testimony for Christ nor do anything that would push someone else further away from Christ.

2. *You Should Not Be a Stumbling Block by Setting a Bad Example or Leading Others Astray.*

> **One man considers one day more sacred than another; another man considers every day alike. Each one should be fully convinced in his own mind. He who regards one day as special, does so to the Lord. He who eats meat, eats to the Lord, for he gives thanks to God; and he who abstains, does so to the Lord and gives thanks to God....Do not destroy the work of God for the sake of food. All food is clean, but it is wrong for a man to eat anything that causes someone else to stumble. It is better not to eat meat or drink wine or to do anything else that will cause your brother to fall. So whatever you believe about these things keep between yourself and God. Blessed is the man who does not condemn himself by what he approves. But the man who has doubts is condemned if he eats, because his eating is not from faith; and everything that does not come from faith is sin (Ro.14:5-6, 20-23, NIV).**

In the ancient world, when people accepted Christ as personal Savior, they faced a critical problem. What were they to do about their circle of unsaved friends and their social activities? Practically every social function served meat that had been offered to idols. And when a significant function was held, such as a marriage or an important business meeting, it was sometimes held in an idol's temple. In addition, no matter where the event was held, an offering was always made to an idol. What were Christians to do? Could they attend such social functions? If they refused, how would it affect their friends? Their jobs? Their business contacts?

- Practically every family had its own idol sitting in a significant place in the home. At mealtime, the family would offer a small sacrifice to its god in order to ensure its blessing. What were Christians to do about fellowship with their neighbors? Were they to cut off all social contact with them?
- The market place was usually filled with meat recently offered to idols. A portion of the animals used in sacrifice was always given to the priests for their upkeep. Then the priests usually sold any excess to the local market places. The markets in turn sold the meat to the public. Some believers felt that it was wrong to purchase meat that had

been used in idol worship, but they could seldom tell if the meat was pure or not. This was the reason many Christians throughout the ancient world became vegetarians. Were they right in their conviction? Or, was it all right to go ahead and eat food that had been used in the worship of idols?

The issue of Christian liberty (freedom) vs. license (lack of restraint) has always been and will always be a challenge for believers who wish to please their Lord. In other words, what can you as a believer *do and not do* personally and socially? Can you...

- use mild profanity or take part in off-colored, suggestive conversations?
- drink socially?
- attend movies, and if so, are any off-limits due to language, violence, or immorality?
- watch television, and if so, are all programs appropriate?
- gamble, and if so, exactly what is considered gambling?
- dance, and if so, is there any form of dance that is offensive or objectionable?
- listen to the world's music, and if so, what is acceptable or unacceptable?
- attend or participate in athletic events on Sunday?

There are a host of social and recreational functions that pose concerns for believers who are truly seeking to please the Lord in *all that they do*. This passage deals with the principles that are to guide you as you face these issues.

a. **First, be fully convinced** of right and wrong behavior, remembering all the while that the commandments and instructions of Scripture are to be obeyed (v.5). The present passage is dealing with the legalistic tendencies of some people: the rules and regulations that some put forth as a requirement or necessity to practice.

   Another fact needs to be mentioned as well: Paul is not suggesting that the Lord's Day is not important. He is not suggesting that it is all right to ignore, neglect, or abuse the Lord's Day. Far from it. What he is attacking is an attitude that substitutes a Christian day for Christianity. The Lord's Day is very important to God, for it is the day set aside for the worship of His Son and for the rest and relaxation of His followers. However, the believer is not to worship the *day* but rather the *Lord* of all days.

You personally must be fully persuaded that something is right and not wrong. You should make the decision for yourself; no one else can decide for you. Ultimately, though...

- You need to make sure that the matter is genuinely questionable, that it is *not actually covered* by a command in the Scripture.
- You need to be honest and intelligent (both are necessary) in deciding if a certain action or behavior is right or wrong.
- You should never violate your conscience, not in the least.

Above all, you should always live as you see and understand God's will. In the above Scripture, the point is very simply stated (vv.5-6): one man dedicates every day to the Lord and sees every day as the Lord's. The other man dedicates every day to the Lord, but he believes Sundays and holy days are more special and meaningful and should be especially set aside for God. Note that the same attitudes prevail toward food: one man *gives thanks* to God and eats everything; the other man *gives thanks* to God and eats only vegetation. The fact to grasp is that...

- both men worship the Lord every day. They differ only in that one man sets aside some days for an extended celebration to God.
- both men thank God for their food. They differ only in what they are eating.

Grasp the crucial factor here: the hearts of both men are focused upon God. Both men are dedicating their lives to worship and serve God and both are thanking God for what they have. Their hearts are right with God. The differences between them—days and food—are external, not matters of the heart. Therefore, both are acceptable to God. Both are fully persuaded that what they are doing is right before God. You, too, need to be fully persuaded *in all things* that what you are doing is right before God.

b. **Do not destroy or hinder** the work of God in another person's life; it is sin to do so (v.20). A person, whether child or adult, is far more important than your having the right to eat and drink certain things or to attend and participate in certain social and recreational activities.

But if you cause one of these little ones who trusts in me to fall into sin, it would be better for you to have a large millstone tied around your neck and be drowned in the depths of the sea (Mt.18:6, NLT).

So if what I eat causes another believer to sin, I will never eat meat again as long as I live—for I don't want to cause another believer to stumble (1 Co.8:13, NLT).

c. **Do nothing to cause** another person to fall (vv.20-21). Note how clearly Scripture speaks: nothing—not food, wine, or anything else—is worth causing a brother, child, or adult to stumble. What is right for you may be the downfall of another, for you do influence other people, a fact that is not debatable. The weak person, whether child or adult, may do something because you are doing it or because he or she...

- ➢ does not want to go against the crowd
- ➢ does not want to be different
- ➢ does not want to be criticized, ridiculed, or unpopular
- ➢ does not want to be rejected or ostracized
- ➢ is weaker in stamina, spiritually immature
- ➢ looks up to and idolizes others (parents, friends, celebrities, sports figures)

We should help others do what is right and build them up in the Lord (Ro.15:2, NLT).

But you must be careful so that your freedom does not cause others with a weaker conscience to stumble (1 Co.8:9, NLT).

d. **Watch—do not condemn** yourself (vv.22-23). There are three ways you can keep from condemning yourself.

- ➢ By keeping your faith. In this context, *faith* means the belief that you can do a certain thing and that it is acceptable to God. If you feel free before God to do a questionable thing that is not forbidden by Scripture, then you are permitted to do it, but it is to be done in *private before God*. It is not to be paraded publicly and done before others lest you cause another to stumble and fall. For instance, if it is food to be eaten or something to be drunk, it is to be done only in private. Doing the thing privately and *offering it up to God with thanksgiving* are the only ways it is acceptable. *If* it cannot be offered up to God with thanksgiving, then *it should not be done*.

- By not going against your conscience. You must not condemn yourself in what you allow in your life and home by acting against your own principles or failing to follow your own standards. For instance, you should not keep intoxicating drinks in your home just to please other family members or guests if you know Scripture forbids such, or if you feel guilty doing so. Such an action would condemn you. Instead, if necessary, you should kindly and quietly explain to your family members or friends that you simply choose not to have any liquor in the home. Remember: children and others in the home are being influenced and impacted by what you say and do.
- By acting on faith, from a conviction that God approves your activity. If there is any question about doing or partaking of something, note how clearly and forcefully Scripture speaks: "Whatsoever is not of faith is sin." If you cannot eat, drink, or do the thing *in faith*—knowing it is acceptable to God—then *doing it is sin*.

And without faith it is impossible to please God, because anyone who comes to him must believe that he exists and that he rewards those who earnestly seek him (He.11:6, NIV).

Therefore, to one who knows *the* right thing to do and does not do it, to him it is sin (Jas.4:17, NASB).

E. YOU AND YOUR WORK (OR EMPLOYMENT)

1. *You Are to Work Hard, As Though You Were Working for the Lord.*

> **"Slaves, obey your earthly masters [employers, managers] with respect and fear, and with sincerity of heart, just as you would obey Christ. Obey them not only to win their favor when their eye is on you, but like slaves [employees, workers] of Christ, doing the will of God from your heart. Serve wholeheartedly, as if you were serving the Lord, not men, because you know that the Lord will reward everyone for whatever good he does, whether he is slave or free" (Ep.6:5-8, NIV).**

This passage deals with the working relationship between people at every level and in every area of society: slave and master, labor and management, employee and employer, workman and supervisor. These verses point out in no uncertain terms that the answer to the basic problems in the workplace is a matter of the heart, not the economy. The discussion concerns slaves and their masters, but the instructions are applicable to every generation of workers, no matter their status. As commentator Francis Foulkes says, "*...the principles of the whole section apply to employees and employers in every age, whether in the home, in business, or in the state.*"[3] Seven specific instructions are given to the Christian worker.

a. **You are to obey** and follow the instructions of your employer (v.5). Whether an individual or a large corporation, your employer provides a job for you...
   - work that enables you to earn money for yourself and your family
   - work that allows you to contribute significantly to society by providing a product or service for others
   - work that helps give you a sense of purpose, responsibility, and satisfaction in life
   - work that helps you fulfill part of God's great call to the human race: to subdue the forces of nature and make the earth a better place in which to live (Ge.1:28; 2:15)

---

3 Francis Foulkes. *The Epistle of Paul to the Ephesians*, "Tyndale New Testament Commentaries," ed. by RVG Tasker. (Grand Rapids, MI: Eerdmans Publishing Co., n.d.), p.167.

When an employer gives you a job that provides these benefits and opportunities, you are obligated to follow his or her instructions. Only as you and your employer work together in a cooperative spirit can the company produce or generate its product or service for the community and guarantee you a job.

b. **You need to work** with an attitude of deep respect and fear (v.5). This does not mean working with the fear of man nor with total, unquestioning obedience, but with the fear of God in your heart. Respect and fear are to be the marks of a Christian worker.

   - You are to respect and fear God lest you perform some irresponsible work and bring reproach upon His holy name.
   - You are to respect and fear your employer (supervisor) by obeying his or her instructions lest your attitude or performance bring rebuke or cause you to lose your job.

c. **You are to work** with a *sincere heart,* with *singleness of purpose* (v.6). This means that you are to work with focused attention, without pretense or slackness. It means that you are not to waste time but instead to be genuinely committed to your work. You should be single-minded, focused upon doing your job and doing it well. And note why: because you are to labor as though you were working for the Lord.

d. **You are always to** work hard, and not only when your supervisor is looking (v.6). There is nothing wrong with seeking to *gain the favor* of your employer. But there are those who slow down when their employers are not looking and speed up when their employers are looking. These people are guilty of seeking favor they do not deserve. Such standards rob labor of its dignity and bring ill repute to the name of Christ. When you return home from a day's work, you need to ask yourself these questions: "Have I done my very best today? Have I pleased the Lord?"

e. **You should work** as though you were an employee of Christ, a worker who does the will of God *from your heart* (v.7). This means that you should labor with enthusiasm, showing great interest and energy. It is the opposite of working in a routine manner and with a listless spirit, having no energy or heart for the work. You should always remember, even if your employer is not looking, Christ sees what kind of work you are doing. In view of this, you need to put your whole heart into your work, even be excited about and thankful for the privilege of working.

f. **You need to keep** in mind that the Lord is going to reward you for your hard work (v.8). In fact, the Lord is going to give you a *reciprocal reward*. That is, He is going to give you *the equivalent of* what you have labored for on this earth, no more and no less (Lu.6:38).

You may have been honest or dishonest, white collar or blue collar, a professional or a laborer, an owner or an employee, gifted or disabled—it matters not. You are going to receive from God exactly what you have put into your day-to-day work. If you have diligently worked as though you were working for Christ, you will be abundantly rewarded. But if you have been careless, negligent, or slack in your work, then you are going to receive a limited reward. With this fact in mind, you ought to make every effort to work hard, work as though you were working for the Lord Himself.

2. *You—the Employer or Manager—Need to Treat Your Workers As You Want Them to Treat You.*

> **"And masters [employers, managers], treat your slaves in the same way. Do not threaten them, since you know that he who is both their Master and yours is in heaven, and there is no favoritism with him" (Ep.6:9, NIV).**

Employers or managers are given two clear commands governing how they are to treat the workers under them:

a. **You must do** the very same things that are required of your workers. This means that you are to treat your employees just as you expect them to treat you. (What a difference this principle would make in labor-management relations if it were truly practiced by both parties!)

As a manager or employer, you must realize that you are...

- to serve both the Lord and the employees under you
- to manage all the workers under you with respect and fear

- to work with a sincere heart, with singleness of purpose
- to work hard all the time and not only when others are watching
- to work as though you were an employee of Christ, managing for the Lord and not for men
- to work knowing that the Lord is going to give you a reciprocal reward for how well you managed those under you

Employers and managers expect at least two things from their employees: hard work and loyalty. God's charge to you as an employer is the same. He requires that you be diligent in your management and in your loyalty to the workers under you. You have a duty to demonstrate your loyalty with fair job evaluations, wages, and job security.

b. **You, as an employer** or manager, are to avoid threats. This does not mean that you cannot correct or release a worker if he or she is not diligent or loyal. God does not encourage slothfulness, license, or indulgence. Indeed, God chastens and disciplines when needed. But note: stern measures are to be taken only after all other corrective measures have been tried. Every person is worth saving and developing into a good worker if at all possible. Even an incompetent worker is a fellow human being. As long as he or she is on the earth, God will continue to reach out to the person. For this reason alone, every step should be taken to reach and train even the most unproductive worker before he or she is released or allowed to go idle, to waste valuable time and resources.

The warning to employers and managers is this: you need to carefully guard against unwarranted threats because you too have a Master in heaven, and He shows no favoritism, no partiality. As an employer or manager, you are supposed to hold every worker accountable; but you must also remember that the Lord holds you accountable to Him. Any threats you make, then, should always be issued carefully and justly, lest God condemn and punish you in the coming day of judgment.

3. *You Are to Withdraw and Stay Away from the Idle, Those Who Shun Responsibility.*

> **"Even while we were with you, we gave you this command: "Those unwilling to work will not get to eat." Yet we hear that some of you are living idle lives, refusing to work and meddling in other people's business. We command such people and urge them in the name of the Lord Jesus Christ to settle down and work to earn their own living. As for the rest of you, dear brothers and sisters, never get tired of doing good. Take note of those who refuse to obey what we say in this letter. Stay away from them so they will be ashamed. Don't think of them as enemies, but warn them as you would a brother or sister" (2 Th.3:10-15, NLT).**

This passage deals with a very relevant subject for our day and time: the problem of idle, unproductive, and irresponsible people. Many workplaces are full of employees who waste time and do as little as possible, workers who are *menpleasers*, working only when they see their employers or supervisors coming. In addition to these, there are increasingly large numbers in society who could be working but choose not to because they are lazy and indifferent. And, sadly, they have found a way to exploit or take advantage of others:

- family
- the government
- social services
- churches
- neighbors

A tragic byproduct of this mindset, this outlook, is the spirit of entitlement, of *"give me"* that has pervaded the workplaces and nations of the world. Scripture addresses four aspects of this relevant and very critical topic.

a. **Those who are idle** need to work or they should lose their right to eat (to be helped and supported by others) (v.10). This is a command of God's Holy Word. The command deals with those who choose to be idle and refuse to work. It is not dealing with individuals who are truly unable to work due to disability or being unable to find employment. If you are able to work, you are to work. If you refuse, you are not to be fed; you are not to be allowed to take advantage of or to exploit your family, community, society, neighbors, church, or government. There is no excuse for your not working if you are able to work—not in the sight of God. If society and the government are unable to train and provide work for you, then almost every church or social service can put you to work on a voluntary basis. Most of these charitable services will help with food and housing if you help them in reaching out to a world of desperate and dying people who need help and attention. Too many in the world—untold numbers—are hopeless and destitute, dying within and without from loneliness, despair, starvation, disease, and sin. You can help these people by doing your part to maintain a productive society. But in God's words: "Those unwilling to work [should] not get to eat."

b. **Those who are idle** tend to be busybodies (v.11). Rather than using their minds to be positive and productive, their minds are idle, open to negative and evil thoughts. In fact, it is often said that *an idle mind is the devil's playground or workshop*. How true! This is the reason so many of the idle—regardless of age—get into trouble. Having nothing significant to occupy their thoughts, they are open to Satan's devious schemes and are easily led astray. Thus, they concern themselves with other people's business and stir up trouble.

The present passage is dealing with believers and the trouble they cause by being busybodies. Too many believers meddle or pry into other people's affairs, tattling, gossiping, and spreading all kinds of rumors. Why? Because they do not work or stay busy helping to meet the needs of those within the community who are hurting, lonely, desperate, dying, and lost.

c. **Those who are idle** need to settle down and get to work. They need to earn their own living (vv.12-13). Again, this is a forceful command, one that comes directly from the Lord Jesus Christ. But the Lord is not cold or hard-hearted about the matter. Rather, the command is a stirring challenge to get up and get to work. If you, as a believer, have been mistaken about how you should work—if you have been idle or negligent in your work—the Lord will forgive you. First, though, you need to confess your wrong and repent; turn your life around. You need to begin to work and earn your own living. And, if you do not have the skills for the jobs that are available, you should make every effort to secure the necessary training that will equip you to work.

Notice how you are to go about earning your living: *by being settled*—quiet, not disruptive. This is in contrast to being an inefficient busybody. You are to work efficiently, with a quiet spirit, minding your own business, not prying into other people's affairs.

Pay special attention to the end of verse 13: never get tired of doing good. Do not let those who are idle discourage you; instead, stick to your job. Be diligent and persevere. No matter what others do, you need to work hard and be responsible. Furthermore, you should help the unemployed who have real needs and are truly unable to work or secure training. Be a dynamic example for the Lord!

d. **Those who are idle** need to be disciplined. As a believer, you are to have no company with the idle; that is, you are to withdraw from them and have no fellowship with them (vv.14-15). Note why: that they may be ashamed. The hope is that their shame will motivate them to get up and get to work.

Even so, the idle are not to be disciplined as enemies, but as brothers and sisters in Christ. This means that the discipline is not to be done in a spirit of superiority, but in the spirit of unity, as a fellow believer, admonishing and warning them of what the Lord has to say about the matter.

The importance of the discipline is seen in the fact that God tells you to *take note of the idlers.* Observe who they are and let them know that their refusal to work is not acceptable. Do not condone or indulge their idleness; instead, warn them. Then, withdraw and have no fellowship with them. Again, warning them is essential because the warning and letting them experience shame may be their only hope for changing. Being warned and feeling shame might stir the idle to repent, get up, and get to work.

4. You Should Not Talk Back to or Steal from Your Employer.

"Slaves [employees, workers] must always obey their masters [employers, managers] and do their best to please them. They must not talk back or steal, but must show themselves to be

entirely trustworthy and good. Then they will make the teaching about God our Savior attractive in every way" (Tit.2:9-10, NLT).

a. **You are to follow** the instructions of the person over you (v.9). In the workplace, there is no instruction that is not to be obeyed. This, of course, does not mean that you are to obey orders that are contrary to the teaching of the Lord, or that do damage to His people or creation. However, it does mean that you are to do what you are told to do when you have been given the privilege of a job.

   Your attitude toward your employer and supervisor is important to the Lord. You are to obey and follow the instructions of your employer.

b. **You are to go beyond** the call of duty. As a believer, you must seek to please your employer in all things (v.9). This includes such things as...

   - *gratitude:* you are to be thankful and show appreciation for the job and for the livelihood it provides you.
   - *positive attitude or spirit*: you are to have a joyful attitude as you work, to be committed and loyal to your employer.
   - *diligence*: you are to think about your work, how to improve it and how to be more efficient.
   - *edification*: you are to build up the company and the work it does.
   - *relationships*: you are to seek to build good relations with all fellow employees and management.
   - *work and labor*: you are to work hard, to be on time and give a full day's labor every day. You should actually seek to increase your own productivity and that of the whole workplace. You should help the company when extra effort or hours are needed and even go beyond what is required.

c. **You should not contradict** or talk back to your manager (v.9). You need to recognize the need for an orderly workplace and for levels of supervision in order to get the work done.

d. **You are not to steal** from your employer (v.10). The Greek word actually stresses the stealing of small items, like pens, tablets, paper clips, and a host of other petty things. How many believers have stooped to stealing, to doing what so many in the world do? How many feel they are not getting what is due them so they feel justified in taking a little here and there? As a true believer, you are not to steal—*not ever*.

e. **You need to be trustworthy**, honorable, and faithful to your employer and manager (v.10). They must know that they can depend upon you in all that you do. In fact, as a follower of the Lord, you should be the most trustworthy person on the job.

f. **You should be a strong witness** for God and the teachings of His Holy Word, both in the workplace and out in the world (v.10). Wherever you work or walk throughout the day, the teachings of God should be evident in your life. You should never bring disgrace to the Lord's name or to His Holy Word.

William Barclay makes a point that every Christian worker needs to heed:

> *It may well be that the man who takes his Christianity to his work with him will run into trouble; but, if he sticks to it, he will end by winning the respect of all men.*
>
> *E.F. Brown tells of a thing which happened in India. "A Christian servant in India was once sent by his master with a verbal message which he knew to be untrue. He refused to deliver it. Though his master was very angry at the time, he respected the servant all the more afterwards and knew that he could always trust him in his own matters."*
>
> *The truth is that in the end the world comes to see that the Christian workman is the only workman worth having. In one sense, it is hard to be a Christian at our work; in another sense, if we would try it, it is much easier than we think, for there is not* [an employer] *under the sun who is not desperately looking for workmen on whose loyalty and efficiency he can rely.*[4]

4 William Barclay. *The Letters to Timothy, Titus, and Philemon*. "The Daily Study Bible." (Philadelphia, PA: Westminster Press, 1960), p.292f.

CHAPTER 5

WHAT GOD EXPECTS OF YOU

Contents

CHAPTER 5

WHAT GOD EXPECTS OF YOU

A. YOU AND THE HOLY SPIRIT

1. *You Should Allow the Holy Spirit to Lead and Teach You Day by Day.*

> **For all who are led by the Spirit of God are children of God (Ro.8:14, NLT).**
>
> **But the Counselor, the Holy Spirit, whom the Father will send in my name, [He] will teach you all things and will remind you of everything I have said to you (Jn.14:26, NIV).**

When you receive Christ as your Savior, the Holy Spirit actually enters your life and indwells your body. Your body becomes the temple of God's Spirit, and He becomes deeply involved in your life day by day (1 Co.6:19-20). Two significant points are seen in the Scripture above:

a. **The Holy Spirit** will lead you as you seek to live for Christ (Ro.8:14). As stated in an earlier chapter, there are several ideas in the Greek word for *lead* or *led* that are well worth emphasizing again.

- ➢ There is the idea of *carrying or bearing along*. The Spirit leads and carries you through the trials of this life. He bears you up through the corruption and death of this world.
- ➢ There is the idea of *leading and guiding along*. The Spirit leads and guides you along the way of righteousness and truth. He guides you by moving in advance and going ahead of you. He blazes the path, making sure you know where to walk (Jn.16:13; see Ga.5:18; 2 Pe.1:21).
- ➢ There is the idea of *guiding you to an end*. The Holy Spirit not only shows you what to do and where to go, but how to get there. The Spirit actually directs in the day-to-day decisions you have to make in order to reach your goal. He guides your steps as you fulfill your daily responsibilities, making sure you reach your *destined end*, that is, heaven, where you will live eternally in the presence of God Himself.

b. The Holy Spirit is your *Teacher* (Jn.14:26). He teaches everything that Jesus taught, everything you need to know in order to overcome the problems and trials of life. The Holy Spirit helps you understand God's Word, both His wonderful promises and His holy commandments that guide you daily as you seek to live righteously.

Also note that the Holy Spirit helps you remember all that has been taught in the Word of God. He helps you especially in the moments of trial and temptation when the truth is needed. In such moments, the Holy Spirit either infuses you with the strength to endure or flashes across your mind the way to escape.

> **No temptation has overtaken you except such as is common to man; but God *is* faithful, who will not allow you to be tempted beyond what you are able, but with the temptation will also make the way of escape, that you may be able to bear *it* (1 Co.10:13, NKJV).**

2. *You Are to Bear the Fruit of God's Spirit All Day Long, Every Day.*

> **But the fruit of the Spirit is love, joy, peace, patience, kindness, goodness, faithfulness, gentleness, self-control; against such things there is no law (Ga.5:22-23, NASB)**

The Holy Spirit's nature is broken down into a list of traits in order to help you understand His work in your life. When you receive Christ, God actually gives you His Spirit, which means that *all* the traits of the Holy Spirit are present within you to help you live each and every day. The traits may not be fully developed in your life yet, but they will become more and more developed if you faithfully live for Christ and allow the Spirit of God to produce them in your life.

a. There is the fruit of *love*. This is agape love, the love of the mind, the reason, the will. This means...

- that you love regardless of feelings, whether you feel like loving or not
- that you love a person even if the person does not deserve to be loved

Picture a spouse, friend, co-worker, acquaintance, or even an enemy. No matter the person's behavior—no matter what he or she may do—as a true believer, the Spirit of God will enable you to love the person.

You may despise the ugly or sinful conduct; nevertheless, you are to love the offender. You need to respond favorably to the urging of God's Spirit: you are to love the person who wrongs you.

b. **There is the fruit** of *joy*. The joy of the Lord is not the same as the joy of the world. The joy of the world is more of a temporary pleasure than joy. The world's joy is always gripped by some sense of incompleteness; there is not a *permanent, lasting* sense of satisfaction. The world's joy is always accompanied by the awareness that something can go wrong: circumstances can change, or trouble can arise to disturb the joy (sickness, death, financial loss, war, or any number of other things). This haunting awareness keeps the world's joy from being complete and lasting. But God's joy does not depend on circumstances or happiness. Happiness depends upon happenings, but the joy that God implants in the believer's heart overrides all, even the matters of life and death (Ps.5:11; 2 Co.6:10; 7:4).

c. **There is the fruit** of *peace*. There are two sources of peace. First, there is the peace of the world. This is a peace of escapism, of avoiding trouble, of refusing to face facts, of unreality. It is a peace that is sought through pleasure, satisfaction, the absence of trouble, positive thinking, or a denial of problems.

Second, there is the peace of God's Spirit. God's peace permeates your mind, body, and spirit. When you have God's peace, your inner spirit is tranquil, whole, and sound. Your spirit is set free from restlessness, uncertainty, incompleteness, and lack of lasting purpose and fulfillment.

- ➢ The peace of God is, first, a *bosom peace*, a peace deep within you. It is the tranquility of your mind, a composure and restfulness that are undisturbed by circumstances.
- ➢ The peace of God is, second, the *peace of conquest* (Jn.16:33). It is the peace that is independent of conditions and environment; the peace that no sorrow, danger, suffering, or experience can take from you.

> **"These things I have spoken to you, that in Me you may have peace. In the world you will have tribulation; but be of good cheer, I have overcome the world" (Jn.16:33, NKJV).**

- The peace of God is, third, the *peace of assurance* (Ro.8:28). It is the peace of unquestionable confidence, a sure knowledge that your life is in the hands of God and that all things will work out for your good because you love God.

 "And we know that God causes all things to work together for good to those who love God, to those who are called according to *His* purpose" (Ro.8:28, NASB).

- The peace of God is, fourth, the *peace of intimacy with God* (Ph.4:6-7). It is the peace that settles your mind, strengthens your will, and establishes your heart. Because your heart is at peace with God, you know that you have access to Him anytime, anyplace. You can call upon God for help as you face the problems, trials, and sufferings of life. And you can rest assured that God will hear and meet your need.

d. There is the fruit of *patience*. The word means bearing and suffering a long time, persevering, being constant, steadfast, and enduring. Patience never gives in; it is never deterred no matter what attacks it.

- Pressure and hard work may fall upon you, but the Spirit of God helps you persevere through it.
- Disease, disability, or old age may afflict you, but the Spirit of God helps you patiently bear up under it.
- Discouragement and disappointment may take hold of you, but the Spirit of God helps you to patiently work through it all.
- People may do you wrong, slander, ridicule, and injure you; but the Spirit of God helps you to endure and overcome the abuse.

Two significant things need to be noted about patience. First, patience never strikes back. Common sense tells you that most people who are attacked by others would strike back and retaliate. *But* God's Spirit gives you the power of patience—the power to tolerate the situation or person for a long, long time.

Second, patience is one of God's greatest traits. If it were not for God's patience, none of us would be saved. And, as pointed out in this verse, it is a fruit of God's very own Spirit, a fruit that is to be one of the traits of your life.

e. There is the fruit of *kindness*. A kind person is thoughtful, gentle, gracious, and helpful through all situations, no matter the circumstances. If you bear this fruit of God's Spirit, you do not act indifferent, harsh, unconcerned, too busy, or bitter.

To the contrary, you are kind to others. You care for their feelings and feel with them. You experience the full depth of sympathy and empathy. You actually show care by getting right into the situation with them. Kindness suffers with those who suffer, struggles with those who struggle, works with those who work, and helps those who need help.

f. **There is the fruit** of *goodness.* A good person is full of virtue and excellence, kindness and helpfulness, peace and consideration. It means that you do good, that you have a good heart and good behavior, that you are a quality person.

If you bear this fruit of God's Spirit, you are a person who treats others just as they should be treated. You do not take advantage of people, nor do you stand by and let others take advantage of them. You stand up and live for what is good, right, and just. This means that goodness involves discipline, rebuke, correction, and instruction as well as love, care, peace, and reconciliation. As a good person, you will not give license to evil nor let evil run rampant. You will not allow evil to indulge itself and treat others unjustly. You will not allow others to suffer evil if it is in your power to prevent it. As a good person, you step forward and do what you can to stop and control evil.

g. **There is the fruit** of *faithfulness.* This means to be truthful and trustworthy; to be loyal and steadfast; to be committed and devoted. It also means to be constant, staunch, and enduring. As a faithful believer, you will deny and sacrifice yourself as needed—all that you are and have—and trust God to work all things out for your good. You believe God and know that He will honor His promises. Therefore, you cast yourself totally upon God and become faithful to Him.

- Faithfulness does not doubt God—not His salvation, provision, or strength to help.
- Faithfulness does not begin with God then back off and give up.
- Faithfulness does not walk with God then give in to the lusts of the flesh.

Faithfulness begins with God and continues with God; it never ceases or surrenders. You are to be faithful to God—steadfast, persevering, enduring—as you walk throughout each and every day.

> **"Moreover it is required in stewards [believers], that a man be found faithful" (1 Co.4:2, KJV).**

h. **There is the fruit** of *gentleness*. A gentle spirit is meek, tender, humble, mild, and considerate, but strongly so. The spirit of *gentleness* has the strength to control and discipline, yet it does so only at the right time.

First, God's Spirit of gentleness has *a humble state of mind*. However, this does not mean you are weak, cowardly, or inferior. It simply means that as a meek person, you love people and love peace. Therefore, you walk humbly among people, regardless of their status or circumstance in life. Associating with the poor and lowly of this earth does not bother you, not if you bear the Spirit's fruit of gentleness. You desire to be a friend to all and to help all people as much as possible.

Second, God's spirit of gentleness has *a strong state of mind*. This means that you look at situations and want justice and righteousness to be enforced. You do not have a weak mind that ignores and neglects evil and wrongdoing, abuse and suffering.

- If someone is suffering, you are gentle. You step in to do what you can to help.
- If evil is being done, your spirit of gentleness does what it can to stop and correct it.
- If evil is running rampant and indulging itself, your gentleness actually strikes out in anger. But note a crucial point: the anger is always at the right time and directed against the right thing.

Third, God's spirit of gentleness has *strong self-control*. As a gentle person, you control your spirit and mind. You control the lusts of your flesh. You do not give way to an ill-temper, retaliation, immoral passions overindulgence, or license. You die to yourself, to what your flesh would like to do, and you do the right thing—exactly what God wants done.

In summary, you walk in a gentle and humble but strong state of mind. You deny yourself, giving utmost consideration to others, and yet you show a controlled and righteous anger against injustice and evil. In a spirit of gentleness, you give to others and forgive them because of what Christ has done for you.

> **"To speak evil of no one, to be peaceable, gentle, showing all humility to all men" (Tit.3:2, NKJV).**

i. **There is the fruit** of *self-control*. The words mean to master or control the body and all of its desires. As a believer, you are to master your appetites and passions, especially your sensual urges and cravings. You must be strong, controlled, and restrained, not yielding to the lust of the flesh, the lust of the eyes, and the pride of life (1 Jn.2:15-16). You are to strenuously exercise self-control, just as any successful athlete does.

> **Now everyone [an athlete] who competes exercises self-control in everything. However, they do it to receive a perishable crown, but we an imperishable one (1 Co.9:25, HCSB).**

In concluding this discussion, you should remember that the fruit of the Spirit is the very nature of God Himself (Ga.2:20; Ep.5:18). Therefore, you are to walk in the Spirit; that is, you are to walk in such a consciousness of God's presence and in open confession that you are kept constantly clean from sin. As you walk with this awareness of God and in such close communion with Him, you will assimilate the very nature of God, and the Holy Spirit's fruit will be produced in your life. No law can ever be justly used to accuse you or any other person who truly bears the fruit of God's Spirit.

3. *You Need to Be Filled with the Holy Spirit—Filled with All the Fullness of Christ Himself.*

> **Do not get drunk on wine, which leads to debauchery. Instead, be filled with the Spirit (Ep. 5:18, NIV).**
>
> **"He who believes in Me, as the Scripture said, 'From his innermost being will flow rivers of living water.' " But this He spoke of the Spirit, whom those who believed in Him were to receive; for the Spirit was not yet *given,* because Jesus was not yet glorified (Jn.7:38-39, NASB).**

You should not seek the highs of pleasure and fleshly stimulation in alcohol or drugs. Neither should you seek to escape the stress, sorrows, and trials of this world through drunkenness. Alcohol and drugs cannot bring *lasting* joy and satisfaction to your soul. Neither can drunkenness give you lasting relief from the constant pressures, demands, and burdens of everyday life. Only God can give you *permanent* joy, peace, and fulfillment. Only God can give the assurance that He has everything under control and is working all things out for your good—even death itself.

God charges you to be filled with His Spirit, and the command is in the present tense, which means that you are to be *continually filled* with the Spirit (Ac.2:4; 4:29-31). The Spirit's infilling is...

- a *personal manifestation* of Christ to the believer who walks obediently day by day (Jn.14:21).
- a strong sense and consciousness of Christ's presence and leadership—moment by moment.
- a deep sense of the Lord's presence exploding in the heart of the believer, those special times when there is a real consciousness and experience of love between the Lord and His faithful follower.

This special manifestation and consciousness of Christ's presence, this infilling of God's Spirit, is the believer's privilege. Even so, the Spirit's filling is not an automatic experience. The responsibility of being filled with the Spirit rests upon your shoulders. You are filled only as you obey Christ and His commandments, His Holy Word. This is exactly what Christ said:

> **"He who has My commandments and keeps them, it is he who loves Me. And he who loves Me will be loved by My Father, and I will love him and manifest [reveal, disclose] Myself to him" (Jn.14:21-22, NKJV).**

When you go through terrible trials, severe crises, and intense temptations, God knows. He knows what you are feeling and thinking; therefore, when you sincerely call upon Him, He moves to meet your need. He moves within your heart, manifesting His presence and giving you a deep sense of His love and care. He helps you and gives you strength, forgiveness, and assurance—whatever He knows you are in need of. The depth of the experience and the intensity of *the special manifestation* depend upon your specific situation. You must always remember that God loves you perfectly, and that He will do whatever is necessary...

- to lift you up
- to strengthen you
- to conform you to the image of His dear Son, the Lord Jesus Christ

Just be responsible; go about your work and duties day by day and God will fill you with His Spirit. And once again, never forget that the infilling of the Holy Spirit—the *special manifestations* of the Lord's presence—is given only to the believer who keeps the commandments of Christ. Knowing this, it is essential that you obey Christ and His Holy Word if you want God to fill you with His Spirit.

When you truly empty and yield yourself to follow Christ, He fills you with His presence and power, the presence and power of the Holy Spirit. And the closer you follow (obey) and draw near Him, the more the Spirit's power will flow through your life unhindered:

- The power to conquer the temptations of your sinful nature.

> **So I say, live by the Spirit, and you will not gratify the desires of the sinful nature (Ga.5:16, NIV).**

- The power to use your spiritual gifts in effective service for the Lord.

> **And they were all filled with the Holy Spirit and began to speak with other tongues, as the Spirit was giving them utterance. Now there were Jews living in Jerusalem, devout men from every nation under heaven....Peter *said* to them, "Repent, and each of you be baptized in the name of Jesus Christ for the forgiveness of your sins; and you will receive the gift of the Holy Spirit....So then, those who had received his word were baptized; and that day there were added about three thousand souls (Ac.2:4-5, 38, 41, NASB).**

- The power to be a bold, effective witness for the Lord.

> **But you shall receive power when the Holy Spirit has come upon you; and you shall be witnesses to Me in Jerusalem, and in all Judea and Samaria, and to the end of the earth" (Ac.1:8, NKJV).**

- The power to be filled with joy and thanksgiving at all times.

> **And do not be drunk with wine, in which is dissipation; but be filled with the Spirit, speaking to one another in psalms and hymns and spiritual songs, singing and making melody in your heart to the Lord, giving thanks always for**

all things to God the Father in the name of our Lord Jesus Christ (Ep.5:18-20, NKJV).

- The power to submit to others.

Be filled with the Spirit....submitting to one another in the fear of God (Ep.5:18b, 21, NKJV).

- The power to bear the fruit of the Spirit.

But the fruit of the Spirit is love, joy, peace, longsuffering, kindness, goodness, faithfulness, gentleness, self-control. Against such there is no law (Ga.5:22-23, NKJV).

- The power to fulfill your duties within your family.

Be filled with the Spirit....Wives, submit to your own husbands, as to the Lord....Husbands, love your wives, just as Christ also loved the church and gave Himself for her....Children, obey your parents in the Lord, for this is right (Ep.5:18b, 22, 25; 6:1 NKJV).

- The power to be a diligent, responsible worker or employer.

Be filled with the Spirit....Bondservants, be obedient to those who are your masters according to the flesh, with fear and trembling, in sincerity of heart, as to Christ....And you, masters, do the same things to them, giving up threatening, knowing that your own Master also is in heaven, and there is no partiality with Him (Ep.5:18b, 6:5, 9, NKJV).

- The power to stand against Satan and his evil forces.

Be filled with the Spirit....Finally, be strong in the Lord and in his mighty power. Put on the full armor of God so that you can take your stand against the devil's schemes (Ep.5:18b; 6:10-11, NIV).

4. *You Must Not Sin Against the Holy Spirit.*

Scripture mentions five major sins against the Holy Spirit.

a. First, you can sin by *grieving* the Holy Spirit.

> **Do not grieve the Holy Spirit of God, by whom you were sealed for the day of redemption (Ep.4:30, NASB).**

To grieve means to pain, sadden, or bring sorrow to the heart. The Holy Spirit is pure, holy, and righteous. You grieve the Spirit when you do such things as...

- allow impure thoughts or behave immorally
- act in a corrupt or unjust manner
- allow or participate in anything contrary to the nature of the Spirit
- covet what others have
- lie, steal, or cheat
- discriminate or oppress
- focus on the sinful pleasures of the world

b. Second, you can sin by quenching the Holy Spirit.

> **Do not quench the Spirit (1 Th.5:19, NASB).**

To quench means to stifle, snuff out, stop. The Holy Spirit is always working in your life, seeking to arouse you to do God's will. You quench and stifle the Spirit's work by...

- ignoring, neglecting, and disobeying Him
- procrastinating
- failing and refusing to do what you should

c. Third, you can sin by lying to the Holy Spirit.

> **Then Peter said, "Ananias, why have you let Satan fill your heart? You lied to the Holy Spirit, and you kept some of the money for yourself. The property was yours to sell or not sell, as you wished. And after selling it, the money was also yours to give away. How could you do a thing like this? You weren't lying to us but to God!" (Ac.5:3-4, NLT).**

There are several ways you can do this:

- You pretend to be something spiritually that you are not.
- You say that you are surrendering your life or money to the cause of Christ, but you fail to follow through. You fail to give yourself or your money to God—just as Ananias did.

- You say that you want the Spirit's presence and power in your life when you are really unwilling to surrender to the Lord.
- You say that you are committed to walk as a brother or sister with other believers when you are not really willing to pay the full price of discipleship. That is, you are unwilling to deny self in order to serve in your church or to reach out to a world of hurting and dying people who do not know Christ.
- You say that you want the fullness of God's Spirit when the acceptance and approval of people are far more important to you.

d. Fourth, you can sin by *insulting* the Holy Spirit.

> **Just think how much worse the punishment will be for those who have trampled on the Son of God, and have treated the blood of the covenant, which made us holy, as if it were common and unholy, and have insulted and disdained the Holy Spirit who brings God's mercy to us (He.10:29, NLT).**

To insult means to abuse, disgrace, snub, disrespect, show contempt. How do you insult the Holy Spirit?

- By sensing the inner pull of the Spirit to repent of some sinful behavior and rejecting it. Instead of following Christ with renewed fervor, you ignore the conviction of the Spirit. This insults and snubs the Spirit and shows that you disrespect Him.
- By professing that you are a follower of Christ yet continuing to live in sin. This insults the Spirit and shows contempt for Him.

Closely note the above verse. The person who knows the truth and still turns to the world and sin will be punished—no matter what he or she professes. And remember: those who falsely professed to be God's people under Moses' law died without mercy (He.10:28). Think how much worse the punishment will be for any of us who lie to the Holy Spirit and turn away from Christ!

e. Lastly, you can sin by committing *blasphemy* against the Holy Spirit.

> **"Therefore I say to you, any sin and blasphemy shall be forgiven people, but blasphemy against the Spirit shall not be forgiven (Mt.12:31, NASB).**

The warning in this verse is unmistakable: blasphemy against the Holy Spirit is unforgivable. But exactly what is blasphemy? Most people think of blasphemy in terms of profane words, words spoken against the Holy Spirit—irreverent, spiteful, wicked words. And this is true. But blasphemy arises out of an evil, irreverent heart, a heart that disbelieves, rejects, and reacts against the Holy Spirit. So people commit blasphemy not only by their words but also by their actions and especially in their hearts. In light of the severity of the warning, people need to take heed, believers and unbelievers alike!

We need to remember that the Holy Spirit is the Person who works in the hearts of people. It is He who "convicts the world of sin, and of righteousness, and of judgment..." (Jn.16:8-11). The word *convicts* is very descriptive of the Spirit's work. When we see, feel, or hear about God's goodness and love and of our own need to surrender to God, it is the Spirit who convicts our hearts to believe. In spite of this, we may go on...

- ➢ insisting on our own way
- ➢ refusing to acknowledge God and to surrender our lives to Him
- ➢ choosing to be blind to what we see, feel, and hear (the convictions of the Spirit)

Tragically, if we continue on in this way, we will eventually become so hardened that we cannot recognize God's truth and goodness. We reach such a point of hardness that we can no longer see, feel, or hear God. In such cases, we blaspheme God's Spirit and count His convictions as worthless. We abuse, revile, neglect, ignore, and harden our hearts to the promptings of God's Spirit permanently. Christ says such blasphemy against God's Spirit is unforgivable. In the clearest terms, this is *stubborn rejection, stiff-necked refusal, obstinate unbelief,* resulting in *a dead spirit.*

What a warning to us all! What a call to stir repentance toward God! We need to totally surrender to God while our hearts are soft enough to be touched!

B. YOU AND YOUR STUDY OF GOD'S HOLY WORD

1. *You Should Diligently Study and Correctly Handle God's Holy Word.*

> **Be diligent to present yourself approved [pleasing] to God, a worker who does not need to be ashamed, rightly dividing the word of truth (2 Ti.2:15, NKJV).**

As a believer, you are to be faithful and diligent in studying the Word of God. You are not to drift off the path and get sidetracked in seeking the truth. You are to go straight to the Word of God, study the truth, and accurately handle it. You are not to rely on...

- your own ideas and thoughts
- the theories and teachings of other people
- the half-truths of false prophets and questionable religions

Your main source for growth and instruction is to be the Word of God. It and it alone should be the basis for judging every other work, theory, or teaching. In light of this and in light of its purity, you must guard against mishandling the Word of God. You must never twist it to fit what you think or want it to say, nor over- or underemphasize its teachings, nor add to or take away from its words. Any person who mishandles God's Word is not pleasing to God. This is the point of this verse: if you want God's approval—if you want to be pleasing to God—you are to be a true student of God's Word. This means you need to diligently study God's Word and handle it for what it is: the Word of Truth. If you are faithful to study and handle God's Word with all the reverence and consideration it is due, you will not be ashamed when you face the Lord Jesus Christ in the great day of judgment.

2. *You Should Not Merely Listen to God's Word but Also Do What God Says.*

> **Do not merely listen to the word, and so deceive yourselves. Do what it says. Anyone who listens to the word but does not do what it says is like a man who looks at his face in a mirror and, after looking at himself, goes away and immediately forgets what he looks like. But the man who looks intently into the perfect law [God's Holy Word] that gives freedom, and continues to do this, not forgetting**

what he has heard, but doing it—he will be blessed in what he does (Jas.1:22-25, NIV).

Contrary to what many people think, it is not enough just to *hear* and to *learn about* the Word of God; you must also live out or obey the Word of God. Scripture makes this very clear.

a. **If you think** that you can hear and learn something about the Word of God and then go out and live any way you want, you deceive yourself (v.22). There are some who study and many who sit under the teaching of the Holy Bible week after week, and they learn or know much about the Bible. They think their listening and learning makes them acceptable to God, that it makes them safe and secure no matter how they live. When they slip into sin, they feel they can just ask God for forgiveness and He will automatically forgive them. They honestly believe that God would never reject them, that they are good enough to be acceptable to God. However, note a critical fact: God does not accept you because you hear and learn about the Bible nor because you confess your sins. Each of these is necessary and very important, but they are not enough.

   God accepts you because you *confess and repent* of your sins. Repentance means that you turn *away* from your sins and turn *toward* God and live for Him. God accepts you because you turn to Him and *live righteously, obeying His holy commandments*. When you believe God—truly believe Him—you trust and follow Him. You do exactly what He says.

b. **If you only hear** and learn God's Word mentally, but fail to do what God says, you soon forget what you have heard (vv.22-23). If you do not practice or carry through with what you learn, it soon fades from memory. It is simply put out of your mind, and it never becomes a part of your life. You are like the person who looks in a mirror to see if anything needs to be done to his or her appearance, then begins to think of something else and walks away, forgetting the wrinkled clothes or tousled hair that needs attention.

   How like so many of us! We hear or think about God's Word and are convicted of some shortcoming, failure, or sin we need to deal with. Yet as soon as we walk out into the world and become engaged in our daily affairs, we quickly forget to do what the Word of God tells us to do.

c. **If you hear** and do what God's Word says, you will be blessed (v.25). Note that the Word of God is called the *perfect law of liberty or freedom.* This means that the Word of God will set you free from the bondages of sin and death. If you truly obey God's Holy Word, He will free you from the condemnation of sin, which is death, and give you the full and victorious life for which your soul longs—a life that will continue on eternally with God.

If you do what God's Word says, you will find that you are set free from all that enslaves your soul upon earth. You will discover love, joy, and peace—a soul that soars with a sense of...

- freedom
- purpose
- security
- victory
- assurance
- fulfillment

It is critical to remember, however, that you must continue to do what the Word of God says. If you do, then God will bless you and give you abundant and eternal joy—no matter what you may face in this world.

3. *You Can Trust God's Word—the Holy Bible: It Was Given to the World by God Himself.*

> **All scripture *is* given by inspiration of God, and *is* profitable for doctrine, for reproof, for correction, for instruction in righteousness (2 Ti.3:16, KJV).**
>
> **"And so we have the prophetic word confirmed, which you do well to heed as a light that shines in a dark place, until the day dawns and the morning star rises in your hearts; knowing this first, that no prophecy of Scripture is of any private interpretation, for prophecy never came by the will of man, but holy men of God spoke *as they were* moved by the Holy Spirit" (2 Pe.1:19-21, NKJV).**

You can trust and have complete confidence in the Word of the prophets (2 Pe.1:19-21). The prophet's words and predictions are part of God's Word, and all Scripture is given by inspiration of God (2 Ti.3:16). In addition, God's prophetic Word has been strongly confirmed and is well-documented in historical records.

Always remember this fact: there are an enormous number of prophecies in the Scripture, many of which predicted the coming Messiah and Savior of the world, Jesus Christ. When these prophecies are studied, it becomes absolutely clear that Jesus Christ is the promised Savior.

He fulfills all the prophecies perfectly. Therefore, the prophetic Word is strong proof that the *account* of salvation and God's Holy Word can be trusted—perfectly trusted. Just by the sheer number of prophecies and their fulfillment in Christ, the Scriptures prove themselves to be true, the very Word of God Himself. In light of this fact, you need to do two things:

a. **You should heed** Scripture very carefully; pay close attention and do exactly what it says. Why? Because the Word of God is like "a light that shines in a dark place, until the day dawns and the morning star rises in your hearts" (2 Pe.1:19). What does this mean?

   - The Word of God is like a light that shows you how to walk in the dark forest of this world. It reveals the narrow path to follow and exposes the stumbling stones, dangerous pitfalls, and poisonous creatures along the path.
   - The Word of God will show you how to walk "until the day dawns." What day? The glorious day of Christ's return. In that day, the Day Star [Christ Himself] will arise in your heart and you will be transformed into Christ's perfect image. Your salvation will then be completely fulfilled and perfected. You will be perfected to live with Christ forever (1 Jn.3:2).

   Commentator Michael Green has an excellent comment on the glorious day when the Morning Star (Christ) will arise in your heart:

   > *Your inner transformation, deepened continually by God's Spirit as you study the Scriptures, will be completed on the great day when you will see Him as He is, and are made like Him.*[1]

   The point is emphatic: you must make every effort possible to study and heed the Scripture. You should study the Old and the New Testaments, the prophecies about Christ and the fulfillment of the prophecies in Christ. You can trust the Scripture as the light of God, the light that will guide you through this dark and dangerous world.

b. **You need to understand** that no prophecy in Scripture came from the prophets' own understanding, reasoning skills, or interpretation (2 Pe.1:20-21). Scripture

---

1 Michael Green. *The Second Epistle of Peter and the Epistle of Jude*. "The Tyndale New Testament Commentaries." (Grand Rapids, MI: Eerdmans Publishing Co., 1968), p.89.

did not come from the will, the plans, or the initiative of men or women. God moved upon the prophets' hearts and gave them visions; then the prophets wrote down exactly what the Spirit of God had shown or spoken to them. The Greek emphasizes the fact that the writers were moved (borne along, inspired, impelled) by God's Holy Spirit to speak and write down the prophecies and words *from God*.

> **I tell you the truth, until heaven and earth disappear, not the smallest letter, not the least stroke of a pen, will by any means disappear from the Law until everything is accomplished (Mt.5:18, NIV).**
>
> **For whatever was written in earlier times was written for our instruction, so that through perseverance and the encouragement of the Scriptures we might have hope (Ro.15:4, NASB).**
>
> **These things I have written to you who believe in the name of the Son of God, so that you may know that you have eternal life (1 Jn.5:13, NASB).**

The great significance of this point cannot be overemphasized. Scripture can be trusted; it is the Word of God. This validates that Jesus Christ is the Savior of the world. You can be saved; your needs can be met. You can now have peace and live eternally. The proof that salvation is available through Jesus Christ is in the *prophetic Scriptures*. They prove beyond any question that Jesus Christ is the Son of God, the Savior and Lord of the entire universe. See the *Prophecies of Jesus and Their Fulfillment*, in the following chart for an exciting study of the prophetic Scriptures.

Old Testament Prophecies of Jesus and Their Fulfillment in the New Testament

Old Testament References	The Prophecies	Their Fulfillment
Ge.3:15	Seed of a Woman	Ga.4:4; Mt.1:20; Lu.1:34, 2:7; Re.12:5
Ge.12:3; 18:18; 22:18	Seed of Abraham	Ac.3:25; Ga.3:8 (Mt.1:1; Lu.3:34)
Ge.17:19; 22:16-17	Seed of Isaac	Mt.1:2; Lu.1:55, 72-74
Ge.28:14 (Nu.24:17)	Seed of Jacob	Lu.3:34 (Mt.1:2)
Ge.49:10[a]	From the Royal Tribe of Judah	Lu.3:33; He.7:14
De.18:15, 18	Will Be a Prophet	Jn.6:14; Ac.3:22-23
2 S.7:13[b] (Is.9:7; 11:1-5; Je.23:5-6)	Will Be Heir to David's Throne	Mt.1:1 (Mt.1:6; Lu.1:32-33)
2 S.7:14[a]	God's Son	Mk.1:1
Is.35:5-6; 61:1-3; Ps.72:2)	Meet People's Needs	Mt.11:4-6
Ps.2:1-2; Is.53:3	Rejected	Jn.19;15; Lu.23:36[a], 38
Ps.2:7	The Son of God	Ac.13:33; He.1:5; 5:5
Ps.8:2	To Be Praised	Mt.21:16
Ps.16:8-11	Resurrected	Ac.13:33-35; 2:25-28, 31 (Mt.28:1-2; Mk.16:6, 12, 14; Lu.24:1-53)
Ps.22:1	Forsaken by God	Mt.27:46; Mk.15:34
Ps.22:7	Mocked at the Cross	Mt.27:39
Ps.22:18	Clothes Gambled for	Mt.27:35; Mk.15:24; Lu.23:34; Jn.19:24
Ps.22:22	To Secure Many Brothers	He.2:12
Ps.31:5	Commends His Spirit to God	Lu.23:46
Ps.40:6-8	Fulfills God's Will	Heb.10:5-7
Ps.41:9	Betrayed by Judas	Jn.13:18; Ac.1:16

Old Testament References	The Prophecies	Their Fulfillment
Ps.45:6, 7	Is Eternal and Preeminent	He.1:8, 9
Ps.68:18	Will Lead Captivity Captive	Ep.4:8-10
Ps.69:21	Offered Drugs on the Cross	Mt.27:34, 48; Mk.15:36; Lu.23:36; Jn.19:28, 29
Ps.69:25; 109:8	Judas' Fate	Ac.1:20
Ps.89:26-27	Exaltation	Ph.2:9 (Re.11:15)
Ps.95:7-11	Hearts Hardened Against	He.3:7-11; 4:3, 5-7
Ps.102:25-27	Is the Creator and Is Eternal	Jn.1:1-3; Col.1:15; He.1:10-12
Ps.110:1	To Be Exalted	Mt.22:44; Mk.12:36; Lu.20:42; Ac.2:34, 35; He.1:13
Ps.110:4	Is the High Priest	He.5:6
Ps.118:22, 23	The Stone	Mt.21:42; Mk.12:10; Lu.20:17; Ac.4:11
Ps.118:25, 26	Triumphal Entry	Mt.21:9; Mk.11:9; Lu.19:38; Jn.12:13
Ps.132:11, 17	Son of David	Lu.1:69; Ac.2:30
Is.7:14	Virgin Birth	Mt.1:23; Lu.1:34-35
Is.9:1, 2	A Light to Those in Darkness	Mt.4:15, 16
Is.11:2	God's Spirit Rests Upon	Lu.4:18-21 (Mt.12:18; Jn.3:34)
Is.11:10	To Save the Gentiles	Ro.15:12
Is.25:8	To Conquer Death	1 Co.15:54
Is.28:16	The Stone	Ro.9:33; 1 Pe.2:6
Is.40:3-5	To Have a Forerunner	Mt.3:3; Mk.1:3; Lu.3:4-6
Is.42:1-4	To Minister to the Gentiles	Mt.12:17-21
Is.49:6	A Light to the Gentiles	Lu.2:32; Ac.13:47, 48; 26:23
Is.53:1	Would Not Be Believed	Jn.12:38; Ro.10:16
Is.53:3-6, 11	To Die for People's Sins	1 Pe.2:23-25

Old Testament References	The Prophecies	Their Fulfillment
Is.53:4	To Heal and Bear People's Sickness	Mt.8:17
Is.53:9	To Be Sinless	1 Pe.2:22
Is.53:12	To Be Counted a Sinner	Mk.15:28; Lu.22:37
Is.54:13	To Teach As God	Jn.6:45
Is.55:3	To Be Raised	Ac.13:34
Is.59:20, 21	To Save Israel	Ro.11:26, 27
Je.31:31-34	To Make a New Covenant	He.8:8-12; 10:16, 17
Ho.1:10-11	To Restore Israel	Ro.11:1-36
Ho.1:10; 2:23	Conversion of the Gentiles	Ro.9:25-26; 1 Pe.2:10
Joel 2:28-32	Promise of the Spirit	Ac.2:16-21
Amos 9:11-12	Lord's Return and Kingdom Established	Ac.15:16, 17
Mi.5:2	Birthplace of Messiah	Mt.2:5, 6; Jn.7:42
Hab.1:5	Jews' Unbelief	Ac.13:40, 41
Hag.2:6	Return of Christ	He.12:26
Zec.9:9	Triumphal Entry	Mt.21:4, 5; Mk.11:1-7; Lu.19:30-35; Jn.12:14, 15
Zec.11:12-13	Judas' Betrayal	Mt.26:14-16; 27:9-10; Zec.11:12b-13;
Zec.12:10	Spear Pierced in His Side	Jn.19:37
Zec.13:7	Disciples Scattered at the Cross	Mt.26:31, 56; Mk.14:27, 50
Mal.3:1	Forerunner, John the Baptist	Mt.11:10; Mk.1:2; Lu.7:27
Mal.4:5, 6	Forerunner, John the Baptist	Mt.11:13, 14; 17:10-13; Mk.9:11-13; Lu.1:16, 17

C. You and Prayer

1. *You Must Pray in Jesus' Name to Receive the Answers to Your Prayers.*

> **And whatever you ask in My name, that I will do, that the Father may be glorified in the Son. If you ask anything in My name, I will do *it* (Jn.14:13-14, NKJV).**

What does it mean to pray "in Jesus' name"? It means far more than just mentioning Jesus' name in a prayer or simply closing your prayer with the words "in Jesus' name." It means that the only Person whose name is perfect enough to approach God is Jesus.

When you approach God in the name of Jesus, you are asking God to hear you because of Christ's righteousness, not because of your goodness. Furthermore, you want God to answer your prayer to honor Christ, not to honor yourself. This is what it means to pray in Jesus' Name. When you ask Christ to hear you and genuinely trust in His name—all He is and has done for you—He promises to answer your prayer.

2. *You Are to Follow Three Simple Rules of Prayer, Rules Laid Down by Christ Himself.*

> **"And when you are praying, do not use meaningless repetition as the Gentiles do, for they suppose that they will be heard for their many words. "So do not be like them; for your Father knows what you need before you ask Him (Mt.6:7-8, NASB).**

Too often, people measure prayer by its fluency or length, thinking that a long or well-worded prayer implies sincerity or devotion. But Christ puts the matter very simply; when you pray, follow these three clear rules.

a. **First, do not use** meaningless or thoughtless repetition. There are several things that lend themselves to meaningless repetition:
   - Memorized prayer: just saying the words of a form prayer, for example, the Lord's prayer. There is nothing wrong with praying a memorized prayer, but it should be prayed through and not just repeated with no thought behind the words.

- Written, well-worded prayers: thinking that what you say is so expressive and so well-worded that it is bound to carry weight with God. The words may be descriptive and beautifully arranged, but the heart must be offering the prayer, not the mind and ego. Such prayer is empty repetition.
- Ceremonial or ritual prayer: saying the same prayer at the same time on the same occasion, over and over again (such as at weddings, funerals, meals, or worship services). This can soon become meaningless repetition.
- Predictable or compulsory prayer: praying in the same way on a rigid schedule can lead to praying strictly as a habit (repeated practice) with little or no meaning to it.
- Thoughtless prayer: speaking words while your mind is wandering. When this happens, you need to ask God to forgive you and immediately begin to focus. No one can control your thoughts but you. It is up to you to concentrate on what you are praying.
- Religious terms or phrases: using certain words or phrases over and over in prayer because they sound religious or pious. (For example, the repeated use of mercy, grace, "I thank thee O God," "dear Lord, I pray").
- Habitual references to God: using repetition mindlessly, such as "Lord this" and "Lord that," or "God this" and "God that," or "Jesus this" and "Jesus that." This shows that a person is giving very little thought to what he or she is praying. Far too little fear and reverence are seen when approaching Him whose name is "the Wonderful Counselor, the Mighty God, the Everlasting Father, the Prince of Peace" (Is.9:6).

Christ is not saying that repetition in prayer is wrong. It is not wrong. What is wrong is vain and empty repetition. Christ Himself used repetition in prayer (Mt.26:44), as did Daniel (Da.9:18-19), and the Psalmist (Ps.136:1f). There are several basic things that will keep you from using meaningless repetition in prayer.

- A genuine heart: knowing God personally and having a moment-by-moment fellowship with Him all day long.
- Concentrated thought: really focusing on what you are saying.
- A desire for fellowship with God: praying sincerely, openly, personally.

- Preparation: when possible, calming your spirit and preparing to meet God by first meditating on His Word.

b. **Second, do not speak** much. Some believers think that length of prayer equals devotion; that is, the longer they pray, the more God will listen to them and the more spiritual they will become. They feel that long prayers show how sincere they are.

God does not hear your prayer because it is long, but because your heart is genuinely poured out to Him. Length has nothing to do with devotion, but a sincere heart does.

Long prayers are certainly not forbidden. What is forbidden is thinking that long prayers are automatically heard by God. Christ prayed all night (Lu.6:12). The early disciples prayed and fasted and sought God for ten days and nights waiting for the coming of the Holy Spirit (Ac.2:1f). Obviously, there *are* special times when an extended prayer time is necessary. Some of these times are clearly seen in Scripture.

- Sometimes, you should sense the needs of the world so much that you are driven to seek God and His intervention for long periods of time, and the seeking should be often (Ep.6:18).
- Sometimes, a very special pull to praise and adore God arises within your heart. When you feel this pull, you should get alone and spend a very special time praising and worshipping God (Ac.16:25).
- Sometimes, a special need will arise in your life. This may be your own need or that of a friend or loved one. You should intercede until God gives the assurance that the need will be met (Ep.6:18; see Ac.12:1-5, esp. v.5).
- Sometimes, an unusual experience or event has taken place, or is about to take place, in either your own or a loved one's life. You should get alone and share the event with God. And you should stay before God until you receive whatever is needed to face the matter: courage, confidence, power, faith, love or assurance (Mt.4:1-11).
- Sometimes, a great trial or temptation is confronting you. A long session of prayer may be needed to gain strength and to keep you away from the trial or temptation (Mt.4:1-11)
- Sometimes, you may need to work through a particular problem, a difficult circumstance, or make a major decision. In these times, you need to seek the

help and guidance of God. God should be acknowledged in all of your ways. You should continue to ask God for help until the answer is given (Ac.13:1-3, esp. 2.).

In concluding this point, always remember that prayer is a matter of the heart, not a matter of words or length of prayer. Praying is sharing with God your thoughts, feelings, praises, and requests as if you were speaking with Him face-to-face.

c. **Third, when you pray,** *trust God.* God knows what you need even before you ask (2 Chr.16:9; Is.65:24). Why, then, should you pray? Because prayer demonstrates your need for God and your dependence upon Him. Prayer gives time for concentrated sharing and communion between you and God. It is *not enough* merely to have a knowledge of God in your mind as you walk throughout life. You need to have times when you are in the presence of God and can concentrate your thoughts in prayer and fellowship with God. You need such time with God just as you need such times with your family and friends. You are not meant to live in isolation from people nor from God. Therefore, you pray not *only* to have your needs met but to share, fellowship, and enrich your life with God.

Always keep in mind that God desires to fellowship with you and to do so often, as well as to hear and answer your prayer and to meet your needs. Just pray and trust Him, for He loves and cares for you (1 Pe.5:7).

3. *You Need to Persevere in Prayer: Ask, Seek, and Knock.*

> **"Ask, and it will be given to you; seek, and you will find; knock, and it will be opened to you. For everyone who asks receives, and he who seeks finds, and to him who knocks it will be opened (Mt.7:7-8; see Lu.18:1-8, NKJV).**

What is persevering prayer? It is *asking, seeking,* and *knocking* until the answer is received, found, or opened. It is being so passionate or fervent about something that you never give up until God responds. The words *ask, seek,* and *knock* are in the present tense. You are to keep on asking, keep on seeking, keep on knocking. You are to persist in prayer. The words *receive, find,* and *open* are also in the present tense (Mt.7:8). This shows that the answer to prayer is more than just a promise for the future.

Perhaps the event has not yet happened nor the problem resolved nor the answer received, but by faith you know that God has heard your prayer. Christ teaches several important lessons about prayer in these two verses.

a. **True prayer is** persevering prayer. When you sense a real need to pray, you should not only ask, but also seek and knock. Do not play around and glibly murmur a prayer, but pray and continue to pray until you receive an answer.
b. **Prayer is** to be often. Christ tells you to "ask... seek... knock," which means to pray repeatedly. Pray often and pray with intensity.
c. **The answers** to your prayers are assured (vv.9-10). Remember, God is not reluctant to give. He is not sitting back, disinterested and unconcerned about your welfare. He is like a loving father who cares deeply for His child. God will never refuse to hear your request, the request of His dear child—not if what you ask is good for your welfare and growth.
d. **The request—**the thing wanted—must be in God's will. You must not ask from selfish desires and motives. God gives only what is good and wholesome for you (1 Jn.5:14-15; see Js.1:17; 4:2-3).
e. **True prayer,** persevering prayer, acknowledges your dependence upon God. It is when you face a desperate need that you are stirred to cry out to God, that you really begin to ask, seek, and knock. The very fact that you keep on asking, seeking, and knocking demonstrates that you are truly dependent upon God.
f. **God does not** always answer your prayers immediately. People frequently wonder why it is necessary to ask, seek, and knock and to keep on asking, seeking, and knocking. There are at least four reasons:
   - Prayer teaches you to communicate and fellowship with God and to seek Him more and more. When God delays answering your prayer, you keep coming to share with Him over and over again. Just as your human father longs for your fellowship, so your heavenly Father longs for your fellowship.
   - Prayer teaches you to be patient and to hope in God and His promises more and more. When God does not answer your prayer immediately, you should continue coming into His presence, waiting and hoping for what He has promised (Mt.21:22; Jn.14:26; 1 Jn.5:14-15). You actually grow more mature in patience and endurance as you learn to place more hope in God and His wonderful promises.

- Prayer teaches you to love God as your Father more and more. Knowing that God is going to answer your prayer and having to wait on the answer causes you to draw closer to Him. Then, when the prayer is answered, your heart is endeared to Him much more than before.
- Prayer demonstrates how deeply you trust God, how much you love and depend upon Him. As you grow in that trust, you will bring more and more concerns to God. If, on the other hand, you are not quite sure that God will answer your prayer, you will only come occasionally, usually in emergencies. Your prayer life easily shows both you and God how much you love and trust Him.

For these reasons and so many more, you need to persevere in prayer. Learn to ask, seek, and knock.

4. *You Should Not Be Anxious About Anything, but Pray: Tell God, and Peace Will Guard Your Heart and Mind.*

> **Be anxious for nothing, but in everything by prayer and supplication with thanksgiving let your requests be made known to God. And the peace of God, which surpasses all comprehension, will guard your hearts and your minds in Christ Jesus (Ph.4:6-7, NASB).**

This is actually a charge: Do not be anxious about anything. The idea is that you are not to worry or fret about a single thing. This is easy to say but hard to do, as we all know. Most of us suffer some degree of anxiety...

- when we lose money, employment, a friendship, a loved one, or anything of value to us
- when we lack or are unable to provide adequate food, clothing, or shelter
- when we live, work, or worship in a divisive or stressful environment
- when we are persecuted, ridiculed, abused, or threatened
- when we face a serious illness or some other major problem

In the midst of such circumstances, we do not have the ability or power within ourselves to keep from worrying. The only way we can keep from being apprehensive or frightened is to receive an injection of supernatural power.

This is the very point of Scripture. There is an answer to worry and anxiety, a supernatural answer: the peace of God. As a true believer, God will *enable* you to conquer your fear and uneasiness. God will *empower* you to overcome and walk through the trials of life no matter how terrible and pressing they may be. God will *infuse* you with peace—the very peace of God Himself—a peace so amazing that it carries you right *through* the trial. Of course, this does not mean that you are not to be concerned about the problems of life or that you will not bear some suffering. You are to be concerned, and you will experience suffering and pain in life; but through it all, God promises to give you peace of heart and mind. How?

a. **The remedy** for anxiety and worry is prayer (v.6). Scripture says: Pray *in everything.*" This means that you are to walk around in a *spirit of prayer,* that you are to pray about everything as you go about your daily affairs.

   Furthermore, you are to pray about every single thing no matter how small or insignificant it may seem. God is interested in the details of your life, in the most minute details. He wants you to acknowledge Him in *all your ways* because He cares about and wants to look after you in everything you do.

   Picture the scene: you are walking through your day, sharing with God every step of the way, and God is right there with you. What, then, can take away the peace of God? Absolutely nothing! For as you walk in prayer and fellowship with God, God is infusing you with His presence and peace. No matter the conflict or trial, He is there for you and with you. You are communing with God, and He is continuing to strengthen you with His presence. *Through prayer,* He is giving you the peace to conquer and walk through the trial. Your relationship with God and His peace is unbroken.

b. **God's great promise** is peace—peace of heart and peace of mind (v.7). To be *at peace* means to be assured, confident, and secure in the love and care of God. It means to have a sense, a consciousness, a knowledge that God will take care of you. Note what God says about the peace He gives.

   First, God's peace passes all understanding. It is beyond anything you can ask or think. It even surpasses all you can imagine (Ep.3:20). Envision the most terrible thing you would ever have to face or endure; then think of the peace you would need as you went through that trial. In all reality, the peace of God is far greater than anything you could ever understand or hope for! The peace of God actually carries the *faithful believer* through the midst of the most devastating trials and temptations.

Second, the peace of God guards your heart and mind. The word *guard* is a military word meaning to garrison, to keep watch and protect. The peace of God is like an elite soldier who guards and protects God's most precious possession: you, one of His dear believers, His own child.

It is imperative to remember, however, that God can keep you—watch over and protect you—only if you are "in Christ Jesus." God cannot look upon sin; therefore, He cannot look at you in your sinful condition. This means that you can know the peace of God only if you have trusted Christ as your Lord and Savior and are covered with His righteousness, only if you walk in prayer and fellowship with Him. To be *in Christ* means to be *at peace*!

> **Peace I leave with you, My peace I give to you; not as the world gives do I give to you. Let not your heart be troubled, neither let it be afraid (Jn.14:27, NKJV).**
>
> **These things I have spoken to you, that in Me you may have peace. In the world you will have tribulation; but be of good cheer, I have overcome the world" (Jn.16:33, NKJV).**

5. *You Should Set Aside Time for Both Prayer and Fasting When a Very Special Need Arises.*

> **"And when you fast, don't make it obvious, as the hypocrites do, for they try to look miserable and disheveled so people will admire them for their fasting. I tell you the truth, that is the only reward they will ever get. But when you fast, comb your hair and wash your face. Then no one will notice that you are fasting, except your Father, who knows what you do in private. And your Father, who sees everything, will reward you (Mt.6:16-18, NLT).**

Fasting means to abstain from food for a particular cause. From a worldly perspective, fasting is rarely undertaken except to protest something, and then it is almost always to attract attention. From a spiritual perspective, though, fasting is usually a deeply personal experience, a time to set aside food in order to concentrate on seeking God. Whether done to intercede on someone's behalf, to seek a solution to a problem, or to praise God for who He is or for what He has done, Biblical fasting involves prayer and intense supplication before God.

Note the words "when you fast" (vv.16, 17). Jesus assumed that believers fasted. In fact, He expects you to fast. He fasted and He taught fasting (Mt.4:2), and the early believers fasted (Mt.17:21; Lu.2:37; Ac.10:30; 13:3; 14:23; 1 Co.7:5; 2 Co.6:5; 11:27). Yet, so few have continued this intense seeking of the Lord. Today, few fast; few truly trust God enough to take time to focus only upon Him. Few consider His help or praising Him to be more necessary than food and all else.

The benefits of spiritual fasting are enormous, but there are also dangers. A person can fast for the wrong reasons. That is why Christ counsels us on the wrong and right motives for fasting.

a. **There is a wrong way to fast.** Fasting in the wrong way or for the wrong reason is hypocritical. There are several reasons people fast, and all but one are misguided and hypocritical.

   ➢ People fast to gain a sense of *God's approval* and of *self-approval.*
   ➢ People fast to fulfill a *religious ritual* or *requirement.*
   ➢ People fast to gain *religious recognition.*
   ➢ People fast to *genuinely meet God* for a specific purpose.

   Fasting is not condemned by Christ, but fasting for any purpose other than to meet with God is condemned. When you fast, make sure no one knows about it except God; make sure you are not fasting to draw attention to yourself. Always remember that fasting poses several serious dangers that must be guarded against with all diligence.

   ➢ The danger of feeling *super-spiritual*. You need to guard against a feeling of pride.
   ➢ The danger of *over-confidence*. After fasting, you usually feel spiritually confident, stronger and more ready to face the problems that confront you. But you must never forget, your confidence is to be in God, not in self. Be certain you are depending upon the strength of Christ and not upon your own energy and effort.
   ➢ The danger of *revealing your fasting experience*. You will sometimes learn so much from being in

God's presence that you will want to share it, especially with those closest to you. The best advice is to say nothing, not even to your dearest friend. If you truly feel led by God to share, be sure to draw attention to God's sufficiency, not yours.

- The danger of *changing your appearance, actions, or behavior*. Any change whatsoever from your normal behavior and routine attracts attention and ruins the whole benefit of the fast. As Christ says, "they make it obvious" (act super-spiritual) (v.16).

Fasting for the wrong reason or in the wrong way has its reward. If you fast for human recognition, you will receive human recognition, but that is all you will ever receive. You may gain the control and discipline of your body through fasting, but you can ruin yourself and your testimony through pride. You can lose your reward in the glorious day of redemption.

b. **There is the right way** to fast. Fasting the right way should be done without notice. You are to fast before God, not before people. There is to be no change in appearance or behavior to indicate that you are fasting. Think about it. Why should there be? Why should anyone know that you are seeking God in a very special way? The matter concerns you and God, not other people. God is the object of your fast. You need to meet Him and Him alone, and in doing so, you are demonstrating your dependence upon God and His provision.

Christ does not say when or how often you should fast, but as has been seen in this discussion, He does tell you how to fast. Therefore, you need to take every precaution to fast exactly as God's Word says. You are to fast before God, in secret, without any pretentiousness or show whatsoever. No one is to see or know that you are fasting.

If you fast in the right way, God will reward you openly in the glorious day of redemption. In closing, there would seem to be at least four times when you should fast.

- There are times when you feel a special pull, an urge, a call within your heart to get alone with God. This is God's Spirit moving within you. When this happens, nothing—not food, not responsibility—should keep you from getting alone with God. You should fast as soon as possible.
- There are times when special needs arise. The needs may concern your own life or the life of a loved one, friend, the world or society in general,

the church, a ministry, or any number of other worthy causes. Again, nothing should keep you from spending a very concentrated time in God's presence when facing such important needs.

- There are times when you need to humble your soul before God. At such times, you learn not only humility but also dependence upon God (Ps.35:13).
- There are times when you need a very special power from God. The Lord promised such power if you pray and fast (Mt.17:21; Mk.9:29).

Finally, there are several excellent benefits to fasting, and God wants you to reap these benefits.

- Fasting keeps you in the presence of God. You fast for a very special purpose, and you remain in God's presence until you feel He has or is going to meet your need.
- Fasting humbles your soul before God. It says that God is the most important thing in all the world to you (Ps.35:13).
- Fasting teaches you to depend more and more upon God. You are seeking God, and in so doing you are demonstrating your conviction that you are dependent upon God.
- Fasting demonstrates to God (by action) a real seriousness. It shows that the matter being considered is a priority.
- Fasting teaches you to control and discipline your life. You do without food for a greater cause and gain a greater blessing.
- Fasting keeps you from being enslaved by habit. You lay aside all substances; in so doing, you break the hold of anything that might have you chained.

D. You and Your Faith

1. *You Are to Live by Faith, Day by Day, Not by Feelings and Emotions.*

> **Now the just [righteous ones] shall live by faith: but if *any man* draw back, my soul shall have no pleasure in him (He.10:38, KJV).**
>
> **And without faith it is impossible to please him, for whoever would draw near to God must believe that he exists and that he rewards those who seek him (He.11:6, ESV).**

How does a believer live by faith? What does it even mean *to live by faith*? In the simplest of statements, living by faith is living by God's Word, not by feelings and emotions. You place your faith in God and in His Holy Word, trusting God to look after and take care of you as you walk obediently day by day (Ro.10:17).

> **Abraham never wavered in believing God's promise. In fact, his faith grew stronger, and in this he brought glory to God (Ro.4:20, NLT).**
>
> **So then faith *comes* by hearing, and hearing by the word of God (Ro.10:17, NKJV).**
>
> **But when you ask him, be sure that your faith is in God alone. Do not waver, for a person with divided loyalty is as unsettled as a wave of the sea that is blown and tossed by the wind. Such people should not expect to receive anything from the Lord. Their loyalty is divided between God and the world, and they are unstable in everything they do (Jas.1:6-8, NLT).**

People with weak, unstable faith waver in their confidence in God's Word, in His provision and power. Like the waves of the sea that are controlled by the wind, they are up-and-down. Their stability is determined by circumstances and by how they feel—their moods and emotions. People who *live* by faith are not like this. They are steady and stable. Feelings and circumstances have no bearing upon their confidence in God. They are single-minded and stable in all they do (Jas.1:8).

Hebrews chapter 11 is the greatest chapter on faith in God's Holy Word. It spells out in great detail how to live by faith. Here is God's manual for living by faith.

a. **Living by faith is** approaching God as He dictates: through the atoning blood of Jesus Christ.

> **It was by faith that Abel brought a more acceptable offering to God than Cain did. Abel's**

> **offering gave evidence that he was a righteous man, and God showed his approval of his gifts. Although Abel is long dead, he still speaks to us by his example of faith (He.11:4, NLT).**

b. **Living by faith is** fellowshipping with God all throughout the day—seeking to *please* Him in all you do.

> **By faith Enoch was taken away so that he did not see death, *"and was not found, because God had taken him";* for before he was taken he had this testimony, that he pleased [walked with] God (He.11:5, NKJV).**

c. **Living by faith is** heeding God's warning—obeying Him out of holy fear and reverence.

> **By faith Noah, being warned by God concerning events as yet unseen, in reverent fear constructed an ark for the saving of his household. By this he condemned the world and became an heir of the righteousness that comes by faith (He.11:7, ESV).**

d. **Living by faith is** obeying God even when you cannot see the way.

> **By faith Abraham obeyed when he was called to go out to a place that he was to receive as an inheritance. And he went out, not knowing where he was going (He.11:8, ESV).**

e. **Living by faith is** trusting God to guide and provide for you as you walk day by day.

> **By faith he made his home in the promised land like a stranger in a foreign country; he lived in tents, as did Isaac and Jacob, who were heirs with him of the same promise (He.11:9, NIV).**

f. **Living by faith is** keeping your eyes focused on the eternal city of God, the place Christ is preparing for you.

> **Abraham was confidently looking forward to a city with eternal foundations, a city designed and built by God (He.11:10, NLT).**

> **In My Father's house are many mansions; if *it were* not *so,* I would have told you. I go to prepare a place for you (Jn.14:2, NKJV).**

g. **Living by faith is** believing and acting on God's promises, even when they seem impossible.

> **By faith Sarah herself received power to conceive, even when she was past the age, since she considered [believed] him faithful who had promised (He.11:11, ESV).**

h. **Living by faith is** obeying God's Word all throughout life, acknowledging that you are only a stranger and exile on earth.

> **These all died in faith, not having received the things promised, but having seen them and greeted them from afar, and having acknowledged that they were strangers and exiles on the earth (He.11:13, ESV).**

i. **Living by faith is** living for heaven, not for this earth.

> **For people who speak thus make it clear that they are seeking a homeland. If they had been thinking of that land from which they had gone out, they would have had opportunity to return. But as it is, they desire a better country, that is, a heavenly one. Therefore God is not ashamed to be called their God, for he has prepared for them a city (He.11:14-16, ESV).**

j. **Living by faith is** offering everything you have to God—even your children.

> **By faith Abraham, when he was tested, offered up Isaac, and he who had received the promises was in the act of offering up his only son (He.11:17, ESV).**

k. **Living by faith is** believing that God will do the miraculous—even raise the dead—to keep His promise.

> **Of whom it was said, "Through Isaac shall your offspring be named." He considered that God was able even to raise him from the dead, from which, figuratively speaking, he did receive him back (He.11:18-19, ESV).**

l. **Living by faith is** believing that God will keep His promise, even if it is not in your lifetime.

> **By faith Isaac invoked future blessings on Jacob and Esau. By faith Jacob, when dying, blessed each of the sons of Joseph, bowing in worship over the head of his staff. By faith Joseph, at the end of his life, made mention of the exodus of the Israelites and gave directions concerning his bones (He.11:20-22, ESV).**

m. **Living by faith is** choosing God over worldly pleasures, prosperity, and power; choosing to suffer the reproach of this world for the reward of knowing God.

> **By faith Moses, when he was born, was hidden for three months by his parents, because they saw that the child was beautiful, and they were not afraid of the king's edict. By faith Moses, when he was grown up, refused to be called the son of Pharaoh's daughter, choosing rather to be mistreated with the people of God than to enjoy the fleeting pleasures of sin. He considered the reproach of Christ greater wealth than the treasures of Egypt, for he was looking to the reward. By faith he left Egypt, not being afraid of the anger of the king, for he endured as seeing him who is invisible (He.11:23-27, ESV).**

n. **Living by faith is** obeying God's instructions and commands, even when they are humanly illogical.

> **By faith he [Moses] kept the Passover and sprinkled the blood, so that the Destroyer of the firstborn might not touch them. By faith the people crossed the Red Sea as if on dry land, but the Egyptians, when they attempted to do the same, were drowned. By faith the walls of Jericho fell down after they had been encircled for seven days (He.11:28-30, ESV).**

o. **Living by faith is** standing with and for the people of God, regardless of the cost.

> **By faith Rahab the prostitute did not perish with those who were disobedient, because she had given a friendly welcome to the spies [men who believed and trusted God] (He.11:31, ESV).**

p. **Living by faith is** being faithful in carrying out whatever task God gives you to do, even if your service leads to death.

> **And what more shall I say? For time would fail me to tell of Gideon, Barak, Samson, Jephthah, of David and Samuel and the prophets—who through faith conquered kingdoms, enforced justice, obtained promises, stopped the mouths of lions, quenched the power of fire, escaped the edge of the sword, were made strong out of weakness, became mighty in war, put foreign armies to flight. Women received back their dead by resurrection. Some were tortured, refusing to accept release, so that they might rise again to a better life. Others suffered mocking and flogging, and even chains and imprisonment. They were stoned, they were sawn in two, they were killed with the sword. They went about in skins of sheep and goats, destitute, afflicted, mistreated—of whom the world was not worthy—wandering about in deserts and mountains, and in dens and caves of the earth (He.11:32-38, ESV).**

These Old Testament believers had one thing in common: they lived by faith. Faith was not merely something they inwardly felt, it was something they outwardly acted upon. They believed God, and they acted and carried on according to God's Word and what He had promised. They did not just proclaim that they believed God, they proved it by their actions. They lived by faith. They obeyed God, even when the promises were not fulfilled during their earthly lives (v.39).

This is living by faith: living in confident, bold obedience to Gods' Word—His call, commands, and promises—regardless of the circumstances and regardless of the consequences.

> **But someone will say, "You have faith, and I have works." Show me your faith without your works, and I will show you my faith by my works (Jas.2:18, NKJV).**

2. *You Should Have Faith in God As You Face the Mountains—the Problems and Trials—of Life.*

> **"Have faith in God," Jesus answered. "I tell you the truth, if anyone says to this mountain, 'Go, throw yourself into the sea,' and does not doubt in his heart but believes that what he says will happen, it will be done for him. Therefore I tell**

you, whatever you ask for in prayer, believe that you have received it, and it will be yours (Mk. 11:22-24, NIV).

Jesus did not say, "Have faith," but "Have faith *in God*." Faith has to have an object. "In God" is where you are to have faith, where you are to place your faith. Note four significant facts:

a. **First, the object of faith** is God Himself (Mk.11:22). The critical words are "in God." The Bible never says to have faith in faith, yet this is the experience of far too many of us. Too often, when a great difficulty or problem arises, we feel we have to *arouse* our faith. We believe that if we can just *stir up* enough faith, we will whip the problem. But in reality, our faith was in faith itself. Our hearts and minds focused on our faith, not upon God.

   Always remember, faith has no power in and of itself; it is the object that has power. Your faith is not going to remove the mountain. God is going to remove the mountain. The strength of faith is not faith, but God. In the Bible, practically everyone who came to God had weak faith. Only a few had strong faith, yet God saved them and granted their requests (Mt.14:22-33).

b. **Second, faith requires knowing** the object. The more you know the object of faith (God), the more you believe in the object (He.11:6; Mk.11:23). For example, consider two men who want to go out on a frozen lake to fish. One man is told to go ahead, walk out on the ice and cut the hole. He is assured by his friend that the ice will hold him up. Yet, when he steps out on the ice, he is cautious and trembling. He takes step after step until he can stand it no more, then nervously makes his way back to shore. The other man walks out boldly on the ice, cuts a hole, sits down, and begins to fish.

   Now, ask yourself several important questions.

   - What supported the man sitting out on the ice? Not his faith, but the ice—the object of his faith.
   - Who had the stronger faith? Of course, the man out on the ice. The one with the weak faith is the man who slowly inched his way back.
   - What made the difference between the faith of the two? One thing. One man *knew* the ice, and the other man *did not know* the ice.

   If you want strong faith—a faith that conquers all the overwhelming problems and trials of life—you must know God and know Him well. You must consistently study and obey God's Holy Word to learn more and more about Him. When you obey Him and live responsibly day by day, you will learn to depend upon God more and more. Your faith in God will grow enormously.

c. **Third, the way to possess faith** is through prayer (Mk.11:24). Jesus explicitly says, if you will not doubt but believe that what you ask will come to pass, you will have whatever you ask. But you must not doubt *at all*. This means not wondering, questioning, or being concerned about God's answering your prayer. Realistically, only God Himself can know if a thing will happen or not. What Christ is after is for you to keep praying and depending upon Him to help you. He wants you to grow in your trust of Him. He wants you to believe that all things are possible through Christ who strengthens you (Ph.4:13).

   You must also believe in God's authority. If you believe, not doubting, then you stand in the authority of God. What you ask will be done if it is truly for your good and for the good of all who genuinely love Him (Ro.8:28).

d. **Fourth, note the astounding promise** of faith (Mk.11:24). If you pray in faith, truly "having faith *in God*," you receive whatever you ask (if it is for your good and the good of all who love God). The mountains—the overwhelming problems and trials that confront you—will be removed by the power of God (Ep.3:20) or else God will use the mountains (problems and trials) for a far greater purpose in your life (Ro.8:28).

E. YOU AND THE CONTROL OF YOUR MIND

1. *You Must Let God Transform You into a New Person by Renewing Your Mind—Changing the Way You Think.*

> **Do not conform any longer to the pattern of this world, but be transformed by the renewing of your mind. Then you will be able to test and approve what God's will is—his good, pleasing and perfect will (Ro.12:2, NIV).**

You must be *transformed*—undergo a radical change within your heart—in order to escape the world and its doom. You must be changed inwardly.

How can you be transformed within your heart, your inner person? The Bible declares as simply as can be stated, "by the renewing of your mind." This means to be regenerated, made new, readjusted, turned around. You have to change the way you think. This is absolutely necessary because your mind has been affected by sin. Your mind is far from perfect. In fact, your thoughts are *basically worldly*, that is, self-centered, materialistic, and prideful.

But once you receive Christ, the most wonderful thing happens. God's Spirit begins to change your mind to focus upon God and living responsibly. Whereas your thoughts used to be centered on the world, they now should be geared toward living in a thoughtful, righteous, and godly manner (Tit.2:12-13). Your mind has been renewed, changed, turned around. As you go about your daily responsibilities, exert all the energy you can to focus upon God. Live a transformed life; that is, walk day by day *renewing your mind more and more*. Allow the Holy Spirit to help focus your mind more and more upon God and spiritual things.

- Love the Lord with all of your mind.

> **Jesus said to him, " *'You shall love the Lord your God with all your heart, with all your soul, and with all your mind'* (Mt.22:37, NKJV).**

- Keep your mind upon spiritual things, not fleshly, carnal things.

> **Those who live according to the sinful nature have their minds set on what that nature desires; but those who live in accordance with the**

Spirit have their minds set on what the Spirit desires. The mind of sinful man is death, but the mind controlled by the Spirit is life and peace (Ro.8:5-6, NIV).

- Strive to captivate every thought for Christ.

We demolish arguments and every pretension that sets itself up against the knowledge of God, and we take captive every thought to make it obedient to Christ (2 Co.10:5, NIV).

- Do not let your mind be corrupted.

But I am afraid that, as the serpent deceived Eve by his craftiness, your minds will be led astray from the simplicity and purity *of devotion* to Christ (2 Co.11:3, NASB).

- Do not fulfill the lustful, sinful desires of your flesh and mind.

Among them [the disobedient] we too all formerly lived in the lusts of our flesh, indulging the desires of the flesh and of the mind, and were by nature children of wrath, even as the rest (Ep.2:3, NASB).

- Do not walk as unbelievers walk, in the futility—the emptiness and senselessness—of their minds.

So I tell you this, and insist on it in the Lord, that you must no longer live as the Gentiles [unbelievers] do, in the futility of their thinking (Ep.4:17, NIV).

- Be renewed in the spirit of your mind.

"And be renewed in the spirit of your mind" (Ep.4:23, KJV).

- Adopt the mind of Christ: deny yourself and walk humbly before God and others.

Let this mind be in you which was also in Christ Jesus....[who] humbled Himself and became obedient to *the point of* death, even the death of the cross (Ph.2:5, 8b NKJV).

- Focus your mind on daily responsibilities and the excellent things of life.

  Finally, brethren, whatever things are true, whatever things *are* noble, whatever things *are* just, whatever things *are* pure, whatever things *are* lovely, whatever things *are* of good report, if *there is* any virtue and if *there is* anything praiseworthy—meditate on these things (Ph. 4:8, NKJV).

- Live by the laws of God, the laws that God has put in your mind and on your heart.

  This is the covenant I will make with the house of Israel after that time [Christ coming], declares the Lord. I will put my laws in their minds and write them on their hearts. I will be their God, and they will be my people (He.8:10, NIV).

- Arm yourself with the same mind and attitude as Christ in bearing suffering.

  So then, since Christ suffered physical pain, you must arm yourselves with the same attitude he had, and be ready to suffer, too (1 Pe.4:1, NLT).

2. *You Should Make a Commitment to Positive Thinking—Focus Your Thoughts Only on the Excellent Things of Life.*

Finally, brethren, whatever things are true, whatever things *are* noble, whatever things *are* just, whatever things *are* pure, whatever things *are* lovely, whatever things *are* of good report, if *there is* any virtue and if *there is* anything praiseworthy—meditate on these things (Ph.4:8, NKJV).

The word *meditate* means to consider, reflect, reason, and ponder. The idea here is that of focusing your thoughts until they shape your behavior.

The excellent Biblical scholar William Barclay says:

> *"...it is a law of life that, if a man thinks of something often enough and long enough, he will come to the stage when he cannot stop thinking about it. His thoughts will be*

quite literally in a groove out of which he cannot jerk them."[2]

If you center your thoughts on the world, you will live for the world: its wealth, property, possessions, power, recognition, social standing, fame, pleasure, fleshly stimulations, recreation, and a host of other worldly pursuits. A mind set upon or preoccupied with the world and the flesh is what leads to anxiety, worry, emptiness, and restlessness. A worldly mind never knows true peace, not the peace of God. And God will never give a worldly mind peace, for it is the restlessness of the human soul that He uses to reach people for salvation.

Once you have been converted to Christ and become a new person, focus your thoughts upon the good things of life and upon God. Give your mind to *positive thinking*. In fact, think only positive thoughts. Do not allow immoral, worldly, selfish, sinful, or evil thoughts to settle in your mind. You cannot keep sinful thoughts from flashing across your mind, but you can reject them—refuse to focus upon them. Sinful and negative thoughts disrupt and destroy your peace. For this reason, struggle to control your mind. Exert however much energy is required to captivate and control every thought. What you think about is so important that God tells you what to focus or concentrate on:

a. **Focus your thoughts** upon things that are *true,* genuine. Many things in the world appear to be true, but they are not; they are false, deceptive, misguided, corrupt, or fabricated. They seem to offer peace, but what they offer is a counterfeit peace, a temporary escape. Therefore, keep your mind on things that are real and genuine. If you do this, you will live a life that is true to both men and God. Furthermore, when your thoughts are centered upon true things, peace will flood your heart.

b. **Focus your thoughts** upon things that are *noble,* honorable, worthy, revered, and highly respected. Many things in this world are imitations, passing fads, or role models that appear respectable or praiseworthy. In reality, though, they are destructive and disgraceful. They will harm you and eventually bring you down. So set your mind on things that are serious, responsible, and honorable—things that are noble.

---

2 William Barclay. *The Letters to the Philippians, Colossians, and Thessalonians,* p.97.

c. **Focus your thoughts** on things that are *just*. To be *just* means to do what is right, to behave righteously, in this case toward other people and toward God. Be a responsible citizen while on earth, responsible toward the earth and toward your fellow human beings. A mind filled with *just and righteous* thoughts will live righteously and know peace.

d. **Focus your thoughts** upon things that are *pure,* chaste, undefiled, free from moral pollution and filth. Your mind should never be filled with unwholesome, indecent, depraved things so prevalent in society and media today. Strive to make every thought and every image in your mind pure.

e. **Focus your thoughts** upon things that are *lovely,* pleasing, endearing, kind, gracious; things that result in more love and kindness. Your thoughts are not to be unkind, mean, critical, or reactionary. Instead, they should be focused on things that are lovely—that build people up, not tear them down.

f. **Focus your thoughts** upon things that are of *good report,* reputable, admirable, worthy things—things of the highest quality. Do not fill your mind with junk, the rumors, gossip, and slander so often shared by others. And never fill your mind with the immoral, lawless, violent, and vulgar so readily available in all forms of media such as radio, television, newspapers, magazines, and elsewhere. Neither should you fill your mind with tasteless or trashy music or off-colored jokes. Focus only upon worthy things—only upon that which is of *good report.*

g. **Focus your thoughts** upon things that have *virtue* and are *praiseworthy.*

Think, concentrate, resolve to keep your mind and thoughts on these things. Positive thinking is the answer to peace for the Christian believer.

F. You and God's Demand for Holiness

1. *You Should Strive to Be Holy in Everything You Do Because God Is Holy.*

> **But now you must be holy in everything you do, just as God who chose you is holy. For the Scriptures say, "You must be holy because I am holy" (1 Pe.1:15-16, NLT)**

To be *holy* means to be righteous, pure, and godly; to be separated and set apart to God; to be different from all other beings and things. You are to be entirely different from all who live selfish, immoral, and lawless lives. There are two reasons for this:

a. **God is holy.** He is totally different and set apart from all else. God is the very embodiment of holiness...
   - of absolute perfection and glory
   - of absolute righteousness
   - of absolute dominion and power

b. **God has called** believers to be holy in *all* of life. God's purpose in saving us is to have a people who will be like Him and who can live with Him eternally.

   God does not want you to be corrupted by the world nor to die with the world. You escape the corruption and death of the world by trusting Christ (2 Pe.1:4; He.2:14-15). When you trust Christ, God accepts you as righteous—holy—before Him. God's purpose is for you to be separated from all the sinful behavior in the world and to be totally committed to Him. Therefore, once you accept Christ, pursue a life of holiness. Seek to be like God while on this earth. If you do, then God gives you the most glorious of hopes: the hope of eternal salvation.

2. *You Are to Pursue a Holy Life: Without Holiness, You Will Never See God.*

> **Because we have these promises, dear friends, let us cleanse ourselves from everything that can defile our body or spirit. And let us work toward complete holiness because we fear God (2 Co.7:1, NLT).**
>
> **Work at living a holy life, for those who are not holy will not see the Lord (He.12:14^{b}, NLT)**

As a believer, you are to be different from the unbelievers of the world. You are to be holy. You are to separate from the world and cleanse yourself from everything that could defile your body or spirit (2 Co.6:17-18; 1 Jn.2:15-16).

You, of course, *live in the world*. You walk and move within the world; you buy, eat, and sleep in the world; you work and play in the world; you associate and fellowship with others in the world. However, you are *not to be of the world*. You are not to be possessed by the world, enslaved to its pleasures and possessions. What does this mean? In very simple terms, do not indulge and give license to your flesh:

- Do not buy without restraint; do not be a materialist.
- Do not eat without restraint; do not be a glutton.
- Do not sit around wasting time; do not be slothful.
- Do not work relentlessly; do not be a workaholic.
- Do not play constantly; do not over-emphasize recreation.
- Do not heap riches upon riches; do not hoard wealth in a world of desperate needs.
- Do not fellowship continuously; do not neglect your duty.

Giving in to the enticement and seductions of the world is not an option for you as a believer and neither is living selfishly and sinfully. You are to live for God and help meet the needs of a desperate world that is dying from sin, disease, hunger, and war. You do this by pursuing a life of holiness. Keep in mind what the Scripture above declares: you will never see the Lord unless you are holy (He.12:14). Holiness—setting your life apart and living for God—is an absolute essential for anyone who wishes to live eternally with God.

G. You and Your Obedience to God

1. *You Need to Focus on Obeying God and Live As God's Obedient Child.*

> **As obedient children, do not conform to the evil desires you had when you lived in ignorance (1 Pe.1:14, NIV).**

The words "obedient children" mean *children of obedience*. That is, you are to be so obedient to God that obedience becomes the basic trait of your life, so characteristic that you could be called a *child of obedience*.

Note the statement that you must not conform or slip back into your old *evil* or *sinful desires*. This is a sharp contrast, for it pictures your former life—the time before you committed yourself to Christ. In those days, you were living in ignorance, *given over* to doing your own thing. You were a child of *evil desires*.

This is not a pretty picture, but it is exactly the way God saw you before you accepted Christ: as a *child of evil desires*, someone who lived as he or she wanted to live. You did what you wanted to do instead of what God says to do. You followed your own path, your own desires, not God and His Holy Word. What kind of desires is Scripture referring to? All kinds. The cravings for...

- money
- recognition
- popularity
- position
- authority
- food
- property
- possessions
- housing
- sex
- stylish clothing

Obviously, you must have the necessities of life. God made you to desire these things. But when you begin to crave these things over and above what you need, it becomes wrong. Your focus in life becomes the desire for these things, getting more and more of them and gratifying your flesh. The lust of the flesh and of the eyes will enslave and consume you. This is a fact of human nature that is too often ignored.

Also, when God looked at you, He saw you alienated from Him. You did not know God—not personally, not in a close relationship, not in an intimate way. As stated above, you felt free to do your own thing and to go your own way in life. Whatever excited you or gave you purpose in this world controlled you. The result was either a spirit of obsession or a feeling of emptiness. You were either controlled by your desires, or you were left with a sense of being incomplete and dissatisfied because your desires could not give you a lasting sense of fulfillment.

But things are different now. Since you have received Christ, you now know God in a personal way and have a relationship with Him, for God has revealed Himself in the Lord Jesus Christ. You are no longer ignorant of God. Thus the world and its evil desires are no longer to control your life. Instead, you are to follow the Lord. You are to obey God in all things so that you can be called a *child of obedience*. Therefore let Jesus Christ dominate your life. Focus upon Him and the glorious hope of salvation that He gives you, both now and eternally.

2. *You Need to Understand This Fact: If You Truly Know God, You Will Obey His Commandments.*

> **By this we know that we have come to know Him, if we keep His commandments. The one who says, "I have come to know Him," and does not keep His commandments, is a liar, and the truth is not in him (1 Jn.2:3-4, NASB).**
>
> **And this is his commandment, That we should believe on the name of his Son Jesus Christ, and love one another, as he gave us commandment (1 Jn.3:23, KJV).**

How can you be absolutely sure that you know God? The answer is really quite simple: Do you obey or keep God's commandments?

a. **God's chief commandment** is this: that you believe on the name of His Son, Jesus Christ, and love other people (1 Jn.3:23). First, if you genuinely believe in God's Son, Jesus Christ, you know God. And if you truly know God, you will diligently seek to obey Him.

   The second part to God's chief commandment is that you should love other people. Love covers all the commandments of God. If you love other people, you will not hurt or cause pain for them; you will not offend or sin against them. Thereby, you will be obeying all the commandments of God. This is exactly what Scripture declares:

> **Let no debt remain outstanding, except the continuing debt to love one another, for he who loves his fellowman has fulfilled the law. The commandments, "Do not commit adultery," "Do not murder," "Do not steal," "Do not covet," and whatever other**

> **commandment there may be, are summed up in this one rule: "Love your neighbor as yourself." Love does no harm to its neighbor. Therefore love is the fulfillment of the law (Ro.13:8-10, NIV).**

b. **If you say** that you know God and do not obey God's commandments, Scripture is very clear: you are a liar (1 Jn.2:3-4). You are making a false profession. How can this be true since you claim to follow Christ, live a fairly good life, and attend church regularly? Because you do not obey God. You do not keep the commandments of God. If you are not walking as Jesus Christ walked, nor doing what God says to do, you are being disobedient. You are making a *false* profession.

> **"Not everyone who says to me, 'Lord, Lord,' will enter the kingdom of heaven, but only he who does the will of my Father who is in heaven (Mt.7:21, NIV).**

3. *You Need to Work Out Your Salvation By Obeying God's Stirrings—His Work—in Your Heart.*

> **Therefore, my dear friends, as you have always obeyed—not only in my presence, but now much more in my absence—continue to work out your salvation with fear and trembling, for it is God who works in you to will and to act according to his good purpose (Ph.2:12-13, NIV)**

While writing the great book of *Philippians*, Paul was in prison being held on false charges. There was a good chance he would be executed. He was not sure he would ever see and share with the Philippians again. Therefore, his words were carefully chosen. So far as he knew, these could be his last words to the Philippian believers. In light of the words' importance, you need to pay close attention to this instruction.

What does it mean to "work out" your salvation? It does *not mean* to work *for* salvation but to work out the salvation God has already given you. That is to say, grow, mature, finish the Christian race, and do it well. Finish the effort and the work begun; bring it to completion.

The point is this: do not go half-way in salvation, being a mediocre Christian. Do not take bits and pieces when there is a whole parcel. Do not be satisfied with a little when you can have much. Go on, grow until salvation is completed and perfected in you. It is *your* salvation. No one else can work it out for you. You alone must do it, and it begins with *obeying God*.

a. **You are to work out** your salvation with *fear and trembling* (v.12). Life is not always easy or pleasant. To the contrary, it is full of trials, tragedies, and temptation. We all experience these things. True, life can also be beautiful, pleasurable, and very rewarding, but the reality is what has just been described: life is a journey of trials until the point of death. And no amount of denial or camouflage can escape the fact. The only thing that can bring abundance of life is the *absolute confidence* that God cares for you and will work all things out for your good and that you will live eternally in a perfect world.

   What is the point of mentioning all this? Because, now that you are saved, it is up to you to complete your salvation, to be sure you don't miss out on all God has planned for you.

   - You are to *fear and tremble* because of the trials and temptations of life. Anyone of them can throw you off or cause you to buckle under. The world's temptations and trials are strong and the flesh is weak. Consequently, you can slip into sin and failure before you know it unless you are constantly working at completing your race—fearing and trembling lest you fail.
   - You are to fear and tremble lest you *disappoint the Lord*. He has saved you, and He has gone to the ultimate limit in order to do it. He has demonstrated a perfect love for you by taking all your sins upon Himself and bearing the punishment for you. So when you sin and fail, it cuts His heart immensely. For His sake—to keep from hurting Him—you should work out your salvation conscientiously, fearing and trembling lest you cut His heart.
   - You are to fear and tremble because you will face the judgment seat of Christ (1 Co.3:11-15; 2 Co.5:10). Though you may try to reason away the fact of coming judgment, your reasoning has no effect on God's judgment whatsoever. If you refuse to live faithfully for Christ, you will be judged and suffer loss—great loss. Scripture teaches this with all certainty. For this reason, that of judgment, you need to grow in Christ and mature in your salvation with fear and trembling.

b. You are to work out your salvation by obeying the stirrings of God within your heart, that is, obeying God's Holy Word and commandments (v.13). We all experience movements and stirrings within our hearts to do something, to take some action, to change some behavior. These stirrings are from God. God is working within you, energizing you, giving you both *the will and the power* to do...

- ➢ what is right
- ➢ what is best

This *stirring* means that God does not leave you alone to work out your salvation. He works within you, arouses you to get up and get to it. God uses the stirring to guide you—never leaving you alone—working and stirring you to complete your salvation.

The tragedy is this: far too often, we ignore or refuse to respond to the movement of God. Far too often, we continue to go about our own affairs instead of heeding the working and stirring of God. When this happens, think how much growth you lose and how you cut the heart of God to the core. You choose to do your own thing and choose the possessions, pleasures, and comforts of this sinful world instead of yielding to God and His movement within you. Your duty is to grab hold of the stirrings—not to let them pass. Remember, when God arouses and energizes you to do something, He will enable you to do it. He will be with you every step of the way. So grab hold and obey the working of God within your heart.

4. *You Need to Obey and Teach God's Commandments to Be Great in the Kingdom of Heaven.*

> **Anyone who breaks one of the least of these commandments and teaches others to do the same will be called least in the kingdom of heaven, but whoever practices and teaches these commands will be called great in the kingdom of heaven (Mt.5:19, NIV).**

Breaking and *obeying* (practicing) God's commandments are continuous actions. No person is perfectly obedient all of the time. Every person fails sometimes (Ro.3:23; Jas.3:2; 1 Jn.1:8, 10). But if you continue to break a commandment, even if it is the least commandment, you will be called least in the kingdom of heaven.

You cannot break a commandment and ask forgiveness, then go out and break the commandment over and over, time and again. You cannot expect God to think that you are serious about His commandments, His Holy Word. No person would think that you are serious. Why should God? You only deceive yourself.

Also, remember that you teach by what you do. Others observe and learn from what you do. If you repeatedly break a law, no matter how small, you teach that God's Word is not important, not worthy to be obeyed. Such behavior is consciously or unconsciously teaching people to disobey God's Holy Word and commandments.

Christ issues a strong warning: if you disobey God's Holy Word and teach others to break the law, even the least commandment, you will be called least in the kingdom of heaven. On the other hand, if you obey and teach God's commandments, you have the most wonderful promise: you will be called great in the kingdom of heaven and richly rewarded (See chapter 10, *Your Death and Rewards* for more discussion*)*.

H. You and God's Power

1. *You Should Pray and Ask God for His Power.*

> **We also pray that you will be strengthened with all his glorious power so you will have all the endurance and patience you need. May you be filled with joy (Col.1:11, NLT).**

God's power is absolutely essential for the follower of Christ. This is easily seen by asking two questions: What benefit is it if you know God's will but do not have the power to do God's will? And, how can you walk worthy of Christ if you do not have the power to walk worthy?

Many in the world believe that they have the strength within themselves—in the flesh—to become spiritually strong, that it is a matter of the will and discipline, that they can apply themselves and conquer the circumstances of life. To some degree, this is true. But the flesh fails in three critical areas.

- ➢ The flesh can never achieve perfection. No matter what a person becomes or does, he or she is still unacceptable to God. Why? Because God is perfect, and being perfect, God can only accept perfection. Therefore, the power of God that has been demonstrated in the cross of Christ (His dying for your sins) is needed if a person is ever to be acceptable to God.
- ➢ The flesh cannot conquer death. No matter what a person does, he or she will end up as dead matter. One thing is certain: death has no part with God. Therefore, God must infuse a person with His power if he or she is to conquer death and live forever.
- ➢ The flesh cannot do what this verse says: it cannot endure and be patient against all the traumatic trials of life and *be joyful at the same time*. Lasting joy, completion, and fulfillment can be experienced only through God's power.

For these three reasons and many more, you need the power of God. You have the mental and physical strength to overcome some of life's problems, but you cannot overcome them all, especially the three mentioned.

Take into account some of the issues you face as you walk through life on a daily basis. There is no way for your flesh to *work up a joyful spirit* through some of the trials of life. But God has the power to give you understanding, peace, strength, hope, joy, assurance, and security through it all. And you can secure His power through prayer and obedience. Therefore, it is necessary for you to ask God for His power and to obey His Holy Word. If you are faithful, you will be strengthened with His glorious power. And you will walk triumphantly through life, conquering the trials and temptations that confront you.

a. **God's power** will give you a spirit of endurance, steadfastness, constancy, perseverance. The word *endurance* is not passive; it is active. It is not the spirit that sits back and merely tolerates the trials of life, taking whatever may come. Rather, it is the spirit that stands up and faces the trials of life, that actively goes about conquering and overcoming them.

b. **God's power** will give you a spirit of patience. Patience means bearing and suffering a long time and never giving up. Patience never gives in; it is never broken, no matter what it comes up against: pressure, hard work, disease, accident, old age, discouragement, disappointment, abuse, slander, or persecution. The Spirit of God infuses you with the power of God and you are able to patiently suffer under it all.

c. **God's power** will give you a spirit of joy through all the problems and trials of life. How is it possible to have a spirit of joy in the face of bad circumstances? Because the joy of the Lord is not the same as the joy of the world. The joy of the world is more of a temporary pleasure than joy. The world's joy is always nagged by incompleteness, a lack, an unfulfilled need or missing ingredient. There is the knowledge—*a haunting awareness*—that something can go wrong. Circumstances can change or a situation can arise to disturb the joy (broken relationship, sickness, death, financial loss, war). This always keeps the world's joy from being full, complete, assuring, and satisfying.

   The *believer's joy* is different. It *lasts* and *endures* and is always assured of God's presence and help. It is permanently satisfying and complete; and God has the power to fill you with His joy even in the midst of life's severest trials.

2. *You Should Trust God's Power, Not Your Own Strength: God Alone Can Keep You from Stumbling and Present You Faultless in the Day of Judgment.*

> **Now to Him who is able to keep you from stumbling, And to present *you* faultless Before the presence of His glory with exceeding joy, To God our Savior, Who alone is wise, *Be* glory and majesty,**

Dominion and power, Both now and forever. Amen (Jude 24-25, NKJV).

This is a great promise on the believer's security. It is God—His *keeping power*—that keeps you secure while you walk on the earth.

a. **God alone is able** *to keep you from falling,* but you must stand watch and *stay close* to the Lord. In a world full of corruption and false teaching, you should make every effort to draw near to God and stay in touch with Him. How? By daily Bible study and prayer, and by walking righteously; by learning to walk moment by moment in *open and unbroken* prayer, communion, and fellowship with Him (see chapter 2; pt.3, pp.34-36 for more discussion).

b. **God alone is able** *to present you faultless* when you come face-to-face with Him. To be *faultless* means to be spotless and pure, without any defilement whatsoever. God has the power to accept you as righteous and faultless because you are covered with the righteousness of Jesus Christ, the spotless Lamb of God.

c. **God alone is able** to infuse you with triumphant joy in the glorious day when you meet Him face-to-face. In that day you will experience...
   - ➢ the amazing glory of God's presence and of heaven
   - ➢ the glorification of Christ and seeing Him face-to-face
   - ➢ the transformation of your body into perfection
   - ➢ the joy of being reunited with your deceased loved ones
   - ➢ the unbelievable privilege of ruling and reigning with Christ forever
   - ➢ the great honor of serving God and Christ forever and ever

d. **God alone is your Savior**, and He alone is wise. He is the only living and true God—the only God who could ever plan and create the world and the human race. Only He could bring about the plan of salvation after we have made such a mess of things. And He alone has the wisdom and power to save you from this corrupt world of sin and evil, disease and death.

Therefore, the only thing left for you to do is to shout the praises of Him who alone has saved you and can keep you from falling. He alone can present you faultless before the presence of His glory. And He will—all because you have trusted His dear Son, the Lord Jesus Christ as your Savior.

I. You and Your Testimony or Witness

1. *You Should Look Upon the Crowds and See the Truth: Many Are Confused and Helpless, Without a Shepherd (Christ).*

> **When he saw the crowds, he had compassion on them because they were confused and helpless, like sheep without a shepherd. He said to his disciples, "The harvest is great, but the workers are few. So pray to the Lord who is in charge of the harvest; ask him to send more workers into his fields" (Mt.9:36-38, NLT).**

When Jesus was on earth, He saw the multitudes. And He still sees them today. When Christ looks upon earth, He sees every living soul wherever they are, and He has compassion on them. Moreover, Christ wants you to look at the multitudes and be moved with compassion. When Jesus sees crowds of people, He sees four things:

a. Jesus sees the crowds weary and confused. You, too, should see people weary and confused, for many are weighed down and ready to collapse.

- ➢ Life itself has weighed down and confused some people. Life can be cruel, hard, lonely, painful, and without real purpose. In some people's eyes, life seems hopeless and worthless.
- ➢ Religion has also weighed down and confused some people. Some religions lay burden after burden, demand after demand upon their followers. These religions require endless ceremonies, rituals, and rules. They also mislead their followers, taking them down paths that do not really lead to God. Thus, the people are not spiritually satisfied.
- ➢ Sin always weighs down and confuses people. The weight of their sins rests upon their hearts and preys upon their minds. Sin weakens whatever confidence and assurance people have. And their sins make them uncertain about the future.

In summary, you need to look upon the crowds and see them weary and discouraged. You need to be stirred with compassion for them.

b. Jesus sees the crowds scattered and helpless. Many are wandering about, not knowing which direction to go. They stop here and there trying to find something that gives lasting satisfaction, but to no avail. They are without meaning, purpose, and significance.

"I am come that they might have life, and that they might have it more abundantly" (Jn.10:10b, KJV).

c. **Jesus sees** the crowds as sheep without a shepherd—sheep who have gone astray and wandered away from God.

d. **Jesus sees** a great harvest of souls—a world of souls that are ready to be reaped. So many in the world are weary and confused, scattered, and helpless. They desperately need someone who can...

- give them rest and peace (save them from their weariness)
- strengthen and hold them up (keep them from fainting)
- give them answers and show them what to do and where to go (solve their bewilderment)
- gather them and give them direction (deliver them from being scattered and give them purpose, meaning, and significance in life)

Only Christ can truly meet the needs of these people. This is the reason He lays before you the vision of a great need for laborers. Tragically, although Christ came centuries ago, the laborers are still few. Christ needs you and He needs men, women, boys, and girls who will truly follow Him. And He needs you *now*. Unless you and other believers go forth immediately as reapers, the harvest will die and rot upon the earth. Therefore, commit yourself to become a laborer for Christ. And begin to pray more than ever before for God to raise up laborers who will reach out to the weary, the fainting, the bewildered, and the scattered.

"Then He said to His disciples, "The harvest truly *is* plentiful, but the laborers *are* few" (Mt.9:37, NKJV).

2. *You Are the Salt of the Earth—the Flavor of Christ Among People.*

"You are the salt of the earth. But if the salt loses its saltiness, how can it be made salty again? It is no longer good for anything, except to be thrown out and trampled by men (Mt.5:13, NIV).

Salt is distinctively different from whatever it is sprinkled on. By nature and by purpose it is different. So are believers. You are distinctively different by nature and by purpose. *By nature,* you are a new creation, born of God (2 Co.5:17; 1 Pe.1:23); *by purpose,* you are to penetrate and change the very taste of the earth. Note three significant points:

a. **First, your character** is to be like salt. You are *called and designed* (made) to be the salt of the earth. Several things can be said about salt that point out precisely what Jesus means.

- Salt is *distinctive.* As stated, it is totally different from the food or object it is sprinkled on. The power of salt lies in this difference. As a believer, you are to be just like salt—to be different from the world. The power of your life and testimony is in being different and distinctive. You are to be "unspotted from the world" (Jas.1:27).
- Salt *preserves.* It keeps things from going bad and decaying. It cleanses and disinfects. Like salt, you are to cleanse and preserve the world. You are to disinfect the world and keep the germs (sins) of the world from causing things to go bad. You are to do all you can to save the world from corruption (2 Pe.1:4).
- Salt *penetrates.* It inserts a new quality, substance, and life. It changes whatever it contacts. You are likewise to penetrate the world and insert a new life into it (2 Co.5:17; Ep.4:24).
- Salt *flavors.* It influences the taste of things. It takes a bland, tasteless, and sometimes undesirable food and makes it enjoyable. As you walk with the Lord day by day, you too can have a powerful influence on the world for Christ. Through your joy, peace, positive attitude and witness, you can touch and strongly impact the lives of many who are bland, tasteless, without Christ. You are to salt them with the love and joy of the Lord, making them enjoyable and desirable within the world (Col.1:28).

b. **Second, your mission** is to salt the earth, so bear strong witness for Christ. Penetrate, flavor, and preserve the earth. Spread your salt out into the world. There is no witness for Christ other than yours and that of other believers. The task is yours and the success of the mission rests upon you and your fellow believers.

> **Let your conversation be always full of grace, seasoned with salt, so that you may know how to answer everyone (Col.4:6, NIV).**

c. **Third, you face** a very serious danger—that of becoming useless and destructive. Salt does not lose its saltiness and flavor. However, in the time of Christ the salt of Palestine was gathered in such a manner that dirt and other impurities were often mixed with it. The salt was thus useless and good for nothing. In fact, it actually destroyed the fertility of the soil. Therefore, it was not only useless but also destructive. This is a picture of a backslider, a believer who loses his or her testimony (saltiness). Shamefully, the backsliding believer...

- ➢ becomes useless just as salt can become
- ➢ is of no value. He or she may as well be cast out and trodden underfoot
- ➢ destroys the fertility of some out in the world by not being able to salt them and even by becoming a stumbling block to them

> **Jesus replied, "No one who puts his hand to the plow and looks back is fit for service in the kingdom of God" (Lu.9:62, NIV).**
>
> **Now the just shall live by faith: but if *any man* draw back, my soul shall have no pleasure in him (He.10:38, KJV).**
>
> **Yet I hold this against you: You have forsaken your first love (Re.2:4, NIV).**

3. *You Are the Light of the World.*

> **"You are the light of the world. A city on a hill cannot be hidden (Mt.5:14, NIV).**

"God is light" (1 Jn.1:5). And Jesus Christ said, "I am the light of the world" (Jn.8:12; 9:5). Now, Christ gives you one of the highest compliments possible. He says, "you are the light of the world." You and God and Christ share an amazing quality: light. No greater honor could be given you as a true believer. But note: to be identified with God and Christ is an enormous responsibility as well as a compliment. Whatever light is and does, you are *to be and do.*

a. **Your character** is to be light. You are to undergo a radical transformation: you are to *become like* Christ more and more and *to reflect* the light of Christ (2 Co.3:18; 4:6-7). Light is and does several things.

- Light is clear and pure. It is clean, that is, good, right, true.

  For you were once darkness, but now you are light in the Lord. Live as children of light (for the fruit of the light consists in all goodness, righteousness and truth) (Ep.5:8-9, NIV).

- Light penetrates. By nature, it cuts through and eliminates darkness.

  For you are all children of the light and of the day; we don't belong to darkness and night (1 Th.5:5, NLT).

- Light enlightens. It enlarges your vision and knowledge of an area.

  Then Jesus told them, "You are going to have the light just a little while longer. Walk while you have the light, before darkness overtakes you. The man who walks in the dark does not know where he is going (Jn.12:35, NIV).

- Light reveals. It opens up the truth of an area, exposing a whole new world. It clears up the way to the truth and the life.

  Jesus said to him, "I am the way, the truth, and the life. No one comes to the Father except through Me (Jn.14:6, NKJV).

  "While you have light, believe in the light, that [you] may be the children of light" (Jn.12:36, KJV).

- Light guides and discriminates between the right way and the wrong way.

  I have come into the world as a light, so that no one who believes in me should stay in darkness (Jn.12:46, NIV)

  Jesus spoke to the people once more and said, "I am the light of the world. If you follow me, you won't have to walk in darkness, because you will have the light that leads to life" (Jn.8:12, NLT).

- Light strips away the darkness.

> **And the judgment is based on this fact: God's light came into the world, but people loved the darkness more than the light, for their actions were evil. All who do evil hate the light and refuse to go near it for fear their sins will be exposed (Jn.3:19-20, NLT).**

- Light defeats the chaos.

> **"That you may become blameless and harmless, children of God without fault in the midst of a crooked and perverse generation, among whom you shine as lights in the world" (Ph.2:15, NKJV).**

- Light exposes. It lays bare the evil done by people in darkness.

> **Take no part in the worthless deeds of evil and darkness; instead, expose them. It is shameful even to talk about the things that ungodly people do in secret. But their evil intentions will be exposed when the light shines on them, for the light makes everything visible. This is why it is said, "Awake, O sleeper, rise up from the dead, and Christ will give you light" (Ep.5:11-14, NLT).**

- Light protects. It warns a person of the dangers that lie ahead in the darkness. It keeps you from stumbling, falling, and injuring oneself.

> **"The night is far spent, the day is at hand: let us therefore cast off the works of darkness, and let us put on the armor of light" (Ro.13:12, KJV).**

b. **You are *now* the light** of the world. Jesus said, "As long as I am in the world, I am the light of the world" (Jn.9:5). Jesus is no longer in the world, not bodily. His light is now in you and in all other believers. Thus, believers are *reflections* of Christ. And your light is to reflect *the light of the Lord.* It is vitally important that you obey the Lord's commandments and live righteously. Remember, you may be the only real example of a believer some people ever see!

> **For once you were full of darkness, but now you have light from the Lord. So live as people of light! (Ep.5:8, NLT).**

c. **Your light sits** on a hill, and it cannot be hid. A candle is placed on a candlestick, giving light to all who are in the house. Your life and words are an unavoidable witness for Christ (vv.14-15). Your light—testimony and witness—is in the world, shining both on a hill and in the house where you live. You must never neglect presenting Christ to your family while you are bearing witness to the world.

d. **You are the light** of God upon the earth; therefore, you are to "*let* your light shine." You can refuse to *let* it shine. You can turn it off, refuse to turn it on, shade it, darken it, turn it away, direct its beam in another direction. There are two purposes for *letting* your light shine.

   - You are to let your light shine in order to show forth good works. You are to show good works to the world, let people know beyond all question that you—as well as God—care for them and want to help them.

     > **In all things showing yourself *to be* a pattern of good works; in doctrine *showing* integrity, reverence, incorruptibility (Tit.2:7, NKJV).**

   - You are to let your light shine in order to stir people to glorify God. This is the supreme reason why your light is to shine before people. God is glorified when people see the good works you do in this dark, sinful world.

4. *You Are an Ambassador for Christ, His Envoy Sent Forth with His Message to the World.*

> **Therefore, we are ambassadors for Christ, as though God were making an appeal through us; we beg you on behalf of Christ, be reconciled to God (2 Co.5:20, NASB).**

The great message of reconciliation is committed to *ambassadors,* to all who truly follow Christ.

a. **You are given** the highest of titles: you are an "ambassador for Christ." As an *ambassador,* an official envoy, you are sent forth to represent the Sender and to announce the message of the Sender. Four things are always true about an ambassador—four things that are true about you:

- An ambassador belongs to the One who sends him or her out. You, too, belong to the One who has sent you out into the world.
- An ambassador is commissioned to be sent out. Your mission exists only for the purpose for which Christ has sent you.
- An ambassador possesses all the authority and power of the One who sent him or her out. You too, possess all the authority and power of Christ who sends you out into the world.
- An ambassador is sent forth with the message of the Sender. You, too, are sent forth with the message of Christ.

> **You did not choose Me, but I chose you and appointed you that you should go and bear fruit, and *that* your fruit should remain, that whatever you ask the Father in My name He may give you (Jn.15:16, NKJV).**

b. **You are given** the greatest of messages: "Be reconciled to God." This message is so critical that you are to *appeal* to people—beg, cry, and plead with them—to be reconciled to God.

It is "for Christ's sake" that you are to plead with people. Christ has paid the ultimate price to make reconciliation available. He has taken the sins of people upon Himself and borne the condemnation for them. Because He has done so much, every person owes his or her life to Christ. Every person needs to be reached and reconciled to God. As Christ's ambassador, you are to take His message of reconciliation to your part of the world and to help others take it to every human being worldwide.

5. *You Have Been Assigned the Greatest Task on Earth: Bearing Witness for Christ Throughout the World.*

> **But you shall receive power when the Holy Spirit has come upon you; and you shall be witnesses to Me in Jerusalem, and in all Judea and Samaria, and to the end of the earth" (Ac.1:8, NKJV).**

The greatest task on earth has been assigned you, the very commission of Christ Himself. It is what is known among believers as the Great Commission. Three significant facts are clear in this passage:

a. **First, you are equipped** with the power of the Holy Spirit. Your power is spiritual and supernatural. It is *the very power* of God Himself, the power of His presence and His Spirit. God's very own Spirit dwells within your heart and life so that you can carry out His great mission on earth.

b. **Second, your task** is the greatest of all missions: to tell people about God. Witnessing about God's love and sharing the glorious salvation found in Him is your great task.

   There is no reason for the world—no reason for any individual—to suffer any longer under the weight and bondage of sin and evil. Since Christ has come, no person should ever have to live with...

   - guilt and shame
   - fear and anguish
   - emptiness and loneliness
   - insecurity and low self-esteem
   - selfishness and hoarding
   - bitterness and hatred
   - killing and maiming
   - war and conquest
   - inadequate food and shelter
   - ignorance and uncertainty

   (God have mercy upon all who know the cure and keep silent! No greater indictment against a person could exist!)

   Pay careful attention to the word *you*: it is *you,* the believer, who is to witness. It is *you* who knows the cure, the truth of being saved from sin, death, condemnation, and hell. Therefore, you must bear strong witness and share the wonderful news with everyone.

c. **Third, Christ gives you** the method that you are to follow in your witness and in the spread of the gospel. You are to witness where you are (Jerusalem) and move progressively outward (Judaea and Samaria) until you are helping to reach the uttermost part of the earth. You are to go as far as you can personally go and give as sacrificially as you can for others to go.

   Never forget, you are to witness where you are first, see to it that Christ is well-known throughout your own home and community before moving on. But once you have borne witness in your home and community, you are to move out, ever pressing outward until the whole world is reached with the glorious message of eternal life.

J. You and Serving Others

1. *You Are God's Workmanship—the Work of His Hands—Created to Do Good Works.*

> **For we are God's workmanship, created in Christ Jesus to do good works, which God prepared in advance for us to do (Ep.2:10, NIV).**

When you believe in Jesus Christ, God *creates you anew in Christ*. What does this mean? It means that God makes your spirit alive. Whereas your spirit was dead to God, it is now alive. God creates it anew because of your belief in His Son, Jesus Christ.

You are now what Scripture calls God's *workmanship.* Through Christ, God fashions your life and creates a masterpiece, a true work of art. The beauty that shows through the canvas of your life was not created by you, but by God and God alone.

However, you show that you are God's workmanship by the life you live before others. Your works are an evidence of your salvation. Those who continue to live in trespasses and sins (Ep.2:1-2) show that they are not God's workmanship, no matter what profession they make. God's people—you who truly believe in Christ—give ample evidence of the *power of the new life* that operates in you.

Note the Scripture: God's purpose for you is to do good works. Doing good works is not an option for you nor for any other believer. If you have truly trusted Christ, you do good works because your very nature dictates it. True, you are not perfect; consequently, you fail sometimes. But when you do, you come back to God and ask for forgiveness. Then you get back up and go forth once again to do all the good that you can. Just like a tree, you bear the fruit of your nature, the fruit of godliness and of good works.

2. *You Should Be Ambitious in Life, Ambitious to Serve People, Not to Be Great and to Lord Authority Over Them.*

> **So Jesus called them together and said, "You know that the rulers in this world lord it over their people, and officials flaunt their authority over those under them. But among you it will be different. Whoever wants to be a leader among you must be your servant, and whoever wants to be first among**

you must be the slave of everyone else (Mk.10:42-44, NLT).

Jesus never said that ambition was wrong. To the contrary, He encourages you to be ambitious—to use your ability to achieve all you can. To do less than your best is sin. At the same time, Christ is quite clear: there is both good and bad ambition, and there is a significant difference between the two.

One is of the world, the other of God. Note exactly what Christ said: good ambition, ambition that is healthy and useful to society, does not seek to lord or flaunt authority over people. There is, of course, nothing wrong with leading people—ruling and holding authority over them. Leaders are absolutely essential in every area of life. And yet the thrust of a leader's heart should not be to rule over people but to serve them. Problems arise when you and society begin to *measure success* by a person's position, title, or influence.

When position or title is exalted over character (honor, morality, justice, compassion, service), then leaders begin to put themselves first and to lord their authority over people. This should never be, especially among you and other believers. Any leadership or greatness you seek *must not* be for yourself but for doing what the Son of God says to do: serve people. Christ made a significant distinction between the terms *leader* and *first*. Note the difference:

- ➢ The *leader* is a *servant.*
- ➢ The *first* among leaders is a *slave*—a person who is totally given over to serving others.

What Jesus is saying is simply this: the *servant* is a person who serves occasionally, whereas the *slave* is a person who is always serving, regardless of hour or difficulty. Not every believer serves the Lord with the same fervor or commitment. Some believers serve with a thirty percent commitment, others sixty percent, and a few one hundred percent (Mt.13:1-9, esp.v.8).

True leadership is not found in your holding a position of leadership or that of a ruler, but in your serving others. If you wish to be truly great—first among leaders—then you must become a *slave* in meeting the needs of people. You have to be totally given over to serving others, whether at work, home, play, or church.

3. *You Are to Practice Hospitality—Open Your Heart and Home to People.*

> **Do not neglect to show hospitality to strangers, for by this some have entertained angels without knowing it (He.13:2, NASB).**

An open door and heart are to be the marks of a believer. As much as possible, you should open your home and reach out to...

- other believers, church groups, and missionaries
- college students and foreigners
- travellers and newcomers
- the young and the aged
- the lonely, homeless, hungry, cold, and needy

The idea is that your home is to be used as an outreach ministry for the Lord: to grow believers, reach unbelievers, and help the needy. *The Amplified New Testament* develops the theme further, saying this:

> **Do not forget or neglect or refuse to extend hospitality to strangers...being friendly, cordial and gracious, sharing the comforts of your home and doing your part generously—for through it some have entertained angels without knowing it (He.13:2, AMP).**

If each of us really carried out this practice, think how many needs would be met in our communities! Think how many people would be influenced for Christ! Think how many future leaders among foreign students might be reached for Christ—future leaders who could help bring peace to the world—if we periodically shared the comfort of our home and meals with them and nurtured them in the Lord!

Communities need believers just like you who will take the lead within their churches to set up *open-home ministries*, using their homes to reach out to people on a *regular basis*. Imagine the impact for Christ! Remember: home evangelism is what Christ and God's Word stress so much (Lu.9:4; 10:5-9; also see the book of *Acts*).

When opening your heart and home to complete strangers, however, you must use discernment. You need to remember that we live in a lawless world, and no matter how honorable your intentions or how much trust you place in people, some will abuse the privilege. For this reason, you must always be wise and vigilant and never endanger yourself or your dear family.

> **Discretion will guard you, Understanding will watch over you (Pr.2:11, NASB).**

4. *You Should Think of Ways to Encourage Fellow Believers, to Love People, and to Do Good Works.*

> **Let us think of ways to motivate one another to acts of love and good works (He.10:24, NLT).**

You have a unique responsibility to other believers, your brothers and sisters in Christ. You are to stir them up—motivate them to love people and to do good works. This would include encouraging your fellow believers to help...

- the poor and the homeless
- the sick and the shut-ins
- the orphans and the fatherless
- the singles and the divorced parent
- the widows and the widowers
- the lonely and the empty
- the unbelieving and the doubtful

Your faith in Christ is not a *dead faith;* it is a living faith that should stir you to action. In all you do, you should set an excellent example for your brothers and sisters in Christ. Through your love for other people and your good works, you will arouse your fellow believers to love one another and to do good works also. And there is no shortage of things to be done and people to be helped. Even young children can participate in many ways. They can go with you to visit shut-ins or help you take a meal or mow a lawn or repair a house. On and on the list could go, but the point to see is that people of all ages can and should minister to others.

Imagine the impact on family members, friends, or co-workers when they see or hear about your selfless commitment to serving others. It will be a powerful motivation and encouragement for them to do likewise. For the sake of a needful and sick world—a world reeling under the weight of corruption, immorality, lawlessness, and death—believers desperately need to be committed to truly loving and ministering to the people of the world.

> **"Let your light so shine before men, that they may see your good works, and glorify your Father which is in heaven" (Mt.5:16, KJV).**

K. You and Your Joy

1. *You Are to Be Filled with the Joy of Christ Himself.*

> **"If you keep My commandments, you will abide in My love; just as I have kept My Father's commandments and abide in His love. "These things I have spoken to you so that My joy may be in you, and that your joy may be made full" (Jn.15:10-11, NASB).**

Joy is an inner happiness, delight, pleasure; a deep sense of lasting comfort, fulfillment, and satisfaction. Joy is a depth of assurance...

- that you have been reconciled to God
- that you have been accepted by God
- that God is working all things out for good in your life
- that God is present with you and will take care of you all throughout life
- that—when the moment of death comes—God will immediately transfer you into His presence where you will live eternally

Again, joy is a deep sense of comfort and the great assurance of all these wonderful gifts of God. This means at least four things for you as a believer.

a. **Your joy is divine.** It is the joy of God Himself, and it is given only by God. Its roots are not in earthly or material things or in the cheap and temporary triumphs you may feel when you achieve something or solve a problem. The joy God gives is the joy of the Holy Spirit, a joy based in the Lord Himself!

b. **Your joy does not depend** on outward circumstances, good feelings, fleshly stimulations, or exciting events. The joy that God implants in your heart overrides all, even the most troublesome matters of life and death.

> **But let all who take refuge in you be glad; let them ever sing for joy. Spread your protection over them, that those who love your name may rejoice in you (Ps.5:11, NIV).**

c. **Your joy will grow** more and more as you study God's Word, the promises and commandments that He has given. In fact, Christ says that He gave us God's commandments for this very reason: that by obeying them, one's heart will be filled with His joy (Jn.15:10-11). God floods your heart with true, lasting joy when you obey His Holy Word. So study and obey God's Word, and your heart will overflow with the joy of Christ Himself.

d. **Your joy of future reward** makes and keeps you faithful. (See Chapter 10 for a discussion of Rewards.)

2. *You Are to Rejoice in the Lord Always As You Walk Throughout Each and Every Day.*

> **Rejoice in the Lord alway: *and* again I say, Rejoice (Ph.4:4, KJV).**
>
> **Whatever happens, my dear brothers and sisters, rejoice in the Lord. I never get tired of telling you these things, and I do it to safeguard your faith (Ph.3:1, NLT).**

You are to rejoice in the Lord always, that is, *continually* and *repeatedly*. This is necessary because you frequently have to deal with difficult circumstances and unexpected trouble. No matter where you go, the trials of life, both minor and major, confront you:

- enticing temptations
- greed and selfishness
- arguments and strife
- broken relationships
- dissension
- abuse and oppression
- lawlessness
- accidents
- disease
- death

The list could go on and on. None of us escapes the trials of life. We are confronted with the grim reality of problems and struggles nearly every day of our lives. Therefore, you need to guard and brace yourself to face these issues. One way to do this is to rejoice in the Lord. If you walk throughout the day rejoicing in the Lord, your mind is upon the Lord.

Rejoicing in the Lord keeps you in the presence of Christ. No matter what confronts you—no matter how terrible the trial—you know that Christ the Lord is looking after you. Nothing can separate you from the Lord and His love. Therefore, no trial, no matter how severe, can ever conquer or overcome you. Christ will give you supernatural power and strength to walk triumphantly through any and all trials. Even if you are called upon to die and move on to heaven, you will never taste or experience death. Jesus Christ is going to escort you into God's presence immediately—quicker than the eye can blink.

You are forever secure in the keeping power of the Lord Jesus Christ. For this reason, walk throughout the day rejoicing in the Lord no matter what confronts you.

> **Can anything ever separate us from Christ's love? Does it mean he no longer loves us if we have trouble or calamity, or are persecuted, or hungry, or destitute, or in danger, or threatened with death? (As the Scriptures say, "For your sake we are killed every day; we are being slaughtered like sheep.") No, despite all these things, overwhelming victory is ours through Christ, who loved us. And I am convinced that nothing can ever separate us from God's love. Neither death nor life, neither angels nor demons, neither our fears for today nor our worries about tomorrow—not even the powers of hell can separate us from God's love. No power in the sky above or in the earth below—indeed, nothing in all creation will ever be able to separate us from the love of God that is revealed in Christ Jesus our Lord (Ro.8:35-39, NLT).**

L. YOU AND HUMILITY OR UNSELFISHNESS

1. *You Should Not Be Selfish or Conceited, but Humble.*

> **Do nothing from selfishness or empty conceit, but with humility of mind regard one another as more important than yourselves; do not *merely* look out for your own personal interests, but also for the interests of others (Ph.2:3-4, NASB).**

As members of the human race, we are basically selfish. Selfishness is ingrained in our nature. Far too often, when we are dealing with our spouses, children, friends, fellow workers, or the public at large, we allow selfishness to rear its ugly head. For example...

- ➢ We want our way, even if it causes dissension and hard feelings.
- ➢ We want to do what we want, when we want, and how we want.
- ➢ We claim we are right even when we are not quite sure.
- ➢ We want to do most of the talking, thinking that what we have to say is more important than what others have to contribute.
- ➢ We show disrespect by interrupting others' conversations or discussions.
- ➢ We have difficulty accepting and admitting that we might not be right.

But God says, do not act selfishly—not if you are a true follower of His. In fact, God gives you five clear charges regarding your behavior.

a. **First, you should guard** against selfishness (v.3). To be selfish simply means showing *too much* concern for your own interests and *too little* concern for others. Of course, you must have concern for your own welfare, but you must also have concern for others. This is God's instruction, the way He wants you to live: do not be self-centered, indulgent, narrow-minded, or prejudicial.

   Simply stated, guard against being wrapped up in yourself. Do not focus only upon your own desires and interests. Control yourself and do nothing in a spirit of selfishness.

b. **Second, you should guard** against conceit (v.3). A conceited person has an inflated sense of self-love, self-admiration, self-importance, and self-exaltation.

Sadly, when conceit is shown, it exposes a person as being...

- arrogant
- egotistical
- stuck-up
- smug
- bigheaded
- cocky
- puffed up
- phony
- full of hot air

As a true believer, you must not be conceited. Do not be egotistical—acting as if you are above, before, and over others.

c. **Third, you should be humble** and do everything in a spirit of humility (v.3). Some people mistakenly look upon humility as a vice. They look upon a humble person as lowly and cowardly, a simple, mindless, and cringing type of person. As a result, these people fear the idea of being humble. They think humility is a sign of weakness and will make them the object of contempt causing them to be shunned and overlooked. Because of this, they ignore and shun the teaching of Christ on humility. This is tragic, because a humble spirit is necessary for salvation (Mt.18:3-4). God's idea of humility is not weakness and cowardice.

To the contrary, humility is strength under God's control. God makes people strong, the strongest they can possibly be. When you truly turn to the Lord, God infuses a new and strong spirit within you, a spirit that causes you to conquer all throughout life. God wants you to walk in humility: *to offer* yourself in a spirit of submissiveness, kindness, and lowliness; never acting high-minded, proud, arrogant, overly assertive, or oppressive.

Contrary to what some people think, humility reaps unbelievable benefits. Humility will result in your being exalted by Christ in that glorious day of redemption. But, presently, humility results in healthy relationships. For example, humility wins friends and influences people for good. Humility acknowledges and boosts others, encourages and helps others, motivates and stirs others to grow and to achieve more and more.

d. **You should walk** in humility day by day (v.3). Practicing humility demands that you honestly evaluate yourself. The excellent commentator William Barclay points this out.[3] Humility comes from knowing yourself, just who you really are. It comes from an honest appraisal of yourself. It takes courage to look at yourself and it

---

3 William Barclay. *The Letters to the Philippians, Colossians, and Thessalonians*, p.39.

takes honesty to see yourself as you really are: basically self-centered. You are like every other human being: you tend to see yourself unrealistically. You would like to see yourself...

- as the center of attention
- as the athlete saving the game in the last second
- as the beauty queen dazzling the crowds
- as the hero of some spectacular discovery, achievement, or rescue
- as the great politician marching to victory
- as a brilliant lawyer arguing the case of the century
- as Prince Charming or Cinderella sweeping others off their feet

Humility begins to come when you honestly face yourself and admit your self-centeredness. Self-centeredness weakens and limits relationships and achievements. Humility reaches its height when you lose your life in the cause of Christ and in the welfare of others.

e. **You should control** focusing so much on yourself and also focus on others (v.4). Very simply, you must quit looking only at your own interests. You must focus upon Christ, on ministering to people and reaching the world with the good news of salvation. The world is too needful and too desperate for you to be focused upon yourself. Every believer is needed to reach the lost and lonely, the shut-ins and helpless, the hungry and cold, the sinful and doomed of your community and world.

2. *You Should Think Highly of Yourself, but Not Too Highly.*

> **For by the grace given me I say to every one of you: Do not think of yourself more highly than you ought, but rather think of yourself with sober judgment, in accordance with the measure of faith God has given you (Ro.12:3, NIV).**

There is a tendency with many people to think too highly of themselves, to think of themselves as *better* than others. They become prideful and arrogant, *puffed up* with their own...

- importance
- appearance
- popularity
- position
- abilities
- performance
- wealth
- possessions
- opinions
- education
- goodness
- title

God stands staunchly against such *puffed-up* attitudes. Think of yourself, but think *soberly*. The word means to be balanced, sane, in one's right mind. You need to be wise and accurate, make a sound and well-balanced evaluation of yourself and your abilities. Note how strong Scripture is: thinking too highly of yourself is, in essence, an insane thought! Thinking that you are more important as a human being than anyone else is insane behavior. Every person is important to God; every person is meaningful and significant, no matter who he or she is.

The reason you are to walk humbly before others is clearly spelled out: all you are and have has come from God. It is God who has given to every person a *measure of faith* (v.3). The word *faith* in this context means a *working faith*. It includes both the gifts and abilities God gives to you and the faith and drive to use the gifts.

Very simply, a *working faith* is the ability and drive within you to get to it and to make your contribution to life and society. God gives you a measure of faith and the abilities and gifts for your special task on earth. Since everything you are and have comes from God, you have no reason to think too highly of yourself.

> **Whatever is good and perfect comes down to us from God our Father, who created all the lights in the heavens. He never changes or casts a shifting shadow. (Jas.1:17, NLT).**
>
> **For who makes you different from anyone else? What do you have that you did not receive? And if you did receive it, why do you boast as though you did not? (1 Co.4:7, NIV).**

Note another fact as well: what you have received from God is *only a measure,* a portion. No person has the full measure of anything. No person is perfect in any area. We all age, deteriorate, and decay; and, eventually, we move aside for others, no matter what our abilities and contributions. Therefore, we have no reason to think too highly of ourselves.

M. You and Your Faithfulness

1. *You Are to Be a Faithful Steward—a Faithful Manager of All God Has Given You.*

Moreover it is required in stewards that one be found faithful (1 Co.4:2, NKJV)

A steward is a manager, someone who is given or entrusted with something to oversee, such as an estate, money, property, a gift, or some area of responsibility.

As a believer, you are God's steward. When you accepted Christ, you acknowledged that God is the Creator and Savior of the world, that God is the Source of every good and perfect gift (Js.1:16). Consequently, everything you have has been given to you by God...

- your life and salvation
- your family and friends
- your skills and talents
- your employment
- God's Holy Word
- the church
- the message of the gospel
- the earth and its resources

Take just a moment and think through the above, all that God has given you. He has entrusted all these into your hands, as well as everything else you oversee in life. Beyond question, you are a choice steward of God. And, remember, God has no one to look after some of these gifts *except* you. As a result, God lays a strong demand upon you: you must be faithful. Being faithful is the one and only duty God lays upon you. He does not require you to be intelligent, shrewd, gifted with ability, or successful. But you must be faithful. All that you have—all that has been entrusted into your hands—you are to look after responsibly. It is a gift, a trust, from God. Therefore, be faithful, steadfast, unwavering in taking care of all that God has given you.

And, when it is time for you to go home to heaven, continue to be faithful: leave your God-given trust—all He has entrusted to you on earth—in the hands of those who will continue to be faithful in using it for Christ and His kingdom.

2. *You Are to Be Steadfast—Let Nothing Move You—Give Yourself Fully to the Lord's Work.*

> **Therefore, my dear brothers, stand firm. Let nothing move you. Always give yourselves fully to the work of the Lord, because you know that your labor in the Lord is not in vain (1 Co.15:58, NIV)**

This is a strong charge. You are to be firm—even inflexible—in your commitment to Christ.

a. **The word *firm*** means steadfast, fixed, determined, purposed, faithful. Stand fast and fixed in your belief and work for the Lord. Be unwavering in your determination to live for Christ and to serve Him.

b. **The phrase** "let nothing move you" means to be immovable, unyielding, unshakable. Do not be fickle in your life and work for the Lord. To be fickle means to be changeable, unpredictable, inconsistent. You should never be fickle by...

   - ➢ professing to be committed to Christ, then uncommitted
   - ➢ repenting of some sinful behavior, then returning to the sin
   - ➢ obeying God's commandments, then disobeying
   - ➢ living righteously, then giving in to friends' seductions and engaging in sinful behavior
   - ➢ serving Christ and His church, then not serving
   - ➢ attending worship services, then not attending
   - ➢ giving to help the church in its mission, then not giving
   - ➢ having a set time for daily worship, then failing to have daily worship
   - ➢ bearing a strong testimony for Christ, then not witnessing at all

   You must not falter in your life and work for the Lord. Be as solid as a rock in living for Christ and in working for Him and His church.

c. **You need to give** yourself fully to the work of the Lord. The word *labor* here means to toil and work to the point of exhaustion—to the point of utter collapse. The idea is that you never stop, never slacken up, never quit, and never retire.

   You serve Christ, the very Son of God Himself. Therefore, be steadfast—never allowing anything to move or keep you from giving yourself fully to the work of the Lord.

3. *You Are to Stand Firm in Christ and Cling to God's Holy Word.*

> **With all these things in mind, dear brothers and sisters, stand firm and keep a strong grip on the teaching we passed on to you both in person and by letter (2 Th.2:15, NLT).**
>
> **All Scripture *is* given by inspiration of God, and *is* profitable for doctrine, for reproof, for correction, for instruction in righteousness (2 Ti.3:16, NKJV).**

The word *teaching* above refers to all the Word of God, whether it is taught or written (2 Th.2:15). The Word of God is not of human origin; consequently, neither the preacher nor the teacher is ever at liberty to substitute his or her own thoughts for that which God says. Nor are you at liberty to do so, regardless of your position or status as a believer.

Always remember that all Scripture is inspired by God (2 Ti.3:16). God has given His Holy Word...

- to teach you the basic doctrines and truths of life
- to reprove and rebuke you
- to correct and discipline you
- to tell you how to live righteously

So stand fast in Christ and cling to the Word of God (2 Th.2:15). Do not buckle under to the world and its temptations nor cave in and begin to disobey God's Holy Word. Never let it be said that you are living in sin, shame, or darkness. Furthermore, do not cave in to the unbelievers of the world—the secularists, humanists, atheists, agnostics, persecutors—any who deny God's existence and His Holy Word. With all this in mind, stand firm in Christ. Never let go. Cling to God's Holy Word.

N. You and Your Physical Body

1. *You Are to Exercise Both Physically and Spiritually.*

> **"Physical training is good, but training for godliness is much better, promising benefits in this life and in the life to come" (1 Ti.4:8, NLT).**

The human body is probably abused more than any other single thing. Consider some of the things that damage and destroy our bodies...

- unhealthy food
- overeating
- laziness, inactivity
- lack of exercise
- overwork and stress
- lack of sleep
- air and water pollution
- abuse and immorality
- smoking, alcohol, drugs
- violence and war

If there is any single thing that proves human depravity, it is how we treat our bodies. Yet God's instruction is clear: we are to exercise our bodies both physically and spiritually.

Olympic athletes, known the world over for their excellence in a specific sport, throw themselves into their training wholeheartedly. Their sport is the focus of their lives—unequivocally so. Their physical training is unmatched; therefore, you as a believer can learn much from them:

a. **First, you should** exercise your body regularly, keeping it physically fit. Many of the physical, mental, and emotional problems that we have are due to physical inactivity and sluggishness. This is sad when just a little physical exercise would strengthen our bodies and give them more energy for a more active and productive life. As a believer, you are to keep your body physically fit, even if you have to take the time to exercise. Discipline (train) your body so that you can be in better health, live longer, perform your duties more effectively, and serve God more energetically and productively.

b. **Second, you need** to exercise and train your body for godliness. Bodily exercise will reap many benefits, but training your body for godliness will reap far greater benefits, both in this life and the next. In light of this, you should do all you can to keep your body physically strong so that you will have the energy to serve God and His church more effectively.

2. *You Are to Control Your Body—Do What Is Beneficial and Profitable, Not Just What Is Allowed.*

> **You say, "I am allowed to do anything"—but not everything is good for you. And even though "I am allowed to do anything," I must not become a slave to anything. You say, "Food was made for the stomach, and the stomach for food." (This is true, though someday God will do away with both of them.) But you can't say that our bodies were made for sexual immorality. They were made for the Lord, and the Lord cares about our bodies. And God will raise us from the dead by his power, just as he raised our Lord from the dead (1 Co.6:12-14, NLT).**

God has made you, your body, and everything in the world, and all that He has created is good. Therefore, you are *allowed* to use everything and to do anything that is not contrary to God's Holy Word. But there are restrictions that God places upon you.

a. **First, not everything is** good for you (v.12). Not everything is beneficial, worthwhile, advisable, or profitable.

b. **Second, you should not** become a slave to anything (v.13). You should control everything within your power and not be enslaved by anything: not food, drink, drugs, desires, urges, or anything else. Self-control or self-restraint needs to be exercised in all things. You are to control the substances of this earth and not be controlled by them.

c. **Third, your body is not** designed for indulgence in selfish desires and urges (vv.13). In Paul's day, fornication and immorality were acceptable among unbelievers and society as a whole (much like today). Sadly, immoral behavior was carried over into the early church by some of its members. The members were apparently using the argument of the society of their day. It was the age-old argument heard so often in every generation: just as the body desires food and must have food for normal functioning, so the body desires sex and must have sex for normal functioning. The reasoning is that the desires of the body are normal and natural; therefore, satisfying these desires is only logical. Every generation has its own way of justifying or rationalizing its bad behavior:

- "I'm just doing my own thing."
- "I'm doing what comes naturally."
- "Everyone else is doing it."
- "Times change. You have to accept it."
- "How could it be wrong when it feels so right?"
- "It could not be wrong, no matter who says it is."

Scripture is forceful in its answer to this argument. Your body *is not designed* for the stomach and food. Contrariwise, the stomach and food are designed for the body, to help keep you healthy, whole and functioning. It is your responsibility to control your appetites. You should never allow your body to become a slave to the urges and desires of your stomach nor to the appeal of food—its looks, smell, or taste. Never forget, when Christ returns, you will be transformed and your body perfected (Ph.3:20-21.) Then you will no longer desire or crave more than you need.

The point is clear: you are to use food to feed the body, not allow food to control or enslave your body.

> **Their destiny is destruction, their god is their stomach, and their glory is in their shame. Their mind is on earthly things (Ph.3:19, NIV).**

Scripture is also forceful in this statement: your body *is not designed* for fornication nor for the purpose of sexual gratification (v.13). Sexual intimacy is part of life, and it has its place in carrying on the human race and in building an intimate, precious, and strong foundation *for the family*. But, again, sexual intimacy was given *for the body*; the body was not created for the purpose of sexual urges and fantasies. You must never be the cause of sexual immorality nor let yourself be drawn into immoral behavior. Instead, you are to yield your body to God, asking Him to help you control your sexual urges and not let them have power over you.

> **And the men, instead of having normal sexual relations with women, burned with lust for each other. Men did shameful things with other men, and as a result of this sin, they suffered within themselves the penalty they deserved (Ro.1:27, NLT).**
>
> **"Now the works of the flesh are manifest, which are these; Adultery, fornication, uncleanness, lasciviousness....[but] they which do such things**

shall not inherit the kingdom of God" (Ga.5:19, 21, KJV).

d. **Fourth, your body *is*** *designed* for the Lord and He cares deeply about your body (vv.13-14). Note these facts:

- God created your body to worship and serve and fellowship with Him. This is the first reason our bodies exist.

  "Get out of here, Satan," Jesus told him. "For the Scriptures say, 'You must worship the Lord your God and serve only him' " (Mt.4:10, NLT).

  What we have seen and heard we proclaim to you also, so that you too may have fellowship with us; and indeed our fellowship is with the Father, and with His Son Jesus Christ (1 Jn.1:3, NASB; see Re.3:20)

- God created your body for the Lord to dwell in, that your body might become the very temple of God's Spirit.

  Do you not know that your body is a temple of the Holy Spirit, who is in you, whom you have received from God? You are not your own; you were bought at a price. Therefore honor God with your body (1 Co.6:19-20, NIV).

- God has destined your body to be resurrected. Your body will not lie in the grave forever. Just as God raised up the Lord Jesus Christ from the dead, so He will raise up your body from the dead. No matter where your body or the various parts of your body may be, the day is coming when God will call together all the minute particles (atoms) of your body and give you a new, perfect, and eternal body.

  Do not marvel at this; for the hour is coming in which all who are in the graves will hear His voice and come forth—those who have done good, to the resurrection of life, and those who have done evil, to the resurrection of condemnation (Jn.5:28-29, NKJV).

O. You and God's Discipline or Correction

1. *You Should Know That God Disciplines You Because He Loves You.*

> **And you have forgotten that word of encouragement that addresses you as sons: "My son, do not make light of the Lord's discipline, and do not lose heart when he rebukes you, because the Lord disciplines those he loves, and he punishes everyone he accepts as a son." Endure hardship as discipline; God is treating you as sons. For what son is not disciplined by his father? (He.12:5-7, NIV).**

God does discipline us. He chastens, corrects, and rebukes us. But we must always remember that God never does evil: "God cannot be tempted by evil, nor does he tempt anyone" (Js.1:13, NIV). God does not cause temptation, sin, devastation, destruction, accidents, sickness, death, suffering, trials, trouble, and problems in people's lives. These things are caused by man's own sinful and selfish desires, or by the corruptible world in which we live, or by that arch-enemy of us all: Satan.

The crucial truth to grasp is that God does not cause wickedness or evil in life. God loves us and loves this world. Hence, His concern is not to cause problems and pain for us; His concern is to deliver us through all the trouble and pain on earth and to save us for heaven and eternity. How does God do this?

When we think of discipline, we usually think of punishment and correction, and it does mean this. But it also means to train, teach, and instruct a person. Both meanings are included in the word *discipline.* As you go through life day by day, pay attention to several key factors dealing with discipline:

a. **First, when you face** a trial or temptation, God stirs you to stand fast and to conquer the trial or to turn away from the sin. He guides, teaches, and instructs you all along the way, making you stronger and drawing you closer and closer to Him. God does not want the trials and temptations of life to defeat you; He wants them to strengthen you. He wants to use them to discipline and teach you ...

- to endure more and more
- to trust and depend upon Him more and more
- to draw closer and closer to Him in prayer and fellowship (1 Jn.1:3)

However, note this: you have to allow God to work in your heart so that He can use the trials to strengthen you. You cannot wallow around in self-pity or react against the trials and problems that attack you. You must sincerely turn to God and ask Him for help and strength. Then you must continue to go about your affairs and trust God to help you.

An illustration is this: an innocent baby who is crippled in an accident by a drunk driver is not being corrected by God. The baby has done nothing wrong to deserve being disciplined. The baby is crippled because a sinful man followed the indulgent path of self and Satan. He is crippled because he lives in a corruptible world. God loves the young child and will look after him as he grows, if the youngster will look to the Lord for help. God will use the child's sufferings to work good for everyone involved if they will simply trust and live for God.

- ➢ God will teach the *growing child* to increase in endurance and strength as he or she grows older.
- ➢ God will teach the growing child to trust and to fellowship and commune with Christ more and more.
- ➢ God will use the endurance and faith of the growing child as a testimony to His love and care—as a testimony to His power that can conquer all the trials and sorrows of life, even that of death.

b. **Second, when you fail** and cave in to some trial or temptation, God lets you reap what you have sown (Ga.6:7). You bear the results of your sin. But never forget, even during sin and failure, God loves and works with you (He.12:6). He uses the suffering to stir you to remember your sin and failure, and to think of Him and repent. God takes the sufferings that are caused by trials and sins and uses them to correct and discipline you. This is a key statement, and it is what you must always remember when dealing with all the bad and evil things in the world. God does not cause them. They are caused by three forces that have already been mentioned and are well-known to most of us: sinful people, the corruptible world in which we live, and the arch-enemy Satan. God loves us and has nothing in mind for us except love and the very best of everything. Therefore, God takes all the bad and evil—all the sufferings of the world—and works it all out for the good of all who truly love Him (Ro.8:28). He uses the suffering caused by sin and trials to correct and discipline us; to stir us to draw near to Him in trust, dependence, and love, and to live as we should.

c. **Third, do not** make light of the LORD's discipline (He.12:5). Too often, we pay little attention to God's discipline and correction in our lives:

- to the tug and pull of God's Spirit
- to the consequences of our sin and the suffering in our hearts
- to the unusual, out of-the-ordinary things that happen to us.

Too often, instead of searching our hearts to learn what God might be saying to us, we just shrug things off or try to explain things away as unrelated. As a result, we continue right on in our irresponsible behavior. The little flaws and sins get bigger and bigger until finally they are too big to handle. The consequences involve so much destruction and suffering that we can no longer ignore them.

If we would heed the discipline of God, then we could correct our small misbehavior and prevent the more serious sins from happening. This would mean that much of the horrible suffering in the world would never come to pass.

The point is this: you should not treat lightly the discipline of God, but rather heed it. As you do, life will become easier and more victorious from day to day.

d. **Fourth, do not faint** or lose heart when you are disciplined, but endure God's correction (He.12:5-7). When God *receives* you as a child of His, He will discipline you when you go astray. Why? Because He loves you. Despite being God's son or daughter, you still have faults and weaknesses. You go astray, disobeying, rebelling, and acting selfishly. Sometimes you hurt and cause pain both for yourself and for others. So God corrects you. He loves you and wants to stop you from harming yourself and other people. He wants you to grow and move through life with as little pain and anguish as possible, to become stronger and stronger within your mind and heart. Therefore, when you go astray, God will correct you.

The point is this: endure the discipline of God. Stand fast against all trials and sufferings. Follow the Word of God and the urgings and convictions of the Holy Spirit within your heart. When you sense these urgings and convictions, God is disciplining you. He is teaching and correcting you because He is your Father and He loves you. He is disciplining you just as a loving father disciplines his child. For this reason, heed the discipline of God and correct your behavior before you harm yourself or others.

> **Now no chastening seems to be joyful for the present, but painful; nevertheless, afterward it yields the peaceable fruit of righteousness to those who have been trained by it (He.12:11, NKJV).**
>
> **I correct and discipline everyone I love. So be diligent and turn from your indifference (Re.3:19, NLT).**

2. *You Should Know Why God Disciplines You: He Prunes You So You Will Bear More Fruit.*

> **"I am the true vine, and My Father is the vinedresser. "Every branch in Me that does not bear fruit, He takes away; and every *branch* that bears fruit, He prunes it so that it may bear more fruit. "You are already clean because of the word which I have spoken to you (Jn.15:1-3, NASB).**

In this picture of the Vine and the Branches, Jesus is the Vine, God is the Vinedresser (Gardener), and the people who claim to believe in Christ are the branches.

a. **The unfruitful branches** are taken away. Note that these are *attached branches.* Jesus said that they are "in Me," but they have a problem: they bear no fruit. The unfruitful branches claimed to be attached to Christ. They seemed to have an *organic* relationship to Him. They joined the church and began to associate with true believers. They appeared to bud and spout:

- They had listened to Jesus and the gospel.
- They had made a profession and were baptized.
- They seemed capable of bearing fruit.
- They appeared to be true branches.

Still, the branches were unfruitful. They were *in* the Vine, a part of it, but they simply bore no fruit.

Very practically, what does this mean? It means that the unfruitful branches are not true believers (see Jn.15:6, 8). They *claimed* to be *in Christ,* but their hearts are not truly committed to Christ. Their profession is...

- more profession than possession
- more pretending than sincerity
- more deception than truth
- more counterfeit than reality

As a result, the unfruitful branches become apostates and deserters. They are the men and women who hear about Christ and for a period of time claims to follow Him, but their claim is false (Jn.6:6; 13:10-11; 1 Jn.2:19.)

> **Such people claim they know God, but they deny him by the way they live. They are detestable and disobedient, worthless for doing anything good (Tit.1:16, NLT).**

God cuts off and *takes away* the unfruitful branches (v.2). This is a severe warning to every branch—everyone who claims to be *in Christ.* You must make sure that your profession is genuine that you do bear fruit or else face severe judgment.

b. **The fruitful branches** are pruned. All bad spots, useless buds, misdirected shoots, and discolored leaves are cut back. We all have some things in our lives that need to be pruned, some...

- conduct
- thoughts
- attitudes
- passions
- motives
- relationships
- commitments
- habits

Now, the purpose for pruning is to prepare you to bear more fruit. The purpose is not to hurt or damage you (the branch). You are pruned—disciplined by God—to correct your behavior. Through the process of pruning or discipline, you are stirred to live more righteously and to bear more of the Holy Spirit's fruit: love, joy, peace, patience, kindness, goodness, faithfulness, gentleness, and self-control (Ga.5:22-23).

Note *how* the fruitful branches are pruned or cleansed (disciplined). You are cleansed by the words Jesus has given you, cleansed by the Word of the Lord Himself. The Word of God washes away all the pollution and dirt of sin that clings to you. It does so by showing you what you are doing and not doing, where you are failing and how, and also your sins of commission and omission.

> **"How can a young man cleanse his way? By taking heed according to Your word" (Ps.119:9, NKJV).**
>
> **"Your word I have hidden in my heart, That I might not sin against You!" (Ps.119:11, NKJV).**

When you look truthfully into the Word of God, you see your shortcomings in comparison with Christ in all His perfection. The Word of God forces you to measure yourself against Christ, and it arouses you to repent and to bear more and more fruit. This is the reason God disciplines you.

P. You and Money

1. *You Should Not Place Your Trust in Wealth but in God.*

> **Teach those who are rich in this world not to be proud and not to trust in their money, which is so unreliable. Their trust should be in God, who richly gives us all we need for our enjoyment. Tell them to use their money to do good. They should be rich in good works and generous to those in need, always being ready to share with others. By doing this they will be storing up their treasure as a good foundation for the future so that they may experience true life (1 Ti.6:17-19, NLT).**

The word *teach* here (*charge,* KJV; *command,* NIV) suggests begging or beseeching a person—strongly so—to the point that the person is commanded to act. God is appealing to you in love and tenderness, but you are expected to do exactly what He says. If you are rich or have a desire to be rich, four strong charges are directed to you.

a. **You should not** be proud or arrogant because you have money (v.17). The world honors money. The great majority of people want and seek more money. Indeed, the idea of being wealthy or the pursuit of wealth is so interwoven in the fabric of this world that it is probably the most honored, most sought after, thing in the world. The result is that the rich are lifted up in most people's minds. They want to be like the rich. Therefore, if you are rich, it is extremely difficult for you to keep a proper perspective of yourself. You face the great danger of thinking too highly of yourself, of esteeming yourself better than others.

   If you are blessed with wealth, you need to guard carefully against egotism and a sense of self-importance. Riches and possessions do not make you a *good person,* a person of excellent character. Trusting in Christ, living righteously, and doing good works are what make you a good person.

   If you are rich, the temptation to be prideful is always confronting you because of the value and high regard people place upon money. But the charge of God is forceful and clear: you are not to be filled with pride.

b. **You should not** trust in the *uncertainty of riches* (v.17). Riches are the most uncertain thing in life. The world's economy fluctuates up and down every few years. In world affairs, one crisis follows another and the markets respond and react to each crisis. Even if you can keep your wealth in this life, disease or an accident can happen overnight, and your wealth is of no value whatsoever when you face God. Riches—their value and benefit—may be here today, but they are just as easily gone tomorrow.

In light of this, you must not play the fool. Do not place your trust in money, which is so unpredictable and unreliable.

c. **You should** *trust in God* instead of riches, focusing your heart and life upon Him (v.17). God is the Creator of the universe; thus, He is the only One who possesses every good and perfect gift. God alone can give you the good gifts necessary for this life, and the perfect gifts necessary for the next life.

In fact, every *good gift* that you receive now—including riches—has come from God. This fact bears repeating: every good gift that you now have has come from God. It stands to reason, then, that if you want more and more of the good things in this life—the things that are of real value—you must trust in God.

> **Every good gift and every perfect gift is from above, and comes down from the Father of lights, with whom there is no variation or shadow of turning (Jas.1:17, NKJV).**

d. **You should** use your money to do good (vv.18-19). You are even to distribute your wealth willingly and be generous in doing so. Too many rich people shut their ears when they hear this command from God. They turn their attention elsewhere, because they do not want to think about giving away large amounts of their money or estate. They reject the fact that God expects them to give to the point of sacrifice just as Christ did when He came to earth. Just imagine: He gave up the glory, worship, and wealth of heaven to come to this sinful, corrupt world to save us. But think about the following facts—think honestly and realistically:

- Think about the millions of people who are dying every day from hunger, disease, and lack of fresh water. Think about those who are hurting due to ignorance, sin, loneliness, and emptiness. When God looks down upon the earth and sees so many uneducated, hurting and dying, and He sees you—the rich of the earth—what do you think He expects you to do? The world is one large community or family. God expects you to help meet the needs of people, and to do so sacrificially.

- Second, why do you think you have wealth? To selfishly waste it on yourself and your family? To hoard it? To bank and store it up and just let it lie around and never be used? You and everyone else—if we are truly objective and honest—know better.

God expects you—the rich of this world—to use your money to do good. He expects you to distribute and to be generous and sacrificial in carrying the gospel of Christ to the lost and in meeting the needs of the uneducated, the poor, the helpless, and the dying of this world.

God's charge and His promise are strong: if you use the wealth God has entrusted into your hands to do good—to help the needy and reach the lost with the good news of eternal life—you store up heavenly treasure for the world to come.

> **But do not forget to do good and to share, for with such sacrifices God is well pleased (He.13:16, NKJV).**

2. *You Should Realize the Secret to Contentment Is Godliness, Not Money.*

> **But godliness with contentment is great gain. For we brought nothing into the world, and we can take nothing out of it. But if we have food and clothing, we will be content with that. People who want to get rich fall into temptation and a trap and into many foolish and harmful desires that plunge men into ruin and destruction. For the love of money is a root of all kinds of evil. Some people, eager for money, have wandered from the faith and pierced themselves with many griefs (1 Ti.6:6-10, NIV).**

Every person strives for contentment. We want to be fulfilled, complete, satisfied, and at peace both within and without. But when we look around, we see a discontented society and a world full of people who are unfulfilled, anxious, and restless. They lie, steal, cheat, hoard, oppress others, and wage war in order to get more and more of this world's possessions, power, and money. Why are so few people truly content? God's Word gives us clear insight into *the secret of contentment*.

a. The secret to contentment is true godliness (vv.6-8). To be *content* means to be fulfilled and complete, at peace within your heart. Imagine feeling wholly complete and fulfilled, being at peace with who and what you are and have. What brings such contentment to the human soul? Scripture states unequivocally that it is *godliness*. Godliness alone can make you content—permanently fulfilled, satisfied, complete, and sufficient. To illustrate the truth, Scripture reminds you about the three stages of life:

- There is the *stage of birth*: when you were born, you brought nothing into this world (v.7).
- There is the *stage of death*: at death, you carry nothing—absolutely nothing—out of this world. You leave the world just as you entered it, with nothing (v.7).
- There is the *stage of life*: This is the stage between birth and death, when you need certain things to sustain you: food, clothing, and shelter. In reality, you *need* nothing else. You can live, sustain life, and be content if you have these things and truly live for Christ. Therefore, you are to be content with the basic necessities (v.8).

Remember the point of these verses: the *secret* to *contentment* is godliness. If you live a truly godly life, God will flood your soul with a deep sense of peace—a lasting sense of fulfillment, satisfaction, and completion. And godliness with contentment is *great gain*.

b. The secret to contentment is not money (vv.9-10). This is shocking, for the rich cling to their money, and the rest of us never seem to have enough or are forever seeking to get more of it. But God is clear about the matter: money and wealth do not bring contentment. There are four reasons this is true.

First, money tempts and enslaves (v.9). How? If you have money, you can usually buy what you want, when you want. Money is power within the world. If you have the power to buy anything, go anywhere, and do whatever you want, you have power—a power that most people desire. They, too, want the wealth to buy, go, and do anything they desire.

If you are rich, you are far more tempted to indulge the flesh and to live extravagantly, far more tempted to live selfishly and to hoard. And if you are in a position of authority, you are far more tempted to control and oppress people through the power of your wealth.

The rich and those who yearn to be rich are rarely free from the bombardment of temptation. Therefore, they seldom have peace—not in a permanent and lasting sense. This is the first reason money does not bring contentment. Money brings a flood of temptation and ensnares people in sin.

Second, money is the source of many foolish and hurtful desires (v.9). Think how foolish and hurtful some of these things are.

- How irrational it is to have a closet full of clothing that is hardly ever worn, and then to replace or add to it every year with new clothing. You can wear only one set of clothing at a time.
- How foolish it is to buy so much junk food that you simply do not need, and to just keep on eating and eating—conditioning your body to crave more and more food. Is it foolish or wise to be so indulgent and to damage your body through gluttony?
- How harmful it is to give your body over to intoxicating drink, drugs, immorality, and greed.
- How hurtful it is to become addicted to work, to make more and more money, to the neglect of your family, friends, and God.

How tragic is it to indulge your desires with the excesses of this world when millions upon millions are hopeless and helpless, uneducated, going to bed hungry, cold, and sick or dying from disease or lack of food, clothing, and shelter? But more tragic than all these are those who are dying without Christ, without the hope of eternal life, when the resources exist to reach every soul with the gospel.

Third, money can plunge you into ruin and destruction (v.9). If you become obsessed with the foolish and harmful desires of this world, you will be utterly destroyed, both in body and soul. And the ruin and destruction will be for eternity.

Fourth, the *love of money* is the root of all kinds of evil (v.10). Note why:

- The love of money can cause you to covet, and covetousness is idolatry.
- The love of money can cause you to wander away from the faith. It causes many people to turn away from the Lord, to seek the entrapments of this world, the world's bright lights and pleasures, authority and honor, comfort and ease.

- The love of money can cause you to pierce yourself with many sorrows and griefs. The things of this world can never fully satisfy your heart nor bring lasting and permanent contentment to your soul.
- The love of money only consumes you with a craving for more and more—a craving that is never satisfied. It even leads to anxiety and insecurity lest you lose your wealth through bad investments, economic slump, or theft. Money cannot buy love, health, or deliverance from death. Money cannot buy God; it cannot buy assurance of God's care, guidance, forgiveness, and gift of eternal life.

In sum, your human nature craves the necessities of life. This is only reasonable. But once you have the necessities of life, you discover that you still crave more. The necessities do not satisfy your inner craving and restlessness for something more. When you realize this, you have a decision to make, a path to choose: What will you turn to in order to satisfy your inner craving?

Unfortunately, the majority of people—and too often believers—look to the things of this world for fulfillment by obtaining more and more food, clothing and whatever else they desire. They go after more pleasure, wealth, and recognition. But what they so often overlook is this fact: the craving within their hearts—the void and hunger—is not for more material possessions. It is for *spiritual satisfaction*.

Their true craving is for an inner peace, one that can only come from a close personal relationship with the Lord. When you walk with God day by day, you learn to trust and lean on Him, and, in doing so, you find the true contentment that only He can give. Obviously, you must have both your physical and spiritual needs met to live and thrive in the world. But one without the other leads to certain death—either physical or eternal death or both. True contentment, then, comes from a life of genuine godliness, seeking God first in all things.

> **But seek first the kingdom of God and His righteousness, and all these things shall be added to you (Mt.6:33, NKJV).**
>
> **But my God shall supply all your need according to his riches in glory by Christ Jesus (Ph.4:19, KJV).**

Q. YOU AND YOUR CIVIC DUTY

1. *You Are to Give to Caesar (the Government) the Things That Are Caesar's and to God the Things That Are God's.*

> **Show Me a denarius [Roman coin]. Whose image and inscription does it have?" They answered and said, "Caesar's." And He said to them, "Render therefore to Caesar the things that are Caesar's, and to God the things that are God's" (Lu.20:24-25, NKJV).**

Christ astounded the world of His day by declaring that there is an earthly kingdom to which some things are to be given, and there is a spiritual, heavenly kingdom to which other things are to be given. In this Scripture, Christ uses the occasion to teach the truth about citizenship, a truth that was earth-shaking to the people of that day. It was shocking because the Jews believed that the loyalty of a citizen belonged only to God, and the rest of the world believed that loyalty belonged only to the ruling monarch of their territory.

As a true believer, you have two citizenships. You are clearly a citizen of this world; therefore, you owe to earthly officials (government) what belongs to them. But you are also a citizen of heaven, of the spiritual world; therefore, you owe to God what belongs to Him (Ph.3:20).

a. **There are some** things that belong to Caesar. The image on the coin was Caesar's; the inscription was Caesar's; and the coin had been made by Caesar's government. Therefore, the coin belonged to Caesar if Caesar said it was due him.

The point is clear: you have an obligation to the government under which you live. As a believer, you receive the benefits of government—even the currency that is used to exchange for goods—just as *unbelievers* do. For example, in industrialized societies, the government provides security, roads, public transportation, sewage, and sometimes health services, food, air, and water safety, and so much more. In fact, without the government and its laws, society would be in utter chaos; lawlessness and violence would be out of control:

- ➢ No one would be safe to walk the streets.
- ➢ People would have to live behind closed doors.
- ➢ Abuse, attacks, murder, and war would be a constant threat.

- No property would be safe.
- There would be no public roads, transportation, water, sewage, or electrical systems, for there would be no law to protect property or to collect taxes. And even if there was, few would honor it.
- There would be no military, police, or fire protection for the same reason.

Without government and its laws, there could be no civilized society or community. Government is an utter necessity to keep people from becoming like wild beasts in a jungle of unrestrained selfishness and lawlessness. In view of this, you are to pay your fair share of taxes for these benefits.

b. There are some things that belong to God. In no uncertain terms, Christ declares that God does exist and that there is a spiritual world. This means that you belong to God, as well as to this world; you are a spiritual being, as well as a physical being; and you are responsible to live as a citizen of heaven, as well as a citizen of this world. Think of all you have received from God! As a responsible citizen of heaven…

- You owe God your very life. You need to show an attitude of gratitude for all He has done.
- You owe God a transformed life that produces the fruit of His Spirit: love, joy, peace… (Ga.5:22-23).
- You should use your mind and body to enjoy and preserve the beauty of the earth and all God has provided.
- You are to work and produce for the betterment and service of all people everywhere.
- You should help support God's church through your tithe and offerings as it carries out its awesome task for Christ.

Considering all God has done in your life, you can never repay Him in full. For this reason alone, be eager to pay your due share to God. Give to Caesar the things that are Caesar's, and to God the things that are God's.

2. *You Are to Submit to the State and Its Authority.*

Submit yourselves for the Lord's sake to every authority instituted among men: whether to the king, as the supreme authority, or to governors, who are sent by him to punish those

who do wrong and to commend those who do right. For it is God's will that by doing good you should silence the ignorant talk of foolish men. Live as free men, but do not use your freedom as a cover-up for evil; live as servants of God. Show proper respect to everyone: Love the brotherhood of believers, fear God, honor the king (1 Pe.2:13-17, NIV).

This is also why you pay taxes, for the authorities are God's servants, who give their full time to governing. Give everyone what you owe him: If you owe taxes, pay taxes; if revenue, then revenue; if respect, then respect; if honor, then honor (Ro.13:6-7, NIV).

Remind the people to be subject to rulers and authorities, to be obedient, to be ready to do whatever is good, to slander no one, to be peaceable and considerate, and to show true humility toward all men (Tit.3:1-2, NIV).

In Peter's day, believers were being severely persecuted by the government. Most, if not all, had been forced to flee their homes. They had to leave everything behind: property, businesses, clothes, furnishings, and jobs. In light of the severe persecution, what was to be the attitude of the believers toward the government and its authorities? This is a critical question because of the *periodic persecution* of believers by government and society.

History reveals that genuine believers are constantly suffering persecution of some sort. But no matter what you may be suffering, God says that you are to *submit* to those in power. Submitting to government authority is difficult, especially if you are in the midst of suffering persecution. Nevertheless, the word *submit* is an imperative; it is a strong command. God expects you to submit yourself to the laws at every level of government. Local as well as state and national governments are to be obeyed.

At this point, a question naturally arises. Is there ever a time when opposition to or rebellion against the government is justified? Yes, there is, and this will be discussed below. However, it is important that one first understand these seven key elements pointed out in Scripture:

a. **You are to submit** to civil authorities because they are *sent* or *ordained* by God (1 Pe.2:13-15; Ro.13:1). It is God's will that government exists and that gifted leaders have the authority to rule within the government. There are three institutions ordained by God:

the family, the church, and the government. All three exist because God set them up as the framework within which people are to relate to each other and to God Himself.

- Within the family, the parents rule and family members share together.
- Within the church, the church leaders exercise authority and people learn about and grow in the knowledge of God as well as worship Him.
- Within the government, government officials exercise authority within their department or jurisdiction and citizens relate to each other as well as to their officials.

People are responsible for how they carry out the functions of these three institutions. Each of the three has leaders who are faithful, obedient to God and do an excellent job; and each has leaders who are disloyal, disobedient to God, and do a terrible job.

The fact to remember is that government is ordained by God, and rulers are answerable to Him. Every ruler will give an account to God. And so will you and all other citizens. We all will give an account for our behavior as citizens, whether good or bad (2 Co.5:10).

To a great extent, you can do little about how the authorities in government conduct their affairs, but you can do a great deal about your behavior as a citizen within the state; and God is very clear about what your behavior is to be. You are to obey all civil authorities no matter who they are. BUT, there is one exception to obeying government and those in authority—one exception that allows you to resist the leaders:

- when the law or leader fails to execute true justice and righteousness, requiring you to act against or to disobey God's law
- when leaders begin to exercise personal and immoral or unjust mastery over human life

In such times, you are to obey God and not man (Ac.5:29). You should always do what is right, moral, and just. You, as a true believer, will serve the highest good of the government by refusing to obey the officials and insisting upon their execution of *true justice* and *righteousness* within society. By resisting the unjust and immoral behavior of officials, you bear a great witness for the Lord and work for greater justice by bringing about change within the state. However, the justice and morality you pursue must be that of God's Holy Word and not of your own making.

b. **You should seek** to silence the critics of Christ by your good behavior (1 Pe.2:15). Most people, even many professed believers, want nothing to do with Christ's demand for self-denial and holy living. Sadly, they want to live as they wish and to do their own thing. The very idea that people are to give all they are and have to Christ is radical to them. They are simply unwilling to accept what, in their minds, is extreme or overzealous behavior. As a result, the government and society sometimes turn against the church and anyone who refuses to turn away from Christ and His cause.

Scripture actually calls anyone who persecutes the church and believers *foolish*. Imagine rejecting people just because they teach...

- love and peace
- patience and kindness
- respect for authority
- morality and purity
- justice and righteousness
- discipline and control
- sacrificial giving

Any person who opposes the great virtues of life or the teaching of them is behaving very foolishly. Still, no matter how badly unbelievers treat you, you need to continue to live for Christ by doing good. Usually, your righteous and godly behavior will overcome the lies and attacks of those who oppose you. This is the second reason you are to obey rulers—so that your lawful and righteous behavior will silence any question about Christ and His great cause.

c. **You are to live** as a free citizen, yet live as a servant of God (1 Pe.2:16). When you receive Jesus Christ as your Savior, you subject yourself to God above all other laws. As stated above, if human law stands against God's law, you are to obey God rather than the man-made law. But you must guard against using your liberty as a cloak to act maliciously against the state. You should never disobey a law and claim it is unjust when in fact it is not. You have no right to disobey a law merely because you do not like the law.

The point is this: you are God's servant, not the servant of your own ideas and thoughts. You are to serve God and His call, not your own lusts and desires. You have no right to break the laws of government unless the laws directly oppose God and His law. All laws of government are to be obeyed unless they violate God's perfect law of love, the Divine law that demands *true justice* and *equal and moral treatment of every citizen.*

d. **You are to respect** all citizens (1 Pe.2:17). Remember the early church and its believers, how they were surrounded by the most corrupt people imaginable. They found themselves among heathen worshippers, people who wallowed around in a cesspool of lawlessness, immorality, injustice, and drunkenness. Yet, Scripture is saying to respect *all citizens*, the bad as well as the good. Of course, this does not mean to respect them because of their sin, but rather...

➢ because they are God's creation
➢ because their souls are of more value than all the wealth in the world
➢ because they contribute to the work, defense, and structure of the nation

You are to respect all people. No person is to be scorned or rejected, no matter who he or she may be: rich or poor, corrupt or clean, bad or good, evil or righteous, destructive or constructive.

Just as Christ showed compassion and reached out to save you, so you should be concerned about reaching every individual you can for Christ. Thus, no person is to be counted beyond reach. God's charge is clear: respect all citizens.

e. **You are to love** your brothers and sisters in Christ (1 Pe.2:17). This means to love all believers whoever they may be, regardless of color, nationality, or beliefs.

Love is the very opposite of prejudice, discrimination, and divisiveness. Love never criticizes, backbites, grumbles, or murmurs. This means loving all believers, everywhere, and at all times—even when they seem unlovable!

f. **You are to fear** God. As a citizen and as a member of God's church, you need to do everything you can to obey God. In fact, Scripture clearly says you should fear what will happen if you disobey God's will and commandments (1 Pe.2:17). The idea is that judgment is coming and disobedience will bring the judgment of God down upon you.

g. **You are to honor** the king or highest authority at every level (1 Pe.2:17). Bear in mind that the evil and infamous Nero was on the throne when this was being written and the believers were being persecuted by the authorities (Nero ruled A.D. 54-68). Nevertheless, God instructs believers to honor those in authority. Think how difficult this must have been for them, yet what a powerful testimony they had before God and before men!

As citizens of this world, you and all other believers are to be a people of order and discipline, of righteousness and justice. You are to set a dynamic example of love and peace so that some can be won to Christ and be saved for eternity.

R. You and Forgiveness of Others

1. *You Must Forgive Those Who Wrong You If You Wish God to Forgive You.*

> **For if you forgive men when they sin against you, your heavenly Father will also forgive you. But if you do not forgive men their sins, your Father will not forgive your sins (Mt.6:14-15, NIV).**

The very idea that you must forgive others in order for God to forgive you is an alarming concept to some people. It is only natural to love those who love you, but to forgive those who hate or have seriously wronged you is quite another matter.

However, think for a moment: How can God forgive an *unforgiving heart*? His nature of love and justice will not permit Him to indulge and give license to the passions of a person's unforgiving spirit. God can forgive you only when your heart is filled with mercy toward others—only when you yourself are willing to forgive. How can you expect otherwise? In the present passage, Christ teaches the basic principle of forgiveness: you must forgive those who wrong you if you wish God to forgive you.

a. **First, you must** acknowledge that you need forgiveness. You have transgressed God's law. Even the most mature among us fail to keep God's law perfectly. We all stumble, fall, blunder, and fail; and we do it much too often. Think of your own daily experience...
   - ➢ how often you come short of what you should do or be. You come short of God's perfection and holiness everyday (Ro.3:23).
   - ➢ how often you *cross over* from the path you should be following and deviate into *a forbidden* area.

In light of your own sin and failure, you desperately need God's forgiveness. And God promises that He will forgive you if you will, first, turn away from your sin and, second, forgive those who wrong you.

The greatest gift in all the world is to be forgiven by God: to be absolved and released from all guilt and condemnation; to be accepted and restored by God and assured of seeing Christ face-to-face. Forgiveness of sins means that you are set free—set at liberty to live abundantly and to live eternally with God in perfection.

But the only way to be forgiven your sins is to forgive others when they sin against you. Forgiving others means several very practical things.

- You are not to be judgmental or critical.
- You are not to become bitter or hostile.
- You are not to take revenge or even to think about it.
- You are not to hold hard feelings against another person.
- You are not to talk about, gossip, or join in spreading rumors about someone. On the contrary, you are to correct the rumors.
- You are not to rejoice in the trouble and trials that fall upon another person.
- You are to love and pray for the person who wrongs you.

Having bitter or angry feelings against another person is sin. It is holding sin within your heart. But forgiving a person who wrongs or harms you is proof that you wish to have a clean heart. You genuinely want God to forgive you.

> **"Blessed are the merciful: for they shall obtain mercy" (Mt.5:7, KJV).**

b. Second, Christ issues a strong warning: refuse to forgive others and you will not be forgiven (Mt.6:14-15). If you pray for forgiveness and hold feelings against another person, you are being hypocritical. If you continue to harbor ill will toward another person, it is clear proof that you are not right with God. Christ is perfectly clear in His warning about forgiving others:

> **Be merciful, just as your Father is merciful. "Do not judge, and you will not be judged. Do not condemn, and you will not be condemned. Forgive, and you will be forgiven (Lu.6:36-37, NIV).**

The warning and the promise are direct and forceful: judge, and you will be judged; condemn, and you will be condemned; be unforgiving, and you will not be forgiven. God could not be any clearer.

2. *You Are to Forgive Those Who Wrong You, Forgive Them Seventy Times Seven—an Unlimited Number of Times.*

> **Then Peter came to him and asked, "Lord, how often should I forgive someone who sins against me? Seven times?" "No, not seven times," Jesus replied, "but seventy times seven! (Mt.18:21-22, NLT).**
>
> **Bearing with one another, and forgiving one another, if anyone has a complaint against another; even as Christ forgave you, so you also *must do* (Col.3:13, NKJV).**

Seventy times seven is four hundred and ninety, but this is not the point Jesus is making. The question is how often should you forgive a brother or sister who continues to wrong you?

- Peter: "Seven times?"
- Jesus: "No. Seventy times seven."

What Jesus means is that there is to be no limit to the number of times you forgive a person. Forgiveness is a matter of the heart, not of the mind. The mind will only keep a record of wrongs. A spirit of forgiveness does not measure or limit the number of times it will forgive. A spirit of forgiveness is longsuffering and tolerant. Why? There are several reasons.

a. **A forgiving** spirit is a quality of the heart. None of the spiritual virtues or realities—such as love, mercy, grace, joy, forgiveness—can be measured or limited. By their very nature, they are spiritual and not physical. So they are to be known and practiced without limit or measure. For example, you should experience and practice love at every opportunity. And you should also experience and practice forgiveness at every opportunity. As a follower of Christ, forgiveness is to be a part of your very nature, one of the virtues of your life. You are to have a spirit of forgiveness that forgives seventy times seven—*ad infinitum* (without limit).

b. **Good relationships** are impossible without a forgiving spirit. Offending others is common to us all. We are sinful beings; therefore, we offend one another often, and sometimes without even knowing it. If we kept score of each other's offenses, there would be little time to do anything else. We offend others by...

- ➢ failing to smile and speak
- ➢ failing to recognize or acknowledge them
- ➢ failing to word things properly
- ➢ failing to be gentle and kind
- ➢ failing to be humble and respectful
- ➢ failing to be generous and giving
- ➢ failing to be patient and controlled

c. **Offending others** is usually unintentional and, as stated, we are often unaware that we have offended them. The reasons we offend others are innumerable, but common causes are preoccupation, a heavy heart, illness, anxiety, weariness, a demanding schedule, or difficulty dealing with problems. Keeping these in mind will help you forgive others when they offend you as well as help you guard against offending them.

Never forget, you are as human as the next person. Remembering that you need forgiveness as much as the next person will help you maintain healthy relationships as much as any other single fact (Ro.12:17-18).

d. **The common response** to being offended is to react. Reactions can range from very minor to very serious in nature. Verbal, emotional, mental, or physical abuse is, of course, very serious and potentially dangerous. Less serious but still unacceptable is arguing, casting blame, verbally attacking, making accusations, withdrawing, or wallowing around in self-pity and a spirit of condemnation. Some even revel in the attention gained by being the object of abuse instead of handling the matter quietly in a true spirit of reconciliation. You should never react against those who offend you nor revel in being the innocent or wounded party. Rather, you must forgive the offender.

This does *not mean* that you are to tolerate true abuse. God forbid! You are never to indulge or sanction someone's rage against you or their mistreatment of you. Instead, you need to seek the help of someone you know you can trust, such as a close friend or a qualified professional. However, you are still to forgive the offender.

e. **An unforgiving spirit** shows that you are basically self-centered and spiritually immature. Unforgiveness reveals that you have not grown to be like Christ in His nature of understanding, compassion, and love. A forgiving spirit...

- ➢ understands God's nature, that He is perfect and holy, yet He forgives our sins

- ➢ understands human nature, that we all are sinful and offend others at times

f. **Peace and health** can be preserved only through a merciful and compassionate spirit. If you have an unforgiving spirit, you cause as much disturbance and division as the offender. You are actually stooping to the level of the offender, and, in fact, you yourself become an offender. And, sadly, as long as you have an unforgiving spirit, there can never be peace. A sense of discord and turmoil will dominate your thoughts and life.

It is the lack of peace—the lack of a good relationship with God and others—that disrupts the normal functioning of your body, mind, and emotions. Tension, anxiety, ulcers, high blood pressure, troubled relationships, and many other physical and emotional problems can, and often do, come from an embittered, resentful spirit. If only for these reasons, you should forgive others. But because Christ has forgiven you of all your sins—past, present, and future—you must forgive others and keep on forgiving them an unlimited number of times (Col.3:13b).

No matter how much wrong a person has done to you, it cannot match the wrong you have done to Christ. Yet, Christ has forgiven you. Therefore, as you grow in your Christian faith day by day, you should do all you can to mature in your spirit of forgiveness. The benefits you gain from your efforts will far outweigh the pain!

Chapter 6

What You Must Do to Overcome Temptation and Sin

Contents

Chapter 6

What You Must Do to Overcome Temptation and Sin

1. *You Need to Understand the Causes of Temptation.*

> **Where do wars and fights *come* from among you? Do *they* not *come* from your *desires for* pleasure that war in your members? You lust and do not have. You murder and covet and cannot obtain. You fight and war. Yet you do not have because you do not ask. You ask and do not receive, because you ask amiss, that you may spend *it* on your pleasures. Adulterers and adulteresses! Do you not know that friendship with the world is enmity with God? Whoever therefore wants to be a friend of the world makes himself an enemy of God (Jas.4:1-4, NKJV).**
>
> **What is causing the quarrels and fights among you? Don't they come from the evil desires at war within you? You want what you don't have, so you scheme and kill to get it. You are jealous of what others have, but you can't get it, so you fight and wage war to take it away from them. Yet you don't have what you want because you don't ask God for it. And even when you ask, you don't get it because your motives are all wrong—you want only what will give you pleasure. You adulterers! Don't you realize that friendship with the world makes you an enemy of God? I say it again: If you want to be a friend of the world, you make yourself an enemy of God (Jas.4:1-4, NLT).**

As human beings, we constantly face temptation, and all too often we find ourselves yielding and doing wrong. But remember, temptation itself is not sin. We sin when we yield to temptation. As believers, we need to prepare and make every effort to overcome whatever temptation confronts us. One of the first preparations we can make is to learn what causes temptation and sin. This passage reveals four causes.

a. **The first cause** of temptation and wrongdoing is *evil desires*—the passion for pleasure and gratification that rages within our bodies (v.1). The picture is that of constant warfare, of craving and grasping after whatever will satisfy our desires. All of us know what it is to experience this conflict, to have our flesh continually yearning for something. Strong desires are difficult to control. In fact, few people control them completely. Some may control their evil desires in what are called the *gross and visible* sins such as adultery, vengeance, and murder. But many more gratify their desires in the so-called *acceptable* things such as overeating, selfishness, wasteful, spending, gambling, social drinking, hoarding, or participating in inappropriate sexual activities or fantasies.

The point is this: your body is a walking civil war with one craving after another waging battle after battle within you, seeking gratification or fulfillment. You sense a deep desire to lift the restraints and to enjoy the guilty pleasure of the enticement you struggle to control.

Notice the shocking result of our evil desires: it is conflict and wars, quarrelling and fighting. And it is those conflicts and wars that create the greatest need of the human race, the need for peace. Imagine what the world would be like if all of our hearts were at peace and if we all lived in peace with one another and with God. There would be no restlessness or uneasiness within the human soul and no conflict or wars between people or nations. There would be no sin or evil committed against others—wife, husband, neighbor, or anyone else—because we would be at peace with God as well as with one another.

So, what is the cause of temptation and wrongdoing? Your own sinful or evil desires. Your desire for pleasure and gratification that rages within your body.

> **"But each one is tempted when he is drawn away by his own desires and enticed. Then, when desire has conceived, it gives birth to sin; and sin, when it is full-grown, brings forth death" (Jas.1:14-15, NKJV).**

William Barclay quotes several of the great thinkers of past history who recognized this point, that strong desires lie at the very root of human problems. These are well worth quoting. (Each man's statement is given in a separate paragraph for easier reading):

> *The root cause of this unceasing and bitter conflict is nothing other than desire.*
>
> - *Philo points out that...desire is the worst of all the passions of the soul. "Is it not because of this passion that relations are broken and...that great and populous countries are desolated by domestic dissensions? and land and sea filled with ever new disasters by naval battles and land campaigns? For the wars famous in tragedy...have all flowed from one source—desire either for money, or glory or pleasure. Over these things the human race goes mad."*
> - *Lucian writes, "All the evils which come upon man—revolutions and wars, stratagems and slaughters—spring from desire. All these things have as their fountain-head the desire for more."*
> - *Plato writes, 'The sole cause of wars and revolutions and battles is nothing other than the body and its desires."*
> - *Cicero writes, "It is insatiable desires which overturn not only individual men, but whole families, and which even bring down the state. From desires there spring hatred, schisms, discords, seditions and wars." Desire is at the root of all the evils which ruin life and which divide men."*
> - [William Barclay himself says,] *This overmastering desire for the pleasures of this world is always a threatening danger to the spiritual life. It is the cares and riches and pleasures of this life which combine to choke the good seed (Luke 8:14). A man can become a slave to lusts and pleasures, and, when he does, malice and envy and hatred enter into life (Titus 3:3).*
>
> *The ultimate choice in life lies between pleasing oneself and pleasing God; and a world in which men's first aim is to please themselves is a world which is a battleground of savagery and division.*[1]

b. **The second cause** of temptation and wrongdoing is distrust and prayerlessness (v.2). You are tempted because you seek to fulfill your desires with the comfort, pleasures, possessions, and power of this world. As a result, your desires are never completely and permanently fulfilled. Things of this world can never bring a lasting peace and satisfaction to your soul. Only God can fulfill the *restless desires* of your heart and life. This

---

1 William Barclay. *The Letters of James and Peter.* "The Daily Study Bible." (Philadelphia, PA: The Westminster Press, 1958), p.116.

is exactly what Scripture says. Indeed, your desires are not met because you do not trust and pray, asking God to fulfill your desires and to meet your every need. It is when God is shoved aside that you begin to covet and crave to the point that you act selfishly and give in to your sinful cravings.

As stated, your desires will never be permanently or completely fulfilled apart from God. For this reason, you have to trust and call upon Him in order to have your needs fulfilled: "You do not have because you do not ask."

God wants to fellowship and commune with you. Prayer and communion with God—trusting and calling upon Him—is the only way you can ever fulfill the deepest and innermost desires of your heart. And once the spiritual craving is permanently satisfied, all the other cravings of your life will be fulfilled. Your desires will be controlled by the power of God's Spirit in your heart. Again, the second cause of temptation and wrongdoing is *distrust and prayerlessness*—not knowing God enough to trust Him, and not praying to God.

c. **The third cause** of temptation and wrongdoing is praying with the wrong motives (v.3). When the motivation in your heart is not pure, God is unable to help you. What does it mean to pray amiss, to pray with the wrong motive? It means to ask for things in order to indulge your own lusts and desires. For example, you ask...

   - for health and a longer life to continue your comfortable lifestyle
   - for more money to be able to purchase more things
   - for success to be recognized and honored
   - for position to hold authority
   - for a suitable spouse and marriage so you can project the right image in public

   You ask for these things and more because you are focusing on self, not on God or the benefit of others. You seek God's help, His blessings so you can have more comfort, enjoyment, material goods, acceptance, recognition, and so forth.

   What is the right motive for prayer? How can you pray and know that God will give you the desires of your heart? By asking for the glory of God. God is glorified when people worship Him and when the desperate needs of the world are being met. When you want something from God, you must want it so that you can glorify God more effectively and be able to reach out to help people more and more.

d. **The fourth cause** of temptation and wrongdoing is *worldliness* (v.4). Scripture uses strong language here. It calls people who are friends with the world *adulterers*. In this case, Scripture is speaking of *spiritual adultery*. God holds His relationship with you in the highest regard. Your relationship with Him is to be so close that it can only be likened to the closeness and intimacy of marriage. Thus, spiritual adultery means that you turn away from God to the world, that you break your commitment to God and turn to other things; that you follow the things of the world instead of following God.

Of course, this cuts God's heart to the core and causes pain beyond description. It is as though you commit adultery against Him, for you turn your love away from Him and give it to the things of this world.

You need to pay close attention to what Scripture asks you: "Do you not know that friendship with the world is enmity with God?" (v.4). In other words, the person who is a friend of the world is an enemy of God! What does it mean to be a friend of the world?

- ➢ It means to live for the world and the things of the world: houses, property, money, position, power, popularity, recognition, and anything else that people focus on and put before God.
- ➢ It means to seek the things of this world so much that you deceive, lie, cheat, steal, or even kill to get them.
- ➢ It means to seek the bright lights, the fleshly pleasures, and the wicked indulgences of the world.

Everything in this world, without exception, passes away. Why? Because it has the seed of corruption in it. In light of this, it stands opposed to God, who is both incorruptible and eternal. It stands to reason, then, that you need to be a friend of God and live for Him and not live for this world (2 Co.6:17-18).

2. *You Need to Use the Sword of God's Spirit—the Word of God—to Fight Temptation.*

But He [Christ] answered and said, It is written [in God's Holy Word],

- **Man shall not live by bread alone, but by every word that proceeds from the mouth of God....**
- **You shall not tempt the Lord your God....**

- **You shall worship the Lord your God, and Him only you shall serve (Mt.4:4, 7, 10, NKJV).**

Put on salvation as your helmet, and take the sword of the Spirit, which is the word of God (Ep.6:17, NLT).

At the beginning of Christ's ministry, He was immediately confronted with three very enticing temptations. In each instance, He used God's Holy Word to combat the devil's seduction. This experience of Christ shows you exactly how you can overcome temptation: you must use the sword of God's Spirit, the Word of God.

Of course, you cannot use a weapon if you do not hold the weapon in your hand. Sadly, many believers do not hold God's Word in their hands often enough or long enough to be of any help. They have not read or studied the Word enough to have its truths at their disposal.

You need to take time to read and study God's Word. You need to learn God's Word—hold it in your heart and mind—so you can meditate on it and quote its wonderful truths when you are tempted.

Three very practical suggestions that believers use to combat temptation are these:

- Find and memorize Scripture that deals with your particular weaknesses, areas that often give rise to temptation.
- Quote or read the Scripture aloud when temptation first arises. Reading or quoting Scripture silently will strengthen your spirit. But, because Satan and his followers are not omniscient or omnipotent, they cannot read your mind. Therefore, do what Christ did: speak the Scripture aloud.
- Flee the temptation—immediately turn away, run away, and completely turn your back on the source of the enticement.

If you will use God's Word to gain victory over temptation, you can overcome all the strategies the devil launches against you. The Sword of the Spirit—God's Holy Word—is the weapon God has given you to use in fighting temptation.

3. *You Must Resist Sin.*

Therefore do not let sin reign in your mortal body so that you obey its evil desires (Ro.6:12, NIV).

This statement is an imperative, a forceful command. It is up to you to resist sin; it is your responsibility to fight it, to stand firmly against it.

a. **You must not let sin** *reign* in your mortal body. You cannot allow it to have authority or control over you. The present tense is used here, so the idea is that of a continuous attitude and behavior. Always keep your mind away from sin and sinful things. Instead, focus on those things that are good and pleasing to the Lord (Ph.4:8). Keep your mind under control by guarding against the lust of the eyes, the lust of the flesh, and the pride of life. Do not let sin dominate or control...

   - your mind: what you think about
   - your eyes: what you look at
   - your mouth: what you say or taste
   - your hands: what you touch
   - your feet: where you go and the company you keep

   Actively resist sin by standing against it and by rebuking and fighting it. Oppose it with all your might.

b. **You must not obey** the evil desires that arise within your body. The pull of sin can sometimes be strong, very strong. We know what it is to lust after things, whether it be money, property, security, position, pleasure, fun, or fleshly stimulation. For this reason, do not *yield* to the pull of these desires and cravings. Do not let the lusts of your eyes and flesh control your mind and behavior or *rule* your life. Resist all the sinful desires of your mortal body so that you can please God. Then, one day, you will inherit the eternal reward God is going to give those who truly love and obey Him (1 Co.15:50-58, Jas.1:12).

4. *You Should Not Yield Any Part of Your Body to Sin, but Rather Yield Every Part to God.*

> **Do not offer the parts of your body to sin, as instruments of wickedness, but rather offer yourselves to God, as those who have been brought from death to life; and offer the parts of your body to him as instruments of righteousness (Ro.6:13, NIV).**

No part of your body, seen or unseen, is to be used as an instrument of wickedness. Think about your body parts, the parts that must be protected from sin: your eyes, ears, mouth, tongue, hands, feet, mind, or any of the covered and dressed parts. Do not give any part of your body over to unrighteousness. The tense is present action, so be constantly on guard against the arousal of evil desires.

Of course, this involves enormous strength because of the sinful and corrupt world in which we live. When we are exposed to so much immoral, lawless, and violent behavior every day of our lives, it is a constant struggle to keep a pure mind and thoughts and to fight against the temptation of sin. But you must fight. You have to do everything you can to control yourself and to protect against giving any part of your body over to sin. How?

a. **First, you need to yield** yourself completely to God. Note a significant fact: in the original Greek, the text is not written in the present tense, but in the *aorist tense*. This simply means that you are to make a *one-time,* permanent decision for God, a *once-for-all* dedication of your life to Him. This presentation of your life to God is to be an unconditional, genuine, and total commitment. You are to yield all of yourself—your body, mind, spirit, and life, all that you are—wholly to God.

b. **Second, you are to yield** your body parts *to* God as instruments of righteousness. Again, this includes your eyes, ears, mouth, hands, feet, mind—all your members, clothed and unclothed. Every part of your body, your whole being, is to be surrendered and given over to God for the purpose of working righteousness.

> **Therefore, I urge you, brothers, in view of God's mercy, to offer your bodies as living sacrifices, holy and pleasing to God—this is your spiritual act of worship. Do not conform any longer to the pattern of this world, but be transformed by the renewing of your mind. Then you will be able to test and approve what God's will is—his good, pleasing and perfect will (Ro.12:1-2, NIV).**
>
> **If your right eye causes you to sin, gouge it out and throw it away. It is better for you to lose one part of your body than for your whole body to be thrown into hell. And if your right hand causes you to sin, cut it off and throw it away. It is better for you to lose one part of your body than for your whole body to go into hell (Mt.5:29-30, NIV; see Mt.18:8-9).**

5. *You Need to Stay Alert! Watch Out for the Devil and Stand Firm Against Him.*

> **Stay alert! Watch out for your great enemy, the devil. He prowls around like a roaring lion, looking for someone to devour. Stand firm against him, and be strong in your faith. Remember that your Christian brothers and sisters all over the world are going through the same kind of suffering you are (1 Pe.5:8-9, NLT).**

This is one of your most important duties as a believer. You must be continually on guard for the devil's schemes, or your life and testimony for Christ will be destroyed.

a. **First, you need to stay** alert and watch for the attacks and temptations of the devil (v.8). In other words, you need to be prepared, focused, controlled, and sober. It means that...

- ➢ you should not become intoxicated with drugs or alcohol or anything else that would keep you from being watchful and prepared.
- ➢ you should be sober in mind and behavior, controlled in all things, not given over to indulgence, license, or extravagance. It means not to overindulge or go to the extreme in anything, even such things as eating, sleeping, or recreation.

If you are not careful, you will give in to the assaults and enticements of the devil. You will be overcome and led into sin and destruction. For this reason, live a sober and controlled life. Be alert enough to see the attacks coming. Develop a mind and spirit strong enough to stand against the devil.

To *watch out* for the devil you have to be observant and awake. It has the idea of being constantly on guard or on the lookout for the devil and his attacks. Again, if your mind and body are dull, sluggish, and weak from overindulgence in any area—drink, drugs, sleep, recreation, pleasure, or anything else—you cannot be alert and watchful.

Scripture is clear: you need to be very serious about the devil. You have to be vigilant, always on guard, in looking for the devil's strategies and traps. This is the only conceivable way you can conquer and overcome in this life; it is the only way you can keep your life and testimony from being destroyed by the devil.

b. **Second, you need to realize** that the devil is your *greatest enemy* or adversary (v.8). He is like a legal opponent in a lawsuit or a common enemy who opposes you every day. The picture is that of the devil's standing against you in every conceivable way.

- Satan stands as an adversary in the court of God, accusing you before God.
- Satan stands as an adversary here on earth, doing all he can to trip you up and to defeat and destroy you.

The devil is a malicious enemy who accuses you before God. Scripture teaches that Satan is constantly bringing up your sins before God, that he is constantly reminding God of your disobedience. But note: the accusations or charges against you are false. How can that be when you are guilty of sin? Through Christ! Christ died for your sins, and when you trust Him for forgiveness, He forgives you. You are no longer guilty of sin. Thus, Satan's accusations and charges against you are false.

Why, then, would Satan continually accuse you before God? Why would he remind God time and again of your sins? Because he seeks to hurt and cut the heart of God. He is the devil, the one who stands most opposed to God and to all that God stands for.

Eons ago, sometime before the world was ever created, he was apparently the highest angel in all of creation. God had created him as the highest spiritual being in the universe. At that time, his name was Lucifer. But he rebelled against God and led other angelic beings to rebel with him. Subsequently, God judged him and cast him from his exalted position in heaven. From what we can glean in Scripture, this is what happened to Satan, how he became the devil, God's most fierce opponent (Re.12:9; Is.14:12-17; Eze.28:11-19).

The point is this: the devil does all he can to seek revenge in order to cut the heart of God. So he constantly reminds God of your sins. This, of course, means that he does all he can to tempt and lead you into sin, for the more you sin, the more he can hurt and cause pain for the heart of God.

Think about this fact for a moment. You are a believer, a person for whom God gave His Son to die. When God paid such an enormous price for your salvation—actually cast His wrath against His own Son because of your sin—think about how much He must hurt when you sin, especially when you profess to love Him!

The devil is a slanderer who is constantly accusing you before God. He will use your sin to hurt God as much as possible. This is the major reason you should stand against the devil's temptations. You should do all you can to protect the heart of God. In fact, your desire should be to never again bring pain to your Father's heart.

c. **Third, you need to understand** that the devil is like a roaring lion seeking to devour you (v.8). The *roaring lion* is a picture of anger, fierceness, and cruelty. Satan is being pictured as angry toward God and all whom God has created. Scripture says he prowls around seeking someone to attack and devour. How does Satan devour a person? Jesus says that the devil consumes people by leading them to do four things (see Jn.8:44 below).

➢ The devil leads people to desire and love the evil things that they do. He tempts people to give in to the lust of the flesh, the lust of the eyes, and the pride of life (1 Jn.2:15-16).

➢ The devil leads people to murder. Satan is behind all war, murder, and maiming of human life. He destroys lives and robs people of all abundant living when he can, depriving them of love, joy, and peace (Ga.5:22-23).

Jesus was saying that one thing is certain: God is not the father of murder (and injury)—the devil is. They who commit murder are children of the devil.

➢ The devil leads people to reject and hate the truth (1 Jn.3:8).

➢ The devil leads people to lie and deceive (2 Co.4:3-4; 2 Co.11:13-15).

Jesus tells us in one of the most shocking statements ever made: people who do not trust God as their Father are actually following the devil as their father! In other words, Jesus says that all unbelievers have the devil as their father.

> **For you are the children of your father the devil, and you love to do the evil things he does. He was a murderer from the beginning. He has always hated the truth, because there is no truth in him. When he lies, it is consistent with his character; for he is a liar and the father of lies (Jn.8:44, NLT).**

d. **Fourth, you need to stand** firm against the attacks and temptations of the devil (v.9). You need to be strong in your faith, *resisting* and *struggling* against the devil. You must make every effort...

- Not to take your eyes off the Lord
- not to let your guard down
- not to slip back one step
- not to look the first time if possible, but never the second
- not to touch the unclean or forbidden thing
- not to listen to one word of Satan's lies
- not to think evil thoughts
- not to give way to any wicked or selfish desire
- not to loosen or diminish righteous or godly restraints

The seduction might look good, taste good, and feel good, but you need to resist the evil desire and be steadfast in doing so. You must not give in at all. Giving in one step leads to a second step, and before you know it, you have caved in and are engaged in the sin. Satan has devoured you.

Your duty is to resist the devil and to be strong in your resistance. Note what it is that Satan is after: your faith. He wants you to deny your faith, to turn away from Christ. The devil's crowd may say...

- "Oh come on! It won't hurt you, not this one time."
- "No one will ever know."
- "Don't let some old-fashion rule keep you from enjoying life."
- "Do your own thing."
- "You're a fool if you don't take advantage of this opportunity."
- "Eat, drink, and be merry."

The flesh usually desires more and more of the possessions and pleasures of this world. The temptation will always be there—at least temporarily—to turn away from Christ and His righteousness, to turn away from your faith and return to the world and its seductions. But your duty is to resist the devil and be strong in your faith.

> **Submit therefore to God. Resist the devil and he will flee from you. Draw near to God and He will draw near to you. Cleanse your hands, you sinners; and purify your hearts, you double-minded (Jas.4:7-8, NASB).**

Never forget, other believers are suffering the same seductions of the devil as you, and many are conquering them. They are faithfully resisting the devil, standing steadfast in their faith. As a result, their example should be an encouragement to you. You are not alone in the world. You are to let their example stir you to resist the devil. You are to use their example to arouse you to stand fast for Christ.

> **No temptation has overtaken you except such as is common to man; but God *is* faithful, who will not allow you to be tempted beyond what you are able, but with the temptation will also make the way of escape, that you may be able to bear *it* (1 Co.10:13, NKJV).**

6. *You Need to Put on the Full Armor of God to Stand Against the Onslaught of the Devil.*

> **A final word: Be strong in the Lord and in his mighty power. Put on all of God's armor so that you will be able to stand firm against all strategies of the devil. For we are not fighting against flesh-and-blood enemies, but against evil rulers and authorities of the unseen world, against mighty powers in this dark world, and against evil spirits in the heavenly places. Therefore, put on every piece of God's armor so you will be able to resist the enemy in the time of evil. Then after the battle you will still be standing firm. Stand your ground, putting on the belt of truth and the body armor of God's righteousness. For shoes, put on the peace that comes from the Good News so that you will be fully prepared. In addition to all of these, hold up the shield of faith to stop the fiery arrows of the devil. Put on salvation as your helmet, and take the sword of the Spirit, which is the word of God. Pray in the Spirit at all times and on every occasion. Stay alert and be persistent in your prayers for all believers everywhere (Ep.6:10-18, NLT).**

Your life is a battlefield. Immediately upon receiving Christ, you find yourself in a constant struggle, an unending war. You are a combatant, a soldier in conflict. Your calling as a believer is not to a life of enjoyment and ease but to a life of hard conflict. There are foes within and foes without. From the cradle to the grave there is a constant struggle against the sinful desires of the flesh and the alluring temptations offered by Satan and the world—a struggle against an excessive corruption that inevitably leads to death (Ro.7:21; Gal.5:17; 6:8; Ep.4:22b;

6:10-12). Furthermore, there are people who will ridicule, mock, provoke, abuse, or even threaten to kill you for your faith.

You must therefore be strong *in the Lord* and in His mighty power. To do so, you must understand your enemy, the devil, and his strategies. The devil will do everything he can to deceive you and to cause you to turn away from God. He will launch strategies that appeal specifically to you...

- to the desires of your eyes and your flesh
- to your need for attention, success, and recognition—the very things that stir excessive pride

In addition, the devil will send false teachers, very impressive teachers, across your path. Never forget that Satan is not a fiery red person with a set of horns, a pointed tail, and a pitchfork in his hands. He is a living being in the spiritual world or dimension—a being who is transformed into a *messenger of light*. Tragically, some people are serving him by walking around and proclaiming a righteousness other than that of Christ. Their message is that of self-righteousness: human goodness and works, ego and self-image, personal development and growth, self-improvement and correction.

Such messages appeal to your flesh, and many are helpful to a certain extent. This fact must be acknowledged, but such messages are not the basic power you need. They cannot deliver you *through* the severe trials and sufferings of life nor from death. The temptations of Satan can only lead you down the path of all flesh—that of death, decay, and eternal judgment.

As a Christian soldier, you must realize that your warfare against Satan and temptation is not human or physical, but spiritual. Your foes are spiritual forces that possess unbelievable power (v.12). Note exactly what is said: you fight...

- against evil rulers and authorities of the unseen world
- against mighty powers in this dark world
- against evil spirits in the heavenly places

The thrust of this verse is to stress the enormous power and great number of evil forces that stand against you as a believer. The list also seems to indicate that the forces of evil are organized into a government or hierarchy of evil. The description points to a ranking of spiritual forces with exceptional authority, position, and rule.

A number of people have always scoffed at the idea of a personal devil and fallen angels (demons) who actually exist in a so-called spiritual world. They feel they are too educated and intelligent to believe such nonsense. They proclaim that such ideas are outdated and belong to the dark ages of human ignorance and superstitions. But note a significant fact: every human being who is both thoughtful and honest is keenly aware of the reality of...

- ➢ *subconscious horrors*—frightening thoughts and fears—that affect both your mind and body
- ➢ *unseen and uncontrollable forces* that greatly affect your behavior
- ➢ *unregulated behavior and urges* that you cannot control, even when you know better and want to behave differently
- ➢ *cosmic forces* that affect and determine your behavior
- ➢ *blind fate* that at times seems to control your life like a puppet

Think for a moment about all the wickedness, lawlessness, violence, wars, evil, injustice, immorality, and selfishness in the world. Sadly, it is usually these sinful themes that dominate the news reports every day. Now, just think about it. Why do so many people behave in such an evil manner? Do people not know better? Are there not enough of us who do know better who could change things? Yes, there are. Why, then, do we not change the world? This passage tells us why:

> **For we are not fighting against flesh-and-blood enemies, but against evil rulers and authorities of the unseen world, against mighty powers in this dark world, and against evil spirits in the heavenly places (Ep.6:12, NLT).**

God has to tell us the truth. He cannot do otherwise. So, God reveals to us a fact that should be understood: there is an evil force that has access to the spirit of the human race—a force that can influence and enslave people to do evil. That evil force is called Satan, and he rules over *the darkness and spiritual wickedness of this world.* Your only hope to stand against Satan and his onslaught of evil strategies is to put on the *full armor of God*. Scripture lists the seven pieces of armor you must wear at all times.

a. ***The belt*** *of truth*. The soldier used a belt to hold his clothing next to his body. This kept his clothing from flapping about and allowed him freedom of movement. The belt was also used to strengthen and support his body. The sign of the Christian soldier is the belt of truth...

- not truth individually or subjectively thought out
- not truth found in some man or woman's novel idea
- not truth taught by religions that have been founded by human beings

Such truth is self-centered and restrictive. God and God alone can possess and give pure truth to the human race. God alone can reveal the truth of abundant and eternal life. What specifically is the belt of truth?

- Christ is the truth. You are to put on Christ.

> **And the Word became flesh and dwelt among us, and we beheld His glory, the glory as of the only begotten of the Father, full of grace and truth (Jn.1:14, NKJV).**
>
> **Jesus answered, "I am the way and the truth and the life. No one comes to the Father except through me (Jn.14:6, NIV).**

- The Word of God is truth. You are sanctified—set apart to God and cleansed—by the Word of God. You are to put on the Word of God.

> **Sanctify them by Your truth. Your word is truth (Jn.17:17, NKJV).**

- A tongue that does not lie and a life that is not hypocritical demonstrates the truth. You are to put on—live and speak—the truth.

> **"Hypocrites! Well did Isaiah prophesy about you, saying: 'These people draw near to Me with their mouth, And honor Me with their lips, But their heart is far from Me. And in vain they worship Me, Teaching as doctrines the commandments of men' " (Mt.15:7-9, NKJV).**
>
> **Therefore, putting away lying, *"Let each one of you speak truth with his neighbor,"* for we are members of one another (Ep.4:25, NKJV).**

b. ***The breastplate*** *of righteousness*. The breastplate covered the body of a soldier from the neck to the thighs. It was used to protect his heart.

The breastplate of the Christian soldier is righteousness. As a soldier, your heart is to be focused upon the Lord Jesus Christ and His righteousness, and that focus must be protected. When you were saved, God *counted you righteous* because you placed your faith in Christ and His righteousness. However, in this battlefield called earth, it is not enough for you to stand in the righteousness of Christ. As a Christian soldier, you must protect your heart. This you do by *living righteously.* Righteousness keeps you from being wounded by Satan's attacks and losing your focus. Thus, you need to strive for victory daily, always pursuing the righteousness of Jesus Christ and living righteously in this present world.

> **"But seek first the kingdom of God and His righteousness, and all these things shall be added to you" (Mt.6:33, NKJV).**
>
> **"Teaching us that, denying ungodliness and worldly lusts, we should live soberly, righteously, and godly in the present age, looking for the blessed hope and glorious appearing of our great God and Savior Jesus Christ" (Tit.2:12-13, NKJV; see 1 Co.15:34)**

c. ***The sandals*** *of the gospel.* Sandals were worn by a soldier as a sign of readiness—readiness to march and to do battle. Interestingly, Roman sandals were made with nails that gripped the ground firmly even when it was slippery or sloping. The sign of the Christian soldier is readiness—a readiness to march and to bear witness to the gospel. Wherever your feet take you, you are to share the gospel of Christ. The gospel alone can firmly ground people in a slippery world of sin and darkness.

> **But in your hearts set apart Christ as Lord. Always be prepared to give an answer to everyone who asks you to give the reason for the hope that you have. But do this with gentleness and respect (1 Pe.3:15, NIV).**

d. ***The shield*** *of faith in God.* This shield is not the small round shield that a soldier held in his hand to fight off the weapons of the enemy. It is the large oblong shield that the soldier used to protect his whole body from the fiery darts thrown by the enemy. The enemy's darts were dipped in pitch or some other combustible material and set afire. When they struck, they served the purpose of small incendiary bombs. Satan too has his fiery darts—things that can cause you...

- to doubt your salvation or worthiness
- to become discouraged, depressed, and defeated
- to burn with passion and desire
- to question if you can really serve God, handle the project, or achieve anything worthwhile in life

Such fiery darts often assault the mind. Doubtful and evil thoughts, one after the other, fight against your will and struggle to get control of your mind. However, the sign of the Christian soldier is that of the *shield of faith, faith* in God—a complete *trust* that God will help you quench the darts of doubt and evil. As you focus your thoughts upon God, He will give you a deep sense of His presence. In fact, *God's presence* itself will become your shield and defender (Ge.15:1). As Scripture says, God is your help and shield (Ps.33:20; 84:9).

> **But You, O Lord, are a shield about me, My glory, and the One who lifts my head (Ps.3:3, NASB).**
>
> **"For the LORD God is a sun and shield: the LORD will give grace and glory: no good thing will he withhold from them that walk uprightly" (Ps.84:11, KJV).**

e. ***The helmet*** *of salvation*. The helmet covered the head of a soldier. The head, of course, was the core of a soldier's capability to wage war. His thinking ability was the most important factor in determining his victory or defeat. Therefore, the soldier needed a helmet to protect his head.

The helmet that protects the mind of the Christian soldier is *salvation* (deliverance). Unless you are saved—unless your mind is protected by God's saving power—you stand no chance against the fiery darts of temptation. The minds of unsaved people are exposed and vulnerable, open to whatever Satan throws their way. Thus, they usually focus on this earth and seldom, if ever, upon God and Christ. It is normal and natural for the unsaved to see nothing wrong with being their own person and doing their own thing, just so they are reasonably considerate of others. Satan's fiery darts of covetousness, self-indulgence, extravagance, self-centeredness, worldliness, license, hoarding, and immorality have complete freedom to zero in and take control of the minds of those who do not trust God to save and help them.

But this is not to be so with you who are saved. As a Christian soldier, you desperately need to be on guard, always armed with the helmet of salvation. Knowing that you are saved and hoping for the glorious day of redemption will stir you...

- to keep your mind on Christ instead of on the seductions of this world
- to focus on Christ and your mission to carry the good news to a lost and dying world

> **We demolish arguments and every pretension that sets itself up against the knowledge of God, and we take captive every thought to make it obedient to Christ (2 Co.10:5, NIV).**
>
> **Therefore, my dear friends, as you have always obeyed—not only in my presence, but now much more in my absence—continue to work out your salvation with fear and trembling, for it is God who works in you to will and to act according to his good purpose (Ph.2:12-13, NIV).**

f. ***The sword*** *of the Spirit, the Word of God*. The soldier's sword was a weapon used for both defense and offense. The weapon of the Christian soldier is his use of the Word of God. By living in the Scriptures, you protect yourself from the onslaught of the enemy; you become empowered to fight and to win battle after battle, day after day. Remember: Jesus Christ Himself overcame the onslaught of the devil by using Scripture (Mt.4:4, 7, 10). The *written Word* is the one weapon that assures victory for the Christian soldier, for "the Word of God is living and powerful, and sharper than any two-edged sword."

> **For the word of God *is* living and powerful, and sharper than any two-edged sword, piercing even to the division of soul and spirit, and of joints and marrow, and is a discerner of the thoughts and intents of the heart (He.4:12, NKJV).**

g. **The supernatural provision of prayer**. Although a soldier entered the conflict fully dressed and armed, something else was required as well: confidence, assurance, and courage. For the Christian soldier, this comes from a spirit of prayer.

- As a Christian soldier, you need to be in *a spirit of prayer at all times*, praying to the only living and true God. Prayer to any other so-called god is empty and useless. Only the living Lord can hear, answer, and protect you from the fierce enemies and temptations that bombard you day after day.
- As a Christian soldier, you need to be *alert in prayer*, always focused. Otherwise, you will take your eyes off of Jesus and allow the enemy to slip in and gain a foothold in your territory (daily activities). Sometimes, when you are faced with a critical situation, you should actually go without sleep in order to pray.
- As a Christian soldier, you have a duty to *pray unselfishly*, for you are not in battle alone. Many are engaged in the same warfare. Indeed, the outcome of the battle is determined by the courageous struggle of all involved. You should pray for those who fight with you, pray as much for your fellow soldiers as for yourself.
- As a Christian soldier, you ought to *pray for leaders* in particular. Their decisions and example often determine the outcome of the battle. You have leaders who teach and preach and administer throughout the church and around the world. You should ask God to give them wisdom, decisiveness, boldness, and purity of life as they lead you through the battle. Then, you will put the enemy to flight and capture souls for Christ with the gospel (Ac.28:20).

7. *You Should Remember That God Always Provides a Way to Escape Temptation.*

> **No temptation has overtaken you except such as is common to man; but God *is* faithful, who will not allow you to be tempted beyond what you are able, but with the temptation will also make the way of escape, that you may be able to bear *it* (1 Co.10:13, NKJV).**

Temptation is common to everyone. The temptations you face are no different from what others experience. This is an encouraging fact. Think about it. No temptation is unique to you; others have faced and already overcome whatever confronts you. Yes, many caved in to the temptation, but some demonstrated the willingness to obey God—

to call upon Him for help—and, through Him, they overcame the temptation. Keep two things in mind at all times:

a. **God is faithful**: He will always limit the temptation that attacks you. He will not allow a temptation to confront you that is (think about each of these)...
   - too enticing
   - too overpowering
   - too exciting
   - too persuasive
   - too appealing
   - too captivating
   - too empowering
   - too stimulating
   - too attractive
   - too irresistible
   - too overwhelming
   - too arousing

   God knows exactly *what* and *how much* you can bear. Therefore, He will limit or restrain every single temptation so that you can overcome it *without sinning*. God is faithful.

b. **God always provides** a way to escape temptation. God will give you the knowledge and strength either to walk triumphantly through every temptation or else to turn and flee from it. But never forget, the choice is up to you. You are the one who must decide to turn away and flee temptation. You are the one who has to take the escape route God has provided. Staying or giving in to temptation is never the only option. So it is up to you to take the route and to flee the enticement—each and every time.

8. *You Should Keep Your Eyes on the Reward for Enduring Trials and Temptations.*

> **God blesses those who patiently endure testing and temptation. Afterward they will receive the crown of life that God has promised to those who love him (Jas.1:12, NLT).**

(See chapter 10, *What Your Future Holds As a Believer—Your Death and Rewards,* pt.5, pp.400-401, for discussion.)

9. *You Need to Persevere in the Great Christian Race, Stripping Off Everything That Hinders You and the Sin That So Easily Trips You Up.*

> **Therefore we also, since we are surrounded by so great a cloud of witnesses, let us lay aside every weight, and the sin which so easily ensnares *us,* and let us run with endurance the race that is set before us, looking unto Jesus, the**

> **author and finisher of *our* faith, who for the joy that was set before Him endured the cross, despising the shame, and has sat down at the right hand of the throne of God (He.12:1-2, NKJV).**

This is one of the most stirring passages in Scripture, one that should be memorized by every Christian. In fact, it should motivate all true believers to run and to keep on running in the great *Christian race of life*. To begin with, however, we need to look at the *purpose* or *goal* of the Christian race. It can be described in several ways.

- It is the race for perfection, a life and world where righteousness, justice, and godliness reign; a place where no suffering, corruption, evil, or death exist.
- It is the race to know God, to commune and to fellowship with Him for all eternity.
- It is the race for the *promised land*, for heaven itself, for the new heavens and earth where we will live and serve God forever and ever.

This is the great goal, the wonderful promise for which you and all other believers strive. It is the incredible hope to which you cling as you make your way through this life. And when you endure to the end of your life here on earth, you will be escorted into the very presence of God where you will live with Him for all eternity.

The end of the Christian race is so glorious that we could go on and on about it. But the point of the present passage demands our attention: the great Christian race, a race like no other, lies before us. If you are willing to run it—and we all must run it—you need first to study and understand it.

a. **The powerful inspiration** for the Christian race is a great cloud of witnesses. The picture is that of a massive coliseum filled to capacity with spectators. The race is about to begin. Two quick instructions are given: get rid of all excess weight and any other worldly or sinful entanglements that slow you down. Run and keep on running, enduring to the end. As you run, remember Jesus (v.2). He formerly participated in the race, and He participated for the joy of winning. He disciplined Himself and endured to the point of death. And He received His reward.

   The crowd, the former heroes of the Christian faith, have also participated in the race. They have run and finished the race themselves, endured to the end and won their reward. Now, they are both witnesses and examples for you. They once were *participants* but now are *spectators*. They are actually witnessing your race and performance because they are vitally interested in how you run the race.

This great cloud of witnesses stood fast against all kinds of trials, temptations, and opposition. Their great faith and endurance should inspire you to believe and to endure in your race. Bear in mind that these believers were not perfect. They made mistakes and slipped just like you and everyone else do. But, they never buckled or crumbled in their faith. They persevered to the end and finished the race well.

- ➢ They endured through great trials and temptations, many even in the face of persecution and martyrdom. No matter how terrible the pain or tribulation, they endured in faith, believing in God and His glorious promises.
- ➢ They endured against all opposition, whether from family, friends, neighbors, fellow workers, or even institutional religionists. No matter how challenging the conflict or how strong the opponent, they believed God and endured in their faith, trusting God's Word and His promises.

Again, the point is this: the faith and endurance of former believers should stir you to believe God and to hold fast to your faith, to persevere through all in the great Christian race of life.

b. **The required disciplines** of the Christian race are threefold. First, you have to strip away every weight and every thing that hinders you. All serious athletes train and strain to remove all excess weight. For you, the Christian runner, this refers to things that may be legitimate and innocent in and of themselves, but they hinder you in the race. They hamper and slow you down instead of helping you run faster. What kinds of things would these be?

- ➢ Seeking entertainment instead of seeking fellowship and communion with God, instead of praying and reading your Bible, instead of worshipping and witnessing to the lost. Realistically, we all need recreation sometimes, but the problem with most of us is that we relax and rest far more than we need. We neglect our fellowship and communion with God, as well as our prayer for others. Too many of us do not even know how to spend a long time *keeping our minds* upon God and communing with Him.

- Seeking the possessions and things of this world instead of *seeking* God.
- Listening to music and other sounds that do not build up our spirits nor focus our minds upon God and upon the truth.
- Watching movies, or reading any type of media that fails to strengthen us.

Anything that does not build you up and make you stronger is excess weight that slows you down. As a Christian runner, you should do exactly what the Olympic runner does: strain to remove all excess weight. Do absolutely nothing that hinders or hampers you from running your best race.

Second, you have to strip off the sin that so easily trips you up. What is the *particular sin* that entangles and entraps you? Self-indulgence, the tongue, the flesh, covetousness, immorality, pride, selfish ambition, possessions, worldly friends, uncontrolled anger, drinking, doing drugs, immoral behavior, lying, or idleness?

What is it that consumes your energy and keeps you from following God fully, that causes you to stumble and fall far, far too often? You must strip it off or else it will catch you off guard and bring you down, and you may never finish the race.

Third, you have to run with perseverance—endure to the end. The word *perseverance* or *endurance* is not passive but active. It is not the spirit that just sits back and puts up with the trials of life, taking whatever may come. Rather, it is the spirit that stands up and faces the trials of life, that actively goes about conquering and overcoming them.

The Christian runner needs to be determined. You need to have staying power. You need to be unwavering in your resolve to complete the race, letting nothing stop or hinder you from finishing well.

c. The supreme example of the well-run Christian race is the Lord Jesus Christ. Many of us see examples of strong believers all around us, people who genuinely live for Christ. And we should look at these examples and learn from them. But above all, we should be *looking at and fixing our attention upon Jesus*. Why? Because Christ Himself ran the race of faith when He was upon earth, and He shows us exactly how to run it. You should remember four things about the race Christ ran.

- Jesus Christ ran the race of life perfectly. He finished His course having lived a perfect, sinless, and righteous life upon earth. He is the ultimate example of faith in God—of utter dependence, obedience, and righteousness—for you and all other believers. Therefore, you are always to be looking to Jesus, the Author and Finisher of your faith.

- Jesus Christ had a great inspiration: the joy that was set before Him. What was that joy? The glorious day of redemption, the day when He will be united and exalted with you and all other believers of all ages. In that glorious day, Christ will experience all the glory and joy for which He suffered and died and will fulfill God's purpose for His death. Joy will flood Christ's heart because, at long last, He will have accomplished God's great plan for the human race.

  The glorious day of redemption should stir and motivate you as well. Christ the Lord is your supreme example as you seek the joy of that glorious day, the day of redemption.
- Jesus Christ is also the supreme example in discipline. He followed the rules of the race even to the point of dying in order to be perfectly obedient to God. He ignored and disregarded the shame of the cross in order to finish the race well. As a matter of fact, He finished it flawlessly and thoroughly. And because He was perfectly obedient, He blazed the path of perfect righteousness, the very path that makes you acceptable to God. Christ did it all willingly, and because He did, He is the supreme example for you. You should endure in believing and obeying God no matter the cost you have to pay, even if it means martyrdom.
- Jesus Christ is the supreme example of receiving the reward of faith. He was exalted to the right hand of the throne of God. Many believers in His day witnessed His ascension and several believers have seen Him in visions and dreams since then (Ac.1:9f; 7:55f; 9:3f). The day is coming when you, too, will receive your reward.

With all this in mind, you ought to do all you can to strip off every weight and the sin that so easily trips you up and run the great Christian race. Just make sure—absolutely sure—that you endure to the very end.

10. *You Need to Learn to Walk in Open Confession Before God—All Day, Every Day.*

> **If we confess our sins, he is faithful and just to forgive us *our* sins, and to cleanse us from all unrighteousness (1 Jn.1:9, KJV).**

You should not sin. But, if you do sin, God wants you to know one important fact: if you sincerely confess your sins, He will forgive your sins. Knowing this, you need to walk in *open confession* before God throughout the day. This is absolutely essential because we all slip, fall, fail, sin, and disobey—every one of us. For this reason, learn to walk in *open confession* before God. As you maintain this close fellowship with God...

- ➢ He will continually forgive your sins, and He will do even more...
- ➢ He will cleanse you from all unrighteousness, all the dirt, filth, pollution, and contamination of sin that you know nothing about.

When you sincerely confess your sins, God forgives you. Not a single stain of sin remains on you. No matter how serious or horrible the transgression, God forgives and cleanses you. You stand before God sinless and perfect in the righteousness of Jesus Christ. But remember why: because you believe in Jesus Christ and trust the blood of God's Son to cleanse you from all sin.

How do you know that God will forgive your sins and cleanse you? How do you know that God will count the death of Jesus Christ as the punishment for your sins? Because God is faithful and just, perfectly so. Therefore, God must condemn and punish sin. But God is also perfect love. He is compassionate and merciful, perfectly so. Hence, God demonstrated His love and mercy and provided a way of forgiveness. This is exactly what He did in Jesus Christ. God demonstrated His love in the most perfect and supreme way possible: He gave His Son to die for your sins (Ro.5:8).

The point is this: having done this—having given His Son to die for your sins—God will forgive you. Because, He is faithful and just, He will keep His Word. He will do exactly what He says. Indeed, He would be unfaithful and unjust if He did not forgive you. God will forgive any repentant sinner who truly confesses, turns away from the sin, and turns to Him. God will forgive your sins if you will simply confess them. He will cleanse you from all unrighteousness

As a true believer, learn to walk throughout the day in *open confession* before God. Maintain a close fellowship with Him by walking in praise and thanksgiving. Make your requests known to Him and ask for forgiveness when you become aware of some shortcoming, failure, or sin.

CHAPTER 7

WHAT YOU MUST DO TO RISE ABOVE TRIALS AND SUFFERING

Contents

CHAPTER 7

WHAT YOU MUST DO TO RISE ABOVE TRIALS AND SUFFERING

A. YOU AND THE TRIALS OF LIFE

1. *You Should Consider All the Trials You Face As an Opportunity for Great Joy and Growth in the Lord.*

> **Consider it pure joy, my brothers, whenever you face trials of many kinds, because you know that the testing of your faith develops perseverance. Perseverance must finish its work so that you may be mature and complete, not lacking anything (Jas.1:2-4, NIV).**

The path of life is not an easy path to walk. It is filled with all kinds of trials, sorrow, suffering, and disappointment. This can be due to sickness, disease, accidents, death, temptation, or any number of other circumstances. What people need is a sure way to rise above all the trials and suffering of life. And the glorious message of this passage is that there is a way to be triumphant no matter how severe the trial or suffering. What is that way? It is approaching all trials as an opportunity for great joy and growth in the Lord. Note three points.

a. **First, you will face** many trials in life (v.2). But if you believe God and allow Him to work in your life, He will use the trials for a good and beneficial purpose. Beneficial because God can take the experiences you go through and make you a far stronger person, both in your moral behavior and in your understanding of others.

   - When you walk triumphantly through the problems and trials of life, you become stronger—more focused, more determined, more steadfast, more confident. Thus, you can be trusted to persevere and to fulfill your duties. Your strength also enables you to help others far more than if you were a weakling who crumbled under life's pressures.

- When you rise above trials, you become a purer person. That is, you develop and mature, having been refined and sharpened by the experience. This process strengthens your character more and more with each triumphant instance.
- When you rise above problems and hardships, you become a dynamic witness to all who see you. You demonstrate the presence and power of Christ in your life, bearing witness that He lives in you.

God wants you to face your trial or hardship by drawing closer to Him and asking for His help. When you call upon Him, He empowers you to become more like Christ and you, in turn, make Christ more fully known to the world.

b. **You are to face** trials and suffering with a spirit of joy (v.2). How is this possible? How can you be joyful when facing great adversity or severe problems? Joy is not what usually fills our hearts when we face these things. When a severe crisis comes our way, too often we despair and lose hope. Most of us certainly do not respond with joy.

There is only one way to face trials and temptations with a spirit of joy: you have to *change your way of thinking*—turn your attitude about the situation completely around. You have to stop focusing on the negative and concentrate on the positive. In the words of Scripture, you must *know* something and you must *do* something.

- You need to know that the testing of your faith during trials develops perseverance (v.3). Keep in mind what point one stressed: God allows trials in your life not to defeat or discourage you but to arouse you to draw closer to Him, making you stronger and more righteous. God uses pain and discomfort to conform you more and more into the image of Christ. As you walk through the experience, you become stronger, not weaker. By looking at the situation as a growing experience, a time to mature and gain wisdom, you can face trials more positively. You can begin to develop a joyful attitude in the face of adversity.
- You need to do something: you need to let perseverance develop within you. Perseverance means far more than just putting up with trials and suffering, resigning yourself to their intrusion and waiting for them to pass. It means far more than just following the advice of medicine and

psychology (to take it easy, to be calm, or to relax in stressful situations). Perseverance means that you endure and keep on enduring, never giving in. It means that you exert the energy and effort to triumph over the hardships that come your way.

If you will look at these troublesome, challenging, and sometimes painful times as opportunities, you can begin to face them with a joyful spirit. And when you learn to persevere and rise above them, you will find yourself walking through them triumphantly in the joy of the Lord.

c. **Third, the results** of facing trials and suffering can be very positive (vv.3-4). When you persevere and rise above the trials of life...

- ➢ you become more *mature*—more *perfect* and *complete*.
- ➢ you eliminate more personal weaknesses, flaws, and shortcomings than you may have done in any other way.

As the last two words of verse four say, you will *lack nothing*. You will experience all the abundance and fullness of life. You will become a conqueror, an overcomer, no matter how severe or stressful the circumstances. Even when you face death, God will make sure that you conquer that ultimate trial. God will reward you with an eternity of perfection—a life perfectly complete and fulfilled—because you will be conformed to the image of Jesus Christ.

2. *You Should Trust the Love of Christ: No Trial or Suffering Can Ever Separate You from His Love.*

> **Who shall separate us from the love of Christ? *shall* tribulation, or distress, or persecution, or famine, or nakedness, or peril, or sword?...Nay, in all these things we are more than conquerors through him that loved us. For I am persuaded, that neither death, nor life, nor angels, nor principalities, nor powers, nor things present, nor things to come, Nor height, nor depth, nor any other creature, shall be able to separate us from the love of God, which is in Christ Jesus our Lord (Ro.8:35, 37-39, KJV).**

Take just a moment and think about people, including believers, who feel that God does not love them, that He simply *could not* love them. Think how often you have felt unworthy of God's love because you came so far short of His glory and perfection. Perhaps you have slipped into sin far too often and feel dirty, disobedient, and unworthy of His love. How could God possibly love you when you disobey His Holy Word and commandments so often? The results of such feelings are...

- self-condemnation
- discouragement
- depression
- a lack of confidence
- low self-esteem
- defeated living

It is during such times that you must remember this wonderful truth: there is no *circumstance*, no force, no influence, no creature—nothing—that can cause Christ to turn away from you. No matter how terrible or severe the situation, it cannot separate you, the true believer, from the love of Christ. Christ loves you and will deliver you regardless of the seriousness of the situation or event.

a. **First, Christ will deliver you** from the severest circumstances (vv.35-37). And no more severe circumstance can be imagined than those listed in Scripture:

- *Tribulation* or *trouble*: to undergo a struggle, trial, temptation, suffering, or affliction.
- *Distress* or *calamity*: to suffer anguish, strain, agony, misfortune, not knowing which way to turn or what to do.
- *Persecution*: to be mocked, scorned, shamed, mistreated, ignored, neglected, abused, harassed, attacked, or injured.
- *Famine* or *hunger*: to have no food; to be starving and have no way to secure food; to have no means to buy food.
- *Nakedness* or *destitution*: to be stripped of all clothes and earthly comforts; to be poverty-stricken, deprived of all necessities.
- *Peril* or *danger*: to be exposed to the most severe risks; to be confronted with the most terrible dangers to your body, mind, soul, property, family, and loved ones.
- *Sword* or *death threat*: to face a real threat of being killed; to suffer the threat of martyrdom.

Imagine if you had experienced all this. What would your thoughts be? Would you feel forsaken by God? In the midst of so much dark trouble, would you believe that God loved you?

Scripture declares loudly and clearly that God does love you! There is absolutely nothing—no matter how dark and depressing, no matter how severe—that can separate you from the love of Christ.

Always remember this fact: difficult circumstances are not evidence that God does not love you. God loves you no matter what the circumstances may be. In fact, you are more than a conqueror through Christ who loves you (v.37). Christ will carry you through any and all situations, strengthening and encouraging you. You cannot lose, no matter the severity of the situation, for Christ loves you and is going to look after and take care of you.

b. **Second, Christ delivers you** from the most extreme experiences and forces. There is nothing in the universe that can separate you from the love of God that is revealed in Christ Jesus our Lord. You can be fully persuaded of this glorious fact. Consider the *experiences and forces* mentioned in Scripture (vv.38-39):

- ➢ *Not death*: confronting death and leaving this world cannot separate you from Christ and His love (Jn.5:24).
- ➢ *Not life*: no trial, suffering or disaster in life; no person, thing, or event in this life can separate you from Christ and His love.
- ➢ *Not angels, principalities, or powers*: no heavenly or spiritual creature, no being from any other dimension or world, no kingdom or realm, no authority or influence can separate you from Christ and His love.
- ➢ *Not anything present nor anything to come*: neither present events, beings, or things, nor future events, beings, or things can cut you off from Christ and His love. Absolutely nothing in existence now or in the future can separate you from God's love.
- ➢ *Not height or depth*: no power in the sky above or in the earth below, nothing from outer space nor from the depths of the earth can ever separate you from Christ and His love.

Note the *grand finale*: if there is any creature or anything in creation other than what is named, that creature or thing cannot separate you from the love of God that is revealed in Christ Jesus. For these reasons and so many more, you need to trust the love of Christ. His love enables you to rise above all the trials and sufferings of life.

If you have fallen into sin, ask God to forgive you and then repent, turn away from the sin, and God will shower His love on you. He will forgive and cleanse you (1 Jn.1:9). And you will personally experience His amazing love, for nothing can ever separate you from His love.

3. *You Should Know That God Works All Things Out for Good—Even Trials and Suffering—for Those Who Truly Love Him.*

> **And we know that all things work together for good to those who love God, to those who are the called according to *His* purpose (Ro.8:28, NKJV).**

What a comforting declaration! Think about this wonderful Scripture: nothing could ever be any more assuring than to know that God is working all things out for your good, for your benefit. Look closely at four details in this verse:

a. **The words** *all things* go well beyond the great events of this world. Of course, God does control the events of the world, but He controls much more. He rules over "all things," all that takes place both in heaven and earth, even the detailed events and happenings in the life of every believer. And He is dramatically working out all things—the trials and the suffering, the good and the bad—for *your good*, the good of His dear child. He does this because He loves you and because you love Him. Never forget this!

b. **The words** *work together* mean to create and eliminate, place and replace, connect and separate, interrelate and intermingle, control and guide. The words *work together* are also present action, which means that all things are *continually working together* for your good. God is in control of your life. Every moment of every day, God is arranging and rearranging all things, all the trials and problems you face, for your good.

c. **The word** *good* here signifies the ultimate good. You cannot see the future; you cannot take a single event and see all the lines and ramifications that run from it. You cannot see all the things that result from one single event, much less see the results of every event. But

God does; hence, He can take all the events of your life and work them out for your ultimate good.

d. There is, however, a limitation on this glorious promise, one that you need to pay close attention to: God works all things out for good *only* for those who *love Him* and are *called* according to His purpose.

The wording in this verse is of critical importance. This is clearly seen in the original Greek language of the Bible. The clause "to those who love God" is placed first in the sentence: "to those who love God all things work together for good." Scripture makes sure the point is not missed. God *only* causes your affairs to work together for good if you truly love Him.

Think about this truth for a moment; it is the only logical conclusion a reasonable and honest person could reach.

- If you do not love God, do not place your life into His hands, how can God take care of you?
- Even after you have received Christ as your Savior, if you turn and walk away from God, how can God look after you? Once you turn away, even when God does something good for you, you do not see it, not clearly, because your back is turned to Him. You reject and disobey Him.

God is not going to force His care upon you or anyone else. He is not going to make a robot out of you, forcing you to live at His beck and call. That is only *mechanical behavior;* it is not love. What God wants is love that flows from your heart, a heart that *chooses* to love Him. The choice is yours: you either turn your life over to Him in love, or you continue to take and keep your life in your own hands.

Note the words, "called according to His purpose." Your deliverance is God's objective, His plan. God calls you for the glorious purpose of saving you for all eternity and delivering you from the struggles and sufferings of this life.

God delivers the person who truly loves Him, the person who seeks to please and obey Him by living righteously. If you truly *love God* and are living a righteous life, you will experience God's working all things out for your ultimate good. God will be with you at all times and He will deliver you through all the trials and sufferings of this corrupt world.

> **Fear not, for I *am* with you; Be not dismayed, for I *am* your God. I will strengthen you,**

Yes, I will help you, I will uphold you with My righteous right hand' (Is.41:10, NKJV).

4. *You Should Seek God's Wisdom When Facing Severe Trials and Suffering.*

> **If any of you lacks wisdom, he should ask God, who gives generously to all without finding fault, and it will be given to him. But when he asks, he must believe and not doubt, because he who doubts is like a wave of the sea, blown and tossed by the wind. That man should not think he will receive anything from the Lord; he is a double-minded man, unstable in all he does (Jas.1:5-8, NIV).**

Right now, what is the worst trial you face? A trial that has just arisen and is, perhaps, about to overwhelm you?

Is there an escape? Is there a way to walk through the trial? A way that can assure victory and deliverance?

Yes, there is! Simply ask God for *wisdom*. God knows exactly what you need to do to walk through the trial and to emerge triumphantly!

a. **First, you need to** understand that wisdom means far more than just knowledge. Wisdom is far more than just being intellectual about some subject or area of life. Knowledge applies to acquiring facts, whether through study, observation, discovery, or personal experience. But it stops there. Without wisdom to know how to use or handle the facts, they are entirely useless. Most people in the world have heads full of facts. Tragically, far too few of them know how to make good use of the facts. Why? Because more is needed: wisdom is needed. What does wisdom mean? Wisdom is...

   - knowing facts and understanding what to do with the facts
   - seeing and knowing the truth and having the insight and good sense to deal with and protect the truth

   Godly wisdom grasps the great truths of life. It sees the trials that surround life and death, God and man, time and eternity, good and evil—the deep things of the universe and of God. Wisdom not only grasps these facts but also knows what to do about them. And then wisdom takes action and does what is needed. Wisdom walks through the trials and sufferings of life because it sees and knows the path of victory.

If you lack this kind of wisdom—if you do not understand or know how to conquer life's problems or to rise above the trials and suffering—there is one sure way to gain the wisdom: Ask God (v.5).

b. **Second, you need to** pay attention to God's wonderful promises when you ask Him for wisdom. Scripture spells them out clearly:

- God will give you wisdom.
- God will give you a generous amount of wisdom.
- God will not rebuke or scold you for not knowing how to handle the trial.

The idea is that God will not even question you for lacking wisdom, for not knowing what to do. God loves you, for you are His son or daughter, and He is your Father. Therefore, God will hear your request and your cry. He will give you the wisdom to conquer or to rise above whatever trial or suffering confronts you.

c. **Third, you have to** seek God's wisdom *in faith and not waver*. You have to believe that God really cares and will hear your prayers and meet your every need. When you pray and cry out to God, you cannot doubt; that is, you cannot ask for wisdom and then...

- wonder if God really exists
- wonder if God really heard your request
- wonder if God really loves and cares for you
- wonder if God can really do what you ask
- wonder if you really know God well enough for Him to hear and answer you
- wonder if the request is the will of God

God will not answer the prayer of a doubting person. If He did, He would be rewarding doubt—rewarding those who do not fully believe or trust Him. He would be rewarding those who have misgivings, who ignore, neglect, distrust and, in many cases, curse, deny, and fight against Him. God will not hear a person who wavers in his or her faith. You must believe that God exists and that He loves and cares for you (He.11:6). You must believe that He will hear you when you ask for wisdom to face the trials and sufferings of life.

Note what Scripture says about you if you waver in your faith. You are just like a wave of the sea, blown by the wind and tossed to and fro. You will not receive anything from the Lord. Why? Because, if you waver back and forth, you show that you do not know the value of God's gifts. As a wavering person, you would misuse and waste whatever God gave you—a terrible abuse of God's gifts!

In fact, Scripture says that if you waver in faith, you are a double-minded person, unstable in all your ways. You are living a life that is up and down, back and forth. Your whole behavior is unstable and unreliable. You are like a person with two minds: you are not sure; you are uncertain; you feel *yes* about something and then you feel *no*. You begin and then back up, then begin again. You believe, then you disbelieve; you act, then you distrust and slip back. You are unstable and inconsistent in your prayer life and behavior before God.

What a descriptive picture of so many! This is the very reason so many of us receive so little from God. We either do not ask or else when we ask, we waver in believing whether God will hear and answer us.

As you face the trials and sufferings of life, you need to ask God for wisdom and genuinely believe that God will hear and answer you. When you pray believing, God will show you the path to victory!

5. *You Should Remember God's Great Provisions When Trials and Suffering Confront You.*

> **But may the God of all grace, who called us to His eternal glory by Christ Jesus, after you have suffered a while, perfect, establish, strengthen, and settle *you* (1 Pe.5:10, NKJV).**

As believers, we sometimes suffer greatly in this world. Not only do we bear the normal afflictions that all people suffer, but we are sometimes attacked because of our faith in Christ. We are attacked because we live righteous lives and proclaim the hope of eternal salvation. Most people want nothing to do with righteous and holy living. They want to live in comfort to indulge their desires, enjoying the pleasures and possessions of this world. Consequently, they reject and oppose anyone who stresses the necessity for genuine faith and commitment to Christ.

As a genuine believer, you have a great promise: God will take care of you through all the trials and sufferings of this life. God will keep and preserve you, and He will eventually take you on home to heaven. This is the wonderful message of this great Scripture.

a. **First, you have** two great resources made available to you at all times: *God's grace* and *His call to eternal* *glory*. Everything God does for you is because of His grace. He is even called the *God of all grace*. Grace means the unmerited favor and strength of God. God favors you; consequently, He wants to bless and strengthen you (2 Co.9:8). He wants to help you through every trial and difficulty you face in life.

Remember, every blessing you have ever received came from the favor of God, even life itself. In fact, all good things come from God and from His grace (Jas.1:17). Ask God right now to pour out His grace (blessings and strength) upon you.

> **Let us therefore come boldly [to] the throne of grace, that we may obtain mercy, and find grace to help in time of need (He.4:16, KJV).**

God also gives you another resource: the hope of eternal glory. He wants you in heaven with Him, free from all the problems, troubles, sin, filth, evil, corruption, disease, and death of this world. God wants you perfected and glorified, made just like His Son, the Lord Jesus Christ. God wants you living with Him forever and ever. He has called you to eternal glory, so He will do anything—whatever is necessary—to save you and to keep you for glory.

> **[You] who are kept by the power of God through faith for salvation ready to be revealed in the last time (1 Pe.1:5, NKJV).**

This is the wonderful truth of God's promise. God's grace and God's call to eternal glory will sustain you through all the sufferings of this life, no matter how severe. God will keep you.

b. **Second, God uses** your trials and sufferings to *perfect* or *restore* you (1 Pe.5:10). The idea is that of adjusting, fitting, and joining together. God takes all of the displaced joints and broken limbs of life and uses them to adjust your character. He uses all the adversities and temptations, difficulties and persecutions, every burden of life, to make you more like Christ. If you are truly called of God and if you truly love God, then He will take all that ever happens to you and work it out for good. He will gradually perfect you, fit all the parts of life together—even the hardships and afflictions—and lead you to glory. This is the amazing grace of God that prepares you for eternal glory.

c. **God uses** your trials and sufferings to *establish* and *support* you (1 Pe.5:10). To *establish* means to make steadfast, firm, and solid. It means to be firmly set, as if in reinforced concrete. It means to be immovable. God is able to attach you to Himself to such a degree that you will be immovable, no matter how severe the trial or suffering. Rest assured of this. No matter what happens to you, God will use the situation to establish you, to make you more solid and secure.

d. **God uses** your trials and sufferings to *strengthen* you (1 Pe.5:10). He will give you all the strength necessary to overcome the trials and sufferings of life. Never forget that it is only God Himself who can give you such enormous strength. And He will, if you will only draw near Him, trusting and obeying Him and crying out for help when the trials of life confront you.

e. **God Himself will** *settle you* (1 Pe.5:10). Used here, *settle* means to secure as in a foundation, to anchor you securely. God is able to make you secure through all the sufferings of life. He is able to settle and secure you. He will calm your anxiety and uneasiness and give you peace in the midst of the storms. God can settle you and place you on a firm foundation, but once again, you must trust and draw near Him and ask for His help.

> **For we do not have a high priest who is unable to sympathize with our weaknesses, but we have one who has been tempted in every way, just as we are—yet was without sin. Let us then approach the throne of grace with confidence, so that we may receive mercy and find grace to help us in our time of need (He.4:15-16, NASB).**

6. *You Should Learn from Other Believers Who Persevered Through Suffering and Severe Trials.*

> **For examples of patience in suffering, dear brothers and sisters, look at the prophets who spoke in the name of the Lord. We give great honor to those who endure under suffering. For instance, you know about Job, a man of great endurance. You can see how the Lord was kind to him at the end, for the Lord is full of tenderness and mercy (Jas.5:10-11, NLT).**

What an encouragement! Look at the prophets. Look at those who have gone before you—men and women who believed God. They placed their hope in God and bore strong witness for Him. They faced all kinds of trials, but they patiently endured through them all. Look at the prophets, and you will have a great example to follow in patient endurance. As *Hebrews* says:

> **"[They suffered] cruel mockings and scourgings, yea...[chains] and imprisonment: they were stoned, they were sawn asunder, were tempted, were slain with the sword: they wandered about in sheepskins and goatskins; being destitute, afflicted, tormented; (of whom the world was not worthy:) they wandered in deserts, and in mountains, and in dens and caves of the earth" (He.11:36-38, KJV).**

The prophets patiently endured all the trials and sufferings of life. They refused to give in or even to question and grumble against God. To the contrary, they continued to proclaim the salvation and hope of God for the world, continued to believe and to speak up for God despite the terrible trials that swarmed in upon them. As you are going through or facing affliction, remember the prophets and all they endured. Use them as an example of patience. Endure and be as steadfast as they were in their afflictions.

Also consider Job, the great Old Testament figure known for his patience. Few people, if any, have ever borne as much suffering in life as Job did. He first suffered utter bankruptcy—the loss of all his wealth, property, livestock, and employees. Then, in the severest blow of all, he lost all ten of his sons and daughters in a natural disaster. In addition to all this, he was afflicted with a horrible disease that was thought to be terminal. Lastly, and in some ways the most tragic, his wife opposed him because he refused to complain and curse God for destroying their lives.

Yet despite the horrible tragedies that struck Job—all on the very same day—Job never gave up under the weight of the trials. He never forsook the LORD, never turned away from his faith in God. He did not understand all that was happening to him, but he refused to turn against God. He patiently endured. As difficult as it was, Job pressed on and persevered through all the trials, and he ultimately overcame them all in the name of the LORD.

> **"Though he slay me, yet will I trust in him" (Jb.13:15, KJV).**

Job kept his eyes fixed upon the end, that is, upon the LORD and the great hope of the LORD (Jb.14:14-17). As a result of Job's faithfulness, the LORD carried him through all the trials. Job was blessed with the very presence of God Himself, with the compassion and mercy of God. Job endured, and, because he did, God blessed and rewarded him tremendously (Jb.42:10-17).

You, too, are to bear the afflictions and trials in your life by focusing your eyes on the end, that is, upon the coming again of the Lord Jesus Christ. As you do, the compassion and mercy of God will flow upon you. God will deliver you with His very own presence. He will deliver you through all the trials and sufferings of life, giving you the most victorious life imaginable, both now and eternally.

7. *You Should Focus on the Endurance of Jesus Christ When Trouble and Afflictions Strike You.*

> **Consider him who endured such opposition from sinful men, so that you will not grow weary and lose heart. In your struggle against sin, you have not yet resisted to the point of shedding your blood (He.12:3-4, NIV).**

When you think about your sufferings and weigh them against the sufferings of Jesus Christ, it is rather humbling. At the same time, it should encourage you to endure whatever threatens you. Christ bore so much more than you will ever have to endure. Let any person compare his or her own situation with the following list, and remember that Jesus bore *all of this*:

- being born to an unwed mother (Mt.1:18-19)
- being born in a stable, the worst of conditions (Lu.2:7)
- being born to poor parents (Lu.2:24)
- having his life threatened by government authorities when He was only a baby (Mt.2:13f)
- being the cause of unimaginable sorrow (Mt.2:16f)
- having to be moved and shifted around as a baby (Mt.2:13f)
- being reared in a despicable place, Nazareth (Lu.2:39)
- having His father die during His youth (Mt.13:53-58)
- having to support His mother, brothers, and sisters as a very young man (Mt.13:53-58)
- having no home as an adult, not even a place to lay His head (Mt.8:20; Lu.9:58)
- being hated and opposed by some people, in particular, religionists (Mk.14:1-2)

- being charged with insanity (Mk.3:21)
- being charged with demon possession (Mk.3:22)
- being opposed by His own family (Mk.3:31-32)
- being rejected, hated, and opposed by audiences to whom He spoke (Mt.13:53-58; Lu.4:28-29)
- being betrayed by a close friend (Mk.14:10-11, 18)
- being left alone, rejected, and forsaken by all His friends (Mk.14:50)
- being tried before the high court of the land on the charge of treason (Jn.18:33)
- being executed by crucifixion, one of the worst possible forms of death (Jn.19:16f)
- bearing the sins of the whole world (1 Pe.2:24)
- being separated from God (Mk.15:34)

Note why you should compare your sufferings with those of Christ: it keeps you from becoming *weary*, from *fainting* and losing heart, from becoming discouraged and dejected. Focusing upon the endurance of Christ will help keep you from drawing back and giving up.

You are to stand firm in the face of trials and temptations even to the point of blood. This is the picture of Christ's ordeal in Gethsemane and upon the cross. In Gethsemane, Christ struggled against the temptation to choose some other way other than the cross, but He endured to the point of sweating drops of blood. On the cross, Christ withstood the trial and suffering to the point of shedding His blood (Mt.26:36-46; Mk.14:32-42; Lu.22:39-53). The point is striking! You, too, must stand strong and refuse to give up under the weight of trials and suffering...

- to the point of sweating blood if necessary
- to the point of death, dying as a martyr if necessary

One of the ways to gain victory over the trials and sufferings of this life is to focus upon the endurance of Jesus Christ. The example of Christ is an encouragement to stand firm against whatever strikes you—even the most severe circumstances and extreme problems imaginable.

8. *You Should Know Why God Comforts You in Your Afflictions: That You Might Be a Testimony—a Comforter—to Other Sufferers.*

Praise be to the God and Father of our Lord Jesus Christ, the Father of compassion and the God of all comfort, who comforts us in all our troubles, so that we can comfort those in any

trouble with the comfort we ourselves have received from God (2 Co.1:3-4, NIV).

God is the Father of compassion and the God of all comfort. To be *compassionate* means to feel sympathy or pity for someone; to have a desire to alleviate or take away a person's pain or problem. It means that you look upon people in need and long to comfort and reach out to help them. Note that God is the *Father* of mercies. His very nature and behavior toward you is that of a Father. He is your Father, a Father who is compassionate and who showers His loving kindness and mercy upon you.

To *comfort* means to be by the side of another; to relieve and support; to console and encourage. But there is always an underlying meaning to the word: the idea of strength. True comfort consoles and relieves you, but it strengthens at the same time. It encourages you to go out and face all the afflictions and trials of this life.

God comforts you so that you might be a testimony to other sufferers. The use of the word *trouble* in these verses is the picture of a beast of burden being crushed beneath a load that is obviously too heavy. It is also the picture of a person with a heavy weight placed on his or her heart—a weight so substantial that it presses and crushes to the point of death.

Note the words "us" and "ours." Paul is *not only talking* about his own trials and sufferings, but about ours as well. God comforts you—you and the rest of us who truly believe in Christ. God does not have favorites; His compassion and comfort are for everyone. And note: He comforts you in *all your troubles,* not in just a few of your trials and afflictions. You do not have to bear a single trial or moment of suffering by yourself. Your Father—the Sovereign LORD and Majesty of the universe who controls all—is not off in the distance someplace, far removed from you. His Spirit, the precious Holy Spirit, is right here with you. He is ready to comfort you in all your suffering. And God's purpose in comforting you is to make you a testimony to others.

- God comforts you so that you can comfort others.
- God carries you through trials so that you can carry others through trials.
- God strengthens you so that you can strengthen others.
- God helps you so that you can help others.
- God encourages you so that you can encourage others.

This is one of the major reasons why God allows you to suffer and why He comforts you in your afflictions: that you might be a strong testimony and a comfort to other sufferers.

9. *You Should Remember That God Will Rescue You from Death Itself and Transfer You into His Heavenly Kingdom.*

> **The Lord will rescue me from every evil attack and will bring me safely to his heavenly kingdom. To him be glory for ever and ever. Amen (2 Ti.4:18, NIV).**

When the Apostle Paul wrote his young disciple Timothy, the situation seemed bleak. Paul had been arrested, imprisoned, and condemned to death on false charges. Both the civil and religious leaders were set on stamping out Christ and His church. Paul was condemned to death by the voices of the world. But note this amazing truth: although the authorities would kill Paul, he would not experience death. Paul proclaimed that he was going to his *coronation*. The Lord Jesus Christ was going to transfer him into the heavenly kingdom of God, the kingdom that is gloriously perfect and that lasts forever. Paul had only one final statement about the matter: "To Christ be glory forever and ever."

The picture of God's transferring Paul right through this world into the next world is both mystifying and exciting! It is a picture of unbroken time. God preserved Paul right through time into eternity. In one moment, Paul was living in this world, conscious and aware; within the same moment, in a split second, he was transported into God's heavenly kingdom. That one moment of time happened quicker than the blinking of an eye (11/100 of a second).

Just imagine! There was no loss of consciousness, no experience or awareness of death. One moment Paul was a citizen of this world, and within the same moment he stood before the Lord as a citizen of His kingdom (2 Co.5:6-8). It is a beautiful picture of the believer's never having to taste or experience death (Col.3:1-4; He.2:9; 2 Co.5:5-8).

No matter what trials or afflictions you have to face, even death, God is going to rescue you. He will deliver you through all the evil and suffering of this world. God is going to transfer you into His heavenly kingdom quicker than the eye can blink. As a true believer, you will ultimately be victorious over all the trials and sufferings of this life—even over death itself. This is God's wonderful promise. Focus on this truth, and it will help you walk through the hardships and troubles of this life.

10. *You Should Keep Your Eyes Fixed on the Hope of Eternal Glory: This Empowers You to Face the Trials of Life.*

> **For our light and momentary troubles are achieving for us an eternal glory that far outweighs them all. So we fix our eyes not on what is seen, but on what is unseen. For what is seen is temporary, but what is unseen is eternal (2 Co.4:17-18, NIV).**

Your trouble and afflictions are light when compared to the glory you will receive in heaven: "an eternal glory that far outweighs them all." Every believer should keep this picture in mind. Visualize a set of scales sitting before you. You balance your afflictions on one end and the eternal glory you are to receive on the other end. The afflictions may be severe and heavy and even constant, but when you place the eternal glory you are to receive on the scales, the afflictions become light. It is as though they weigh nothing.

In light of the severe persecution some believers endure, how could this be possible? Remember, in heaven there will be no more tears, no death, no sorrow, no crying, no pain. All of these things will be gone (Re.21:4). Everything in heaven will be perfected, beautiful, and eternal. With this in mind, you should not focus your eyes on the physical and temporal, but on the spiritual and eternal. You should fix your attention on the goal of spending eternity with God in the new heavens and earth (2 Pe.3:10-13). Instead of looking at the things that are seen (the physical and corruptible), concentrate on those things that are not seen (the spiritual and incorruptible). The reason is strikingly clear: the things that are seen are temporary (worldly, fading, fleeting), but the things that are not seen are eternal (endless, immortal, glorious). Keep your eyes focused on the hope of eternal glory. It will make you stronger and more able to walk victoriously through all of life's trials and sufferings. (See chapter 10 for a complete list of rewards.)

B. You and Persecution

1. *You Need to Be Aware of This Fact: As a Follower of Christ, You Will Be Persecuted.*

> **"Behold, I send you out as sheep in the midst of wolves. Therefore be wise as serpents and harmless as doves. But beware of men, for they will deliver you up to councils and scourge you in their synagogues. You will be brought before governors and kings for My sake, as a testimony to them and to the Gentiles. But when they deliver you up, do not worry about how or what you should speak. For it will be given to you in that hour what you should speak; for it is not you who speak, but the Spirit of your Father who speaks in you. Now brother will deliver up brother to death, and a father *his* child; and children will rise up against parents and cause them to be put to death. And you will be hated by all for My name's sake. But he who endures to the end will be saved. When they persecute you in this city, flee to another. (Mt.10:16-23[a], NKJV).**
>
> **Yes, and all who desire to live godly in Christ Jesus will suffer persecution (2 Ti.3:12, NKJV).**

When you receive Christ as Savior and Lord, you become a sheep in the midst of wolves—a world of unbelievers. You can expect to be persecuted, sometimes severely. This is Christ's own statement, so you must listen and stay alert. Within the world, some people will be like wolves. They *will* oppose the gospel of Christ and His Holy Word and reject His demand for righteousness. Consequently, as a true believer, you will be looked at scornfully and suffer some degree of abuse, ridicule, and isolation, perhaps even rejection. How can you prepare for persecution? Christ encourages you to do seven things:

a. **You need to be** as wise as serpents and as harmless as doves (Mt.10:16). To be as *wise as serpents* means to maneuver quietly with caution and with intelligence—with a planned strategy; to be quick in seeing danger and quick to escape from it. In other words, it means to be a person of vision and initiative. You need to know what your resources are, when to strike, and when to withdraw. And you need to strike with your message when opportunity arises.

   All the while you are also to be like a dove: to be as gentle and harmless as a dove; to cause no damage; to be known as a symbol of peace.

b. **You need to be** on guard with people at all times (Mt.10:17-18). There are some people in this world who will persecute you, and you do not always know who they are. Christ warns about three specific classes of persecutors.

- People (men and women) just like yourself will persecute you. When people do not like something, they can turn into vicious creatures. Their dark and evil qualities can begin to manifest themselves. Sadly, they become two-faced and devious, plotting and scheming behind your back. Sometimes they even attempt to hurt or destroy you by ruining your reputation or by force. The attack may be over a job, a promotion, a specific action, a belief, or anything else they oppose. Therefore, you must always be on guard with everyone.
- Religionists—people in the synagogues, temples, and churches—may persecute you. The church is full of people who have not really committed their lives to God. They do not know Him personally, not in a real way. So, if you truly live and take a stand for God and His mission of reaching the world, you may be persecuted by those within the church who do not understand God or His mission. They can quickly become hypocritical, speaking evil against you, gossiping, slandering, reviling, and insulting you. They might also scold, mock, and attack you. Any or all of this might be done to try to destroy your reputation and life, depending on the society in which you live. The great tragedy is that persecution can and too often does take place within the walls of God's house. Religionists can be so deceived that they think they do God a service by persecuting the believer (Jn.16:2).
- Civil authorities within the state may persecute you. Within every generation, believers all over the world are dragged before state authorities and persecuted. Always be alert to the laws and threats of civil authorities against Christ and His Holy Word.

c. **You need to keep** in mind why God allows you to be persecuted: that you might be a testimony to the persecutors (Mt.10:18). There is no greater testimony for Christ than your standing up for Him in the face of persecution (see Ac.24:1f; 25:1f; 25:13f; 26:1f).

- You demonstrate the truth of the gospel. The persecutor clearly sees the message of love and salvation in your life.

- ➢ You give the Holy Spirit a unique opportunity to reach those standing by with the truth of the gospel.
- ➢ You are a testimony against the persecutors. Their abuse of you exposes their hearts, how deeply wickedness and evil are rooted in their hearts. Their abuse will stand as a testimony against them in the day of judgment.

d. **You should not** worry about a defense when people are threatening you (Mt.10:19-20). You will never be left alone to defend yourself against persecution. God promises to give you exactly what you need to say. In fact, God's Spirit will speak through you and God Himself promises to stand with you. He will give the answer you need in the very hour it is to be spoken.

e. **You need to be aware** that families will be divided (Mt.10:21). A person's own family—either individuals or the family as a unit—can become your greatest persecutor. Why? There are three reasons:

- ➢ Because the family may live a worldly life and cannot understand your godly life. The family subsequently opposes a family member who ceases to participate in certain functions and traditions (2 Co.6:17-18; 1 Jn.2:15-16).
- ➢ Because of the family's orthodox religion or church. The converted family member may wish to change religions or churches. The family opposes such a move.
- ➢ Because of the believer's commitment to Christ. You should become a dynamic witness to your own family, sharing the Lord's graciousness and love with them. Such an active witness is sometimes an embarrassment to a family.

f. **You must endure** to the end (Mt.10:22). Again, you should expect persecution. Some of the world will oppose you. Why? "For My name's sake." As a genuine believer, you are a living witness to the name of Christ, who is our example of perfect righteousness and supreme self-denial. The world and its people oppose any lifestyle that demands self-denial. Therefore, when you endure, you give strong evidence of your salvation. Remember several facts:

- ➢ There is an end to persecution. It is only temporary; it will not last.
- ➢ Enduring persecution is possible. You can persevere. God will bear you up through it all.

- Deliverance awaits the person who endures. A life of glory and reward is promised.

You should always remember that persecutors are just people. They can oppose and cause trouble; they can even kill the body. But never forget...

- Persecutors cannot kill your soul.
- Your body will die one day anyway. Why sacrifice eternity for what amounts to just a little more time here on earth?
- The persecutors *are mere people* who will die themselves, and then they will face the eternal judgment of God (He.9:27; see Is.51:12). You and your faith will be vindicated.

g. **You need to flee** persecution (Mt.10:23a). There are at least three reasons why Christ instructs you to flee.

- Christ cares for you, for your safety.

> **Cast all your anxiety on him because he cares for you (1 Pe.5:7, NIV).**

- Christ wants other people to observe the righteousness of your life and to hear the gospel. Some are receptive. It is better to minister to those who are receptive than to cast your pearls before swine (Mt.7:6). Christ is saying that you are not to be foolish and jeopardize your life by trying to share the gospel (pearls) with hypocrites and mockers who will not receive you or listen to the Word of God. They will only hurt you and abuse the glorious message of the gospel, so flee as quickly as you can.
- Christ wants you to bear a strong witness against all who reject Him. They need to know just how terrible their sin and shame is, how cold and hard, how bitter and hostile they are against God. If they can see their true hearts in this way, perhaps they will surrender to God and His love. If not, then their persecution of you will stand against them in the terrible day of judgment.

2. *You Must Stand Up Under the Fiery Trial of Persecution.*

> **Dear friends, do not be surprised at the painful trial you are suffering, as though something strange were happening to you. But rejoice that you participate in the sufferings of Christ, so that you may be overjoyed when his**

glory is revealed. If you are insulted because of the name of Christ, you are blessed, for the Spirit of glory and of God rests on you. If you suffer, it should not be as a murderer or thief or any other kind of criminal, or even as a meddler. However, if you suffer as a Christian, do not be ashamed, but praise God that you bear that name. For it is time for judgment to begin with the family of God; and if it begins with us, what will the outcome be for those who do not obey the gospel of God? And, "If it is hard for the righteous to be saved, what will become of the ungodly and the sinner?" So then, those who suffer according to God's will should commit themselves to their faithful Creator and continue to do good (1 Pe.4:12-19, NIV).

Persecution is a strange thing. Why would God ever allow a follower of His to suffer persecution, especially when it can be so fiery, so painful? The purpose of this passage is to address the question of persecution, the intense and traumatic trials that you as a believer sometimes have to endure.

a. **First, do not be** surprised when you are persecuted and have to bear affliction (v.12). God allows your painful trial for one very basic reason: to test and prove your faith. This means at least four things.

- Persecution measures how strong your faith in Christ really is. Your faith can be measured by how much you are willing to sacrifice and bear for Christ.
- Persecution proves your trust in God. The more you suffer for Christ, the more you draw near to God and plead for His help and strength. This, of course, teaches you to trust and depend upon Him more and more.
- Persecution strengthens your endurance. The more you are tried and persecuted, the more you have to endure; and the more you endure, the more you are *able to* endure.
- Persecution attracts others to Christ. When you suffer and are persecuted, others can see the strength of Christ in you. They see that your faith in Christ is a living reality, that you are actually suffering for the hope of salvation and eternal life. As a result, the Holy Spirit uses your suffering to speak to the hearts of both the persecutors and the observers. He convicts them, and some eventually turn to Christ. Your faith is proven to be true, and it bears fruit.

b. **Second, rejoice** in persecution (v.13). This is difficult to do, for no person likes to suffer abuse or pain of any sort. This is especially true when it is inflicted by family, friends, or co-workers. No one likes to be isolated, ridiculed, bypassed, scorned, imprisoned, or called upon to face death. Hence, it is difficult to rejoice in persecution. But Scripture indicates there is a way: by keeping your eyes and mind upon two things.

- When you suffer, you are sharing in Christ's sufferings. Christ was rejected by people because He lived and proclaimed the truth of God's righteousness and salvation. So, when you suffer for following Christ—for living righteously and bearing witness to God's salvation—you are suffering for the same reason that Christ suffered. You are actually *sharing* in the sufferings of Christ Himself! You become identified with Christ, associated with Him in the *deepest devotion* possible, the sacrifice of yourself for the righteousness of God and His glorious salvation. To be identified in such a way with Christ, the very Son of God Himself, is the height of privileges, a great reason for joy and rejoicing.
- When Christ returns in glory, you will be greatly rewarded for your suffering. This is exactly what Scripture declares time and again.

The Spirit Himself testifies with our spirit that we are children of God, and if children, heirs also, heirs of God and fellow heirs with Christ, if indeed we suffer with *Him* so that we may also be glorified with *Him* (Ro.8:16-17, NASB).

For our light and momentary troubles are achieving for us an eternal glory that far outweighs them all (2 Co.4:17, NIV).

He [Moses] thought it was better to suffer for the sake of Christ than to own the treasures of Egypt, for he was looking ahead to his great reward (He.11:26, NLT).

c. **Third, know** that *God's Spirit* and the *glow of God's glory* rest upon you when you are persecuted (v.14). You are given a special closeness, a oneness with Christ that is beyond imagination—totally unexplainable (Ac.7:54-60). The Holy Spirit infuses you with a deep, intense consciousness of the Lord's presence. In fact, the Holy Spirit actually causes a *glow of God's glory* to shine in and through your body! It is the same glory that Stephen experienced when he was martyred (Ac.7:55-56). It is *an anointing, a consciousness* so deep that it cannot be experienced apart from some severe experience of suffering.

d. **Fourth, do not bring** suffering and persecution upon yourself by breaking a law or doing some evil deed (v.15). If you violate the laws of God or of your nation and harm others, then you deserve to suffer. This is not suffering for Christ's name. Suffering for Christ means that you are persecuted because you are living for Christ and proclaiming His glorious salvation.

e. **Fifth, do not be** ashamed to suffer for being a Christian (v.16). The name *Christian* was given to the early believers by unbelievers. It was a name of derision and ridicule. If you are being scorned, mocked, cursed, or persecuted because you are a Christian, do not be ashamed. No believer should ever be ashamed of the fact that he or she is a Christian, for Christ has given us the wonderful hope of salvation and glory. Take a stand for Christ and stand firm.

f. **Sixth, accept** persecution as the purifying judgment of God (vv.17-18). This does not mean that all persecution is God's judgment on believers, but that God *uses* all persecution to further purify believers. However, as Scripture says, judgment must begin at the *house or church of God.* What does this mean?

   ➢ When things are going well, some believers tend to feel more secure in themselves and are more inclined to partake of the bright lights, sinful pleasures, and covetous ways of the world.
   ➢ When things are going well, believers sometimes fail to focus upon Christ as they should. They fail to pray and worship, fellowship and commune with Him. Their focus shifts to themselves and they gradually become contaminated by the things of the world.

When either of the above happens, God has to do something to awaken and stir us up. He often uses persecution to arouse us to repent. God uses the persecution as a means of judgment, as a means of arousing us to clean up our lives and draw closer to Him.

Think about it: When you are persecuted, to whom can you turn? There is only one sure *deliverer,* and that is God. Therefore, persecution causes you to flee to God for deliverance and protection; it causes you to turn your attention from self and the world to focus more fully upon God.

- You forget self and self-sufficiency and you acknowledge that you are totally dependent upon God.
- You clean up your life. You turn away from the lures of worldliness and focus upon God. You fellowship and commune with Him more and more.

Remember that God uses persecution as a purifying judgment, as a means of stirring us to evaluate our lives and to draw closer and closer to Him. So stand fast against persecution. Know that God wants to use it to draw you closer and closer to Christ.

g. **Seventh, keep** on doing good and commit yourself to God (v.19). Note that your suffering is in *the will of God*. God is either glorifying the name of Christ by drawing unbelievers to Himself or purifying your life by the suffering. Therefore, do two things:

- keep on doing good.
- *commit* the keeping of your soul to God.

The word *commit* means to deposit, to entrust. It is a picture of putting money into the hands of a trusted banker or friend. You need to commit or entrust yourself into God's care. God can be trusted; He will not fail you. He will either deliver you *through* the persecution or else take you on home to be with Christ forever.

God will save your soul. You can trust Him far more than any friend on earth. God never fails. He is your faithful Creator who has created you to be with Him eternally. And God's plan will not be defeated. If you commit your soul to Him, no matter what people may do to you, God will save you. He will fulfill His plan and purpose in your life—both now and eternally.

3. *You Are Not to Fear Persecutors but Rather Fear God.*

> **And do not fear those who kill the body but cannot kill the soul. But rather fear Him who is able to destroy both soul and body in hell. Are not two sparrows sold for a copper coin? And not one of them falls to the ground apart from your Father's will. But the very hairs of your head are all numbered. Do not fear therefore; you are of more value than many sparrows. "Therefore whoever confesses Me before men,**

him I will also confess before My Father who is in heaven. But whoever denies Me before men, him I will also deny before My Father who is in heaven (Mt.10:28-33, NKJV).

a. **You are not** to fear mockers or persecutors because they can kill only the body, not the soul (v.28). Their power is limited, and they can go no further. They cannot touch your true being, not your soul or spirit. Neither can they keep you out of heaven. And, remember, "to be with Christ...is far better" (Ph.1:23; 3:20-21).

   Never forget, persecutors can only separate you from this world, not from life. You already have eternal life; death will never be a part of your experience, not if you are a genuine believer (He.2:9). You have already passed from death to life and are in the process of living forever (Jn.5:24). When death confronts you—quicker than the eye can blink—you will be transferred from this world into the next, the heavenly or spiritual dimension of being, where you will live eternally.

b. **You are not** to fear mockers and persecutors because God cares for you (vv.29-31). Christ is clear: if the God of all creation cares for the common sparrow, how much more He cares for you! He cares for every event, every concern, even the most minute detail in your life. In light of this, there is no need for you to fear when enemies or persecutors confront you. Just cast your anxiety and welfare upon God, because God truly cares for you (1 Pe.5:7).

c. **You must be** loyal to Christ: confess Him before people. Admit you are a follower of Christ (vv.32-33). And Christ is talking about confessing Him in the most difficult moment imaginable—while being persecuted. You are sometimes called upon to confess Christ by those who reproach, sneer, mock, curse, question, slander, abuse, and avoid you because of your witness for Christ. Do not be ashamed of Christ or of His Holy Word. If you confess Him, He gives you a most wonderful promise: He will confess that He knows you in the glorious day of redemption. He will accept you into His eternal kingdom.

CHAPTER 8

WHAT YOUR DUTY IS TO THE CHURCH

Contents

CHAPTER 8

WHAT YOUR DUTY IS TO THE CHURCH

A. YOUR DUTY TO UNDERSTAND WHO AND WHAT THE CHURCH IS

1. You Need to Understand That the Church Is Built Upon This One Truth: Jesus Is the Christ, the Son of the Living God.

> **When Jesus came to the region of Caesarea Philippi, he asked his disciples, "Who do people say the Son of Man is?" They replied, "Some say John the Baptist; others say Elijah; and still others, Jeremiah or one of the prophets." "But what about you?" he asked. "Who do you say I am?" Simon Peter answered, "You are the Christ, the Son of the living God." Jesus replied, "Blessed are you, Simon son of Jonah, for this was not revealed to you by man, but by my Father in heaven. And I tell you that you are Peter, and on this rock I will build my church, and the gates of Hades [hell] will not overcome it (Mt.16:13-18, NIV).**

Jesus was facing imminent death, so His time on earth was very limited. Therefore, He had much to teach and reveal to His disciples. It was time for them to learn that He was *building a church*—an assembly of people who believed and confessed Him to be the true Messiah, the promised Savior of the world. The present passage contains one of the most dramatic revelations ever made. It also includes one of the most demanding questions ever asked. Demanding because it forces a person to confess either that Jesus is the Son of God or that He is not. And such a confession demands that a person commit his or her life to Christ. In addition, your confession and commitment to Christ determines where you will spend eternity—with God in heaven or apart from God in a place called hell. And there is only one answer to the question that can qualify you for heaven.

a. **Listen to the question** Jesus asked: "Who do people say the Son of Man is?" (vv.13-14). There were and still are false confessions regarding Christ. Popular opinions show that Christ was highly esteemed and greatly respected. He was considered one of the greatest men who had ever lived. However, these beliefs were dangerous because they contained only *half truths*. The result was tragic; many people were deceived and misled by them. Sadly, the same false confessions about Christ exist in every generation.

- There are some people who think that Jesus is a man just like John the Baptist—a great man of righteousness who was martyred for His faith. As such, He leaves us a great example of how to live and stand up for what we believe.
- There are other people who think that Jesus is like Elijah, only one of many great teachers and prophets of history.
- There are still others who think that Jesus is a great man like Jeremiah, who revealed some important things to us about God and religion. Hence, Jesus Christ can make a significant contribution to people in their search for God.
- Then there are others who think that Jesus was a great man and prophet sent only to the people (Jews) of His day. And just as we learn from all great men of history, we can learn some important lessons by studying the life of Jesus Christ.

> **He came into the very world he created, but the world didn't recognize him. He came to his own people, and even they rejected him (Jn.1:10-11, NLT).**

The world is not unanimous in its opinion of Christ. Consider this fact for a moment: if Jesus Christ is not the Son of God, then He is neither a good nor a great man. He is the worst deceiver and biggest liar ever to arrive on the world scene. Why? Because He claimed to be the Son of God and the promised Savior of the world, and He built His following on that claim. If Jesus Christ is not the Son of God, the true Messiah, then every true follower of His is living in a *dream world* of *false hope,* and death will be the end of life. If there is any possibility whatsoever that Christ could not be the Son of God, then He is not worth following.

However, anyone who studies the record of Jesus Christ knows what the facts show: Christ was far from a liar or deceiver. He was, in fact, a very upright and moral man, a person with an unblemished character. For this reason, you can trust the claims of Jesus Christ. Furthermore, Scripture emphatically declares that Jesus Christ is the Messiah, the Son of the living God. He is precisely who He claimed to be.

b. **Jesus asked a second question,** and He asked this question much more emphatically: "But what about you, who do you say I am?" Without hesitation, Peter blurted out, "You are the Christ, the Son of the living God"—a simple but momentous confession arising from a deep personal conviction (vv.15-16). Peter was thoroughly convinced that Jesus Christ is the Savior of the world.

It is this same confession that saves your soul and lays the foundation for the church. The very life and survival of your soul and of the church as a whole rests upon this simple, yet profound, conviction.

- Jesus is the *Christ,* the Messiah, the anointed One of God.
- Jesus is both the *Son of God* and fully God. He is of the same being, the same essence as God. Jesus Christ is One with the Father, possessing the very same nature of perfection.
- Jesus is the *Son of the Living God*. He is the very source and being of life. He possesses the energy and power of life within Himself (Jn.5:26; 17:2-3; 1 Th.1:9).

Obviously, Peter did not understand all that was involved in Christ's being the Son of God (the cross and resurrection had not yet taken place). But his confession was made in simple trust. It arose from a heart that was truly convinced that Jesus is the Christ, the promised Messiah, the Son of the living God. Never forget, it is simple trust that God desires and longs for—nothing more and nothing less. Peter was simply confessing step by step, "I believe you are more than a mere man. I believe you are the true Messiah, the Son of God who was sent by God to fulfill all that the prophets foretold."

The question is personal: "What about you?...Whom do you say I am?" You have to answer, and your eternal destiny depends upon your response, the response of both your word and your life.

c. **Peter's confession** that Jesus is the Christ is the foundation of the church (vv.17-18). Christ replied, "You are Peter and on this rock [petra] I will build my church." This was a tremendous compliment to Peter, but what did Jesus mean? Probably this: the rock was both *Peter himself and his confession,* not just one or the other. The rock was *both,* but in a very special sense.

First, Peter himself was the rock in that he was the first person to *fully* grasp who Jesus really was. He was the first to confess with *full* understanding that Jesus is the Christ (Messiah), the Son of the living God. Others had made similar confessions before (Jn.1:41, 45, 49; 6:69), but they had not yet been with Jesus long enough to *fully* grasp what being *the Son of God* really meant. Their confessions had been those resulting from a simple child-like faith. But now Peter understood more fully; he *fully* grasped who Jesus is. Therefore, he became the first man, the first rock, the foundation *upon* which the church and all other *living stones*, (believers) were to be built (1 Pe.2:5).

Great weight is given to this meaning in Ep.2:20. The apostles and prophets are said to be part of the *foundation* of the church upon which all future believers or *living stones* are built. But always remember that Jesus Christ is the *chief cornerstone*. It is Christ's power and work that establishes the church (1 Co.3:11; 1 Pe.2:4-8).

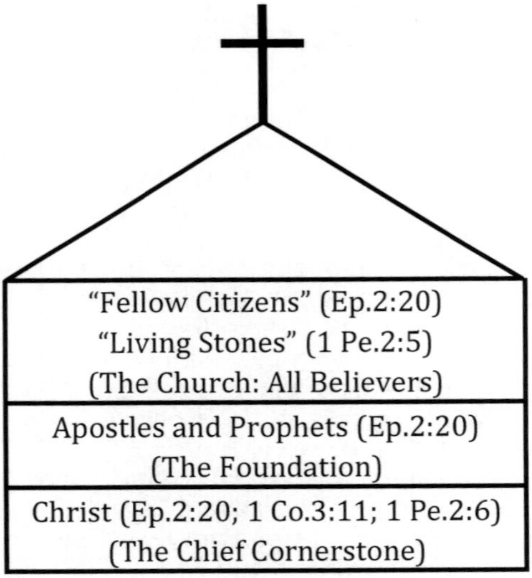

Peter was also the one who launched and laid the foundation of the church. He was the early leader of the church who stood forth at Pentecost when three thousand souls were saved (Ac.2:41), and at Caesarea when the door of salvation was opened to the Gentiles (Ac.10:1f). He was also the rock and the foundation in that he was the first man who ever opened the doors of the church to both Jew and Gentile.

Second, Peter's confession (that Christ is the Son of God) was the rock upon which the church was built. Christ said, "You are Peter, and on this rock [the great truth of your confession] I will build my church" (Mt.16:18). There is no question that the church is built upon Christ, and that He is the builder of the church as well as the power behind its structure (1 Co.3:11). It is He who takes every believer, all the *living stones*, and places them into the structure of His church (1 Pe.2:4-8). The church *depends* upon Christ, not upon Peter nor any other person or combination of people. The church was first called together by Peter after Pentecost; but it is *built, held up, and held together* by Christ, the Chief Cornerstone. Note the facts revealed by Christ:

- Fact 1: "My church." The church is Christ's, not man's.
- Fact 2: "I will build." Christ builds the church.
- Fact 3: "The gates of hell shall not prevail." Christ Himself protects the church.

d. The word *church* (ekklesia) means to call out a gathering, an assembly. There is no spiritual significance ascribed to the word itself (Ac.19:32, 39, 41). What is the difference, then, between secular gatherings and the church of God?

- It is God who calls together and gathers His church. His church is the body of people called out from the world by Him. They are His body of people, a people set apart by Him to form the church of the living God.
- God dwells within the very presence of believers when they gather together (1 Co.3:16-17).
- God's people gather and meet together for the purpose of worship, praise, and mission. God is the object of worship and praise and His mission becomes the objective of the church. Or, put another way, God's church, the local assembly, gathers together to worship and to pool its resources in order to carry out the mission of Christ Himself. It should be noted that this is the first mention of the church in the New Testament (v.18).

2. *You Should Remember What the Church Is, the Seven Pictures God Uses to Describe His Church.*

Consequently, you are no longer foreigners and aliens, but fellow citizens with God's people

> **and members of God's household, built on the foundation of the apostles and prophets, with Christ Jesus himself as the chief cornerstone. In him the whole building is joined together and rises to become a holy temple in the Lord. And in him you too are being built together to become a dwelling in which God lives by his Spirit (Ep.2:19-22, NIV).**
>
> **Husbands, love your wives, just as Christ loved the church and gave himself up for her to make her holy, cleansing her by the washing with water through the word, and to present her to himself as a radiant church, without stain or wrinkle or any other blemish, but holy and blameless (Ep.5:25-27, NIV).**

This is an excellent description of the church. Seven pictures are given in these two Scripture passages.

a. **First, the church** is pictured as a *new nation or society* (Ep.2:19). Note the words *fellow citizens.* Before you accepted Christ, you were a foreigner and an alien. You were not a citizen of God's nation of people and did not obey God's laws. You had no relationship or fellowship with God, and no home or rights to citizenship in His kingdom and nation.

   But here is the glorious news: as a genuine believer, you are no longer a foreigner or an alien to God. Jesus Christ has made you acceptable to Him. You are now a *fellow citizen* with all of God's people. You now have a home and all the rights of citizenship in the nation being created by God, a nation of people who believe God with all of their hearts and obey Him. This new nation of people, true believers, will be the citizens who live in the new heavens and earth (2 Pe.3:10-13; Re.21:1; 21:27).

b. **Second, the church** is pictured as the *family of God*—"God's household" (Ep.2:19). Jesus Christ has brought you and all other believers into the family of God. This involves the wonderful privilege of adoption. You have been adopted as a true son or daughter of God. You now live in the same house with God and His family, and all the experiences of God's family are now available to you:

   - love
   - care
   - compassion
   - help
   - provision
   - protection
   - guidance
   - training
   - fellowship
   - friendship
   - spiritual bond and unity

At the same time, being a member of a household also includes responsibility and service. Every person in the family has duties to perform, some service to render for the sake of the family. You are responsible to love and help, provide and protect, guide and teach other members of God's family. You should do all the things mentioned above and everything else that will build up and strengthen the family of God.

c. **Third, the church** is pictured as *God's building* (Ep.2:20). Believers are pictured as the building stones being used to construct a building for God. Jesus Christ Himself is the *chief cornerstone*. The cornerstone is the first stone laid. All other stones are placed after it. It is the preeminent stone. So it is with Christ. He is *the first* of God's great movement in building the church.

You and other believers are the stones that are placed upon the cornerstone of Christ and held up by Him. As the chief cornerstone, Christ is the support and foundation of God's new building, the church. And Christ is the *only true foundation* upon which you can build your life (see pt.1,c, pp. 329-330 for more discussion).

Any life that is not built upon Christ will crumble in the day of God's judgment. And any church that removes Christ as the chief cornerstone of its structure will collapse. No Christ, no church. Christ holds everything within the church together. Thus, it is an absolute necessity that He and He alone be preached, taught, and lived.

Also remember that you and all other believers—the church—are built upon the foundation laid by the testimonies of the apostles and prophets. They served and lived with Christ and were taught by Him. It is their inspired record—the Word of God itself—that is the foundation upon which the church is built.

d. **Fourth, the church** is pictured as a body or a *growing organism* (Ep.2:21; 1 Co.12:12-31). The word *rises* in Greek actually means *grows* and conveys the idea of a living organism. Thus, the church is pictured as a union of various parts of a living being, of a growing dynamic body. This may seem strange to speak of a building in biological terms, a building that grows. The point is simply this: more and more parts (believers) are brought in and placed into the building as each day passes. The church—the body of true believers—grows and will continue to grow until the Lord Jesus Christ returns.

Peter also refers to the church as a living organism. He calls Jesus Christ the *living stone*. Christ is the *living stone* upon which all other believers are built up into a spiritual house. All believers have to be built upon Christ—the *living stone*—if they wish to live with God and have their spiritual sacrifices accepted by God.

> **And coming to Him as to a living stone which has been rejected by men, but is choice and precious in the sight of God, you also, as living stones, are being built up as a spiritual house for a holy priesthood, to offer up spiritual sacrifices acceptable to God through Jesus Christ (1 Pe.2:4-5, NASB).**

e. **Fifth, the church** is pictured as a *worldwide temple,* as the *universal church* (Ep.2:21). Note the words *whole building*. All believers make up the holy temple of God and are pictured as a building, a universal church being structured for God's presence. Each new believer and each new generation of believers are seen as being placed into God's universal structure. As the little chorus says, "Red and yellow, black and white, they are precious in His sight." All believers of every generation from across the world are being placed into God's universal temple. We, the church—all of us who have been truly saved throughout the generations—will be building stones. We will be the worshipers of God in the new universe when God makes the new heavens and earth (2 Pe.3:10-13; Re.21:1-27; 22:1ff).

It is key to understand, though, that each person is placed into the structure *only by Christ.* Only the person and the body of people who come to Christ as the chief cornerstone are fitted into the building. You must build upon the foundation laid by the apostles and the prophets, which is the foundation of Christ Himself. If you lay your life upon any other cornerstone or any other foundation, you are helping to construct some other kind of building, not God's building. You may follow your own strategy or even someone else's well-thought-out ideas, but it is not God's building that you are constructing. God's building is being structured upon Christ and Christ alone.

The gospel of Jesus Christ is open to all people everywhere. There is no place for division or prejudice, privilege or partiality, classes or caste systems in the temple or church of God. Every nation, even to the uttermost part of the earth, is to be given the privilege of hearing the gospel (good news) of Jesus Christ and the opportunity to become a part of God's universal temple or church (Mt.28:19-20).

f. **Sixth, the church** is pictured as a *local temple*, the *local church* (Ep.2:21). Note that Paul now uses the word "you," in referring to the Ephesian church. Each local church is pictured as a building structured for God's presence. And each member is pictured as being placed and fitted into the building (Ep.4:16; 1 Pe.2:5). The strength of each local church lies in the individual believer's (stone's) being placed into the building and fit by the Lord, holding up its load, and fulfilling its purpose in the structure.

Scripture teaches that the local church exists for the purpose of providing a dwelling or home for the presence of God's Spirit. The church is to allow the Spirit of God to live out His life through the ministry of the local body of believers. The Holy Spirit dwells within all believers to help them when they are...

- troubled or confused
- suffering or dying
- fearful or doubtful
- weary or complacent
- discouraged or dispirited
- witnessing
- teaching or preaching
- ministering

When believers assemble together, the Spirit of God dwells within the church. The Spirit stirs and encourages each member to worship and serve God faithfully and to conform the church to the image of God's will. The effectiveness of any local church depends upon how much it allows the Holy Spirit to dwell within and to control its body of believers.

Don't you realize that all of you together are the temple of God and that the Spirit of God lives in you? God will destroy anyone who destroys this temple. For God's temple is holy, and you are that temple (1 Co.3:16-17, NLT).

g. **Seventh, the church** is pictured as the bride of Christ (Ep.5:25-27). Christ loves the church with a perfect love, loves the church far more than any husband or wife could ever love the other. Just think! The relationship Christ wants with you is to be closer than that between husband and wife. For this reason, Christ calls the church *His bride.*

With the church as His bride, the Lord's purpose is to cleanse or sanctify it through the cleansing power of His Holy Word (Ep.5:25-26). To be sanctified means to be set apart. All believers are set apart to establish a very special relationship with God.

When Christ promises to receive us as we are—no matter what we have done—it is His Word (promise) that cleanses us from all past sinful behavior. And it is the promise, His Word, that continues to cleanse us. With believers as His bride, the Lord's purpose is...

- to make us (His bride) a glorious church, a church that has no spot or wrinkle or any such thing.
- to make sure the church is presented to Him holy and without blemish (v.27). He wants His dear bride kept pure and untouched by evil.

It is the sacrificial love of Christ that stirs us to keep ourselves holy and unblemished for Him. As true believers, we should long to be presented to Him as a glorious church, a bride that pleases and honors the Lord's wonderful name.

B. YOUR DUTY TO BE FAITHFUL TO THE CHURCH

1. *You Should Be Faithful to the Local Church—Faithful to Worship and Serve Together with Other Believers.*

> **And let us not neglect our meeting together, as some people do, but encourage one another, especially now that the day of his return is drawing near (He.10:25, NLT).**

You should not neglect meeting with other believers, not even for a brief time. You are to assemble together for five very specific purposes:

- for worship
- for prayer
- for the study of God's Word
- for ministry and witnessing
- for fellowship

Read the verse closely and it becomes clear that you are to assemble often and not forsake coming together. As genuine believers, you need one another—the presence, fellowship, strength, encouragement, care, and love of one another.

Sadly, some have forsaken the church, even as they did in the days of the early church. For this reason, you should encourage one another, especially since every passing day brings the day of the Lord's return a little closer. You also need to exhort unbelievers lest they miss the glorious return of Christ's coming and have to face His judgment.

However, in a society where Sunday is not always honored as the day of worship and people have to work on the Lord's Day, the church should arrange worship and Bible study meetings at other times for believers. This is a duty some churches have neglected—a responsibility that needs attention by church leaders.

William Barclay has an excellent application on this point that merits your attention as you encourage people to be faithful to the local church. He takes the three points from the scholar James Moffatt in the *International Critical Commentary*. He says there are three reasons that keep a person from worshipping with other Christian believers.

1) *"He may not go to Church because of fear. He may be ashamed to show his loyalty by being seen going to church. He may live or work among people who laugh at those who go to Church. He may have friends who have no use*

for that kind of thing, and he may fear their criticism and their contempt. He may try to be a secret disciple; but it has been well said that to be a secret disciple is impossible because either 'the discipleship kills the secrecy, or the secrecy kills the discipleship.' It would be well if we remembered that, apart from anything else, to go to Church is to demonstrate where our loyalty lies. Even if the sermon be poor and the worship tawdry, the Church still gives us the chance to show to men what side we are on.

2) *"He may not go because of fastidiousness. He may dislike the common people; he may shrink from contact with people who are 'not like himself.' There are churches, even in this country, which are as much clubs as they are churches. They may be in neighbourhoods where the social status has come down; and the members who have remained faithful to them would be as much embarrassed as delighted if the poor people and the slum-dwellers in the area came flooding in. We must never forget that there is no such thing as a 'common' man in the sight of God. It was for all men, not only for the respectable classes, that Christ died.*
3) *"He may not go because of conceit. Frankly, he may believe and state that he does not need the Church; that he is intellectually beyond the standard of preaching there. Social snobbery may be bad, spiritual and intellectual snobbery is worse. The wisest man is a fool in the sight of God; and the strongest man is weak in the moment of temptation. There is no man who can live the Christian life and neglect the fellowship of the church. If any man feels that he can do so let him remember that he comes to Church, not only to get, but to give. He ought to come not only to receive, but to make his own contribution to the life of the church. If he feels that the Church has faults, it is his duty to come in and to help to mend them."*[1]

God's instruction to you is very straightforward. You must not neglect meeting and worshipping together with other believers.

> **And he [Jesus] came to Nazareth, where he had been brought up: and, as his custom was, he went into the synagogue on the sabbath day (Lu.4:16, KJV).**

---

1 William Barclay. *The Letter to the Hebrews*, p.136f.

2. *You Should Worship God in Spirit and in Truth.*

> **God *is* a Spirit: and they [who] that worship him must worship *him* in spirit and in truth (Jn.4:24, KJV).**

God's nature is not physical or material substance like ours. God is Spirit, and He is present everywhere throughout the universe (omnipresent). This means that God is not limited by space or time. You can worship God anyplace and anytime. If you and your fellow believers do not have a church building in which to worship, you can worship God wherever you can gather together—by a river or in a field, in a hut, a house, or anywhere else. As Jesus said,

> **"For where two or three are gathered together in my name, there am I in the midst of them" (Mt.18:20, KJV).**

What is important is not *where* you worship God but *how* you worship Him. You are to worship God in spirit and in truth.

a. **To worship God** *in spirit* means that you approach God sincerely, with an open and honest heart. Do not just go through the motions of worship to please, impress, or seek the favor of others. Instead, truly submit to God and worship Him from the depths of your heart. Seek the most intimate communion and fellowship possible with God, trusting and resting in His acceptance, love, and care.

b. **To worship God** *in truth* means that you worship the LORD God Himself, the only true and living God. This means...

- ➢ that you approach God in the right way. And there is only one way, through God's Son, the Lord Jesus Christ.

> **Jesus saith unto him, I am the way, the truth, and the life: no man cometh unto the Father, but by me (Jn.14:6, KJV).**

- ➢ that you worship God whole-heartedly and truthfully, not half-heartedly, with a wandering mind and sleepy eyes. As the verse above says:

> **God *is* a Spirit: and they [who] worship him must worship *him* in spirit and in truth. (Jn.4:24, KJV).**

3. *You Should Understand That the Church Is God's House of Prayer.*

> **And He said to them, "It is written, '*My house shall be called a house of prayer*" but you have made it a '*den of thieves*' " (Mt.21:13, NKJV).**

The church is the temple of God, and it angers Christ to see His temple abused (1 Co.3:16-17). This fact is often de-emphasized or ignored by believers and overlooked by the world. But Christ declared that the church belongs to God no matter how people treat it. It is God's holy temple.

a. **Christ called** the church *God's house*. When a church is established by a group of people, Christ says that it becomes the place where God lives and dwells. However, considering that God is present everywhere, what could Christ have meant? Very simply, the church is a special place that has been *founded* and designated specifically for God's presence. It is different from all other places in that it is the place set aside where people can meet for worship and prayer and to gain a deep sense of God's presence.

   The words *My temple* or *My church* show possession. The church (temple) is the Lord's; it belongs to Him. He possesses and owns it. The people in the temple are only worshippers or servants, not owners. Accordingly, whatever is done in the church is to be what God wants done. His house is to be operated as He wills, and His servants are to do His bidding.

b. **Christ called** the church a *house of prayer.* He did not call it a house of sacrifice and offerings or a house of teaching, prophecy, or preaching. Everything done within the House of God is to lead to prayer, that is, the worship of God—fellowship and communion with Him. It is true that you are to pray everywhere, but you are also to attend church and to join other believers in offering up prayer and worship to God. The church, wherever it is, is *the special place* where you, along with other believers, are to meet with God. This makes the church unique, for it alone is God's established House of Prayer.

c. **Christ clearly demonstrated** that the church is *not to be profaned or defiled*. It is not to be a place of commotion, loud noises, or commercialism but a place of reverence, quietness, and meditation. It is not to be a place of buying and selling, dealing and negotiating, or stealing and cheating. Rather, the church is the House of God, God's House of Prayer. It is to be a place of sanctity, refined and purified by God Himself, a place set aside for praise, worship, and prayer. It is to be a place where sinful, broken, or distressed hearts can come to meditate, worship, and seek to meet God face-to-face.

4. *You Should Receive the Word of God When It Is Taught—Receive It As the Word of God and Not As the Mere Ideas of Human Beings.*

> **And we also thank God continually because, when you received the word of God, which you heard from us, you accepted it not as the word of men, but as it actually is, the word of God, which is at work in you who believe (1 Th.2:13, NIV).**

What a phenomenal statement! Paul declares unequivocally that the Word he proclaimed was not the word of men, but the Word of God Himself. And he emphasizes the truth: "it actually is, the Word of God...at work in [those] who believe." Do you personally believe that the Word (the Bible) is God's Word?

- The Thessalonians believed it.
- Paul believed it.
- Do *you* really believe it?

Remember: what Paul preached was the Old Testament Scriptures and the truths that Christ had revealed directly to him (Ro.16:25-26; 1 Co.2:7; Ep.1:9; 3:4, 9; Col.1:27; 2:2; 4:3; 2 Ti.3:16). Most people—by far most—do not believe that the Word of God (the Bible) is literally God's Word. They receive the Word of God only as the ideas and words of mere human beings. For example...

- Some think that the New Testament is only what the early apostles and believers could remember about Christ and could conclude from His teaching.
- Others think that the Old Testament is only a religious book and religious fables passed down by word of mouth and written by the Jews' great religious leaders.
- Still others believe that the Bible is a great religious book chosen by God to use in the lives of people when it is proclaimed. They actually say

> that the Bible, when sitting on the shelf, is not the Word of God, but when it is read or proclaimed, it becomes the Word of God. It becomes God's Word in the sense that He uses it to stir people to live more righteously.

However, note a crucial point, a point that could affect your eternal destiny: both the Bible and Paul claim that the Word of God is not the words of mere human beings, but the *very Word of God Himself.* Again, as the above verse says, "the Word of God...*actually is...the Word of God.*" And the Thessalonian church and its believers received it as the Word of God.

When the Thessalonian believers received God's Word, a wonderful thing happened. Its truth began to work and operate in the lives of those who truly believed. As this Scripture says, it is God who *works in you who believe.* Believe what? The Word of God.

If you do not believe the Word of God, then there is no objective way to be absolutely sure that Jesus Christ is the Savior of the world, or that anything else in the Bible is true. If the Bible is not truly the Word of God, there is nothing left to believe but the limited and imperfect words of mere human beings. And the best that we as human beings can offer is messages and ideas that stir us to...

- improve ourselves
- boost our self-image
- do good works
- practice kindness
- promote morality
- pursue justice
- strive for equality
- become more committed

All of this is very good, but it has three serious flaws: it is all subjective. It is restricted to what our finite minds know, and it all ends. Everything about us is imperfect and ends when we die. Our message and words cannot exceed what human beings can do, and, on their own, human beings can do no more than die and continue in their terrible separation from God.

As human beings, we cannot save ourselves. This is the reason you need to hope and trust that God is love, and that He has loved you enough to speak to you truthfully and clearly. If God cared no more for you than to leave you in the dark about how to become acceptable to Him, then you would never want to face Him. Why? Because He would not be a God of love—not if He has left you in this dark, hostile, and destructive world—left you groping and grasping to find your way to Him. God would then be a god of evil, not of love. A God of love would speak to you honestly and openly, without any error, so that you could know *with conviction* the truth about Him and the truth about yourself and the world:

- who you are
- why you are here
- why things are the way they are
- where you are going

This is the glorious gospel (good news): God is not a god of evil but a God of love—the only living and true God—who has given you His Word, the very Word of God itself, the Holy Bible. And He has given His Son, the Lord Jesus Christ, to save you. As a consequence, you must do what the Thessalonians did: believe that the Word of God...*really is the Word of God,* which means that Jesus Christ *truly is the Son of God,* your personal Savior and Lord. When you genuinely believe, then God will work in your heart and life, nurturing you to be more like His dear Son, Jesus Christ. And then when your life on earth is done, He will transfer you into heaven—quicker than the eye can blink—where you will live with Him eternally.

5. *You Should Be Baptized and Observe the Ordinance of Baptism in Your Church.*

> **Peter *said* to them, "Repent, and each of you be baptized in the name of Jesus Christ for the forgiveness of your sins; and you will receive the gift of the Holy Spirit (Ac.2:38, NASB).**

Baptism is one of the ordinances of the church. It is the outward sign, the validation or evidence that you have truly repented of your sins and trusted Jesus Christ as your Savior. In fact, baptism is God's first command after you receive Christ. If you are truly repenting and turning to Christ, you should be baptized as soon as possible. Baptism is not an option. It is as much of a command as repentance is.

Now, note a critical fact that is often overlooked or misunderstood: just because you are baptized does not mean you are saved. A person can very simply request to be baptized. And, to a certain extent, a person can even change his or her life through discipline and self-control. Many have and will continue to do this. In reality, a great number of people live what society calls good, upright, and moral lives, and they have been baptized. But there is more to being saved than merely changing your life and being baptized. What is it? It is the very basis of salvation, that critical key to being truly forgiven and receiving the Holy Spirit:

➢ It is *faith, believing* "in the name of Jesus Christ."

Before repentance and baptism, there must be true faith to be saved. You must genuinely believe *in the name of the Lord Jesus.* It is the one absolute essential for salvation.

But never forget, there is no real faith *without true repentance* and there is no forgiveness by God *without trusting or committing* your life to God's dear Son, the Lord Jesus Christ. Once you truly trust Christ to save you, the very first act of following Christ is that of repenting and being baptized. And if you honestly believe in Jesus Christ, you will willingly, even eagerly, do just what Christ says.

6. *You Should Celebrate Communion or the Lord's Supper Regularly.*

> **When the hour had come, He sat down, and the twelve apostles with Him. Then He said to them, "With *fervent* desire I have desired to eat this Passover with you before I suffer; for I say to you, I will no longer eat of it until it is fulfilled in the kingdom of God." Then He took the cup, and gave thanks, and said, "Take this and divide *it* among yourselves; for I say to you, I will not drink of the fruit of the vine until the kingdom of God comes." And He took bread, gave thanks and broke *it,* and gave *it* to them, saying, "This is My body which is given for you; do this in remembrance of Me." Likewise He also *took* the cup after supper, saying, "This cup *is* the new covenant in My blood, which is shed for you (Lu.22:14-20, NKJV).**

Communion or the Lord's Supper is another ordinance of the church. Jesus Christ instituted the communion service as a remembrance of His death. When you partake of the bread and wine, you are proclaiming that you have trusted Christ's broken body (the bread) and blood (the wine) to save you.

a. **Christ reveals the meaning** of the bread (v.19). Jesus took the bread and broke it. This symbolized His own broken body. Just as the innocent, unblemished animals were sacrificed in the Old Testament as a token payment for the people's sins, so Christ's innocent and blameless body was broken and sacrificed once-for-all for the sins of the whole world. He was broken as a victim for your deliverance (Is.53:5). This act was so significant that the early church sometimes called the Lord's Supper simply *the breaking of bread* (Ac.2:42, 46; 1 Co.10:16).

Under the Old Testament celebration of Passover, the broken bread pictured the sufferings of the Israelites. Now, under the New Testament, the bread pictures the broken body of Christ (1 Co.11:24).

Remember: Jesus said that His body was broken and given for you (1 Co.11:24). He suffered and died *for you*: in your behalf, in your place. He died as your substitute and bore the judgment of God that was due you.

> **But he was wounded for our transgressions, he was bruised for our iniquities: the chastisement of our peace was upon him; and with his stripes we are healed (Is.53:5, KJV).**

b. Christ reveals the meaning of the cup (v.20). Jesus identified the cup as His blood of the New Covenant. He simply meant that His blood establishes a *new covenant* with God; His blood allows a new relationship between God and the human race. Note the Lord's exact words.

- "This is my blood": His blood, shed from His body, was to become the sign or symbol of the new covenant. The sacrifice of His life was to take the place of the sacrifice of animals.
- "The new covenant": His blood established the *New Testament*, the *New Covenant* between God and human beings (He.9:11-15). Faith in Christ's blood and sacrifice is the way you are now to approach God. Under the Old Testament, people who wanted a right relationship with God approached God through the sacrifice of the animal's blood. Now, under the New Testament, all who want a personal relationship with God must approach Him through Christ's sacrifice. This is what Jesus said: "This is my blood of the new covenant, which is shed for many" (Mt.26:28; Mk.14:24; 1 Jn.2:1-2; He.9:22.) Your sins are forgiven and you become acceptable to God by believing that Christ's blood was shed for you.

> **In whom we have redemption through his blood, the forgiveness of sins, according to the riches of his grace (Ep.1:7, KJV).**
>
> **But if we walk in the light, as he is in the light, we have fellowship one with another, and the blood of Jesus Christ his Son [cleanses] us from all sin (1 Jn.1:7, KJV).**

7. *You Should Tithe—Financially Support God's Church—Weekly (Regularly) and Generously.*

> **On the first day of every week, each one of you should set aside a sum of money in keeping with his income, saving it up, so that when I come no [special] collections will have to be made (1 Co.16:2, NIV).**

God is very clear about the support of His church. Four details clearly stand out in this verse.

a. **When is your offering** to be given to the church? "On the first day of every week," which is Sunday. The Jews worshipped on the Sabbath, which is Saturday; but the early Christian believers switched the day of worship to commemorate the resurrection of the Lord, which took place on the first day. In fact, they even began to call the first day of the week *the Lord's Day* (Jn.20:19; Ac.20:7; Re.1:10).

   God is very specific about your support of His church and its mission. You are not to give only occasional offerings; you are to give regularly, every Lord's day. This does not mean that you cannot tithe on a monthly or bimonthly basis, depending on when you get paid. But you must be every bit as diligent about your tithing when you receive your income.

   In addition. you need to make sure that the amount you give is what it should be—an amount "in keeping with [your] income." Old Testament believers gave *at least* one tenth of their earnings, a good starting point for you as a New Testament believer. You certainly would not want to give less in light of all Christ has done for you.

> **Now this *I say,* he who sows sparingly will also reap sparingly, and he who sows bountifully will also reap bountifully. Each one *must do* just as he has purposed in his heart, not grudgingly or under compulsion, for God loves a cheerful giver (2 Co.9:6-7, NASB).**

b. **Who is to give?** "Each one of you." Why would God expect the poor to give as well as the middle class and the rich? Scripture gives five strong reasons why everyone is to be involved in helping the church meet the needs of the world (2 Co.9:12-14).

- ➢ Giving helps meet the needs of other believers both locally and worldwide (2 Co.9:12).
- ➢ Giving stirs people to praise God (2 Co.9:12).
- ➢ Giving is a strong testimony of your obedience to Christ (2 Co.9:13).
- ➢ Giving and helping people stirs the recipients to pray for you (2 Co.9:14).
- ➢ Giving builds a strong fellowship among believers (2 Co.9:14).

> **This service that you perform is not only supplying the needs of God's people but is also overflowing in many expressions of thanks to God. Because of the service by which you have proved yourselves, men will praise God for the obedience that accompanies your confession of the gospel of Christ, and for your generosity in sharing with them and with everyone else. And in their prayers for you their hearts will go out to you, because of the surpassing grace God has given you (2 Co.9:12-14, NIV).**

c. **How is your offering** to be given? By setting aside a portion of your income as an offering to the Lord and His church. This could not mean that you are to keep your offering "stored up" or set aside for long periods of time before giving it. Paul explicitly says that it is to be given to the church every week *so there will be no need for a special offering* when he comes to the church. Therefore, to set aside a portion of your income must mean...

- ➢ to put the offering in the *storehouse,* that is, the treasury of the church
- ➢ to lay the money aside when you receive your income during the week so that you will not spend the offering

The importance of this point can never be overstressed. Think how often some believers spend the Lord's money simply because they failed to set it aside.

> **Honor the Lord from your wealth and from the first of all your produce [income] (Pr.3:9, NASB).**

d. **Why are you to give** to the Lord and His church? Because God has blessed you with life and has sacrificed His Son to save you. God looks after and cares for you. Every good and perfect gift you have ever received has come from God (Jas.1:17). Furthermore, Christ taught that all the necessities of life would be provided for those who truly seek first the kingdom of God and His righteousness (Mt.6:33). Therefore, God expects you to give as He has prospered you. Closely note the principle: you are to give on the basis of your prosperity. This definitely means that the rich are to give very generously, compassionately, and sacrificially.

8. *You Should Give Yourself Wholly to the Great Commission: Do All You Can to Reach the World for Christ.*

> **Go therefore and make disciples of all the nations, baptizing them in the name of the Father and of the Son and of the Holy Spirit, teaching them to observe all things that I have commanded you; and lo, I am with you always, *even* to the end of the age." Amen (Mt.28:19-20, NKJV).**

This was the final commission Jesus Christ gave to His followers. It is known as the *Great Commission*, a charge that is given to every generation of believers and to every individual believer.

a. **Christ commissions** you to "go...and make disciples of all the nations." Interestingly, the Lord is telling you not only to go and bear witness to people, but also *how to go* and *how to evangelize*: by making disciples. He is giving *the method* to use to evangelize the world.

Think about the term *make disciples*. This is exactly what Christ did: He *made disciples*! He is telling us to do exactly as He did, and He did more than just save a person; He *attached* Himself to new believers. Christ began to mold and make new believers into His image.

The word *attach* is key. It is probably the word that best describes discipleship. Christ made disciples of people by attaching Himself to them, and through that personal attachment, they were able to observe His life and conversation. In seeing and hearing, they began to absorb and assimilate His very character and behavior. They then began to follow Him and to serve Him more closely.

There is another way to describe what Christ did. Christ envisioned something beyond Himself and beyond His day and time. He envisioned an *extension* of Himself, an *extension* of His mission and method. The way He chose to extend Himself was *discipleship, attaching Himself* to committed individuals. These believers, in turn, attached themselves to others and discipled them. They, too, expected their disciples to make disciples of others who were willing to commit their lives to Christ. In this manner, the glorious message of Christ was to march down through the centuries (2 Ti.2:2).

There is no question but that our Lord's commission is for you to go. But more than that, you are to make disciples, to *attach* yourself to those individuals who will follow the Lord until they in turn can make disciples (2 Ti.2:2).

> **You have heard me teach things that have been confirmed by many reliable witnesses. Now teach these truths to other trustworthy people who will be able to pass them on to others (2 Ti.2:2, NLT).**

b. Christ commissions you and your church to baptize all nations. Baptism is of crucial importance. Christ says that it is essential despite the fact that it is a one-time act. It is as much a part of the commission of Christ as discipling and teaching. And it is confirmation that baptism is to be the immediate sign that a person is turning away from a selfish and sinful lifestyle and taking a stand with Christ. (See pt.5, pp. 343-344 for more discussion.)

Notice that baptism "in the name of the Father and of the Son and of the Holy Spirit" means more than just saying a formula as you are baptized, much more. It means...

- that you are making a statement of faith. You believe in God as the true Father of Jesus Christ; and in Christ as the true Son of God, the Savior of the world; and in the Holy Spirit as your Comforter and Helper.
- that you are making a commitment to follow God.

Your commitment is to follow God as revealed in the Father, the Son, and the Holy Spirit.

c. **Christ commissions** you to teach all that He has commanded in God's Holy Word. Teaching is a very critical part of making disciples; therefore, its importance cannot be overstressed. It is an essential part of the Great Commission of our Lord. Note what is to be taught: "all things that I have commanded you."

d. **Christ promises** to be with you always. Note the emphatic assurance: not "I will be with you," but "I am with you." Christ is with you as you go forth to bear witness and make disciples in your neighborhood, city, state, nation, and the world. Wherever you go, if you faithfully bear witness for Christ, He is with you...

- every step and decision
- every trial and joy
- every day and hour
- whether rich or poor
- whether abused or loved
- whether sick or healthy
- when facing death

Christ's promise is endless, "always, even to the end of the age." There is not a moment when Christ is not with you as you bear witness for Him, even if your witness brings abuse, persecution, or martyrdom.

> **When you pass through the waters [afflictions], I *will be* with you; And through the rivers [trials], they shall not overflow you. When you walk through the fire [persecution], you shall not be burned, Nor shall the flame scorch you (Is.43:2, NKJV).**

9. You Should Watch Out for Divisive People and Avoid Them.

> **I urge you, brothers, to watch out for those who cause divisions and put obstacles in your way that are contrary to the teaching you have learned. Keep away from them. For such people are not serving our Lord Christ, but their own appetites. By smooth talk and flattery they deceive the minds of naive people (Ro.16:17-18, NIV).**

This is a rather startling and severe warning to the local church. You and other members of your church must guard against a situation that is bound to happen: the seeping in of divisive people. A divisive person is someone who...

- grumbles
- complains
- criticizes
- gossips
- causes strife
- is argumentative
- acts out of pride or selfish ambition
- is unforgiving
- is uncompromising

The most effective way for Satan to get a foothold into a strong church is to quietly move a divisive person into a teaching or leadership position. From there, he or she can influence immature believers. This is God's warning that must be heeded by all churches if they are to keep their witness for the Lord: a divisive person must be watched for and avoided.

a. **A divisive person** causes tension and discord and puts obstacles in the way of growth. He or she teaches things that are contrary to God's Word, "contrary to the teaching you have learned." For example, he or she may present some secondary issue or teaching that opposes or denies...

- the death and resurrection of Christ
- the Lordship of Christ
- the teaching or miracles of Christ
- the virgin birth
- the importance of the church
- the relevance of old-fashioned morality
- the legitimacy of all men being created equal
- the truth of heaven and hell

You must avoid contentious people because of the terrible devastation they can do within your church. If you associate with such a divisive person, you run the risk of being influenced by what he or she says and does. You also give the appearance of condoning the divisive behavior. Guard yourself and your church by having nothing to do with a divisive person.

b. **A divisive person** does not serve Christ but his or her own desires (v.18). This type of person is gripped by...

- selfish whims
- personal ambition
- greedy urges
- shameful appetites
- dishonorable intentions
- stubborn pride

Scripture clearly says that divisive people do not serve Christ. They may call themselves *Christians*, but their Lord is not Christ. They are not committed to His honor, glory, and mission but to their own—to getting and doing what they want. The contentious person is still given over to the things of this carnal, sensual, and secular world.

> **For many walk, of whom I have told you often, and now tell you even weeping, that they are the enemies of the cross of Christ: whose end is destruction, whose God is their belly, and whose glory is in their shame, who mind earthly things (Ph.3:18-19, KJV).**

c. **A divisive person** uses smooth talk and flattery to deceive others. He or she uses persuasive and reasonable words to secure people's support. This person talks and acts in a godly manner showing interest and concern for those who need convincing. But Scripture says that the motive of divisive people is to deceive. They want others to think as they think and to believe as they believe.

The impact of divisive people on a church and its members is tragic: they deceive the hearts of the unsuspecting, the innocent, the immature, the carnal, the newborn believers. Do not let this happen in your church. Watch out for divisive people and shun them. If necessary, the leadership of the church must discipline them (see pt.1, pp. 353-355 for discussion).

C. Your Duty in Church Discipline

1. *You Should Correct Offending Believers by Seeking Reconciliation and, Then, by Church Discipline.*

> **"If another believer sins against you, go privately and point out the offense. If the other person listens and confesses it, you have won that person back. But if you are unsuccessful, take one or two others with you and go back again, so that everything you say may be confirmed by two or three witnesses. If the person still refuses to listen, take your case to the church. Then if he or she won't accept the church's decision, treat that person as a pagan or a corrupt tax collector (Mt.18:15-17, NLT).**

Sinning against a Christian brother or sister is a matter of great concern to God. In fact, if the offending party refuses to resolve the matter, he or she is to be *firmly disciplined* (v.17).

God has one concern: He wants peace restored. He wants peace between His sons and daughters, all who truly follow Him, and He wants peace within the church. The disturbance caused by an offending believer is so damaging that God lays down very specific steps as to how the matter is to be handled. And if the sinning party refuses to be reconciled and to correct the wrong, God says the disturbance is not to be tolerated.

a. **The first step** in correcting an offending believer is to attempt reconciliation (v.15). You are not to wait for the *offending brother or sister* to come to you. You are to immediately go to any believer who offends you.

Go and point out the wrong done. This seems to indicate that the offending believer may not know the wrong done to you. If your fellow believer does not know you are offended, he or she cannot correct the situation. Hence, the breach remains, and the sting of the offense continues. The damaging effects of the division can only grow and deepen.

Something else can happen: your heart and mind can brood, become resentful, even bitter and revengeful toward the individual who wronged you. Knowing this, you desperately need to do all you can to resolve the matter. When you go to the offending believer...

- ➢ you are first to approach him or her alone. You are not to share the matter with anyone else, nor are you to openly rebuke the person. This will only deepen the division, causing bitterness and hostility for both parties.

- ➢ you are to go humbly. You must search your own heart to see if you have done anything to cause the offending behavior, knowing that you too can offend others very easily.
- ➢ you are to be soft spoken and gentle.
- ➢ you are to express your desire for understanding and for straightening out the matter so that you can be reconciled together before Christ.

Sadly, some Christian brothers and sisters are prideful and stubborn; others are immature; still others are gripped by selfish and sinful motives and behavior. If this is the case, the offending party may not be willing to be reconciled or willing to admit the wrong. Still, you should continue to pursue reconciliation.

b. **The second step** in correcting an offending believer is to take one or two fellow believers with you (v.16). Of course, these should be wise and caring believers who are gifted in counseling others. This act does several things.

- ➢ It shows the offending believer there is deep concern; a number of people do care and want to help.
- ➢ It shows that the offense is known by more than one or two people. At least several know.
- ➢ It also provides objective and wise counsel between you and the offending believer. Agreement and reconciliation are more likely to arise from this.
- ➢ It helps to prevent bias, one-sidedness, and a hasty or angry reaction.

Remember, though, this step should never be taken until you have first approached the offending believer. You are never to talk about a brother or sister's wrong against you with anyone else—not until you have met with the offender face-to-face in the love of Christ.

Then again, this step of taking others with you is to be attempted if the offender continues to be divisive. But it is always to be done in a spirit of humility, love, concern, and with a sense of personal unworthiness before Christ.

c. **The third step** in correcting an offending believer is to go before the church so the church as a whole can make an appeal for reconciliation (v.17). Then, if the offender still refuses to correct the wrong behavior, he or she is to be disciplined.

The church is to discipline a member if one of three conditions exist: if the offender...

- continues in open rebellion against the Lord.
- continues to be gripped by selfishness, stubbornness, and worldly pride.
- refuses reconciliation with a Christian brother or sister after three attempts have been made, as spelled out by Christ in this Scripture.

What is the discipline? The divisive believer is to be treated as an outsider—as an unbeliever or a corrupt tax collector. The offender is refusing to listen or to respond to the humble and loving appeals for reconciliation. Subsequently, there is no choice: the offender is to be left alone and not bothered until he or she is ready to listen and be reconciled. Until such time, the church can do nothing but treat the contentious believer as an outsider.

In time, *as the church deems wise,* appointed believers should continue seeking out the offending believer, just as the church seeks to reach all outsiders. Realistically, however, the attempts at future reconciliation will probably be less often. The heart of the offending believer will have fewer opportunities to be stirred by those who love and care for him or her so deeply.

2. *You Should Settle Legal Disputes with Other Believers Among Yourselves—Not in the World's Secular Courts.*

> **If any of you has a dispute with another, dare he take it before the ungodly for judgment instead of before the saints? Do you not know that the saints will judge the world? And if you are to judge the world, are you not competent to judge trivial cases? Do you not know that we will judge angels? How much more the things of this life! (1 Co.6:1-3, NIV).**

This Scripture is an eye opener—a point that few believers have ever heard discussed or taught. Nevertheless, it is God's clear instruction. And, once the passage is studied and understood, it seems to make perfect sense and to be the very behavior that believers should practice in settling legal disputes. When a conflict arises between you and another believer, God's Word says that you should ask two questions.

a. **First, do you dare go** before the ungodly instead of before other saints (believers) to settle your dispute? The Greek is forceful: How dare you—you who are the saints, the holy followers of God—go to law before the unbelievers of the world!

   You and other believers are not to be arguing over rights and authority nor over the possessions and issues of this world. You are to be working and using what you earn for Christ and His cause. Masses of humanity are lost and dying from starvation, disease, poverty, and sin. They desperately need to be reached for Christ.

   Tragically, this was not the case within the Corinthian church. The church was divided, and some apparently sought legal judgment against others. Whether the judgment involved rights within the church, actual property, or a dispute over some matter between two or more individuals is not known. A problem existed regarding a legal dispute, and the opposing parties had sought secular judgment.

   As believers, you are to settle your disputes among yourselves within your own Christian society (the church) and be governed by the life of Christ and the law of God. In God's eyes, it is wrong for *believers*—you who truly believe and seek to follow God—to go to court against each other before the world's judges. Consider this:

   - As believers, if you settle differences before the world, you reproach the name of Christ and the testimony of the church. There is no disputing this fact. The name of Christ is always hurt when you *carry your differences* before the world. The Lord's call to you and to His church is to live a life of love, joy, and peace, bearing all the fruit of God's Spirit. But what the world receives from disputing Christians is anything but love, joy, and peace. Think of the *devastating* damage done by a testimony given in anger, hostility, and mistrust!

     Picture the scene as God sees it: two believers, people who truly trust God, stand before an unbelieving judge who rejects and rebels against the very idea of God. Then, they ask him to judge between them instead of asking God or another Christian leader to help them see the matter more clearly. Imagine what God thinks of the behavior of these two conflicting brothers or sisters!

- ➢ As believers, if you settle differences before the world, you fail to govern your affairs by the *life of Christ and the law of God*. You fail the Lord and fail Him miserably. How? You and your fellow believers are to live by Christ's standards spelled out in God's Holy Word, far higher standards of *morality* and *justice* than the standards and rules of the world. You are to salt and permeate the world, not the other way around. You are not to set the world as your standard. You are to be the standard for the world.
- ➢ As believers, you have the Holy Spirit and Christ-centered leaders to help you seek God's wisdom and discern God's will. God has given His Spirit for the very purpose of guiding and teaching you. He has given spiritual leaders for the same purpose. It is God's will for you and other believers who have conflicts to go through godly channels to resolve your differences.

What God wants is for you to live a different lifestyle from that of the world: a lifestyle of love and purity, care and concern, discipline and justice. A godly lifestyle must be held up high, above reproach, for all the world to see. This is the only conceivable way the world can ever witness and grasp the love of God and godly justice and have its desperate needs met. For this reason, you and other believers of the church must surrender your lives and do everything possible to live as God instructs. You will be held accountable to make sure that the love, joy, peace, and wisdom of God are revealed and shared with the unbelievers of the world.

> **Let no debt remain outstanding, except the continuing debt to love one another, for he who loves his fellowman has fulfilled the law. The commandments, "Do not commit adultery," "Do not murder," "Do not steal," "Do not covet," and whatever other commandment there may be, are summed up in this one rule: "Love your neighbor as yourself." Love does no harm to its neighbor. Therefore love is the fulfillment of the law (Ro.13:8-10, NIV).**

b. **Second, when a conflict arises** between you and another believer, you should ask yourself this question: Are you aware of the great authority God has given you? As a true believer, a day is coming when you will judge and govern the world (v.3). In fact, you are even to govern angels in the next world. Never lower yourself or lose your dignity as a saint (one of God's holy people) by going before the world for judgment. When you secure a verdict from the world, you walk out of your exalted position.

To *judge* means to govern, administer affairs, rule, supervise, oversee, and exert judgment. In order to judge others or to govern other things, you must first be given the right and authority to do so. This glorious right is to be given to you as a believer when Christ returns to rule the universe. In that day, God will assign you an area of responsibility over which to execute judgment—an area to govern, supervise, and oversee. All this activity and responsibility is, of course, under the authority of Christ.

Never forget, *eternal life* is not some dreamy sleep or semi-conscious type of existence in the future that puts you on a fluffy cloud. Eternal life is not an eternal state of inactivity. Rather, eternal life is life that goes on and on, although there is one basic difference. Life will be perfected, perfected in body, mind, and spirit. Eternal life is life lived before Christ and with Christ and under Christ's direction in all that is assigned (Jn.3:16; 5:24; Ro.8:19-23; 2 Pe.3:9-18; 1 Jn. 5:11-13; Re.21:1). In light of all this—with God's promise of a new heavens and earth in mind—you should settle legal disputes with other believers among yourselves, not in the legal courts of unbelievers, the legal courts of the world.

D. Your Duty to Support Your Minister

1. You Should Respect Your Ministers and Pay Them Well, Especially Those Who Preach and Teach the Gospel.

> **The elders who direct the affairs of the church well are worthy of double honor, especially those whose work is preaching and teaching. For the Scripture says, "Do not muzzle the ox while it is treading out the grain," and "The worker deserves his wages" (1 Ti.5:17-18, NIV).**

Within society, ministers are sometimes attacked because of their stand and witness for Christ. The teaching of God's Word often conflicts...

- with the behavior and beliefs of unbelievers
- with the beliefs and expectations of society
- with laws and actions approved by governments

So when ministers of God take a stand for the truth of God's Word, unbelievers often oppose them. But as sad as the world's opposition is, even sadder is the opposition that ministers sometimes face within the church. Far too often, people within the church murmur, complain, gossip, oppose, or even attack the minister. They may not like the minister's personality, family, style of preaching, or some proposed change or position.

As a result, ministers can end up being neglected, opposed, and persecuted by church members even more than by the unbelievers of the world. Then, when controversy, gossip, or rumors start spreading about the minister, many church members quickly fall away. And when it comes to honoring and respecting the minister and meeting his or her financial needs, a group of opponents can easily dash a minister's hopes and crush his or her spirit.

The mistreatment of God's ministers is both sad and shameful. As a true believer, never be guilty of causing hardship for the minister of God's church. Treat God's minister exactly as God says, and do precisely what God instructs: honor, esteem, respect, and acknowledge him or her.

In fact, note what Scripture says: count your minister worthy of double honor. There is a condition attached to giving double honor to ministers, however. They must labor hard in directing the affairs of the church and in preaching and teaching the Word of God. They have to spend hours on their faces before God and in the Word in order to preach and teach—this in addition to taking the lead in all the other duties and ministries of the church. If they truly are committed men and women of God, ministers who labor diligently for Christ and the church, then they are worthy of double honor. Give them their due respect.

Note one other significant fact. To *honor* a person means more than just to esteem and respect. It means to pay and bestow what is due. A minister is due compensation or wages for his or her labor. And, if the minister performs his or her duty well, then double honor.

Is this to be taken literally? Is the church to pay the minister a double salary? A.T. Robertson states that there are "numerous examples of Roman soldiers who received double pay for unusual services."[2] One thing is sure: double pay means sufficient and generous financial support. Whatever you and your church do, you must take care of your minister financially—make sure he can adequately take care of his family.

An example to consider is this: the ox that was used to grind out the corn in the East pulled a tremendously heavy millstone around and around over the grain. The ox was never muzzled. He was allowed to eat as much grain as he wished since he was considered to have earned all the grain he ate. So it is to be with the minister of God. He is worthy of his labor. As he grinds and grinds away to reap the harvest of souls for God and His church, the minister is to be given more than enough financial support.

Keep in mind that few people labor as faithfully as committed ministers. For instance, compare their work with any other profession (accountant, attorney, physician, executive, and others). How much time would other professionals take away from their regular duties...

- if they had to speak for thirty or more minutes at a conference this week?
- if they had to speak two or three times at the conference *to the same people*?
- if they had to speak two or three times every week of every year *to the same people,* and they could never use the same speech?
- if they had to attend several committee meetings every week to plan and oversee all future conference work?
- if they had to visit everyone who attended the conference when he or she went into the hospital?

2 A.T. Robertson. *Word Pictures in the New Testament*, Vol.4, p.588.

- if they had to visit all the family members and close relatives of the conference members when they went into the hospital?
- if they had to counsel all the conference members and their family members when they had a serious problem?
- if they had to conduct all the funerals of the conference members and their families?
- if they had to conduct all the weddings of the children of conference members?
- if they were expected to visit in the homes of most, if not all, of the conference members?
- if they were expected to visit all the newcomers and prospective members within the community of the conference?

The list could go on and on. And bear in mind that while the professionals are doing all of this, they still have to work and manage the administration of their businesses (just as the minister has to manage the church). For the committed minister, the hours are endless.

The point is this: respect your ministers, even giving them double honor if they are faithful and work hard. Pay them well. They deserve your respect and adequate pay.

2. *You Should Obey Church Leaders and Pray for Them.*

> **Obey your spiritual leaders, and do what they say. Their work is to watch over your souls, and they are accountable to God. Give them reason to do this with joy and not with sorrow. That would certainly not be for your benefit (He.13:17, NLT).**

Note exactly what Scripture says, for there are people who have entered the ministry only as a means of livelihood or to serve society and who do not proclaim the Word of God. These ministers are not to be followed or obeyed. Their service to society is usually commendable and even helpful. But such individuals belong elsewhere in the community, not in the pulpits of churches. True, the church and its pulpit do *exist* to minister to the social needs of the world, but they do not exist *solely* for social ministry.

God's Word is clear and strong: the church and its pulpit exist first and foremost to *proclaim* the redemption that is in Christ Jesus. Ministers who have been truly called by God exalt Christ and the redemption that is in

Him. It is these ministers who are to be obeyed. Note four significant points:

a. **Church leaders** are called to watch over your souls. They are concerned about your personal welfare, your spiritual growth and faith, as well as your trials and triumphs, your pain and joy. Listen to them and obey their counsel and exhortation.

b. **Church leaders** are accountable to God. This keeps godly leaders from abusing you or their position. Church leaders must never forget: they will stand before God to give an account for how they led. Consequently, if leaders are truly called of God, they will not mislead you. God will hold them responsible for everything they do in His name, and they know it.

c. **Church leaders** can be grieved and hurt. If you follow their lead and grow in the Lord, they are filled with joy because the work of Christ is going forth. People are being reached for Christ and ministered to under their leadership. But if you fail to follow your leaders, they are hurt and grieved, for the work of Christ is hampered and you are not growing in Christ as you should. When you oppose your leaders, you hinder your own growth as well as the growth of other believers. You begin to cause pain and division in the body of Christ and become a tool of destruction instead of an instrument of love and growth.

   Tragically, your disobedience and rebellion damage the church. Members then lose out on whatever growth the leaders could have contributed to their lives.

d. **Church leaders** need your prayers and those of all church members. Why would you not pray for the man or woman who gives you counsel and guidance from God's Holy Word? Ministers are constantly under attack by Satan, constantly being tempted to fall away and to hurt God's name. So lift up the names of your church leaders and their ministries. Pray for all ministers who are living for Christ, whether present or absent, whether ministering to your local church or elsewhere in the world (Ep.6:18-19).

E. Your Duty Regarding False Teaching

1. *You Need to Guard Against False Teachers Who Secretly Introduce Destructive Heresies.*

> **But there were also false prophets among the people, just as there will be false teachers among you. They will secretly introduce destructive heresies, even denying the sovereign Lord who bought them—bringing swift destruction on themselves. Many will follow their shameful ways and will bring the way of truth into disrepute (2 Pe.2:1-2, NIV; see 1 Jn.4:1-3).**
>
> **For the time will come when men will not put up with sound doctrine. Instead, to suit their own desires, they will gather around them a great number of teachers to say what their itching ears want to hear. They will turn their ears away from the truth and turn aside to myths (2 Ti.4:3-4, NIV).**

If the world ever needed a warning it is this: you need to guard against false teachers. Why? Because false teachers lead people to doom themselves quicker than any other single thing. Far too many people are quick to believe a lie. They deny the truth so they can go ahead and live as they wish. They want some excuse to get away from the restraints and demands that Jesus Christ puts on them. So, they grope after any teaching that lowers or diminishes the Person of Christ. The more Christ is lowered in their minds, the less binding His demands are. However, there is one obvious problem with false teaching: it is not the truth. A person dooms himself to eternal separation from God if he or she follows false teaching. This is the critical importance of this Scripture.

a. **False teachers** have been present from the beginning of human history and have carried on their destructive work ever since (2 Pe.2:1). Note the following verses of Scripture along with the above verses:

> **For prophecy [God's Word] never had its origin in the will of man, but men spoke from God as they were carried along by the Holy Spirit. But there were also false prophets among the people, just as there will be false teachers among you... (2 Pe.1:21–2:1, NIV).**

Imagine! Even while God was speaking through the prophets and giving His Word to the world, there were already people who were denying His Word, teaching destructive heresies, and misleading people. Far more important to us, though, is the warning issued by Scripture: "there will be false teachers among you." False teachers have continued right on through the generations, and they will continue to introduce their destructive heresies until the world ends. You must, therefore, be alert to what every man and woman teaches. This does not mean that you should be on a witch hunt; it means that you should test all preaching and teaching by the Word of God.

> **"Beware of false prophets who come disguised as harmless sheep but are really vicious wolves (Mt.7:15, NLT).**

b. **False teachers** secretly introduce and teach destructive heresies (2 Pe.2:1). They do not do it openly. They do it deceptively, quietly, secretly, slipping in a false teaching or doctrine here and there.

Many of the false teachers are not out in the world but in the church, teaching their destructive heresies among believers. They have joined the church and most likely been outstanding members long enough to become teachers and preachers within the church. They often hold leadership positions from which they can teach their destructive heresies. What are the heresies being referred to? Any teaching that goes contrary to the Scripture, the Word of God, the Holy Bible. This is clear from the exhortation given: "pay attention to it [the Scripture]" (2 Pe.1:19-21).

> **"[Scripture is] the word of the prophets...and you will do well to pay attention to it....For prophecy never had its origin in the will of man, but men spoke from God as they were carried along by the Holy Spirit (2 Pe.1:19, 21, NIV).**

The point is this: any teaching that is contrary to God's Word is a destructive heresy. It corrupts God's purpose for the church and destroys the lives of people therein. No matter how personable or charismatic an individual may be, no matter how much you may like him or her, if the person is teaching a destructive heresy, the church and the lives of people are in grave danger. William Barclay states it well:

> *A heretic [is]...a man who believes what he wishes to believe instead of accepting the truth of God which he must believe.*
>
> *What was happening in the case of Peter's people was that certain men, who claimed to be prophets, were insidiously persuading men to believe the things they wished to be true rather than the things which God has revealed as true. They did not set themselves up as opponents of Christianity. Far from it. Rather they set themselves up as the finest fruits of Christian thinking. Insidiously, unconsciously, imperceptible, so gradually and so subtly that they did not even notice it, people were being lured away from God's truth to men's private opinions, for that is what heresy is.*[3]

False teachers also bring destruction *upon themselves* (v.1). They are responsible for their own actions, because they do not *have* to teach false doctrine; they make the *choice* to teach it. Rather than teach the Holy Scriptures, they make a deliberate decision to teach contrary to God's Word. Ultimately, they will face God's condemnation, and there will be no discussion about the matter—no questioning, no leniency, no mercy, no love. There will be true justice: swift, immediate judgment and destruction.

c. **False teachers** mislead many people and, by such, encourage people to live immoral and depraved lives (v.2). This is what is meant by *shameful ways. Shameful* actually refers here to the ways of immorality and of the flesh. How do false teachers lead people to live worldly and fleshly lives?

   First, false teachers may say that Christ is not the Son of God and that the Bible is not the Word of God. If this is so, then there is no Lord over our lives: no absolute authority, no absolute Word from God that tells us how to live and how to become acceptable to Him. The only authority we have is the best thinking that we, as humans, can do.

   This teaching, of course, leads to worldly and fleshly living, for no one can lead people to become more than what they themselves are. And by nature, we are all both fleshly and worldly. Our bodies are made of flesh and we live in a corruptible world. If there is no absolute truth, no instructions telling us how to live, then we are free to live basically as we want. And if God has not clearly instructed us how to live, then He cannot hold us accountable when we slip up or fail.

---

3 William Barclay. *The Letters of James and Peter*, p.374.

Simply stated, if Christ is not the Son of God and the Bible is not God's Holy Word, then people can do what they want and not be held accountable. When false teachers deny Christ and God's Word, they are actually encouraging people to live decadent and immoral lives.

Second, false teachers take the love of God and twist it. They say that God is so loving that He would never condemn you to an eternity of hell. Their approach is something like this: you should believe in Christ and follow Him, but if you fail, God still loves you and will accept you despite your immoral, lawless, or violent behavior. They claim God would certainly never condemn or punish you for eternity in a place called *hell*.

Of course, the consequences of this teaching are devastating. If people are not to be judged and punished for their sin, they can go ahead and live as they wish because there will be little, if any, consequence to selfish, sinful behavior.

Third, false teachers say that Jesus Christ is not the *only Savior*, the *only Mediator*, the *only way* a person can be saved and become acceptable to God. For example, they talk about the people who never hear about Christ, like isolated natives, or those who are followers of other religions that claim to know God. If Christ is the *only* Savior, what about those who do not know Him or who reject Him? Are they doomed?

Fourth, false teachers take *the grace of God* and *faith in Christ* and pervert them. Their position is that you must believe in Jesus Christ, but that once you make a profession, you are safe forever. Even if you fail to live for Christ and return to the world to live in sin, you are still saved because you claim that you believe in Jesus Christ and have been baptized. False teachers say that God accepts us even if we live like the devil—just so we believe in Jesus Christ. In other words, these impostors maintain that faith exists without ever producing fruit; so you can believe in Christ without any permanent repentance or change in your life, without ever separating from the world or denying your flesh.

False teachers declare that God's love and grace are so inexhaustible that you are free to sin, just so you believe in Jesus Christ. The tragic result of this teaching is that it leads to a life of indulgence and gives a person the license to sin.

You need to be on guard against such false teaching at all times. The truth is that once you profess faith in Christ, you are to live for Christ by obeying God's Holy Word and living righteously (He.5:9; Jas.2:17-18).

> **I am astonished that you are so quickly deserting the one who called you by the grace of Christ and are turning to a different gospel—which is really no gospel at all. Evidently some people are throwing you into confusion and are trying to pervert the gospel of Christ. But even if we or an angel from heaven should preach a gospel other than the one we preached to you, let him be eternally condemned! As we have already said, so now I say again: If anybody is preaching to you a gospel other than what you accepted, let him be eternally condemned! (Ga.1:6-9, NIV).**

In sum, false teachers cause the name of Christ to be damaged. They cause people to weaken and devalue the Person, the power, and the authority of God and His Holy Word. They mock or distort the Scriptures.

God's name is further slandered because of church members who are hypocrites, who profess to believe in Christ but disobey God's Holy Word and live immoral, ungodly lives. How often we hear comments such as "the church is full of hypocrites" as an excuse as to why someone will not come (or come back) to church. It is a tragedy, and most of the blame lies at the feet of false teachers. It is they who mislead people and bring shame to the way of truth.

2. *You Need to Guard Against Being Captivated by a False Philosophy or by Astrology.*

> **See to it that no one takes you captive through hollow and deceptive philosophy, which depends on human tradition and the basic principles of this world rather than on Christ. For in Christ all the fullness of the Deity lives in bodily form, and you have been given fullness in Christ, who is the head over every power and authority (Col.2:8-10, NIV).**

People have always asked questions about life and the world in which we live. Very practically, we need to know...

- What is the origin of life and of the universe in which we live?
- Who are we and where did we come from? Why are we here and where are we going?

- Where did evil come from? Can it be controlled? Or better yet, abolished?
- Why is there so much immorality, lawlessness, and violence on earth?
- Is there a God? How can we really know?
- Is life on this planet all there is?
- Is there life after death? Even the possibility of living forever?

The questions could go on and on. The point to see is this: a philosophy that seeks to find the answers to these questions *only in the world* is empty and hollow. It is empty and hollow because it looks only at those elements in the universe that the finite human mind can discover or identify. For example, from the earliest of times, some people have looked at the stars and planets and suggested that they determine the fate of human beings. But astrology and the signs of the Zodiac are to be guarded against just as much as any other worldly philosophy. The basis for saying this is that everything in the world—every element of it—passes away.

It is clear that when a philosophy bases itself only upon the elements of the world, there is no *permanent answer or solution* to life. Why? Because we die. Even the universe itself is physical and wasting away, granted, more slowly than we are; nevertheless, it is still wasting away. (Eventually, it will be destroyed; however, not by man, but by God. See 2 Pe.3:3-18, esp.10-13.) In any event, a philosophy based upon the world is useless in finding *permanent answers and solutions to life*. The very best that a worldly philosophy or science can ever do is...

- make life more comfortable and safer
- make life last longer

But this is not permanent or eternal comfort and safety. It is not permanent truth or reality. We need something much more than a worldly philosophy that offers only *partial* answers and *temporary* solutions to life.

What is it that we require? What is it that can meet our needs better than the sharpest-thinking technologies and sciences of this world? We need *life*—life that is both abundant and eternal, that does not become diseased or experience suffering or death. We need a never-ending world that does not collapse under the weight of corruption, decay, and death and does not erupt in natural disasters that result in catastrophic damage and loss.

How can we secure such a world? How can we find permanent and eternal life? If worldly philosophy is correct, the answer is simple: we cannot. Human philosophy says that such a world does not exist. Obviously, then, we can never find it if it is not there to be found.

On the other hand, what if a *permanent world* does exist in a *spiritual dimension*? How can we find it? We cannot. If a *spiritual world* exists, we cannot find it because we are physical beings living in a material world. And the physical cannot penetrate or move over into the spiritual regardless of what some persons may claim or think.

We cannot know the spiritual world because we and our world are physical, corruptible, weak, and dying. This is significant: if the physical world cannot penetrate the spiritual world, it means there is only one way we can ever know the spiritual world and dimension. The spiritual world must *reveal* itself to the physical world. God must *reveal* Himself to us. This is exactly what God has done in Christ, and this is the startling and glorious message of this passage.

Jesus Christ is the source of reality and truth, the very presence of God Himself. Consider this fact: reality and truth—the answers to all of life's questions—are not found in a human philosophy or human ideas. They are found in a Person, the Person of the Lord Jesus Christ.

Think for a moment: if a Being (God) truly created the world, then the answers to life (truth and reality) are bound to be wrapped up in Him, not in the world He made. He is the source to understanding the world; the world is not the source to understanding Him. This truth is so important to grasp that it bears repeating: God is the source to understanding the world; the world is not the source to understanding God. True, we can look at the world and learn some things about God, but not all that we need to know. For example, the world cannot tell us how to conquer evil and death, not perfectly. In light of this, if we seek the truth only in the world, we are left short, unfulfilled, and still asking questions. Thus, we must seek truth and the answer to all things in the Supreme Being who made all things. He alone knows all the answers and all the details.

The glorious message of the gospel and of this passage is that God does exist. He exists and He has revealed Himself in Christ. Christ is the revelation of God, the truth and reality of life itself in all its origin, purpose, meaning, and destiny. Three wonderful truths stand out.

a. **Christ is the fullness** of God (v.9). Christ is God Himself who came to earth: "For in Christ *all the fullness of [God] lives in bodily form.*" All that God is dwells in Christ.

God the Father and God the Son have the same being and nature, that of God. The word *fullness* means that not a single part of God's nature is lacking in the nature of Christ.

What does all this mean to you in practical day-to-day living? It means that God is not far off in outer space somewhere. God is not unconcerned about you or disinterested with the world. He has not just created the world, wound it up, and left it on its own to fly throughout space. God is interested in the world and you—so much so that He has come to earth to show you how concerned He is.

It also means that God is a God of love, not of evil. Only a god of evil would leave you in the dark where you would have to grope and stumble about in order to find God, the truth about the world, and the presence of both good and evil in the world. A God of love would reveal Himself and show you...

- ➢ the way to God
- ➢ the truth of God and the world
- ➢ the life that you are to live (Jn.14:6)

b. You are complete in Christ. *Complete* in this sense means to be made full. When you truly believe in Christ, you receive the fullness of Christ. Just what is the fullness of Christ? Scripture describes it in several ways.

1) You receive wisdom, righteousness, sanctification, and redemption.

> **But of Him you are in Christ Jesus, who became for us wisdom from God—and righteousness and sanctification and redemption—(1 Co.1:30, NKJV).**

2) You receive the fullness of Christ's nature. The divine nature of God is actually placed in you, and you become a new creature in Christ.

> **"Therefore if any man be in Christ, he is a new creature: old things are passed away; behold, all things are become new" (2 Co.5:17, KJV).**

3) You receive fullness of life now. From the time you receive Christ, you should have no need that God will not take care of. If you ever again lack the fullness of life, it is because you have taken your eyes off of Christ and have begun to focus on the world.

> **"I am come that they might have life, and that they might have it more abundantly" (Jn.10:10, KJV).**
>
> **"These things have I spoken [to] you, that my joy might remain in you, and that your joy might be full" (Jn.15:11, KJV).**

4) You receive the fullness of life eternal.

> **For God so loved the world that He gave His only begotten Son, that whoever believes in Him should not perish but have everlasting life (Jn.3:16, NKJV).**

Note the critical importance of this point: the fullness of life and the answers to truth and reality do not come from a worldly philosophy but from the Person of Jesus Christ.

c. **Christ is the Head** of all principality and power; that is, no rule, authority, or power stands between you and God. In fact, absolutely nothing stands between you and God, who is the ultimate Truth and Reality...

- no force
- no power
- no energy
- no person
- no science
- no law of the universe
- no zodiac sign
- no sign or spirit of the stars and planets
- no astrological energy

Your fate—and that of all humanity—is found in Jesus Christ and in Him alone. He is the only Intermediary between you and God, which means you can approach God only through Christ. No one else—no person or force—can present you to God or make you acceptable to Him. For this reason, you need to do everything possible to guard against being captivated by any false philosophy or by astrology.

Chapter 9

What You Should Know and Do in Light of Christ's Return

Contents

Chapter 9

What You Should Know and Do in Light of Christ's Return

1. *You Need to Trust Christ: He Is Preparing an Eternal Home—a Mansion—for You.*

> **"Let not your heart be troubled; you believe in God, believe also in Me. In My Father's house are many mansions; if *it were* not *so,* I would have told you. I go to prepare a place for you. And if I go and prepare a place for you, I will come again and receive you to Myself; that where I am, *there* you may be also" (Jn.14:1-3, NKJV).**

Christ made several amazing claims above.

a. **First, Christ called** God "My Father." Just as a son knows his father, so Christ knows His Father, the Lord God of the universe. That is, He has lived with God, His Father, through the ages and has a personal relationship with God. Note that Jesus Christ was claiming to be the Son of God. As God's Son, Jesus knew *His Father's house,* the truth and reality of it. God's house is real; it exists in another dimension, the spiritual dimension, a place called heaven. This world—the physical and material world—is the property of God, but it is not His house. This earth is not the eternal and permanent dwelling place of God. Heaven is the spiritual world or dimension, the *home* of God where the mansions for believers exist.

b. **Second, Christ claimed** that there are many mansions in His Father's house (v.2). The word *mansion* means an abiding place, a residence, a dwelling; it even implies a large, stately home. What a glorious hope! How much clearer could Christ be: *a place* for every one of us. Just as you have a home here on earth, so Christ promises you a home (mansion) in heaven. For those not fortunate enough to have a home in this world, Christ's promise of a home in heaven is a blessing beyond measure! And there is no shortage of homes. There are "*many* mansions."

Some people question the existence of heaven, a place where life is perfected and continues on eternally. But note how Jesus stressed the truth and reality of

God's house and its *mansions*: "If it were not so, I would have told you." Jesus did not lie. You are to be given a mansion when you arrive in heaven. However, one thing is essential to inherit your home in heaven: belief in Christ (v.1).

c. **Third, Christ claimed** that He was leaving this earth to "prepare a place for you." Where was He going?

➤ Jesus Christ was first going to the cross to prepare redemption for you, the forgiveness of sins.

> **"Christ suffered for our sins once for all time. He never sinned, but he died for sinners to bring you safely home to God. He suffered physical death, but he was raised to life in the Spirit" (1 Pe.3:18, NLT)**
>
> **In him we have redemption through his blood, the forgiveness of sins, in accordance with the riches of God's grace (Ep.1:7, NIV).**

➤ Jesus Christ was next going to be raised from the dead, resurrected to conquer death for you and to give you a new life and power.

> **"And God [has] both raised up the Lord, and will also raise up us by his own power" (1 Co.6:14, KJV).**

➤ Jesus Christ was finally going to ascend into heaven to prepare an eternal home for you.

> **"Through whom [Christ] also we have access by faith into this grace in which we stand, and rejoice in hope of the glory of God (Ro.5:2, NKJV).**

Such a magnificent work on our behalf is bound to deliver us from this corruptible world with all its trouble and afflictions. But remember that Jesus laid down a condition: "You believe in *God, believe* also in me."

d. **Fourth, Christ claimed** that He will come again (v.3). He will return for you and take you to heaven to live with Him eternally. There are two times when Christ will come for you, as well as for all other future believers.

Christ will come for you at death, and your spirit will immediately be taken to heaven. You will pass from this world into the next world, into heaven itself;

and you will pass quickly, never *tasting the pain of death,* never losing a moment's consciousness. One moment you are in this world; the next moment you are in the presence of the Lord. This will be your personal, face-to-face presentation to the Lord, your very first sight of your Savior. Note the following examples...

- Stephen, while being stoned to death, anticipated going immediately to be with the Lord (Ac.7:59).
- Stephen even "saw the glory of God, and Jesus standing on the right hand of God" (Ac.7:55).
- Paul said: "to be absent from the body is to be present with the Lord" (2 Co.5:8).
- Paul even said "he had a desire" to depart, and to be with Christ, which is "far better" (Ph.1:23).
- Jesus promised the thief: "today you will be with me in paradise" (Lu.23:43).
- The believers of Thessalonica, who had already died, are said to "sleep in Jesus," indicating they are finally at rest in the presence of the Lord (1 Th. 4:14).

> **The Lord will rescue me from every evil attack and will bring me safely to his heavenly kingdom. To him be glory for ever and ever. Amen (2 Ti.4:18, NIV).**

Christ will also come for you when He returns at the end of the world. In that day, the bodies of all believers, both dead and alive, will rise to meet Christ in the air. Then we will receive our glorified bodies—dramatically and instantaneously. Christ will gather all His dear followers together and take us home to live in transformed bodies forever. This glorious event will take place as quickly as the blinking of an eye (1 Co.15:52).

Jesus promises that He will come again, and He will. We must never forget: God promised that His Son would come the first time, and He came. So He will come again, despite the skepticism of the vast majority of people.

Jesus Christ is coming again for a glorious reunion with His people and a triumphant march over sin, death, and hell. The triumphant reunion will be so glorious that it will far exceed all that we can think or dream. The event will be a demonstration of indescribable perfection and joy, a reunion when all of the dear followers of Christ will be gathered together before Him for the very first time. Each of us will experience the presence and joy of all the dear saints who have gone before and who will come after, whether they are well-known servants of God or the multitudes of unknown laborers who serve so faithfully in seemingly insignificant positions. There, before the Lord Jesus Christ, you and all other believers will stand together for the very first time in glorious perfection, transformed into the perfect image of Christ your Lord. What a glorious day that will be!

> **"But we are citizens of heaven, where the Lord Jesus Christ lives. And we are eagerly waiting for him to return as our Savior. He will take our weak mortal bodies and change them into glorious bodies like his own, using the same power with which he will bring everything under his control" (Ph.3:20-21, NLT).**

2. *You Should Encourage Other Believers with the Hope of the Lord's Glorious Return.*

> **"And now, dear brothers and sisters, we want you to know what will happen to the believers who have died so you will not grieve like people who have no hope. For since we believe that Jesus died and was raised to life again, we also believe that when Jesus returns, God will bring back with him the believers who have died. We tell you this directly from the Lord: We who are still living when the Lord returns will not meet him ahead of those who have died. For the Lord himself will come down from heaven with a commanding shout, with the voice of the archangel, and with the trumpet call of God. First, the Christians who have died will rise from their graves. Then, together with them, we who are still alive and remain on the earth will be caught up in the clouds to meet the Lord in the air. Then we will be with the Lord forever. So encourage each other with these words" (1 Th.4:13-18, NLT).**

The Lord's return is a subject that intrigues people and offers the most glorious hope to you as a believer. Christ declared that He was coming again to get those who believe in Him and take them to heaven to live with Him eternally (Jn.14:1-3; also see Jn.5:28-29; Ph.3:20-21; Col.3:4; Tit.2:12-13; 1 Pe.5:4).

But what about your loved ones who have already died? What will happen to them? Will they have a part in the spectacular return of Jesus Christ to earth? Will they have the privilege of sharing in the majestic display of God's power and in the glorious reunion of living believers with Christ? What about their bodies? We know that our bodies—the bodies of believers who are living when Christ returns—will be transformed. They will never lie in the ground and decay.

But what about the bodies of loved ones who have already decayed and in some cases have body parts scattered elsewhere in the world due to war, disease, accidents, or maiming? Are they going to share in the glorious resurrection and transformation when Christ returns? This Scripture speaks clearly to this very subject. Hence, we should all study and grasp what God teaches and be comforted in the glorious hope He gives.

You should not grieve excessively over loved ones who die before Christ returns—not if they have trusted Christ. You are bound to experience some sorrow, but you should not suffer grief like unbelievers who have no hope. They have reason to suffer the most agonizing sorrow and hopelessness, but not you. You have hope in Christ.

Your loved ones—all who have trusted Christ—will be raised up to meet the great God and Savior, our Lord Jesus Christ. This is the glorious message to you and to all who truly follow Christ. The events of the Lord's return and of the resurrection are clearly spelled out in these verses.

a. **First, the *Lord Himself*** will descend with a commanding shout from heaven (v.11). Christ will split the skies and miraculously appear in all the spectacular glory, pomp, and power of heaven itself. The word *shout* here refers to a military command. The Commander-in-Chief of the universe will shout louder than any voice has ever done—shout out a command just as He did when He raised Lazarus from the grave: "[Believers] come forth" (Jn.11:43).

The voice of the archangel will also cry out. His shout will probably be the rallying cry for all the armies of the heavenly angels to join in the praise of the glorious event. Christ taught that the heavenly angels would be with Him when He returned to earth (Mt.24:31; 25:31; 2 Th.1:7).

The trumpet of God will sound. The trumpet has always been for the purpose of arousing attention and giving warning. The whole universe—both heaven and earth, including all believers, unbelievers, and angels—will be aroused. And all unbelievers will be warned. The Lord Himself will be present and the events of the end time will then be launched upon the earth.

b. **Second, the dead in Christ** will rise from their graves (v.16). Why will dead believers be the first to be caught up to meet the Lord? Because of the Lord's great love and care. The first expression of love and care will be shown to those dear saints who have passed through the shadow of death. It is the very nature of Christ to show tenderness and love to those who suffer the most; therefore, those who had to face the fate of death will be the first to meet the Lord in the air.

   Only departed believers will arise; no unbeliever will be resurrected, not at this time. Only those who died believing in Jesus Christ will be resurrected when the Lord splits the skies. The believers themselves, that is, their spirits, are already with the Lord. Their bodies are being raised, reunited with their spirits, and transformed to live forever with God. The shout of the Lord to "*come forth*" will call together all the particles of a person's body, no matter where the various parts may lie. All the particles will be transformed to structure an eternal and perfect body.

c. **Third, we who are alive** will be caught up in the air immediately after the dead have risen (v.17). There will be a glorious transformation of our bodies just as there will be of those whose bodies have decayed in the earth. The change will be as Scripture declares: the making of a totally new nature.

> **"For this corruptible must put on incorruption, and this mortal must put on immortality" (1 Co.15:53, KJV).**

The nature of your present body is corruptible and mortal; the nature of your new body will be incorruptible and immortal.

- ➢ The *corruptible* and *mortal* nature refers to your physical, earthly being. Your body ages, deteriorates, dies, decays, and decomposes. No matter who you are, your body is earthly and will return to the earth unless Jesus returns while you are living.
- ➢ The *incorruptible* and *immortal* nature refers to your heavenly being: you will be transformed and given a *perfect body and nature* that will never age, deteriorate, die, or decompose. You will be

completely free from defilement and depravity. You will be given a body that is diametrically opposed to your present body, a body that will be perfected forever to live with God in the new heavens and earth (1 Co.15:42-44).

d. **Fourth, the great gathering** of the living with the dead will take place. Note the emphatic declaration: "Together with them, we…will be caught up in the clouds to meet the Lord in the air." You will be united with all believers. We will all be there together rejoicing in the presence of Him who has saved and transformed us into perfect and eternal beings. What a day of rejoicing that will be!

e. **Fifth, the experience** of living face-to-face with the Lord will begin. You will be caught up to be with the Lord forever (v.17). As wonderful as the gathering of all believers will be, the most wonderful event will be seeing all believers of all generations lift up their praises to the Lord together for the very first time. What will your first thoughts be? Your first response?

Seeing your loved ones will not be the first focus of your attention. Christ will be! The Lord God Himself, in all His majestic glory and power, will consume your attention and praise. You will be lifting up His name in the most perfect hymn of praise and adoration ever arranged.

In light of the Lord's glorious return, you should encourage other believers. God does not reveal the events of the end time to satisfy curiosity. He reveals these glorious events so that you can prepare for His return and encourage others with this most wonderful hope. There is no need for discouragement on this earth, no need for extreme sorrow or grief, no need for hopelessness, and no need for ignorance. The Lord Himself has given you and all believers the most wonderful hope imaginable—the hope of being perfected and living forever with Him, worshipping and serving Him for all eternity in the new heavens and earth.

"If a man keep my saying, he shall never see death" (Jn.8:51, KJV).

"And God shall wipe away all tears from their eyes; and there shall be no more death, neither sorrow, nor crying, neither shall there be any more pain: for the former things are passed away" (Re.21:4, KJV; see Lu.20:35; Jn.11:26; 2 Co.5:1; 2 Ti.1:10).

3. *You Are to Say "No" to All Evil Behavior and Live for God While You Look for Christ's Return.*

> **"[God] teaching us that, denying ungodliness and worldly lusts, we should live soberly, righteously, and godly in the present age, looking for the blessed hope and glorious appearing of our great God and Savior Jesus Christ" (Tit.2:12-13, NKJV).**

God's Word is very clear about how to live in light of Christ's return. You are to say "No" to ungodliness and worldly lusts, and "Yes" to living soberly, righteously, and godly while in this world. Reject, renounce, and give up, anything that is unholy, unrighteous, or impure. Turn away from any behavior, passion, or possession that is not fit for heaven, that could not be presented to God. This includes all the desires and lusts that pull you away from God, that stir you...

- to look when you should not look
- to act when you should not act
- to seek and hoard more for yourself when you should be giving more to meet the needs of others
- to be carnal and mean-spirited when you should be sacrificial and kind
- to be sensual and immoral when you should be disciplined and pure
- to seek praise and honor for yourself when you should be giving praise and honor to the Lord

The passions and possessions that attach you to this world need to be turned away from *now.* One day you will die and move on, but those things will be left behind. *Now* is the time to rid yourself of the selfish pleasures of this world, the very things that you would never want God to see.

God's Word teaches you to say "No" to worldly lusts. Instead, live soberly. Control and discipline yourself. Restrain desires, lusts, and appetites, never giving in to excess. Turn away from everything that you cannot present to God when you meet Him face-to-face.

> **And what do you benefit if you gain the whole world but lose your own soul? Is anything worth more than your soul? (Mt.16:26, NLT).**

Remember, you should always be looking for the *blessed hope,* the return of your great God and Savior, Jesus Christ. Someday in the future—no one knows when—Christ will appear in all the glory and majesty of His Being. Be ready if that day comes during your lifetime. But if it does not, you still need to be ready to meet the Lord whenever He takes you home. If He returns during your lifetime, you may be caught unaware, but there is no excuse to be caught unprepared. Live as if the glorious appearing of the Lord will be today.

4. *You Should Keep in Mind That Jesus Christ Will Execute Perfect Justice on Earth.*

> **"And God will provide rest for you who are being persecuted and also for us when the Lord Jesus appears from heaven. He will come with his mighty angels, in flaming fire, bringing judgment on those who don't know God and on those who refuse to obey the Good News of our Lord Jesus. They will be punished with eternal destruction, forever separated from the Lord and from his glorious power. When he comes on that day, he will receive glory from his holy people—praise from all who believe. And this includes you, for you believed what we told you about him (2 Th.1:7-10, NLT).**

As a believer, you may suffer all kinds of trouble at the hands of your neighbors, community, or government. Unbelievers often want nothing to do with Christ and His demand for righteousness, so they seek to stamp out His name, threatening and persecuting all who believe in Him.

No matter how mild or terrifying your suffering, no matter how unfair or unjust your treatment, you can be greatly encouraged by this one fact: one day God is going to rectify all the injustices of the world. All of those guilty of unjust behavior toward others will bear the terrible judgment of God for their...

- ridicule
- abuse
- scorn
- cursing
- criticism
- gossip
- deception
- lying
- cheating
- stealing
- fighting
- murder

Logically, God *must judge* the world, because judgment is the righteous and just thing to do. Not to judge would be wrong and unjust. Remember, God is perfectly just and righteous Himself; accordingly, His very nature demands that He judge and punish the people who have inflicted injustices and wrongs upon others. This is a fact that must be heeded.

a. **First, the executor** of judgment will be Jesus Christ Himself (v.7). Note that Christ is coming to give rest to your soul as well as to judge the world. You will be released from all the injustices, sufferings, and death here on earth.

> **"There remains therefore a rest for the people of God" (He.4:9, NKJV).**
>
> **"And God shall wipe away all tears from their eyes; and there shall be no more death, neither sorrow, nor crying, neither shall there be any more pain: for the former things are passed away" (Re.21:4, KJV).**

When Christ comes back to execute justice and judgment, He will make a spectacular appearance from heaven. He will rend or tear the skies and come in flaming fire, in all the blazing holiness and power of God Himself (v.8). He will be revealed as the Supreme Majesty and Judge of the universe. Accompanying Christ will be all the angels of heaven. They will add to the majestic glory and triumph of His person and presence. And they will carry out His orders to execute either justice or mercy upon every human being.

b. **Second, the people** to be judged are all who do not know God and those who refuse to believe and obey the Good News of our Lord Jesus Christ (v.8). Who are these persons? They are those who sin against *natural revelation,* who look at creation and fail to see God or to live by the laws that are clearly seen in nature and creation.

> **"The heavens declare the glory of God; the skies proclaim the work of his hands" (Ps.19:1, NIV).**
>
> **"But God shows his anger from heaven against all sinful, wicked people who suppress the truth by their wickedness. They know the truth about God because he has made it obvious to them. For ever since the world was created, people have seen the earth and sky. Through everything God made, they can clearly see his invisible qualities—his eternal power and divine nature. So they have no excuse for not knowing God" (Ro.1:18-20, NLT).**

The point is this: you can look at nature and know that some Being [God]—a Supreme Intelligence and Power—created the universe. And you can see that God operates everything in an orderly and lawful way, giving purpose and meaning to life. You can also observe that God cares and provides for you, which means that He is both good and great.

In light of all the things that naturally reveal God, every human being should acknowledge, worship, and praise Him. Nevertheless, instead of seeing God and coming to know Him, many people have rejected God. Instead of worshipping God, some worship the creation, that is, science and the ability of people to control their own lives and welfare—a humanistic worship (Ro.1:25). Others worship the god of their own imagination, some idea or image of what a god is like (a god that allows them to live as they desire).

It is these people who are to be judged. They are the ones who do not know the only living and true God, not in a personal day-to-day relationship. Still another class of people is to be judged as well: those who do not obey the *Good News* of our Lord Jesus Christ. Who are these?

- Every person who has ever heard the gospel of Christ and rejected it.
- Every person who has professed the gospel of Christ but refuses to obey the gospel (God's Holy Word).
- Every person who has placed his or her trust in rituals or procedures such as baptism or church membership but does not obey God.

> **"But among you there must not be even a hint of sexual immorality, or of any kind of impurity, or of greed, because these are improper for God's holy people. Nor should there be obscenity, foolish talk or coarse joking, which are out of place, but rather thanksgiving. For of this you can be sure: No immoral, impure or greedy person—such a man is an idolater—has any inheritance in the kingdom of Christ and of God. Let no one deceive you with empty words, for because of such things God's wrath comes on those who are disobedient" (Ep.5:3-6, NIV).**

c. **Third, the penalty** of judgment will be terrible, but it will be deserved. Why? Because those who are to be judged had the opportunity to know God, but they chose to deny Him or to curse Him or to walk as they desired throughout life (vv.8-9).

The words *eternal destruction* do not mean annihilation or ceasing to exist. They mean exactly what they say in this verse: to be forever separated from the Lord and from His glorious power—an eternity of anguish and despair. They mean to suffer complete ruin and loss; to be cut off, excluded, removed, separated, and banished from God's presence and from all the good things of life.

> **Let both grow together until the harvest. At that time I will tell the harvesters: First collect the weeds and tie them in bundles to be burned; then gather the wheat and bring it into my barn' " (Mt.13:30, NIV).**
>
> **"So shall it be at the end of the world: the angels shall come forth, and sever the wicked from among the just" (Mt.13:49, KJV).**

d. **Fourth, the time** of the judgment is set. Unbelievers are going to be judged on that day when Jesus Christ returns to earth. At the same time, He will receive glory and praise from His holy people, from all who truly believe in Him (v.10). This includes you, if you have truly trusted Him. Be encouraged! Jesus Christ is coming to execute perfect justice on earth. And He will give you rest from all the mistreatment, the injustices, and the trials of this life—right then and forevermore.

5. *You Need to Stand Against Scoffers Who Deny the Coming Again of Jesus Christ and the End of the World.*

> **First of all, you must understand that in the last days scoffers will come, scoffing and following their own evil desires. They will say, "Where is this 'coming' he promised? Ever since our fathers died, everything goes on as it has since the beginning of creation."...But do not forget this one thing, dear friends: With the Lord a day is like a thousand years, and a thousand years are like a day. The Lord is not slow in keeping his promise, as some understand slowness. He is patient with you, not wanting anyone to perish, but everyone to come to repentance. But the day of the Lord will come like a thief. The heavens will disappear with a roar; the elements will be destroyed by fire, and the earth**

> **and everything in it will be laid bare. Since everything will be destroyed in this way, what kind of people ought you to be? You ought to live holy and godly lives as you look forward to the day of God and speed its coming. That day will bring about the destruction of the heavens by fire, and the elements will melt in the heat. But in keeping with his promise we are looking forward to a new heaven and a new earth, the home of righteousness. So then, dear friends, since you are looking forward to this, make every effort to be found spotless, blameless and at peace with him (2 Pe.3:3-4, 8-14, NIV).**

The first coming of Jesus Christ to earth was the pivotal point of human history. Scripture is very clear about this fact:

- Jesus Christ came in "the fullness of time" (Ga.4:4).
- Jesus Christ came "in these last times for you" (1 Pe.1:20).
- God has "in these last days spoken to us by His Son" (He.1:2).
- John the Apostle says, "it is the last time" (1 Jn.2:18).

When Christ first came to earth, history began its last or final stage. This final period of human history is called the *age of grace*—the age when God's mercy and salvation began flowing out to the world through His Son, the Lord Jesus Christ. For our present discussion, the fact to remember is that this period of history is also called "the last days" (2 Pe.3:3; 2 Ti.3:1).

The final chapter of human history is now being written. Someday, Jesus Christ will return to earth and the world as we know it will be no more. When? Jesus Christ said that no person knows; only God knows. In light of this, you should not be projecting dates. What you should do is obey the Lord's exhortation to *watch and be ready.* You are to look every day and be prepared any moment for His return.

While you wait for Christ's return, though, you need to be aware that scoffers will arise—people who will ridicule the return of Jesus Christ (vv.3-4). They scoff because it has been thousands of years since Jesus Christ came to earth the first time. They ask:

> *Where is this 'coming' He promised? It has been thousands of years since He first came, and Christians have always been proclaiming that He was coming soon. Even*

today, you are declaring that His coming is just around the corner, that everyone must expect His return today. What has happened? Where is He? If He was coming back to earth, surely He would have returned by now.

Scoffers also point to the fact that the universe continues just as it always has. They argue that the universe and its laws are stable and usually functioning in an orderly way. The laws of nature have kept the universe running on and on since its beginning. Not surprisingly, scoffers ask:

Why should people get excited and become concerned about the world's ending? The laws of nature run the universe, not an imaginary God. Nothing has ever changed the world; the world has been going on for millions of years. In fact, it has been continuing for thousands of years since Jesus Christ came. Why, then, get concerned about a change now? The laws of nature will continue to run the universe and keep it stable for millions, if not billions, of years.

One fact is indisputable: it has been over two thousand years (at the time of this writing) since Christ promised He would return. Does this mean that Christ will never come back to earth? Have Christians been wrong in declaring that Christ would return soon? How can thousands of years be said to be soon?

There are people who ask questions like these, and there are even people who use these questions to mock the return of Christ. So what are the answers to these questions?

a. **First, why has Christ** not yet returned to earth? Quite simply, because God does not measure time the same as we do. To God, one day is like a thousand years and a thousand years are like one day (v.8). God is eternal. Think of thousands upon thousands of years. Now, multiply that by ten thousand years and keep on multiplying, never quitting. That is eternity.

   What, then, is one thousand years? Time is relative; it has no span with God. But this is not so with us. We measure time by days and years, and we walk minute by minute throughout the day, 365 days of the year. Time is linear to us, like a straight line. Time either stretches forward into the future or backward into the past. Yet to God, who is eternal, one thousand years seems like a day. So to ask why Jesus Christ has not yet returned after two thousand years is ridiculous. To

God, it may seem like only two days since Christ died and arose! Two thousand years may seem like a long time to us, but not to God. To God, two days (two thousand years) is like a drop in the ocean.

The point is this: you should not be discouraged because Christ has not yet returned. God may want a lot more to take place on earth before He sends Christ back to earth. Your task is not to question when He is returning, but to watch and be ready in case He returns before you depart this life and go to Him.

b. **Second, why has Christ** not yet returned to earth? Because God loves every human being on earth and does not want any person to perish, not a single person (v.9). God is not slow in fulfilling His promise nor is He powerless to return to judge the earth. He has not returned because He wants more and more people to repent—to turn away from their selfish, sinful ways and turn to Him.

   Very simply, God is patient with us, very slow to judge and condemn us. God loves and cares for us despite our sin and rejection. This is the very reason He sent Christ the first time to save us. With this in mind, He is patiently suffering a long time with us, waiting and waiting for more people to repent and turn to Him.

c. **Third, the return of Christ** and the day of the Lord will come as a thief in the night (v.10). You never know when a thief is going to enter your house. No thief tells you ahead of time that he is going to strike. If you knew, you would watch and prepare. This is just the point: the Lord Jesus Christ has told you that He is coming back to earth. He has forewarned you, but He has not told you when. Why?

   ➢ Not knowing when Jesus is returning keeps you focused upon Him and His return. It keeps you looking and longing for Him. It keeps you watching, and it stirs you to live righteously before Him.
   ➢ Not knowing when Jesus is returning serves as a warning to unbelievers. It warns them that they need to repent now—without delay—for He could return today and catch them unprepared.

The day of the Lord is coming, but it is coming as a thief in the night. Christ's return is going to be totally unexpected by most people.

d. **Fourth, the heavens and universe** will pass away: all the elements will melt and be destroyed with intense heat (v.10). Based upon what we know about the universe today—the basic elements such as the atom—nothing really needs to be said about how the universe is going to be destroyed. It is rather a matter of belief in God, that God is the Supreme Intelligence and Force of the universe. If you believe in God, then you know that God can destroy the universe. How? By doing what He did when He created the world, simply speaking (or thinking) the command. He will command the event—perhaps a universal explosion—and the event will take place.

When scientists have enough intelligence to burst the atom and to cause a chain reaction that can destroy and melt the elements of the earth with intense heat, why not God? Why doubt God? All God has to do is speak the Word and all the atoms throughout the universe will explode in a chain reaction. Scripture declares that the day of the Lord *"will come,"* that God is going to speak the word and the amazing event will occur.

e. **Fifth, you should strive to live** a holy and godly life (v.11). In fact, there should be no area of your life, no thought or act, that is not holy and godly. Why such an emphasis upon holiness and godliness? Because of our sin nature and our tendency to sin. Sin and evil have put a curse on the universe. Due to our immoral, lawless, and violent behavior, the world has become so corrupt that it is beyond repair. And to the shame of mankind, God will be forced to destroy the world. The wicked will do nothing to stop the decline and depravity from taking place, so you as a believer must take a stand: hate sin and evil. Be holy and godly in all of your behavior. Live in the reverence and fear of God. In summary, be *Christlike*. Live upon earth just as Christ lived.

f. **Sixth, you should look** for the *day of God* and speed up its coming (v.12). The *day of God* refers to the day when God will dissolve and destroy the heavens and earth, the day when the universe will be set aflame and dissolved, and the elements will melt with intense heat (v.12). What should be your attitude toward the *day of God*? You should be *looking for* the day of God. The word means to wait patiently but expectantly, to eagerly anticipate and long for the *day of God*.

You should also *speed up* the *day of God.* You can actually rush the coming of Christ and cause the *day of God* to come sooner! You have a part in bringing about the eternal kingdom of God. How? God's Word does not say specifically, and any theories suggested would be sheer speculation. But, whatever the case, you can hasten the return of Christ and the end of the world by living a more holy and godly life and reaching more and more people for Christ. The more that people see *Christ in you,* His presence and power carrying you through the trials and temptations of life, the more they are going to want Christ and His power in their lives. And the more holy and godly you live, the more people will see those things for which they long...

- strength to conquer the trials and temptations of life
- hope for the future
- assurance and confidence of living forever
- conviction, purpose, and meaning in life
- love, joy, and peace

As more and more people are attracted to Christ, more and more souls will be won for Christ. And since God in His providence (His omniscience, His knowing all things) already knows the number of people who will ultimately trust Christ as Savior, the sooner that number is reached, the sooner Christ will come!

g. **Seventh, you need to look** forward to the new heavens and earth. No matter what people may think and say about the issue, God declares as simply as human language can describe that He is going to make *new heavens and a new earth*. Why? So the world will be perfect with nothing but righteousness existing there. God has *preordained* a perfect world, a world in which only righteous people will live. God wants a world where there will be no more sin or evil, no more accidents, disease, suffering, murder, drunkenness, drugs, adultery, sexual perversion, war, or death. God wants a society of people who know only the fullness of love, joy, and peace; a people who worship and serve Him forever and ever.

You should make every effort to be prepared for the coming of Christ and the terrifying *day of God.*

- You need to be *without spot*: clean, pure, and unsoiled; having no dirt, pollution, or contamination of sin whatsoever. As you walk day by day, you should be in constant communion and fellowship with Christ, walking in *open confession*. Just being in the world means that some of the pollution of sin catches your eyes or ears and causes sinful thoughts to cross your mind. Pray for the power of Christ's blood to cleanse you and to keep you pure.

This is the only way you can be found spotless by Christ when He returns (1 Jn.1:9).

- You need to be found *blameless*: faultless, above reproach and rebuke. No one should be able to point to you and accuse you of any sin. Strive to be holy, righteous, and pure before God and people.
- You need to be found *living in peace* with *both God and man*. No rebellion against God nor discord with fellow believers or any others should be discovered in your life.

When Christ comes, you are to be spotless, blameless, and at peace with everyone. In particular, you must not be found at odds with Christ or failing to live for Him. Such sinful behavior will be severely judged.

6. *You Need to Walk Faithfully in Christ Day by Day So That When He Returns, You Will Not Be Ashamed.*

> **And now, dear children, remain in fellowship with Christ so that when he returns, you will be full of courage [confidence] and not shrink back from him in shame (1 Jn.2:28, NLT).**

Jesus Christ is coming back again; He will return to earth just as He promised. No matter what the agnostics, atheists, unbelievers, and mockers of this earth say, Jesus Christ is going to rend or tear the skies above and return to earth as the Lord God of the universe.

Never forget this fact: the prophecies that predicted His first coming—hundreds of prophecies predicted hundreds of years before the event occurred—each took place exactly as foretold. So it will be with the return of Christ. Hundreds of prophecies that predict His return will occur exactly as God's Holy Word says. Jesus Christ is coming again. God has forewarned you. As a believer, therefore, you need to walk faithfully in Christ day by day.

> **Whoever claims to live in him must walk as Jesus did (1 Jn.2:6, NIV)**

Consider a fact that is often ignored by believers, a fact that is seldom even thought about: there will be shame, disgrace, and embarrassment for some believers when Christ returns. Some will shrink back from Christ. The notion that there will be nothing but joy and rejoicing when Christ returns is inaccurate. There is going to be judgment: the judgment of every believer's works, no matter what the works are. And never forget, there will also be the judgment of all unbelievers, no matter who they are, even our own family members (if they fail to trust Christ).

On the other hand, always remember this fact: you *can* be filled with joy and rejoicing in *that day.* All who have *continued in fellowship* with Christ and served Him faithfully day by day will be greatly rewarded. So, be careful to walk faithfully. Obey God's Holy Word and commandments every day. Then, when Christ returns, you will have confidence and not be ashamed before Him. You will not shrink back in humiliation and disgrace.

> **For the Son of man shall come in the glory of his Father with his angels; and then he shall reward every man according to his works (Mt.16:27, KJV).**
>
> **For we must all stand before Christ to be judged. We will each receive whatever we deserve for the good or evil we have done in this earthly body (2 Co.5:10, NLT).**

CHAPTER TEN

WHAT YOUR FUTURE HOLDS AS A BELIEVER—YOUR DEATH AND REWARDS

Contents

Chapter Ten

What Your Future Holds as a Believer—Your Death and Rewards

---

1. *You Will Be Carried Safely into Heaven, Transferred Quicker Than the Blink of an Eye into God's Heavenly Kingdom.*

> **The Lord will rescue me from every evil attack and will bring me safely to his heavenly kingdom. To him be glory for ever and ever. Amen (2 Ti.4:18, NIV).**
>
> **We are confident, yes, well pleased rather to be absent from the body and to be present with the Lord (2 Co.5:8, NKJV).**

When you face death, God will transfer you from this world into the next world instantaneously. The idea is that of unbroken time. Picture this: in one moment of time you are living in this world, and within the same moment—in a split second—you will be transported into God's heavenly kingdom. That one instant will happen quicker than the blinking of an eye (11/100 of a second).

As a true believer, you will never encounter death or the terrifying pain of being separated from God. One second you are a citizen of this world, and within that very same second you will stand before the Lord as a citizen of heaven itself (2 Co.5:6-8). This is a beautiful picture of you as a believer never having to taste or experience death (Col.3:1-4; He.2:9; see 2 Co.5:5-8.)

2. *You Will Receive Eternal Life.*

> **"For God so loved the world, that He gave His only begotten Son, that whoever believes in Him shall not perish, but have eternal life (Jn.3:16, NASB; 1 Jn.5:11-12).**

As a believer, you have already inherited eternal life. God has given you eternal life through His Son, the Lord Jesus Christ. Yet, eternal life does not apply only to the future;

you have already begun your eternal journey here on earth with God. But remember, this earth is not your eternal home; you are only a temporary resident passing through on your way home to God's heavenly kingdom.

In fact, while on this earth, you are no different from anyone else in your desire to live a full and fruitful life and in not wanting to die. This is the reason you accepted Christ as your Savior. Yet to live forever in a corrupt world such as ours—a world of evil and death—would not necessarily be a good thing. So, what you now have is not the *ideal life,* not the fullest or best life. It is certainly not what life was meant to be. The life that God gives is the fullest and best life possible. God's life is perfect, perfect in both quality and time (eternal). It is a life that overflows with an abundance of everything that is both *good* and *perfect* and that continues on and on without end. This is the life for which people crave; this is the life you were meant to live.

Never forget, God alone knows what life is really meant to be (Jn.3:36; 5:24; 6:47). This is to be expected and it is logically true, for God is the Creator of all life. Indeed, the reason He sent His Son, the Lord Jesus Christ, into the world was to show you life's true meaning and purpose. When you look at Jesus Christ, you see what a perfect life is, exactly what it involves. A perfect life is existence and activity, yes, but with permanent purpose, fulfillment, completion, and assurance. The life that Christ lived and the life that He gives is a life of...

- ➢ love
- ➢ joy
- ➢ peace
- ➢ patience
- ➢ kindness
- ➢ goodness
- ➢ faithfulness
- ➢ gentleness
- ➢ self-control (Ga.5:22-23)

(Think through each of the above for a moment in relation to people and the world at large to gain the full impact of the life that Christ offers.)

3. *You Will Receive a Glorious New Body, a Transformed, Incorruptible Body.*

> **But our citizenship is in heaven. And we eagerly await a Savior from there, the Lord Jesus Christ, who, by the power that enables him to bring everything under his control, will transform our lowly bodies so that they will be like his glorious body (Ph.3:20-21, NIV).**

> **So also *is* the resurrection of the dead. *The body* is sown in corruption, it is raised in incorruption. It is sown in dishonor, it is raised in glory. It is sown in weakness, it is raised in power. It is sown a natural body, it is raised a spiritual body. There is a natural body, and there is a spiritual body (1 Co.15:42-44, NKJV).**

As a believer, you are to be focused upon the return of Christ. You should actually be watching for and eagerly awaiting the Lord's return every day of your life. To *eagerly await* means to yearn, to look fervently for the coming of the Lord Jesus to take you to heaven.

You should also focus upon the glorious body you will receive when Christ returns. Right now, your body is imperfect, inadequate, coming up well short of what you want it to be. It is inadequate...

- ➢ because its origin is in the earth: it is corruptible, aging, deteriorating, and dying
- ➢ because it is subject to sin, selfishness, evil, and destruction.
- ➢ because it is so weak: it is subject to mental and physical illness, injury, and death.
- ➢ because it offers no hope whatsoever of lasting beyond a few short years.

Despite all this, the Lord Jesus Christ is going to change your body and fashion it to be just like His. Imagine your transformed body: it will be permanent and incorruptible, unchanging and perfect, holy and righteous—all like the glorious body of Christ!

How is this possible? By the power of God, the very power that raised Jesus Christ from the dead and is able to subdue all things under Christ. The power of God that created the world is able to transform your temporary, earthly body into a glorious, incorruptible body.

4. *You Will Receive the Crown of Righteousness.*

> **In the future there is laid up for me the crown of righteousness, which the Lord, the righteous Judge, will award to me on that day; and not only to me, but also to all who have loved His appearing (2 Ti.4:8, NASB).**

This is an amazing reward, a *crown of righteousness*. The crown of righteousness will make you acceptable to

God and enable you to always live like you should—in perfect righteousness—throughout all eternity. No matter who you are, you can never live before God unless you are crowned with righteousness—covered completely with righteousness and perfection. Why? Because God is perfect and only perfection can live in the presence of God. Remember, though, the only way you or anyone else can ever become acceptable to God is by receiving the crown of righteousness from Him. You are to receive the crown for one reason and for one reason only: because you have given your life to Christ, committed yourself to be...

- a soldier for Christ, one who stands strongly for Him (Ep.6:10-18; 2 Ti.2:3-4)
- an athlete for Christ, one who runs strenuously in the race of life (1 Co. 9:24-27; He.12:1-4).
- a manager for Christ, one who faithfully oversees the affairs of life (1 Co.4:2).

Think about it: the crown of righteousness makes you perfect before God and enables you to live righteously before Him forever and ever. You will be enabled to worship and serve God in perfection—never failing and never coming up short, never grieving and never cutting His heart again. What a day of rejoicing that will be! What a glorious contrast with the weaknesses and failures you face today! What a contrast with the fading crowns and trophies given by this world!

Note that the crown of righteousness will be given by the Lord Jesus Himself. You can trust Him, for He is the righteous and perfect Judge. He is the only Judge who can execute perfect justice, for He alone knows the truth about you and everyone else. He knows your heart, and He has observed your behavior day by day. In fact, the Lord has seen every act you have done and heard every word you have ever spoken or even thought. He knows all. Therefore, if you truly trust Christ and long for His coming, you can be assured that the Lord will give you the crown of righteousness in that glorious day of redemption.

5. *You Will Receive the Crown of Life.*

> **God blesses those who patiently endure testing and temptation. Afterward they will receive the crown of life that God has promised to those who love him (Jas.1:12, NLT; see Re.2:10).**

You are to be greatly rewarded for enduring the temptations and trials of this life. If you persevere in this life, two specific rewards will be given to you.

First, you will be *blessed*. This refers to the here and now, to your present life on earth. To be *blessed* means to have inward joy and satisfaction, an inner confidence that carries you through all the trials and temptations of life no matter the pain, sorrow, or loss. Simply stated, you will be secure in this life. You will know that God is looking after and caring for you. He is going to strengthen and deliver you through all the corruption and evil of this life, including death.

Second, you will receive the *crown of life* in the next world. The verb "will receive" is in the future tense, so this crown definitely refers to the gift of *eternal life. Life itself* is the crown. If you trust Christ and endure the trials of life, you will be crowned with *eternal life*—life that never ends. Furthermore, when you pass from this world of sin and death into the world of eternity, your crown will shine more brightly than all the earthly crowns that have ever been worn by the rulers of this world.

Visualize the actual moment when Christ crowns you. The crown of life . . .

- will bestow honor and dignity upon you
- will give you a perfect sense of victory and completion
- will conform you to the image of eternal royalty
- will fill you with unbroken joy and rejoicing

6. *You Will Receive the Crown of Incorruption, the Crown That Will Last Forever.*

> **Everyone who competes in the games goes into strict training. They do it to get a crown that will not last; but we do it to get a crown that will last forever (1 Co.9:25, NIV).**
>
> **Blessed be the God and Father of our Lord Jesus Christ, who according to His great mercy has caused us to be born again to a living hope through the resurrection of Jesus Christ from the dead, to *obtain* an inheritance *which is* imperishable and undefiled and will not fade away, reserved in heaven for you (1 Pe.1:3-4, NASB).**

As a believer, you are in a race to obtain an *incorruptible crown*, a crown that can never perish. The athletes in Paul's day ran for a crown or wreath of leaves, leaves that quickly withered and died, an honor that swiftly faded. Our athletes today strive for the same earthly fame and crowns that quickly pass away. However, the crown and honor you receive from Christ will never fade. Rather, the *crown of incorruption* will bestow on you eternal honor and distinction with which nothing on earth can compare.

7. *You Will Receive the Crown of Rejoicing or of Soul-Winning.*

> **For what is our hope, our joy, or the crown in which we will glory in the presence of our Lord Jesus when he comes? Is it not you? Indeed, you are our glory and joy (1 Th.2:19-20, NIV).**

Paul clearly says that the Thessalonian believers were his hope and joy and *crown* in which he would glory. When? In the day when the Lord Jesus Christ returns. In that day, Paul and all other believers will stand before the Lord face-to-face.

- What a hope! The return of the Lord Jesus Christ.
- What a joy! Living with the Lord eternally and with all the believers whom we have known and helped to reach and grow in Christ.
- What a crown! To offer to Christ all the dear people we have *had a part* in reaching and growing for the Lord.

Think about who it is that wears a *crown*. It is the victor. The crown is worn by a competitor after he or she has won a contest. You too are in a contest—a spiritual struggle against Satan for the souls of people. Therefore, you must discipline yourself, strain and struggle to be a strong witness for the Lord. Remember, a crown awaits you in heaven, one you will miss unless you have helped reach people for Christ and grow them in the Lord.

Each of us needs to apply this lesson to him- or herself and be very honest about the matter: How many individuals have I helped reach for Christ and grow in the Lord? In *that day*, how many people will stand before Christ and thank Him for my help and witness? How many people will be in heaven and be greatly rewarded because of what I am doing on earth?

- One soul?
- Ten souls?
- Twenty souls?
- Fifty souls?
- One hundred souls?
- Thousands of souls?

The crown of rejoicing and of soul-winning awaits you if you are able to present souls to the Lord in *that day.* Ask God to touch your heart and to help you reach and grow people for Him. He will help if you will ask sincerely.

> **The first thing Andrew did was to find his brother Simon and tell him, "We have found the Messiah" (that is, the Christ) (Jn.1:41, NIV).**
>
> **Remember this: Whoever turns a sinner from the error of his way will save him from death and cover over a multitude of sins (Jas.5:20, NIV).**

8. *You Will Receive the Crown of Glory.*

> **And when the Chief Shepherd appears, you will receive the crown of glory that does not fade away (1 Pe.5:4, NKJV).**

Jesus Christ is the Chief Shepherd; and He is going to appear, that is, return, to earth. The idea is that nothing will stop His return; He is going to appear and reward all who have truly followed Him and obeyed His Holy Word.

Your reward will be astounding: it is to be a crown of glory. What does this mean? It means that you will share in the glory of heaven and be crowned with a very *special portion* of glory. To be *crowned* here means to be given the authority to rule and reign, to be entrusted with the assignment of heavenly service for Christ. (see point 10 below for a list of rewards.)

> **His lord said to him, 'Well *done,* good and faithful servant; you have been faithful over a few things, I will make you ruler over many things. Enter into the joy of your lord' (Mt.25:23, NKJV).**

9. *You Will Live in a State of Perfection in a Perfect World.*

> **But the day of the Lord will come like a thief. The heavens will disappear with a roar; the elements will be destroyed by fire, and the earth and everything in it will be laid bare. Since everything will be destroyed in this way, what kind of people ought you to be? You ought to live holy and godly lives as you look forward to the day of God and speed its coming. That day will bring about the destruction of the heavens**

by fire, and the elements will melt in the heat. But in keeping with his promise we are looking forward to a new heaven and a new earth, the home of righteousness (2 Pe.3:10-13, NIV; see Mt.24:35; Ps.102:25-27; Is.51:6; 65:17; 66:2).

Now I saw a new heaven and a new earth, for the first heaven and the first earth had passed away. Also there was no more sea....And God will wipe away every tear from their eyes; there shall be no more death, nor sorrow, nor crying. There shall be no more pain, for the former things have passed away" (Re.21:1, 4, NKJV).

Amazing! These passages reveal the most astonishing news you could ever hear. The heavenly bodies in outer space and the earth as you know it are going to pass away. God clearly says there is to be a new creation of the heavens and the earth. All things are to be made *again*, made *anew*; and the new creation is to be perfected. Three significant facts in the Scriptures need to be addressed.

a. **All the heavens above**—the sun, moon, stars, and planets—are going to be destroyed. God is then going to create a brand new universe.

   Think how beautiful and awesome the heavens look when you observe them on a starry night. It is impossible even to conceive what they will be like when God creates them again. Try to imagine the majesty and magnificence of a perfect universe! All things will be alive and reflect the glory and splendor of God Himself. The universe will be perfect, a place where nothing burns out, wears down, wastes away, or dies. Picture the light, brilliance, and splendor of all the heavenly bodies when God creates the new heavens. Envision what it will mean to have a universe full of *living planets and stars and solar systems.* We cannot begin to comprehend its beauty; it is beyond our finite minds. Nevertheless, Scripture declares emphatically that God is going to create a new and perfect universe (Is.66:22).

b. **The earth is going** to be totally destroyed along with the heavens. Even so, believers can rejoice, for God is also going to create a new and perfect earth. The present earth is defective; it is cursed. The earth suffers under all kinds of natural disasters such as earthquakes, volcanic eruptions, hurricanes, tornados, floods, scorching heat, and other destructive forces. But when God creates the new earth, there will be...

- no more natural disasters or destruction
- no more infertile or unproductive soil
- no more diseased or ruined crops
- no more abuse of the land by humanity

The new earth will flourish and be fruitful, producing more than the human mind can fathom. Just think how beautiful, lush, and bountiful it will be! Imagine for a moment how peaceful and comfortable it will be. Now consider the full and fruitful life that will be possible upon earth—the security and provision of every good and perfect gift. The earth will be new, perfected by God in every conceivable way.

Note the statement, "there was no more sea" (Re. 21:1). This can mean one of two things. First, it can mean that the sea will be eliminated, done away with, and that the new earth will have no sea. Or, second, it can mean the same thing that is meant with the heavens and the earth. That is, the heavens and the earth and the sea are to pass away and all be made anew. The seas that now cause devastation and destruction will naturally be destroyed right along with the earth and the heavens. But when the earth and the heavens are created again, the seas, which are a part of the earth now, will also be part of the new earth, part of the new creation.

A perfected earth is beyond our comprehension. Yet it is exactly what Scripture proclaims is going to happen. God is going to create a new earth as well as new heavens, the home of righteousness.

c. **Life will be perfected** (Re.21:1, 4). This means that your body will be perfected as well as the environment and earth. Life will be totally different from what it is now. The very life and utopia (paradise) for which you have longed will be a living reality. All the sufferings of life such as disease, pain, and death will be gone. All the evil and negative experiences of life will be gone. No crime, violence, lawlessness, hate, or intolerance will exist. Scripture explains the change in the most beautiful and striking way: it declares, "He [God] will wipe away every tear from their eyes."

10. *You Will Receive an Eternal Inheritance, Be Made an Heir of God and a Co-heir with Christ.*

The Spirit Himself bears witness with our spirit that we are children of God, and if

> **children, then heirs—heirs of God and joint heirs with Christ, if indeed we suffer with *Him*, that we may also be glorified together (Ro.8:16-17, NKJV).**
>
> **So that, having been justified by his grace, we might become heirs having the hope of eternal life (Tit.3:7, KJV).**
>
> **Blessed be the God and Father of our Lord Jesus Christ, who according to His great mercy has caused us to be born again to a living hope through the resurrection of Jesus Christ from the dead, to *obtain* an inheritance *which is* imperishable and undefiled and will not fade away, reserved in heaven for you (1 Pe.1:3-4, NASB).**

Once you trust Christ as your Savior and Lord, God adopts you as one of His sons or daughters. As God's dear child, you immediately become an heir of God. Scripture actually says that you are a *co-heir* with Christ.

This is an astounding promise and truth. You will be given the magnificent privilege of sharing all things with the Son of God Himself.

However, to be a *co-heir* does not mean that you will receive an equal amount of the inheritance with Christ. Rather, it means that you are a fellow-heir with Christ and, as such, you will share Christ's inheritance with Him.

Being a fellow-heir with Christ means at least three glorious things: it means that you will share in the *nature*, in the *position*, and in the *responsibility* of Christ. The following chart shows this at a quick glance.

FELLOW HEIRS BY NATURE

Christ is the Son of God, the very being and energy of life and perfection. Therefore, you will share in the inheritance of His nature. You will receive . . .

- ➢ the adoption as a child of God (Gal.4:4-7; 1 Jn.3:1)
- ➢ a nature that is sinless and blameless (Ph.2:15)
- ➢ eternal life (Jn.1:4; 3:16; 10:10; 17:2-3; 1 Ti.6:19)
- ➢ valued property and possessions that will last forever (He.10:34)
- ➢ a glorious body (1 Co.15:42-44; Ph.3:21;)
- ➢ eternal glorification, honor, and peace (Ro.2:10)
- ➢ eternal rest and peace (He.4:9; Re.14:13)
- ➢ an incorruptible body (1 Co.9:25)
- ➢ a nature that is perfected in righteousness (2 Ti.4:8)

Fellow Heirs by Position

Christ is the exalted Lord, the Sovereign Majesty of the universe, the Lord of lords and King of kings. Therefore, you will share in the inheritance of His position and all the riches that so high a position enjoys. You will receive...

- the position of an exalted being (Re.7:9-12)
- citizenship in the Kingdom of God (Mt.25:34; Js.2:5)
- enormous treasures in heaven (Mt.19:21; Lu.12:33)
- unsearchable riches (Ep.3:8)
- the right to surround the throne of God (Re.7:9-13; 20:4)
- the position of a king (Re.1:5; 5:10)
- the position of a priest (Re.1:5; 5:10; 20:6)
- the position of glory (1 Pe.5:4)

Fellow Heirs by Responsibility

Christ is the Supreme Ruler of heaven and earth, the One who is ordained to rule and oversee all. Therefore, you will share in the inheritance of His responsibility. You will receive...

- rulership over many things (Mt.25:23)
- the right to rule and hold authority (Lu.12:42-44; 22:28-29)
- eternal responsibility and joy (Mt.25:21, 23)
- rule and authority over cities (Lu.19:17, 19)
- thrones and the privilege of reigning forever (Re.20:4; 22:5)

The above Scriptures will give some idea of what God means when He speaks of your being a fellow-heir with Christ. Note how your inheritance is described in 1 Pe.1:4 above. You will be given "an inheritance which is imperishable and undefiled and will not fade away, reserved in heaven for you" (1 Pe.1:4, NASB). This is most descriptive, an astounding picture of the new heavens and earth that are coming and of your life in God's eternal world.

a. **Your inheritance will** *never perish*. This means that the inheritance does not age, deteriorate, or die; it does not have the seed of corruption within it. In this present age, everything on earth changes from better to worse, that is, everything is in the process of deteriorating, even if only slightly. But not in the future age. In the coming world, your inheritance will be perfect and incorruptible. It will never change; it will never cease to be the most perfect inheritance and gift imaginable.

b. **Your inheritance will** *never spoil.* This means that the inheritance cannot be polluted or defiled, dirtied or infected. Your inheritance will be without any flaw or defect; it will be perfectly free from sickness, disease, infection, accident, pollution, dirt—from any defilement whatsoever. Never again will there be any pain, suffering, or tears over what happens to you or over the damage or loss of some possession.

c. **Your inheritance will** *never fade away.* It will last forever and ever. The splendor and beauty of it all—of life and of all the positions and possessions that God will give you—will never fade or diminish whatsoever. Nothing, not your body or even your energy, will diminish or waste away.

d. **Your inheritance is** *in heaven.* It is reserved there, and it is actually being held in trust by God for you. God is simply waiting for you to finish your task here on earth and come to Him. Then, He will grant you your inheritance (Jn.14:2-3).

God counts you as a co-heir with His very own Son, the Lord Jesus Christ. God has willed the treasures of heaven to you.

Take just a moment and think about this astounding truth. What a glorious hope and privilege—all made possible through the Lord Jesus Christ!

> **...you know that you will receive an inheritance from the Lord as a reward. It is the Lord Christ you are serving (Col.3:24, NIV).**
>
> **And God raised us up with Christ and seated us with him in the heavenly realms...in order that in the coming ages he might show the incomparable riches of his grace, expressed in his kindness to us in Christ Jesus (Ep.2:6-7, NIV).**

Amen and Amen!

Chapter 11

What You Need Day by Day— God's Promises and Guidance

When you long to please and live for God, or face some troubling trial or temptation, you often need guidance and encouragement. You yearn for help and the assurance that all will work out for good. To whom can you turn for help? Where can you go for answers? The answer is obvious: you need to turn to God and His Holy Word. You need to know God's promises and be assured of His presence and guidance. But how do you go about finding God's promise or answer to your specific need or question?

This last chapter, Chapter 11, is the very resource you need: *What You Need Day by Day: God's Promises and Guidance.* This is a topical resource of God's promises and answers to most, if not all, questions and concerns, longings and needs that we face as human beings. Be sure to refer to it often when you want to hear what God has to say about your particular situation or need:

- ➢ First, look for the specific subject below and meditate on God's wonderful promises to you.
- ➢ Second, look for the specific topic in the Subject Index at the back of the book. Turn to that page to find a discussion of what God's Word says about your need.
- ➢ Third, in areas where you have a recurring need or desire, memorize one or two verses that speak strongly to your heart.

1. *Abortion* ***(See Life, Sanctity and Value of)***

You made all the delicate, inner parts of my body and knit me together in my mother's womb. Thank you for making me so wonderfully complex! Your workmanship is marvelous—how well I know it. You watched me as I was being formed in utter seclusion, as I was woven together in the dark of the womb (Ps.139:13-15, NLT).

"Before I formed you in the womb I knew you, before you were born I set you apart" (Je.1:5a, NIV).

2. *Abuse* ***(See Forgiveness of Sins; Healing; Helper, God My; Hope; Thoughts, Control of)***

3. *Accident* ***(See Helper, God My; Healing; Hope; Power; Weakness)***

4. *Accomplishment* ***(See Achievement; Diligence; Work)***

5. *Achievement* ***(See Diligence; Goals; Trust)***

I have fought the good fight, I have finished the race, I have kept the faith. Finally, there is laid up for me the crown of righteousness, which the Lord, the righteous Judge, will give to me on that Day, and not to me only but also to all who have loved His appearing (2 Ti.4:7-8, NKJV).

Blessed is everyone who fears the LORD, who walks in his ways! You shall eat the fruit of the labor of your hands; you shall be blessed, and it shall be well with you (Ps.128:1-2, ESV).

LORD, you establish peace for us; all that we have accomplished you have done for us (Is.26:12, NIV).

6. *Activities, Too Many* ***(See Peace; Purpose of Life; Rest; Rewards; Service)***

7. *Addiction—Drugs—Drunkenness* ***(See Deliverance; Helper, God My; Power)***

"But watch yourselves lest your hearts be weighed down with dissipation [carousing] and drunkenness and cares of this life, and that day come upon you suddenly like a trap (Lu.21:34, ESV).

Let us walk properly as in the daytime, not in orgies and drunkenness, not in sexual immorality and sensuality, not in quarreling and jealousy. But put on the Lord Jesus Christ, and make no provision for the flesh, to gratify its desires (Ro.13:13-14, ESV).

Do you not know that the wicked will not inherit the kingdom of God? Do not be deceived: Neither the sexually immoral nor idolaters nor adulterers nor male prostitutes nor homosexual offenders nor thieves nor the greedy nor drunkards nor slanderers nor swindlers will inherit the kingdom of God. And that is what some of you were. But you were washed, you were sanctified, you were justified in the name of the Lord Jesus Christ and by the Spirit of our God (1 Co.6:9-11, NIV).

And do not get drunk with wine, for that is debauchery, but be filled with the Spirit (Ep. 5:18, ESV).

Wine is a mocker, strong drink a brawler, and whoever is led astray by it is not wise (Pr.20:1, ESV).

"Woe to him who gives drink to his neighbors, pouring it from the wineskin till they are drunk, so that he can gaze on their naked bodies (Hab.2:15, NIV).

8. *Adultery* *(See Condemnation; Guilt; Forgiveness of Sins; Immorality; Love for Others; Repentance)*

9. *Afraid* *(See Fear)*

10. *Alcoholism* *(See Addiction; Deliverance)*

11. *Alienation* *(See Fellowship; Friendship; Forgiveness of Sins; Love for Others; Reconciliation; Salvation; Unity)*

12. *Anger* *(See Love for Others; Reconciliation; Unity)*

Get rid of all bitterness, rage, anger, harsh words, and slander, as well as all types of evil behavior. Instead, be kind to each other, tenderhearted, forgiving one another, just as God through Christ has forgiven you (Ep.4:31-32, NLT).

Everyone must be quick to hear, slow to speak *and* slow to anger; for the anger of man does not achieve the righteousness of God (Jas.1:19b-20, NASB).

A hot-tempered man stirs up strife, But the slow to anger calms a dispute (Pr.15:18, NASB).

13. *Anxiety* *(See Worry)*

14. *Apostasy* *(See Backsliding)*

15. *Arrogance* *(See Pride; Humility)*

16. *Assault* *(See Healing; Helper, God My)*

17. *Assurance* *(See Believe; Salvation; Security)*

I give them eternal life, and they shall never perish; no one can snatch them out of my hand (Jn.10:28, NIV).

The Spirit Himself testifies with our spirit that we are children of God, and if children, heirs also, heirs of God and fellow heirs with Christ, if indeed we suffer with *Him*

so that we may also be glorified with *Him* (Ro.8:16-17, NASB).

Being confident of this very thing, that He who has begun a good work in you will complete *it* until the day of Jesus Christ (Ph.1:6, NKJV).

But the Lord is faithful, who shall stablish you, and keep *you* from evil (2 Th.3:3, KJV).

18. *Authority (See Great; Humility; Power; Service)*

19. *Backsliding (See Obedience; Protection, God's; Security)*

"Return, you backsliding children, *And* I will heal your backslidings." "Indeed we do come to You, For You are the LORD our God" (Je.3:22, NKJV).

Be careful then, dear brothers and sisters. Make sure that your own hearts are not evil and unbelieving, turning you away from the living God. You must warn each other every day, while it is still "today," so that none of you will be deceived by sin and hardened against God. For if we are faithful to the end, trusting God just as firmly as when we first believed, we will share in all that belongs to Christ (He.3:12-14, NLT).

20. *Bankruptcy (See Helper, God My; Hope; Provision of Life's Necessities; Trust)*

21. *Behavior, Questionable (See Questionable Behavior and Functions)*

22. *Believe – Belief (See Confidence; Faith; Trust)*

But as many as received Him, to them He gave the right to become children of God, to those who believe in His name (Jn.1:12, NKJV).

Most assuredly, I say to you, he who believes in Me has everlasting life (Jn.6:47, NKJV).

They replied, "Believe in the Lord Jesus and you will be saved, along with everyone in your household" (Ac.16:31, NLT).

23. *Benevolence (See Giving)*

24. *Bible (See Word, God's)*

25. *Birth, New (See Nature, Believer's New)*

26. *Bitterness* (*See Anger; Forgiveness of Others; Reconciliation*)

27. *Blended Family* (*See Marriage*)

28. *Bless* (*See Praise*)

29. *Blessings, God's* (*See Prosperity; Protection; Provision of Life's Necessities; Trust*)

Praise be to the God and Father of our Lord Jesus Christ, who has blessed us in the heavenly realms with every spiritual blessing in Christ (Ep.1:3, NIV).

For there is no difference between Jew and Gentile—the same Lord is Lord of all and richly blesses all who call on him, for, "Everyone who calls on the name of the Lord will be saved" (Ro.10:12-13, NIV).

Every good thing given and every perfect gift is from above, coming down from the Father of lights, with whom there is no variation or shifting shadow (Jas.1:17, NASB).

Oh, how great *is* Your goodness, Which You have laid up for those who fear You, *Which* You have prepared for those who trust in You In the presence of the sons of men! (Ps.31:19, NKJV).

"But blessed is the man who trusts in the LORD, whose confidence is in him (Je.17:7, NIV).

30. *Boastful* (*See Speech; Pride; Self-Sufficiency*)

31. *Body, Discipline of*

I beseech you therefore, brethren, by the mercies of God, that you present your bodies a living sacrifice, holy, acceptable to God, *which is* your reasonable service. And do not be conformed to this world, but be transformed by the renewing of your mind, that you may prove what *is* that good and acceptable and perfect will of God (Ro.12:1-2, NKJV).

For bodily exercise profits a little, but godliness is profitable for all things, having promise of the life that now is and of that which is to come (1 Ti.4:8, NKJV).

I discipline my body like an athlete, training it to do what it should. Otherwise, I fear that after preaching to others I myself might be disqualified (1 Co.9:27, NLT).

32. *Body, New and Glorified*

But our citizenship is in heaven, and from it we await a Savior, the Lord Jesus Christ, who will transform our lowly body to be like his glorious body, by the power that enables him even to subject all things to himself (Ph.3:20-21, ESV).

It is the same way with the resurrection of the dead. Our earthly bodies are planted in the ground when we die, but they will be raised to live forever. Our bodies are buried in brokenness, but they will be raised in glory. They are buried in weakness, but they will be raised in strength. They are buried as natural human bodies, but they will be raised as spiritual bodies. For just as there are natural bodies, there are also spiritual bodies (1 Co. 15:42-44, NLT).

33. *Boldness (See Courage)*

34. *Bondage (See Freedom)*

35. *Born Again (See Nature, Believer's New)*

36. *Brokenhearted (See Depression; Discouragement; Helper, God My; Hope; Power)*

He heals the brokenhearted and bandages their wounds (Ps. 147:3, NLT).

37. *Broken Relationships (See Forgiveness of Others; Helper, God My; Hope)*

38. *Brotherly Love (See Love for Others)*

39. *Burdens (See Comfort; Helper, God My; Peace; Rest)*

Cast your burden on the Lord, And He shall sustain you; He shall never permit the righteous to be moved (Ps. 55:22, NKJV).

Then Jesus said, "Come to me, all of you who are weary and carry heavy burdens, and I will give you rest. Take my yoke upon you. Let me teach you, because I am humble and gentle at heart, and you will find rest for your souls. For my yoke is easy to bear, and the burden I give you is light" (Mt. 11:28-30, NLT).

Carry each other's burdens, and in this way you will fulfill the law of Christ (Ga.6:2, NIV).

40. *Busy, Too* (See Peace; Rest)

41. *Carnal—Carnality* (See Nature, Believer's New)

42. *Chastening* (See Discipline of God)

43. *Cheating* (See Honesty; Integrity; Repentance; Stealing)

44. *Childless* (See Prayer; Purpose in Life)

45. *Children*

Fix these words of mine in your hearts and minds; tie them as symbols on your hands and bind them on your foreheads. Teach them to your children, talking about them when you sit at home and when you walk along the road, when you lie down and when you get up. Write them on the doorframes of your houses and on your gates, so that your days and the days of your children may be many in the land (De.11:18-21[a], NIV).

Train up a child in the way he should go, Even when he is old he will not depart from it (Pr.22:6, NASB).

Correct your son, and he will give you rest; Yes, he will give delight to your soul (Pr.29:17, NKJV).

46. *Children, Duties*

"Honor your father and your mother, that your days may be long upon the land which the LORD your God is giving you" (Ex.20:12, NKJV).

Children, obey your parents in the Lord, for this is right. Honor your father and mother (which is the first commandment with a promise), So that it may be well with you, and that you may live long on the earth (Ep.6:1-3, NASB).

"Now therefore, listen to me, *my* children, For blessed *are those who* keep my ways. Hear instruction and be wise, And do not disdain *it* (Pr.8:32-33, NKJV).

The father of the righteous will greatly rejoice; he who fathers a wise son will be glad in him. Let your father and mother be glad; let her who bore you rejoice. My son, give me your heart, and let your eyes observe my ways (Pr.23:24-26, ESV).

47. *Children of God* (See Assurance; Believe)

48. *Christian Liberty* *(See Discernment; Freedom; Questionable Behavior and Functions)*

49. *Christlikeness*

Dear friends, now we are children of God, and what we will be has not yet been made known. But we know that when he appears, we shall be like him, for we shall see him as he is (1 Jn.3:2, NIV).

But we all, with unveiled face, beholding as in a mirror the glory of the Lord, are being transformed into the same image from glory to glory, just as by the Spirit of the Lord (2 Co.3:18, NKJV).

I have been crucified with Christ and I no longer live, but Christ lives in me. The life I live in the body, I live by faith in the Son of God, who loved me and gave himself for me (Ga.2:20, NIV).

50. *Christ's Return* *(See Return, Christ's)*

51. *Church*

All the believers devoted themselves to the apostles' teaching, and to fellowship, and to sharing in meals (including the Lord's Supper), and to prayer (Ac.2:42, NLT).

Not staying away from our meetings, as some habitually do, but encouraging each other, and all the more as you see the day drawing near (He.10:25, HCSB).

52. *Comfort*

Yea, though I walk through the valley of the shadow of death, I will fear no evil; For You *are* with me; Your rod and Your staff, they comfort me (Ps.23:4, NKJV).

I, I am he who comforts you (Is. 51:12a, ESV).

All praise to God, the Father of our Lord Jesus Christ. God is our merciful Father and the source of all comfort. He comforts us in all our troubles so that we can comfort others. When they are troubled, we will be able to give them the same comfort God has given us (2 Co.1:3-4, NLT).

53. *Companionship* *(See Fellowship; Friendship)*

54. *Compassion for Others* *(See Service)*

55. *Compassion, God's* *(See Mercy, God's)*

Just as a father has compassion on *his* children, So the LORD has compassion on those who fear Him (Ps.103:13, NASB).

Though the mountains be shaken and the hills be removed, yet my unfailing love for you will not be shaken nor my covenant of peace be removed," says the LORD, who has compassion on you (Is.54:10, NIV).

Because of the LORD's great love we are not consumed, for his compassions never fail (La.3:22, NIV).

56. *Complete, Made* *(See Life, Abundant; Maturity)*

57. *Condemned – Condemnation, Feeling*

For God did not send His Son into the world to condemn the world, but that the world through Him might be saved. He who believes in Him is not condemned; but he who does not believe is condemned already, because he has not believed in the name of the only begotten Son of God (Jn.3:17-18, NKJV).

"I tell you the truth, whoever hears my word and believes him who sent me has eternal life and will not be condemned; he has crossed over from death to life (Jn.5:24, NIV).

Jesus straightened up and asked her [the adulteress], "Woman, where are they? Has no one condemned you?" "No one, sir," she said. "Then neither do I condemn you," Jesus declared. "Go now and leave your life of sin" (Jn.8:10-11, NIV).

There is therefore now no condemnation to those who are in Christ Jesus, who do not walk according to the flesh, but according to the Spirit (Ro.8:1, NKJV).

Let us draw near to God with a sincere heart in full assurance of faith, having our hearts sprinkled to cleanse us from a guilty conscience and having our bodies washed with pure water (He.10:22, NIV).

58. *Confession* *(See Forgiveness of Sins; Repentance)*

59. *Confidence* *(See Assurance; Trust)*

And I am sure of this, that he who began a good work in you will bring it to completion at the day of Jesus Christ (Ph.1:6, ESV).

Let us therefore come boldly to the throne of grace, that we may obtain mercy and find grace to help in time of need (He.4:16, NKJV).

Now this is the confidence that we have in Him, that if we ask anything according to His will, He hears us (1 Jn.5:14, NKJV).

For the LORD will be your confidence, And will keep your foot from being caught (Pr.3:26, NKJV).

60. *Conflict* *(See Anger; Love for Others; Strife; Unity)*

61. *Confusion – Disorder*

For where envy and self-seeking *exist,* confusion and every evil thing *are* there. But the wisdom that is from above is first pure, then peaceable, gentle, willing to yield, full of mercy and good fruits, without partiality and without hypocrisy. Now the fruit of righteousness is sown in peace by those who make peace (Jas.3:16-18, NKJV).

For God is not *the author* of confusion but of peace (1 Co.14:33[a], NKJV).

62. *Conquest* *(See Victory)*

63. *Contentment* *(See Joy; Satisfaction)*

I am not saying this because I am in need, for I have learned to be content whatever the circumstances (Ph.4:11, NIV).

***Let your* conduct *be* without covetousness; *be* content with such things as you have. For He Himself has said, *"I will never leave you nor forsake you"* (He.13:5, NKJV).**

But godliness with contentment is great gain (1 Ti.6:6, 8, NIV).

64. *Correction, God's* *(See Discipline of God)*

65. *Counsel, Seeking* *(See Decisions; Guidance; Helper, God My; Wisdom)*

66. *Courage*

"Be strong and courageous, do not be afraid or tremble at them, for the LORD your God is the one who goes with you. He will not fail you or forsake you." (De.31:6, NASB).

Be of good courage, And He shall strengthen your heart, All you who hope in the LORD (Ps.31:24, NKJV).

Fear not, for I *am* with you; Be not dismayed, for I *am* your God. I will strengthen you, Yes, I will help you, I will

uphold you with My righteous right hand.' (Is.41:10, NKJV).

67. *Covet - Covetousness* ***(See Contentment; Provision of Life's Necessities; Purpose of Life; Satisfaction)***

68. *Cravings* ***(See Lust)***

69. *Creature - Creation, New* ***(See Nature, New; Salvation)***

70. *Crime - Criminal* ***(See Repentance)***

71. *Crisis* ***(See Helper, God My; Trouble)***

72. *Crying - Weeping* ***(See Sorrow - Grief)***

73. *Cursing* ***(See Profanity; Speech)***

74. *Dating* ***(See Holiness; Immorality; Integrity; Marriage; Obedience; Questionable Behavior; Righteousness; Self-Control)***

75. *Dead, Reunion with the* ***(See Reunion with Love Ones)***

76. *Death*

- You will not face death alone

Yea, though I walk through the valley of the shadow of death, I will fear no evil; For You *are* with me; Your rod and Your staff, they comfort me (Ps.23:4, NKJV).

- Dying is painless

I tell you the truth, if anyone keeps my word, he will never see [experience] death" (Jn.8:51, NIV).
"O Death, where is your sting? O Hades, where is your victory?" (1 Co.15:55, NKJV).

- You will be immediately with the Lord

But God will redeem my soul from the power of the grave, For He shall receive me. (Ps.49:15, NKJV).

We are confident, *I say*, and willing rather to be absent from the body, and to be present with the Lord (2 Co.5:8, KJV).

- Dying is gain

For to me to live *is* Christ, and to die *is* gain (Ph.1:21, KJV).

The Lord will [immediately] rescue me from every evil attack and will bring me safely to his heavenly kingdom. To him be glory for ever and ever. Amen (2 Ti.4:18, NIV).

77. *Death of Loved One* *(See Death; Helper, God My; Hope; Sorrow)*

78. *Deceive – Deception* *(See Lying)*

79. *Decisions* *(See Guidance; Wisdom)*

Trust in the LORD with all your heart And do not lean on your own understanding. In all your ways acknowledge Him, And He will make your paths straight (Pr.3:5-6, NASB).

"See, I have set before you today life and good, death and evil, in that I command you today to love the LORD your God, to walk in His ways, and to keep His commandments, His statutes, and His judgments, that you may live and multiply; and the LORD your God will bless you in the land which you go to possess (De.30:15-16[a], NKJV).

Thus says the LORD: "Stand in the ways and see, And ask for the old paths, where the good way *is,* And walk in it; Then you will find rest for your souls. But they said, 'We will not walk *in it.*' (Je.6:16, NKJV).

80. *Dejection* *(See Downcast; Depression; Helper, God My; Praise; Prayer)*

81. *Deliverance* *(See Helper, God My; Salvation)*

Yes, and the Lord will deliver me from every evil attack and will bring me safely into his heavenly Kingdom. All glory to God forever and ever! Amen (2 Ti.4:18, NLT).

No temptation has overtaken you except such as is common to man; but God *is* faithful, who will not allow

you to be tempted beyond what you are able, but with the temptation will also make the way of escape, that you may be able to bear *it* (1 Co.10:13, NKJV).

When the righteous cry for help, the LORD hears and delivers them out of all their troubles (Ps.34:17, ESV).

82. *Depression (See Helper, God My; Hope; Thoughts, Control of; Praise; Prayer)*

Why are you downcast, O my soul? Why so disturbed within me? Put your hope in God, for I will yet praise him, my Savior (Ps.42:5, NIV).

But they that wait upon the LORD shall renew *their* strength; they shall mount up with wings as eagles; they shall run, and not be weary; *and* they shall walk, and not faint (Is.40:31, KJV).

For I am persuaded, that neither death, nor life, nor angels, nor principalities, nor powers, nor things present, nor things to come, Nor height, nor depth, nor any other creature, shall be able to separate us from the love of God, which is in Christ Jesus our Lord (Ro.8:38-39, KJV).

He heals the brokenhearted and binds up their wounds (Ps.147:3, ESV).

83. *Desires (See Lust)*

84. *Despair (See Helper, God My; Hope)*

85. *Despondency (See Depression; Downcast; Helper, God My; Hope; Praise; Prayer)*

86. *Diligence (See Perseverance; Work)*

Not lagging behind in diligence, fervent in spirit, serving the Lord (Ro.12:11, NASB).

Nevertheless we, according to His promise, look for new heavens and a new earth in which righteousness dwells. Therefore, beloved, looking forward to these things, be diligent to be found by Him in peace, without spot and blameless (2 Pe.3:13-14, NKJV).

The soul of a lazy *man* desires, and *has* nothing; But the soul of the diligent shall be made rich (Pr.13:4, NKJV).

87. *Direction (See Decisions; Discernment; Guidance; Wisdom)*

88. *Disabilities* *(See Helper, God My; Power)*

89. *Disappointment* *(See Discouragement; Hope)*

90. *Discernment* *(See Holy Spirit; Wisdom)*

The man without the Spirit does not accept the things that come from the Spirit of God, for they are foolishness to him, and he cannot understand them, because they are spiritually discerned. The spiritual man makes judgments about all things, but he himself is not subject to any man's judgment: "For who has known the mind of the Lord that he may instruct him?" But we have the mind of Christ (1 Co.2:14-16, NIV).

Test all things; hold fast what is good. Abstain from every form of evil (1 Th.5:21-22, NKJV).

91. *Discipline of Body* *(See Body, Discipline of)*

92. *Discipline of God*

For the Lord disciplines the one he loves, and chastises every son whom he receives" (He.12:6, ESV).

Our fathers disciplined us for a little while as they thought best; but God disciplines us for our good, that we may share in his holiness. No discipline seems pleasant at the time, but painful. Later on, however, it produces a harvest of righteousness and peace for those who have been trained by it (He.12:10-11, NIV).

"Blessed is the man whom God corrects; so do not despise the discipline of the Almighty. For he wounds, but he also binds up; he injures, but his hands also heal" (Jb.5:17-18, NIV).

93. *Discouragement* *(See Downcast; Helper, God My; Thoughts, Control of)*

Have I not commanded you? Be strong and courageous. Do not be terrified; do not be discouraged, for the LORD your God will be with you wherever you go" (Jos.1:9, NIV).

O LORD, you hear the desire of the afflicted; you will strengthen their heart; you will incline your ear (Ps.10:17, ESV).

Hear my cry, O God; listen to my prayer. From the ends of the earth I call to you, I call as my heart grows faint; lead me to the rock that is higher than I. For you have been my refuge, a strong tower against the foe. I

long to dwell in your tent forever and take refuge in the shelter of your wings. Selah (Ps.61:1-4, NIV).

Don't be afraid, for I am with you. Don't be discouraged, for I am your God. I will strengthen you and help you. I will hold you up with my victorious right hand (Is.41:10, NLT).

94. *Discrimination (See Equality, Human)*

95. *Disease (See Healing; Helper, God My; Hope; Power; Prayer; Strength)*

96. *Dissatisfied, Feeling (See Contentment; Hope; Joy; Purpose of Life; Satisfaction)*

I know what it is to be in need, and I know what it is to have plenty. I have learned the secret of being content in any and every situation, whether well fed or hungry, whether living in plenty or in want. I can do everything through him who gives me strength (Ph.4:12-13, NIV).

Bless the LORD, O my soul; And all that is within me, *bless* His holy name! Bless the LORD, O my soul, And forget not all His benefits: Who forgives all your iniquities, Who heals all your diseases, Who redeems your life from destruction, Who crowns you with lovingkindness and tender mercies, Who satisfies your mouth with good *things, So that* your youth is renewed like the eagle's (Ps.103:1-5, NKJV).

My people shall be satisfied with my goodness, declares the Lord" (Je.31:14b, ESV).

97. *Dissension (See Reconciliation; Speech; Strife; Unity)*

98. *Distress – Distraught (See Helper, God My; Hope; Worry)*

99. *Disturbed (See Helper, God My; Hope; Worry)*

100. *Division (See Love for Others; Reconciliation; Unity)*

101. *Divorce (See Helper, God My; Hope; Loneliness; Marriage; Provision of Life's Necessities)*

102. *Doubt (See Faith; Trust; Victory)*

103. *Downcast* *(See Depression; Discouragement; Helper, God My; Hope; Nerves, Unsettled; Thoughts, Control of)*

Why are you downcast, O my soul? Why so disturbed within me? Put your hope in God, for I will yet praise him, my Savior and my God (Ps.42:11, NIV).

My flesh and my heart may fail, but God is the strength of my heart and my portion forever (Ps.73:26, ESV).

104. *Drunkenness—Drugs* *(See Addiction; Helper, God My; Power)*

105. *Emotional Disturbance* *(See Nerves Unsettled)*

106. *Emptiness* *(See Contentment; Hope; Purpose of Life; Satisfaction)*

107. *Encouragement* *(See Discouragement; Helper, God My; Hope)*

108. *Endurance* *(See Patience; Perseverance)*

109. *Enemies* *(See Deliverance; Forgiveness of Others; Helper, God My; Security; Protection)*

So we can say with confidence, "The Lord is my helper, so I will have no fear. What can mere people do to me?" (He.13:6, NLT).

But love your enemies, and do good, and lend, expecting nothing in return, and your reward will be great, and you will be sons of the Most High, for he is kind to the ungrateful and the evil. Be merciful, even as your Father is merciful. "Judge not, and you will not be judged; condemn not, and you will not be condemned; forgive, and you will be forgiven (Lu.6:35-37, ESV).

But you shall fear the LORD your God, and he will deliver you out of the hand of all your enemies" (2 K.17:39, ESV).

Let those who love the LORD hate evil, for he guards the lives of his faithful ones and delivers them from the hand of the wicked (Ps.97:10, NIV).

And the Lord will deliver me from every evil work and preserve *me* for His heavenly kingdom. To Him *be* glory forever and ever. Amen! (2 Ti.4:18, NKJV).

110. *Enticement* *(See Temptation; Victory)*

111. *Envy* ***(See Contentment; Life, Abundant; Love for Others; Satisfaction; Service)***

112. *Equality, Human*

The rich and poor meet together: the LORD *is* the maker of them all (Pr.22:2, KJV).

And he said to them, "You yourselves know how unlawful it is for a Jew to associate with or to visit anyone of another nation, but God has shown me that I should not call any person common or unclean (Ac.10:28, ESV).

But you are not to be called rabbi, for you have one teacher, and you are all brothers. And call no man your father on earth, for you have one Father, who is in heaven. Neither be called instructors, for you have one instructor, the Christ. The greatest among you shall be your servant. Whoever exalts himself will be humbled, and whoever humbles himself will be exalted (Mt.23:8-12, ESV).

There is neither Jew nor Greek, there is neither slave nor free, there is neither male nor female, for you are all one in Christ Jesus (Ga.3:28; ESV; see Ro.10:12).

Listen, my beloved brothers, has not God chosen those who are poor in the world to be rich in faith and heirs of the kingdom, which he has promised to those who love him? (Jas.2:5, ESV).

113. *Equity* ***(See Honesty; Justice)***

114. *Eternal Life*

For God so loved the world that He gave His only begotten Son, that whoever believes in Him should not perish but have everlasting life (Jn.3:16, NKJV).

My sheep hear my voice, and I know them, and they follow me. I give them eternal life, and they will never perish, and no one will snatch them out of my hand (Jn.10:27-28, ESV).

For the wages of sin *is* death; but the gift of God *is* eternal life through Jesus Christ our Lord (Ro.6:23, KJV).

These things I have written to you who believe in the name of the Son of God, that you may know that you have eternal life, and that you may *continue to* believe in the name of the Son of God (1 Jn.5:13, NKJV).

115. *Exhaustion* ***(See Tired—Weary)***

116. *Failure* *(See Backsliding; Guilt; Power; Stability)*

If we confess our sins, he is faithful and just to forgive us our sins and to cleanse us from all unrighteousness. If we say we have not sinned, we make him a liar, and his word is not in us. My little children, I am writing these things to you so that you may not sin. But if anyone does sin, we have an advocate with the Father, Jesus Christ the righteous (1 Jn.1:9–2:1, ESV).

For though a righteous man falls seven times, he rises again, but the wicked are brought down by calamity (Pr.24:16a, NIV).

If the Lord delights in a man's way, he makes his steps firm; though he stumble, he will not fall, for the Lord upholds him with his hand (Ps.37:23-24, NIV).

117. *Fair – Fairness* *(See Honesty; Integrity; Justice)*

118. *Faith* *(See Believe; Trust; Victory)*

For truly, I say to you, if you have faith like a grain of mustard seed, you will say to this mountain, 'Move from here to there,' and it will move, and nothing will be impossible for you" (Mt.17:20[b], ESV).

Be on your guard; stand firm in the faith; be men of courage; be strong (1 Co.16:13, NIV).

Now faith is being sure of what we hope for and certain of what we do not see (He.11:1, NIV).

And without faith it is impossible to please God, because anyone who comes to him must believe that he exists and that he rewards those who earnestly seek him (He.11:6, NIV).

For everyone born of God overcomes the world. This is the victory that has overcome the world, even our faith. Who is it that overcomes the world? Only he who believes that Jesus is the Son of God (1 Jn.5:4-5, NIV).

119. *Faithfulness, Believer's* *(See Perseverance)*

Now it is required that those [believers] who have been given a trust must prove faithful (1 Co.4:2, NIV).

Let us hold fast the confession of our hope without wavering, for he who promised is faithful (He.10:23, ESV).

Be faithful until death, and I will give you the crown of life (Re.2:10[c], NKJV).

A faithful man shall abound with blessings (Pr. 28:20[a], KJV).

120. *Faithfulness, God's*

And those who know your name put their trust in you, for you, O LORD, have not forsaken those who seek you (Ps.9:10, ESV).

But the Lord is faithful, and he will strengthen and protect you from the evil one (2 Th.3:3, NIV).

If we are faithless, he will [still] remain faithful, for he cannot disown himself (2 Ti.2:13, NIV).

121. *Fall – Falling (See Backsliding; Failure; Protection; Security; Stability)*

122. *False Teaching (See Truth; Word of God)*

Whosoever therefore shall break one of these least commandments, and shall teach men so, he shall be called the least in the kingdom of heaven: but whosoever shall do and teach *them*, the same shall be called great in the kingdom of heaven (Mt.5:19, KJV).

"Beware of false prophets, who come to you in sheep's clothing but inwardly are ravenous wolves (Mt.7:15, ESV).

For the time is coming when people will not endure sound teaching, but having itching ears they will accumulate for themselves teachers to suit their own passions, and will turn away from listening to the truth and wander off into myths (2 Ti.4:3-4, ESV).

I am astonished that you are so quickly deserting him who called you in the grace of Christ and are turning to a different gospel—not that there is another one, but there are some who trouble you and want to distort the gospel of Christ. But even if we or an angel from heaven should preach to you a gospel contrary to the one we preached to you, let him be accursed. As we have said before, so now I say again: If anyone is preaching to you a gospel contrary to the one you received, let him be accursed (Ga.1:6-9, ESV).

123. *Falsehood (See Lying)*

124. *Family, Blended (See Marriage)*

125. *Famine (See Provision of Life's Necessities)*

They [believers] will not be disgraced in hard times; even in famine they will have more than enough (Ps.37:19, NLT).

126. *Fatherless (See Helper, God My)*

A father of the fatherless, a defender of widows, *Is* God in His holy habitation (Ps.68:5, NKJV).

You are the helper of the fatherless (Ps.10:14c, NKJV).

127. *Fatigue (See Tired – Weary)*

128. *Favoritism (See Equality, Human; Love for Others; Service)*

129. *Fear (See Courage; Confidence)*

Fear not, for I *am* with you; Be not dismayed, for I *am* your God. I will strengthen you, Yes, I will help you, I will uphold you with My righteous right hand' (Is.41:10, NKJV).

When I am afraid, I put my trust in you (Ps.56:3, ESV).

And do not fear those who kill the body but cannot kill the soul. But rather fear Him who is able to destroy both soul and body in hell (Mt.10:28, NKJV).

For God has not given us a spirit of fear, but of power and of love and of a sound mind (2 Ti. 1:7, NKJV).

130. *Fear of God*

Praise the LORD. Blessed is the man who fears the LORD, who finds great delight in his commands. His children will be mighty in the land; the generation of the upright will be blessed (Ps.112:1-2, NIV).

The fear of the Lord *leads* to life, And *he who has it* will abide in satisfaction; He will not be visited with evil (Pr.19:23, NKJV).

131. *Fellowship (See Friendship; Loneliness)*

What we have seen and heard we proclaim to you also, so that you too may have fellowship with us; and indeed our fellowship is with the Father, and with His Son Jesus Christ (1 Jn.1:3, NASB).

But if we walk in the light, as he is in the light, we have fellowship one with another, and the blood of Jesus Christ his Son [cleanses] us from all sin (1 Jn.1:7, KJV).

I *am* a companion of all who fear You, And of those who keep Your precepts (Ps.119:63, NKJV).

132. *Finances* *(See Giving; Helper, God My; Money; Provision of Life's Necessities)*

133. *Financial Problems* *(See Helper, God My; Provision of Life's Necessities)*

134. *Fleshly* *(See Nature, Believer's New)*

135. *Forgiveness of Others*

For if you forgive men when they sin against you, your heavenly Father will also forgive you (Mt.6:14, NIV).

Be kind to one another, tenderhearted, forgiving one another, as God in Christ forgave you (Ep.4:32, ESV).

Bear with each other and forgive whatever grievances you may have against one another. Forgive as the Lord forgave you. And over all these virtues put on love, which binds them all together in perfect unity (Col.3:13-14, NIV).

136. *Forgiveness of Sins* *(See Redemption; Repentance; Salvation)*

In Him we have redemption through His blood, the forgiveness of sins, according to the riches of His grace (Ep.1:7, NKJV).

If we confess our sins, he is faithful and just to forgive us *our* sins, and to cleanse us from all unrighteousness (1 Jn.1:9, KJV).

But if we walk in the light as He is in the light, we have fellowship with one another, and the blood of Jesus Christ His Son cleanses us from all sin (1 Jn.1:7, NKJV).

For the LORD your God is gracious and merciful and will not turn away his face from you, if you return to him (2 Chr.30:9c, ESV).

As far as the east is from the west, *So* far has He removed our transgressions from us (Ps.103:12, NKJV).

Let the wicked forsake his way, And the unrighteous man his thoughts; Let him return to the LORD, And He will have mercy on him; And to our God, For He will abundantly pardon (Is.55:7, NKJV).

137. *Foul Speech* *(See Profanity; Speech)*

138. *Freedom*

"If you abide in my word, you are truly my disciples, and you will know the truth, and the truth will set you free" (Jn.8:31-32, ESV).

But now that you have been set free from sin and have become slaves to God, the benefit you reap leads to holiness, and the result is eternal life (Ro.6:22, NIV).

Where the Spirit of the Lord is, there is freedom (2 Co.3:17b, ESV).

The Spirit of the LORD God is upon me, because the LORD has anointed me to bring good news to the poor; he has sent me to bind up the brokenhearted, to proclaim liberty to the captives, and the opening of the prison to those who are bound (Is.61:1, ESV).

139. *Friendship (See Fellowship; Love for Others)*

***Be* devoted to one another in brotherly love; give preference to one another in honor (Ro.12:10, NASB).**

Whoever walks with the wise becomes wise, but the companion of fools will suffer harm (Pr.13:20, ESV).

A friend loves at all times, and a brother is born for adversity (Pr.17:17, ESV).

Two are better than one because they have a good return for their labor. For if either of them falls, the one will lift up his companion. But woe to the one who falls when there is not another to lift him up (Ec.4:9-10, NASB).

140. *Friendship, Ungodly (See Holiness; Separation, Spiritual)*

141. *Frustration (See Downcast; Helper, God My; Hope; Nerves, Unsettled; Thoughts, Control of)*

142. *Fulfillment (See Contentment; Purpose of Life; Satisfaction)*

143. *Full – Fullness (See Life, Abundant; Maturity)*

144. *Functions, Questionable (See Discernment; Freedom; Questionable Behavior and Functions)*

145. *Generosity (See Giving)*

146. *Giving (See Serving Others)*

In everything I did, I showed you that by this kind of hard work we must help the weak, remembering the words the Lord Jesus himself said: 'It is more blessed to give than to receive' " (Ac.20:35, NIV).

Give, and it will be given to you. A good measure, pressed down, shaken together and running over, will be poured into your lap. For with the measure you use, it will be measured to you" (Lu.6:38, NIV).

Whoever brings blessing will be enriched, and one who waters will himself be watered (Pr.11:25, ESV).

He who has a generous eye will be blessed, For he gives of his bread to the poor (Pr.22:9, NKJV; see Ps. 19:17).

Bring all the tithes into the storehouse, That there may be food in My house, And try Me now in this," Says the LORD of hosts, "If I will not open for you the windows of heaven And pour out for you *such* blessing That *there will* not *be room* enough *to receive it (*Mal.3:10, NKJV).

147. *Glory (See Heaven)*

I consider that our present sufferings are not worth comparing with the glory that will be revealed in us (Ro.8:18, NIV).

For our light and momentary troubles are achieving for us an eternal glory that far outweighs them all (2 Co.4:17, NIV).

148. *Goals (See Achievement; Diligence; Work)*

Don't you realize that in a race everyone runs, but only one person gets the prize? So run to win! (1 Co.9:24, NLT).

So we make it our goal to please him, whether we are at home in the body or away from it (2 Co.5:9, NIV).

But one thing *I do:* forgetting what *lies* behind and reaching forward to what *lies* ahead, I press on toward the goal for the prize of the upward call of God in Christ Jesus (Ph.3:13b-14, NASB).

149. *God My Helper (See Helper, God My)*

150. *Gossip (See Speech)*

151. *Grace*

Let us therefore come boldly [to] the throne of grace, that we may obtain mercy, and find grace to help in time of need (He.4:16, KJV).

And God is able to make all grace abound to you, so that in all things at all times, having all that you need, you will abound in every good work (2 Co.9:8, NIV).

And He said to me, "My grace is sufficient for you, for My strength is made perfect in weakness." Therefore most gladly I will rather boast in my infirmities, that the power of Christ may rest upon me (2 Co.12:9, NKJV).

For by grace you have been saved through faith. And this is not your own doing; it is the gift of God (Ep.2:8, ESV).

152. *Great – Greatness* *(See Humility; Service)*

Anyone who breaks one of the least of these commandments and teaches others to do the same will be called least in the kingdom of heaven, but whoever practices and teaches these commands will be called great in the kingdom of heaven (Mt.5:19, NIV).

Therefore, whoever humbles himself like this child is the greatest in the kingdom of heaven (Mt.18:4, NIV).

But he who is greatest among you shall be your servant. And whoever exalts himself will be humbled, and he who humbles himself will be exalted (Mt.23:11-12, NKJV).

Therefore humble yourselves under the mighty hand of God, that He may exalt you at the proper time (1 Pe.5:6, NASB).

Both riches and honor come from you, and you rule over all. In your hand are power and might, and in your hand it is to make great and to give strength to all (1 Chr.29:12, ESV).

153. *Greed* *(See Contentment; Giving; Life, Abundant; Satisfaction)*

154. *Grief* *(See Sorrow)*

155. *Grow – Growth* *(See Maturity; Word of God)*

156. *Grudge* *(See Forgiveness of Others; Reconciliation)*

157. *Guidance* *(See Decisions; Holy Spirit; Wisdom)*

When the Spirit of truth comes, he will guide you into all truth. He will not speak on his own but will tell you what he has heard. He will tell you about the future (Jn.16:13, NLT).

Your ears shall hear a word behind you, saying, "This *is* the way, walk in it," Whenever you turn to the right hand Or whenever you turn to the left (Is.30:21, NKJV).

I will instruct you and teach you in the way you should go; I will guide you with My eye (Ps.32:8, NKJV).

Trust in the LORD with all your heart, And lean not on your own understanding; In all your ways acknowledge Him, And He shall direct your paths (Pr.3:5-6, NKJV).

158. *Guilt* *(See Condemnation, Feeling; Failure; Forgiveness of Sins)*

There is therefore now no condemnation to those who are in Christ Jesus, who do not walk according to the flesh, but according to the Spirit (Ro.8:1, NKJV).

Just think how much more the blood of Christ will purify our consciences from sinful deeds so that we can worship the living God. For by the power of the eternal Spirit, Christ offered himself to God as a perfect sacrifice for our sins (He.9:14, NLT).

Let us draw near to God with a sincere heart in full assurance of faith, having our hearts sprinkled [with Christ's blood] to cleanse us from a guilty conscience and having our bodies washed with pure water (He.10:22, NIV).

For whenever our heart condemns us, God is greater than our heart, and he knows everything (1 Jn.3:20, ESV).

159. *Habits, Bad* *(See Addiction; Helper, God My; Hope; Power)*

160. *Handicaps—Infirmities* *(See Helper, God My; Hope; Power; Strength; Weakness)*

161. *Happiness* *(See Joy; Life, Abundant; Praise)*

Blessed [Happy] *is* every one who fears the LORD, Who walks in His ways. When you eat the labor of your hands, You *shall be* happy, and *it shall be* well with you (Ps.128:1-2, NKJV).

Happy *is that* people, that is in such a case: *yea*, happy *is that* people, whose God *is* the LORD (Ps.144:15, KJV).

She [Wisdom] *is* a tree of life to those who take hold of her, And happy *are all* who retain her (Pr.3:18, NKJV).

He who heeds the word wisely will find good, And whoever trusts in the LORD, happy *is* he (Pr.16:20, NKJV).

If you know these things, blessed [happy] are you if you do them (Jn.13:17, NKJV).

As an example of suffering and patience, brothers, take the prophets who spoke in the name of the Lord. Behold, we consider those blessed [happy] who remained steadfast. You have heard of the steadfastness of Job, and you have seen the purpose of the Lord, how the Lord is compassionate and merciful (Jas.5:10-11, ESV).

162. *Hard Work* *(See Diligence; Work)*

163. *Hate – Hatred* *(See Equality, Human; Love for Others; Reconciliation; Unity)*

164. *Healing* *(See Power; Prayer)*

A thorn was given me in the flesh, a messenger of Satan to harass me, to keep me from being too elated. Three times I pleaded with the Lord about this, that it should leave me. But he said to me, "My grace is sufficient for you, for my power is made perfect in weakness." Therefore I will boast all the more gladly of my weaknesses, so that the power of Christ may rest upon me (2 Co.12:7b-9, ESV).

And we know that God causes all things to work together for good to those who love God, to those who are called according to *His* purpose (Ro.8:28, NASB).

Is anyone among you sick? *Then* he must call for the elders of the church and they are to pray over him, anointing him with oil in the name of the Lord; and the prayer offered in faith will restore the one who is sick, and the Lord will raise him up, and if he has committed sins, they will be forgiven him (Jas.5:14-15, NASB).

And this is the confidence that we have toward him, that if we ask anything according to his will he hears us. And if we know that he hears us in whatever we ask, we know that we have the requests that we have asked of him (1 Jn.5:14-15, ESV).

O LORD my God, I cried out to You, And You healed me (Ps.30:2, NKJV).

Bless the LORD, O my soul, and forget not all his benefits, who forgives all your iniquity, who heals all your diseases, who redeems your life from the pit, who crowns you with steadfast love and mercy (Ps.103:2-4, ESV).

Heal me, O LORD, and I shall be healed; Save me, and I shall be saved, For You *are* my praise (Je.17:14, NKJV; see 1 Pe.2:24; Ps.103:3).

165. *Heart, New (See Nature, Believer's New)*

I will give you a new heart and put a new spirit within you; I will take the heart of stone out of your flesh and give you a heart of flesh (Ez.36:26, NKJV).

166. *Heaven*

"In My Father's house are many dwelling places; if it were not so, I would have told you; for I go to prepare a place for you. "If I go and prepare a place for you, I will come again and receive you to Myself, that where I am, *there* you may be also (Jn.14:2-3, NASB).

But our citizenship is in heaven, and from it we await a Savior, the Lord Jesus Christ, who will transform our lowly body to be like his glorious body, by the power that enables him even to subject all things to himself (Ph.3:20-21, ESV).

God will wipe away every tear from their eyes; there shall be no more death, nor sorrow, nor crying. There shall be no more pain, for the former things have passed away" (Re.21:4, NKJV).

167. *Hell (See Judgment)*

168. *Help – Helper, God My*

Let us therefore come boldly unto the throne of grace, that we may obtain mercy, and find grace to help in time of need (He.4:16, KJV).

But my God shall supply all your need according to his riches in glory by Christ Jesus (Ph.4:19, KJV).

For God has not given us a spirit of fear, but of power and of love and of a sound mind (2 Ti.1:7, NKJV).

Casting all your care upon him; for he careth for you (1 Pe.5:7, KJV).

The LORD also will be a refuge for the oppressed, A refuge in times of trouble (Ps.9:9, NKJV).

For I am persuaded, that neither death, nor life, nor angels, nor principalities, nor powers, nor things present, nor things to come, Nor height, nor depth, nor any other creature, shall be able to separate us from the love of God, which is in Christ Jesus our Lord (Ro.8:38-39, KJV).

Many are the afflictions of the righteous, but the LORD delivers him out of them all (Ps.34:19, ESV; see Ps.18:2; Ps.28:7).

But I *am* poor and needy; *Yet* the LORD thinks upon me. You *are* my help and my deliverer; Do not delay, O my God (Ps.40:17, NKJV).

Fear not, for I *am* with you; Be not dismayed, for I *am* your God. I will strengthen you, Yes, I will help you, I will uphold you with My righteous right hand' (Is.41:10, NKJV).

"Fear not, for I have redeemed you; I have called *you* by your name; You *are* Mine. When you pass through the waters, I *will be* with you; And through the rivers, they shall not overflow you. When you walk through the fire, you shall not be burned, Nor shall the flame scorch you (Is.43:1-2, NKJV).

169. *Helplessness* *(See Provision, God's; Helper, God My; and Specific Need Being Faced)*

170. *Holiness*

But as he who called you is holy, you also be holy in all your conduct, since it is written, "You shall be holy, for I am holy" (1 Pe.1:15-16, ESV).

For God did not call us to be impure, but to live a holy life. Therefore, he who rejects this instruction does not reject man but God, who gives you his Holy Spirit (1 Th.4:7-8, NIV).

Therefore, having these promises, beloved, let us cleanse ourselves from all filthiness of the flesh and spirit, perfecting holiness in the fear of God (2 Co.7:1, NKJV).

Follow peace with all *men*, and holiness, without which no man shall see the Lord (He.12:14, KJV).

171. *Holy Spirit*

But the fruit of the Spirit is love, joy, peace, longsuffering [patience], gentleness, goodness, faith, Meekness, temperance [self-control]: against such there is no law (Ga.5:22-23, KJV).

Be filled with the Spirit; Speaking to yourselves in psalms and hymns and spiritual songs, singing and making melody in your heart to the Lord; Giving thanks always for all things [to] God and the Father in the name of our Lord Jesus Christ (Ep.5:18b-20, KJV).

If you then, being evil, know how to give good gifts to your children, how much more will *your* heavenly Father give the Holy Spirit to those who ask Him!" (Lu.11:13, NKJV).

And I will pray the Father, and He will give you another Helper, that He may abide with you forever—the Spirit of truth, whom the world cannot receive, because it neither sees Him nor knows Him; but you know Him, for He dwells with you and will be in you (Jn.14:16-17, NKJV).

Howbeit when he, the Spirit of truth, is come, he will guide you into all truth: for he shall not speak of himself; but whatsoever he shall hear, *that* shall he speak: and he will show you things to come (Jn.16:13, KJV).

Now we have received not the spirit of the world, but the Spirit who is from God, that we might understand the things freely given us by God (1 Co.2:12, ESV).

172. *Homelessness* *(See Provision of Life's Necessities; Service)*

173. *Honesty* *(See Integrity; Lying; Speech; Truthfulness)*

Therefore, having put away falsehood, let each one of you speak the truth with his neighbor, for we are members one of another (Ep.4:25, ESV).

Do not lie to one another, since you laid aside the old self with its *evil* practices, and have put on the new self who is being renewed to a true knowledge according to the image of the One who created him (Col.3:9-10, NASB).

A full and fair weight you shall have, a full and fair measure you shall have, that your days may be long in the land that the LORD your God is giving you. For all who do such things, all who act dishonestly, are an abomination to the LORD your God (De.25:15-16, ESV).

The man of integrity walks securely, but he who takes crooked paths will be found out (Pr.10:9, NIV).

The righteous hates falsehood, but the wicked brings shame and disgrace (Pr.13:5, ESV).

He who walks righteously and speaks what is right, who rejects gain from extortion and keeps his hand from accepting bribes, who stops his ears against plots of murder and shuts his eyes against contemplating evil—this is the man who will dwell on the heights, whose refuge will be the mountain fortress. His bread will be supplied, and water will not fail him (Is.33:15-16, NIV).

174. *Honoring Parents* *(See Children, Duties)*

175. *Hope*

Why are you in despair, O my soul? And *why* have you become disturbed within me? Hope in God, for I shall again praise Him *For* the help of His presence. O my God, my soul is in despair within me; Therefore I remember You (Ps.42:5-6, NASB).

But those who wait on [hope in] the LORD Shall renew *their* strength; They shall mount up with wings like

eagles, They shall run and not be weary, They shall walk and not faint (Is.40:31, NKJV).

Such things were written in the Scriptures long ago to teach us. And the Scriptures give us hope and encouragement as we wait patiently for God's promises to be fulfilled (Ro.15:4, NLT).

For I am persuaded [living in hope], that neither death, nor life, nor angels, nor principalities, nor powers, nor things present, nor things to come, Nor height, nor depth, nor any other creature, shall be able to separate us from the love of God, which is in Christ Jesus our Lord (Ro.8:38-39, KJV).

Blessed be the God and Father of our Lord Jesus Christ, who according to His great mercy has caused us to be born again to a living hope through the resurrection of Jesus Christ from the dead, to *obtain* an inheritance *which is* imperishable and undefiled and will not fade away, reserved in heaven for you (1 Pe.1:3-4, NASB).

Therefore my heart is glad and my tongue rejoices; my body also will live in hope, because you will not abandon me to the grave, nor will you let your Holy One see decay (Ac.2:26-27, NIV).

The LORD *is* good to those who wait for Him, To the soul *who* seeks Him. *It is* good that *one* should hope and wait quietly For the salvation of the LORD (La.3:25-26, NKJV).

Be of good courage, And He shall strengthen your heart, All you who hope in the LORD (Ps.31:24, NKJV; see Ps.52:9).

Why are you cast down, O my soul? And why are you disquieted within me? Hope in God; For I shall yet praise Him, The help of my countenance and my God (Ps.42:11, NKJV).

You are my hiding place and my shield; I hope in your word....Uphold me according to your promise, that I may live, and let me not be put to shame in my hope! (Ps.119:114, 116, ESV).

176. *Hopelessness* *(See Provision, God's; Helper, God My; Hope)*

177. *Hospitality*

Do not neglect to show hospitality to strangers, for by this some have entertained angels without knowing it (He.13:2, NASB).

Offer hospitality to one another without grumbling. Each one should use whatever gift he has received to

serve others, faithfully administering God's grace in its various forms (1 Pe.4:9-10, NIV; see Mk.9:41).

178. *Humility*

Humble yourselves in the sight of the Lord, and He will lift you up (Jas.4:10, NKJV).

He leads the humble in what is right, and teaches the humble his way (Ps.25:9, ESV).

Do nothing from selfishness or empty conceit, but with humility of mind regard one another as more important than yourselves; do not *merely* look out for your own personal interests, but also for the interests of others (Ph.2:3-4, NASB).

Therefore humble yourselves under the mighty hand of God, that He may exalt you at the proper time (1 Pe.5:6, NASB).

179. *Hunger* *(See Provision of Life's Necessities; Service; Work)*

180. *Hypocrisy* *(See Integrity; Nature, Believer's New; Self-Righteousness)*

181. *Immorality—Sexual Sins* *(See Forgiveness of Sins; Guilt; Redemption)*

"You shall not commit adultery" (Ex.20:14, NKJV).

For this is the will of God, your sanctification: that you abstain from sexual immorality (1 Th.4:3, ESV; see 1 Co.6:13).

Marriage *is* honorable among all, and the bed undefiled; but fornicators [all sexually immoral people] and adulterers God will judge (He.13:4, NKJV).

The scribes and the Pharisees brought a woman who had been caught in adultery, and placing her in the midst they said to him, "Teacher, this woman has been caught in the act of adultery. Now in the Law Moses commanded us to stone such women. So what do you say?" This they said to test him, that they might have some charge to bring against him. Jesus bent down and wrote with his finger on the ground. And as they continued to ask him, he stood up and said to them, "Let him who is without sin among you be the first to throw a stone at her." And once more he bent down and wrote on the ground. But when they heard it, they went away one by one, beginning with the older ones, and Jesus was left alone with the woman standing before him. Jesus stood up and said to her, "Woman, where are they? Has no one condemned you?" She said,

"No one, Lord." And Jesus said, "Neither do I condemn you; go, and from now on sin no more" (Jn.8:3-11, ESV).

182. *Infirmity (See Healing; Helper, God My; Hope; Power; Strength; Weakness)*

183. *Injury (See Helper, God My; Healing; Hope; Power; Strength; Weakness)*

184. *Injustice (See Helper, God My; Justice)*

"Because of the devastation of the afflicted, because of the groaning of the needy, Now I will arise," says the LORD; "I will set him in the safety for which he longs" (Ps.12:5, NASB; see Ps.72:4).

Who executes justice for the oppressed; Who gives food to the hungry. The LORD sets the prisoners free (Ps.146:7, NASB; see Is.54:14).

185. *Insecurity (See Confidence; Nerves, Unsettled; Peace; Security)*

186. *Integrity (See Honesty; Truthfulness)*

For the LORD God *is* a sun and shield; The LORD will give grace and glory; No good *thing* will He withhold From those who walk uprightly (Ps.84:11, NKJV).

He stores up sound wisdom for the upright; *He is* a shield to those who walk in integrity, Guarding the paths of justice, And He preserves the way of His godly ones (Pr.2:7-8, NASB).

Those who walk uprightly enter into peace; they find rest as they lie in death (Is.57:2, NIV).

But you have upheld me because of my integrity, and set me in your presence forever (Ps.41:12, ESV; 1 Chr. 29:17).

Whoever walks in integrity walks securely, but he who makes his ways crooked will be found out (Pr.10:9, ESV).

187. *Jealousy (See Contentment; Life, Abundant; Love for Others; Satisfaction)*

188. *Job, Loss of (See Confidence; Helper, God My; Hope; Provision of Life's Necessities; Worry)*

189. *Job, Too Demanding* (See Peace; Purpose in Life; Rest; Strength; Work)

190. *Joy* (See Praise; Rejoicing)

And though you have not seen Him, you love Him, and though you do not see Him now, but believe in Him, you greatly rejoice with joy inexpressible and full of glory, obtaining as the outcome of your faith the salvation of your souls (1 Pe.1:8-9, NASB).

These things I have spoken to you, that my joy may be in you, and that your joy may be full (Jn.15:11, ESV).

Until now you have asked nothing in my name. Ask, and you will receive, that your joy may be full (Jn.16:24, ESV).

Consider it all joy, my brethren, when you encounter various trials, knowing that the testing of your faith produces endurance (Js.1:2-3, NASB).

For you make me glad by your deeds, O LORD; I sing for joy at the works of your hands (Ps.92:4, NIV; see Ps.89:15-16; Ps.97:11-12).

191. *Judgment*

Marvel not at this: for the hour is coming, in the which all that are in the graves shall hear his voice, And shall come forth; they that have done good, [to] the resurrection of life; and they that have done evil, [to] the resurrection of damnation (Jn.5:28-29, KJV; see Mt.25:31-34).

And as it is appointed [to] men once to die, but after this the judgment (He.9:27, KJV).

So you see, the Lord knows how to rescue godly people from their trials, even while keeping the wicked under punishment until the day of final judgment (2 Pe.2:9, NLT).

And I saw the dead, small and great, stand before God; and the books were opened: and another book was opened, which is *the book* of life: and the dead were judged out of those things which were written in the books, according to their works. And the sea gave up the dead which were in it; and death and hell delivered up the dead which were in them: and they were judged every man according to their works. And death and hell were cast into the lake of fire. This is the second death. And whosoever was not found written in the book of life was cast into the lake of fire (Re.20:12-15, KJV).

And, behold, I come quickly; and my reward *is* with me, to give every man according as his work shall be (Re.22:12, KJV; see Jude 14-15).

192. *Justice*

And will not God bring about justice for his chosen ones, who cry out to him day and night? Will he keep putting them off? (Lu.18:7, NIV).

This is what the Lord says: "Maintain justice and do what is right, for my salvation is close at hand and my righteousness will soon be revealed (Is.56:1, NIV).

The Lord executes righteousness And justice for all who are oppressed (Ps.103:6, NKJV).

Slaves [employees], in all things obey those who are your masters on earth, not with external service, as those who *merely* please men, but with sincerity of heart [justly, doing what is right], fearing the Lord (Col.3:22, NASB).

Masters [employers], treat your slaves justly and fairly, knowing that you also have a Master in heaven (Col.4:1, ESV).

193. *Labor* *(See Diligence; Work)*

194. *Lawlessness* *(See Repentance)*

195. *Lazy – Laziness* *(See Diligence; Work)*

Even while we were with you, we gave you this command: "Those unwilling to work will not get to eat." Yet we hear that some of you are living idle lives, refusing to work and meddling in other people's business. We command such people and urge them in the name of the Lord Jesus Christ to settle down and work to earn their own living (2 Th.3:10-12, NLT).

I passed by the field of the sluggard And by the vineyard of the man lacking sense, And behold, it was completely overgrown with thistles; Its surface was covered with nettles, And its stone wall was broken down. When I saw, I reflected upon it; I looked, *and* received instruction. "A little sleep, a little slumber, A little folding of the hands to rest," Then your poverty will come *as* a robber And your want like an armed man (Pr.24:30-34, NASB).

Not lagging behind in diligence, fervent in spirit, serving the Lord (Ro.12:11, NASB).

196. *Leader – Leadership* *(See Diligence; Great – Greatness; Power; Service; Work)*

197. *Liberty* *(See Freedom)*

198. *Liberty, Christian (See Discernment; Freedom; Questionable Behavior and Functions)*

199. *Life, Abundant (See Blessings, God; Joy; Provision of Life's Necessities)*

Then Jesus declared, "I am the bread of life. He who comes to me will never go hungry, and he who believes in me will never be thirsty (Jn.6:35, NIV).

I am come that they might have life, and that they might have *it* more abundantly (Jn.10:10b, KJV).

You have made known to me the paths of life; you will fill me with joy in your presence' (Ac.2:28, NIV).

But my God shall supply all your need according to his riches in glory by Christ Jesus (Ph.4:19, KJV).

For in Christ all the fullness of the Deity lives in bodily form, and you have been given fullness [made complete] in Christ, who is the head over every power and authority (Col.2:9-10, NIV).

But seek first the kingdom of God and His righteousness, and all these things [necessities of life] shall be added to you (Mt.6:33, NKJV).

200. *Life, Demanding (See Life, Abundant; Peace; Purpose of Life; Rest; Service; Worry)*

201. *Life, Sanctity and Value of (See Abortion; Love for Others; Purpose of Life)*

So God created man in his own image, in the image of God created he him; male and female created he them (Ge.1:27, KJV; see Ge.5:1; 9:6; Jas.3:9).

Know that the LORD, he is God! It is he who made us, and we are his; we are his people, and the sheep of his pasture (Ps.100:3, ESV).

For what will it profit a man if he gains the whole world, and loses his own soul? (Mk.8:36, NKJV).

Don't you realize that your body is the temple of the Holy Spirit, who lives in you and was given to you by God? You do not belong to yourself, for God bought you with a high price [the death of God's Son for you. So you must honor God with your body (1 Co.6:19-20, NLT).

Are not two sparrows sold for a penny? And not one of them will fall to the ground apart from your Father. But even the hairs of your head are all numbered. Fear not, therefore; you are of more value than many sparrows (Mt.10:29-31, ESV).

For God so loved the world that He gave His only begotten Son, that whoever believes in Him should not perish but have everlasting life (Jn.3:16, NKJV).

202. *Loneliness (See Comfort; Fellowship; Friendship)*

The LORD himself goes before you and will be with you; he will never leave you nor forsake you. Do not be afraid; do not be discouraged" (De.31:8, NIV; see He. 13:5).

What we have seen and heard we proclaim to you also, so that you too may have fellowship with us; and indeed our fellowship is with the Father, and with His Son Jesus Christ (1 Jn.1:3, NASB).

I *am* a companion of all who fear You, And of those who keep Your precepts (Ps.119:63, NKJV).

Let us not give up meeting together, as some are in the habit of doing, but let us encourage one another--and all the more as you see the Day approaching (He.10:25, NIV).

Therefore *"Come out from among them And be separate, says the Lord. Do not touch what is unclean, And I will receive you."* "I will be a Father to you, And you shall be My sons and daughters, Says the LORD Almighty" (2 Co.6:17-18, NKJV).

203. *Love for God*

You shall love the LORD your God with all your heart and with all your soul and with all your might (De.6:5, ESV).

What does the LORD your God require of you, but to fear the LORD your God, to walk in all his ways, to love him, to serve the LORD your God with all your heart and with all your soul (De.10:12, ESV).

Oh, love the LORD, all you His saints! *For* the LORD preserves the faithful, And fully repays the proud person (Ps.31:23, NKJV).

Keep yourselves in the love of God, looking for the mercy of our Lord Jesus Christ [to] eternal life (Jude 21, KJV).

"Teacher, which is the great commandment in the Law?" And he said to him, "You shall love the Lord your God with all your heart and with all your soul and with all your mind (Mt.22:36-37, ESV).

"Because he has set his love upon Me, therefore I will deliver him; I will set him on high, because he has known My name (Ps.91:14, NKJV).

The Lord protects all those who love him, but he destroys the wicked (Ps.145:20, NLT).

"I love those who love me; And those who diligently seek me will find me (Pr.8:17, NASB).

204. *Love for Others* *(See Service)*

"A new commandment I give to you, that you love one another, even as I have loved you, that you also love one another. "By this all men will know that you are My disciples, if you have love for one another" (Jn.13:34-35, NASB; see Col. 3:12-14).

Let love be genuine. Abhor what is evil; hold fast to what is good. Love one another with brotherly affection. Outdo one another in showing honor (Ro.12:9-10, ESV).

Love is patient and kind; love does not envy or boast; it is not arrogant or rude. It does not insist on its own way; it is not irritable or resentful; it does not rejoice at wrongdoing, but rejoices with the truth. Love bears all things, believes all things, hopes all things, endures all things (1 Co.13:4-7, ESV).

But the fruit of the Spirit is love, joy, peace, patience, kindness, goodness, faithfulness....If we live by the Spirit, let us also walk by the Spirit. Let us not become conceited, provoking one another, envying one another (Ga.5:22, 25-26, ESV).

Owe nothing to anyone except to love one another; for he who loves his neighbor has fulfilled *the* law. For this, "YOU SHALL NOT COMMIT ADULTERY , YOU SHALL NOT MURDER , YOU SHALL NOT STEAL , YOU SHALL NOT COVET," and if there is any other commandment, it is summed up in this saying, "YOU SHALL LOVE YOUR NEIGHBOR AS YOURSELF." Love does no wrong to a neighbor; therefore love is the fulfillment of *the* law (Ro.13:8-10, NASB).

And above all things have fervent love for one another, for *"love will cover a multitude of sins"* (1 Pe.4:8, NKJV; Pr.17:9).

205. *Love of God*

For God so loved the world that He gave His only begotten Son, that whoever believes in Him should not perish but have everlasting life (Jn.3:16, NKJV).

But God demonstrates his own love for us in this: While we were still sinners, Christ died for us (Ro.5:8, NIV).

And I am convinced that nothing can ever separate us from God's love. Neither death nor life, neither angels nor demons, neither our fears for today nor our worries about tomorrow—not even the powers of hell can separate us from God's love. No power in the sky above or in the earth below—indeed, nothing in all creation will ever be able to separate us from the love of God that is revealed in Christ Jesus our Lord (Ro.8:38-39, NLT).

206. *Lust*

For the grace of God that brings salvation has appeared to all men, teaching us that, denying ungodliness and worldly lusts, we should live soberly, righteously, and godly in the present age, looking for the blessed hope and glorious appearing of our great God and Savior Jesus Christ (Tit.2:11-13, NKJV).

For all that *is* in the world--the lust of the flesh, the lust of the eyes, and the pride of life--is not of the Father but is of the world. And the world is passing away, and the lust of it; but he who does the will of God abides forever (1 Jn.2:16-17, NKJV; see 2 Pe.1:3-4).

His divine power has given us everything we need for life and godliness through our knowledge of him who called us by his own glory and goodness. Through these he has given us his very great and precious promises, so that through them you may participate in the divine nature and escape the corruption in the world caused by evil desires (2 Pe.1:3-4, NIV).

So flee youthful passions and pursue righteousness, faith, love, and peace, along with those who call on the Lord from a pure heart (2 Ti.2:22, ESV).

Where do wars and fights *come* from among you? Do *they* not *come* from your *desires for* pleasure that war in your members? You lust and do not have. You murder and covet and cannot obtain. You fight and war. Yet you do not have because you do not ask. You ask and do not receive, because you ask amiss, that you may spend *it* on your pleasures. Adulterers and adulteresses! Do you not know that friendship with the world is enmity with God? Whoever therefore wants to be a friend of the world makes himself an enemy of God (Jas.4:1-4, NKJV; see Tit.3:3-5).

207. *Lying (See Honesty; Speech)*

Do not lie to one another, seeing that you have put off the old self with its practices and have put on the new self, which is being renewed in knowledge after the image of its creator (Col.3:9-10, ESV).

"You shall not steal; you shall not deal falsely; you shall not lie to one another (Le.19:11, ESV).

No one who practices deceit shall dwell in my house; no one who utters lies shall continue before my eyes (Ps.101:7, ESV).

Lying lips *are* an abomination to the LORD, But those who deal truthfully *are* His delight (Pr.12:22, NKJV).

But the cowardly, unbelieving, abominable, murderers, sexually immoral, sorcerers, idolaters, and all liars shall have their part in the lake which burns with fire and brimstone, which is the second death" (Re.21:8, NKJV).

208. *Marital Problems* *(See Broken Relationships; Marriage)*

209. *Marriage*

Therefore a man shall leave his father and his mother and hold fast to his wife, and they shall become one flesh (Ge.2:24, ESV).

But because of the temptation to sexual immorality, each man should have his own wife and each woman her own husband. The husband should give to his wife her conjugal rights, and likewise the wife to her husband. For the wife does not have authority over her own body, but the husband does. Likewise the husband does not have authority over his own body, but the wife does (1 Co.7:2-4, ESV).

So I would have younger widows [and widowers] marry, bear children, manage their households, and give the adversary no occasion for slander (1 Ti.5:14, ESV).

Let marriage be held in honor among all, and let the marriage bed be undefiled, for God will judge the sexually immoral and adulterous (He.13:4, ESV).

Submit to one another out of reverence for Christ. Wives, submit to your husbands as to the Lord. For the husband is the head of the wife as Christ is the head of the church, his body, of which he is the Savior....Husbands, love your wives, just as Christ loved the church and gave himself up for her....In this same way, husbands ought to love their wives as their own bodies. He who loves his wife loves himself. After all, no one ever hated his own body, but he feeds and cares for it, just as Christ does the church—for we are members of his body. "For this reason a man will leave his father and mother and be united to his wife, and the two will become one flesh" (Ep.5:21-23, 25, 28-31, NIV).

In the same way, you wives must accept the authority of your husbands. Then, even if some refuse to obey the Good News, your godly lives will speak to them without any words. They will be won over (1 Pe.3:1, NLT).

210. *Maturity* *(See Life, Abundant; Word of God)*

It was he who gave some to be apostles, some to be prophets, some to be evangelists, and some to be pastors and teachers, to prepare God's people for works of service, so that the body of Christ may be built up until we all reach unity in the faith and in the knowledge of the Son of God and become mature, attaining to the whole measure of the fullness of Christ (Ep.4:11-13, NIV).

And I am certain that God, who began the good work within you, will continue his work until it is finally finished on the day when Christ Jesus returns (Ph.1:6, NLT).

As newborn babes, desire the pure milk of the word, that you may grow thereby (1 Pe.2:2, NKJV).

211. *Meditation* *(See Thoughts, Control of)*

Blessed *is* the man Who walks not in the counsel of the ungodly, Nor stands in the path of sinners, Nor sits in the seat of the scornful; But his delight *is* in the law of the LORD, And in His law he meditates day and night. He shall be like a tree Planted by the rivers of water, That brings forth its fruit in its season, Whose leaf also shall not wither; And whatever he does shall prosper (Ps.1:1-3, NKJV).

I rise before dawn and cry for help; I have put my hope in your word. My eyes stay open through the watches of the night, that I may meditate on your promises (Ps.119:147-148, NIV).

Do not let this Book of the Law depart from your mouth; meditate on it day and night, so that you may be careful to do everything written in it. Then you will be prosperous and successful (Jos.1:8, NIV).

212. *Meekness* *(See Humility)*

213. *Mental Disturbance* *(See Downcast; Helper, God My; Hope)*

214. *Mercy, God's*

Seek the LORD while He may be found, Call upon Him while He is near. Let the wicked forsake his way, And the unrighteous man his thoughts; Let him return to the LORD, And He will have mercy on him; And to our God, For He will abundantly pardon (Is.55:6-7, NKJV).

Behold, it was for my welfare that I had great bitterness; but in love [mercy] you have delivered my life from

the pit of destruction, for you have cast all my sins behind your back (Is.38:17, ESV).

Who *is* a God like You, Pardoning iniquity And passing over the transgression of the remnant of His heritage? He does not retain His anger forever, Because He delights *in* mercy (Mi.7:18, NKJV).

For the LORD your God is a merciful God. He will not leave you or destroy you or forget the covenant with your fathers that he swore to them (De.4:31, ESV).

215. *Mercy Shown Others (See Service)*

216. *Mind (See Thoughts, Control of)*

217. *Misery (See Depression; Helper, God My; Hope; Purpose of Life; Praise; Prayer)*

218. *Money*

Command those who are rich in this present age not to be haughty, nor to trust in uncertain riches but in the living God, who gives us richly all things to enjoy. *Let them* do good, that they be rich in good works, ready to give, willing to share (1 Ti.6:17-18, NKJV).

But remember the LORD your God, for it is he who gives you the ability to produce wealth, and so confirms his covenant, which he swore to your forefathers, as it is today (De.8:18, NIV).

He who trusts in his riches will fall, But the righteous will flourish like the *green* leaf (Pr.11:28, NASB).

219. *Morality (See Holiness; Immorality; Integrity; Nature, Believer's New; Righteousness)*

220. *Murder (See Love for Others; Repent)*

"You shall not murder (Ex.20:13, NASB).

Everyone who hates his brother is a murderer; and you know that no murderer has eternal life abiding in him (1 Jn.3:15, NASB).

221. *Nature, Believer's New*

Now the works of the flesh are evident: sexual immorality, impurity, sensuality, idolatry, sorcery, enmity, strife, jealousy, fits of anger, rivalries, dissensions, divisions, envy, drunkenness, orgies, and things like these. I warn you, as I warned you before, that those who do such things will not inherit the kingdom of God. But the fruit of the Spirit is love, joy, peace, patience, kindness, goodness, faithfulness, gentleness, self-control; against such things there is no law. And those who belong to Christ Jesus have crucified the flesh with its passions and desires. If we live by the Spirit, let us also walk by the Spirit (Ga.5:19-25, ESV).

And do not be conformed to this world, but be transformed by the renewing of your mind, that you may prove what *is* that good and acceptable and perfect will of God (Ro.12:2, NKJV).

Since you have heard about Jesus and have learned the truth that comes from him, throw off your old sinful nature and your former way of life, which is corrupted by lust and deception. Instead, let the Spirit renew your thoughts and attitudes. Put on your new nature, created to be like God—truly righteous and holy (Ep.4:21-24, NLT).

Put to death therefore what is earthly in you: sexual immorality, impurity, passion, evil desire, and covetousness, which is idolatry. On account of these the wrath of God is coming. In these you too once walked, when you were living in them. But now you must put them all away: anger, wrath, malice, slander, and obscene talk from your mouth. Do not lie to one another, seeing that you have put off the old self with its practices and have put on the new self, which is being renewed in knowledge after the image of its creator (Col.3:5-10, ESV).

And because of his glory and excellence, he has given us great and precious promises. These are the promises that enable you to share his divine nature and escape the world's corruption caused by human desires (2 Pe.1:4, NLT).

Do not love the world or the things in the world. If anyone loves the world, the love of the Father is not in him. For all that is in the world— the desires of the flesh and the desires of the eyes and pride in possessions—is not from the Father but is from the world (1 Jn.2:15-16, ESV).

Therefore if any man *be* in Christ, *he is* a new creature: old things are passed away; behold, all things are become new (2 Co.5:17, KJV).

Being born again, not of corruptible seed, but of incorruptible, by the word of God, which liveth and abideth for ever (1 Pe.1:23, KJV; see Jn.3:3-8).

222. *Nature, Old* (*See Nature, Believer's New*)

223. *Needs—Necessities* (*See Provision of Life's Necessities; Trust*)

224. *Nerves, Unsettled – Emotional Disturbance* (*See Confidence; Courage; Hope; Peace*)

For God has not given us a spirit of fear, but of power and of love and of a sound mind (2 Ti.1:7, NKJV).

But may the God of all grace, who called us to His eternal glory by Christ Jesus, after you have suffered a while, perfect, establish, strengthen, and settle *you* (1 Pe.5:10, NKJV).

But the wisdom that is from above is first pure, then peaceable, gentle, willing to yield, full of mercy and good fruits, without partiality and without hypocrisy. Now the fruit of righteousness is sown in peace by those who make peace (Jas.3:17-18, NKJV).

Do not be anxious about anything, but in everything, by prayer and petition, with thanksgiving, present your requests to God. And the peace of God, which transcends all understanding, will guard your hearts and your minds in Christ Jesus (Ph.4:6-7, NIV).

225. *New Birth* (*See Nature, Believer's New*)

226. *New Creation* (*See Nature, Believer's New*)

227. *New Self* (*See Nature, Believer's New*)

228. *Obedience*

Anyone who breaks one of the least of these commandments and teaches others to do the same will be called least in the kingdom of heaven, but whoever practices and teaches these commands will be called great in the kingdom of heaven (Mt.5:19, NIV).

He who has My commandments and keeps them, it is he who loves Me. And he who loves Me will be loved by My Father, and I will love him and manifest Myself to him" (Jn.14:21, NKJV).

If you keep My commandments, you will abide in My love, just as I have kept My Father's commandments and abide in His love. These things I have spoken to you, that My joy may remain in you, and *that* your joy may be full (Jn.15:10-11, NKJV).

He replied, "Blessed rather are those who hear the word of God and obey it" (Lu.11:28, NIV).

"Therefore everyone who hears these words of Mine and acts on them, may be compared to a wise man who built his house on the rock. "And the rain fell, and the floods came, and the winds blew and slammed against that house; and *yet* it did not fall, for it had been founded on the rock (Mt.7:24-25, NASB).

229. *Old Age* ***(See Helper, God My; Protection)***

230. *Old Nature* ***(See Nature, Believer's New)***

231. *Old Self* ***(See Nature, Believer's New)***

232. *Oppression* ***(See Freedom; Helper, God My; Injustice; Justice)***

233. *Orphan* ***(See Fatherless; Helper, God My)***

234. *Overcomer* ***(See Victory)***

235. *Pardon of Sins* ***(See Forgiveness of Sins)***

236. *Parents*

Fathers, do not provoke your children to anger, but bring them up in the discipline and instruction of the Lord (Ep.6:4, ESV).

Therefore you shall keep his statutes and his commandments, which I command you today, that it may go well with you and with your children after you, and that you may prolong your days in the land that the Lord your God is giving you for all time" (De.4:40, ESV).

"And these words which I command you today shall be in your heart. You shall teach them diligently to your children, and shall talk of them when you sit in your house, when you walk by the way, when you lie down, and when you rise up (De.6:6-7, NKJV).

237. *Partiality* ***(See Equality, Human; Love for Others; Service)***

238. *Passion, Evil* ***(See Lust)***

239. *Patience* *(See Perseverance)*

We do not want you to become lazy, but to imitate those who through faith and patience inherit what has been promised (He.6:12, NIV).

Wait on the Lord; Be of good courage, And He shall strengthen your heart; Wait, I say, on the Lord! (Ps.27:14, NKJV).

I wait for the LORD, my soul waits, And in His word I do hope (Ps.130:5, NKJV).

I waited patiently for the LORD; he inclined to me and heard my cry. He drew me up from the pit of destruction, out of the miry bog, and set my feet upon a rock, making my steps secure (Ps.40:1-2, ESV; Mi.7:7; Is.25:9).

But those who wait on the LORD Shall renew *their* strength; They shall mount up with wings like eagles, They shall run and not be weary, They shall walk and not faint (Is.40:31, NKJV).

Be patient, therefore, brothers, until the coming of the LORD. See how the farmer waits for the precious fruit of the earth, being patient about it, until it receives the early and the late rains (Jas.5:7; ESV).

240. *Peace* *(See Thoughts, Control of)*

Therefore being justified by faith, we have peace with God through our Lord Jesus Christ (Ro.5:1, KJV).

Peace I leave with you, My peace I give to you; not as the world gives do I give to you. Let not your heart be troubled, neither let it be afraid (Jn.14:27, NKJV).

"I have told you these things, so that in me you may have peace. In this world you will have trouble. But take heart! I have overcome the world" (Jn.16:33, NIV).

Do not be anxious about anything, but in everything, by prayer and petition, with thanksgiving, present your requests to God. And the peace of God, which transcends all understanding, will guard your hearts and your minds in Christ Jesus (Ph.4:6-7, NIV).

And let the peace of Christ rule in your hearts, to which indeed you were called in one body. And be thankful (Col.3:15, ESV).

Great peace have those who love Your law, And nothing causes them to stumble (Ps.119:165, NKJV)

You will keep *him* in perfect peace, *Whose* mind *is* stayed *on You,* Because he trusts in You (Is.26:3, NKJV).

241. *Perfect – Perfection* *(See Maturity; Word of God)*

242. *Persecution*

Blessed *are* they which are persecuted for righteousness' sake: for theirs is the kingdom of heaven (Mt.5:10, KJV; see 1 Pe.4:12-13).

For [to] you it is given in the behalf of Christ, not only to believe on him, but also to suffer for his sake (Ph.1:29, KJV).

If you are reviled for the name of Christ, you are blessed, because the Spirit of glory and of God rests on you (1 Pe.4:14, NASB).

243. *Perseverance – Endurance (See Patience)*

You need to persevere so that when you have done the will of God, you will receive what he has promised (He.10:36, NIV).

And let us not be weary in well doing: for in due season we shall reap, if we faint not (Ga.6:9, KJV; Jas.5:7-8).

Let us hold fast the profession of *our* faith without wavering; (for he *is* faithful that promised;) (He.10:23, KJV).

But the one who endures to the end will be saved (Mt.24:13, ESV).

Therefore, my beloved brethren, be steadfast, immovable, always abounding in the work of the Lord, knowing that your labor is not in vain in the Lord (1 Co.15:58, NKJV).

244. *Physical Problems (See Body, Discipline of; Healing; Helper, God My; Hope; Power; Strength)*

245. *Plans, Life's (See Purpose of Life)*

246. *Positive Thinking (See Meditation; Thoughts, Control of)*

247. *Poverty (See Provision of Life's Necessities)*

For He will deliver the needy when he cries, The poor also, and *him* who has no helper. He will spare the poor and needy, And will save the souls of the needy (Ps.72:12-13, NKJV).

He regards the prayer of the destitute and does not despise their prayer (Ps.102:17, ESV).

He raises the poor out of the dust, *And* lifts the needy out of the ash heap (Ps.113:7, NKJV).

248. *Power (See Strength)*

I pray that from his glorious, unlimited resources he will empower you with inner strength through his Spirit (Ep.3:16, NLT).

Now to Him who is able to do exceedingly abundantly above all that we ask or think, according to the power that works in us (Ep.3:20, NKJV).

And Jesus looking upon them saith, With men *it is* impossible, but not with God: for with God all things are possible (Mk.10:27, KJV).

But you will receive power when the Holy Spirit has come upon you; and you shall be My witnesses both in Jerusalem, and in all Judea and Samaria, and even to the remotest part of the earth" (Ac.1:8, NASB).

Concerning this thing [some weakness] I pleaded with the Lord three times that it might depart from me. And He said to me, "My grace is sufficient for you, for My strength is made perfect in weakness." Therefore most gladly I will rather boast in my infirmities, that the power of Christ may rest upon me (2 Co.12:8-9, NKJV).

Then he said to me, "This is the word of the LORD to Zerubbabel: Not by might, nor by power, but by my Spirit, says the LORD of hosts (Zec.4:6, ESV).

249. *Praise*

Bless [Praise] the LORD, O my soul, And forget not all His benefits: Who forgives all your iniquities, Who heals all your diseases (Ps.103:2-3, NKJV).

I will praise you forever for what you have done; in your name I will hope, for your name is good. I will praise you in the presence of your saints (Ps.52:9, NIV).

Whoever offers praise glorifies Me; And to him who orders *his* conduct *aright* I will show the salvation of God" (Ps.50:23, NKJV).

Because your steadfast love is better than life, my lips will praise you. So I will bless you as long as I live; in your name I will lift up my hands. My soul will be satisfied as with fat and rich food, and my mouth will praise you with joyful lips (Ps.63:3-5, ESV).

But you are A CHOSEN RACE, A royal PRIESTHOOD, A HOLY NATION, A PEOPLE FOR *God's* OWN POSSESSION, so that you may proclaim the excellencies of Him who has called you out of darkness into His marvelous light (1 Pe.2:9, NASB).

By him [Christ] therefore let us offer the sacrifice of praise to God continually, that is, the fruit of *our* lips giving thanks to his name (He.13:15, KJV).

And be not drunk with wine, wherein is excess; but be filled with the Spirit; Speaking to yourselves in psalms and hymns and spiritual songs, singing and making melody in your heart to the Lord; Giving thanks always for all things unto God and the Father in the name of our Lord Jesus Christ (Ep.5:18-20, KJV).

250. *Prayer*

"Ask, and it will be given to you; seek, and you will find; knock, and it will be opened to you. For everyone who asks receives, and he who seeks finds, and to him who knocks it will be opened (Mt.7:7-8, NKJV).

Now this is the confidence that we have in Him, that if we ask anything according to His will, He hears us. And if we know that He hears us, whatever we ask, we know that we have the petitions that we have asked of Him (1 Jn.5:14-15, NKJV).

Pray without ceasing (1 Th.5:17, KJV).

And pray in the Spirit on all occasions with all kinds of prayers and requests. With this in mind, be alert and always keep on praying for all the saints (Ep.6:18, NIV).

If you abide in Me, and My words abide in you, you will ask what you desire, and it shall be done for you (Jn.15:7, NKJV).

Watch and pray that you may not enter into temptation. The spirit indeed is willing, but the flesh is weak" (Mt.26:41, ESV).

Seek the LORD and his strength, seek his face continually (1 Chr.16:11, KJV).

251. *Pregnancy, Unwanted (See Abortion; Murder; Purpose of Life)*

252. *Prejudice (See Equality, Human; Love for Others; Reconciliation)*

253. *Pressure (See Helper, God My; Peace; Rest; Worry)*

254. *Pride (See Humility; Self-Righteousness; Self-Sufficiency)*

Pride *goeth* before destruction, and an haughty spirit before a fall (Pr.16:18, KJV).

For all that *is* in the world, the lust of the flesh, and the lust of the eyes, and the pride of life, is not of the Father, but is of the world (1 Jn.2:16, KJV).

Haughty eyes, a proud heart, and evil actions are all sin (Pr.21:4, NLT).

To fear the LORD is to hate evil; I hate pride and arrogance, evil behavior and perverse speech (Pr.8:13, NIV).

You rebuke the proud--the cursed, Who stray from Your commandments (Ps.119:21, NKJV).

"Let the one who boasts, boast in the Lord." For it is not the one who commends himself who is approved, but the one whom the Lord commends (2 Co.10:17-18, ESV).

255. *Profanity (See Speech)*

Do not misuse the name of the LORD your God, because the LORD will punish anyone who misuses His name (Ex.20:7, HCSB)

But I say to you, Do not take an oath at all, either by heaven, for it is the throne of God, or by the earth, for it is his footstool, or by Jerusalem, for it is the city of the great King. And do not take an oath by your head, for you cannot make one hair white or black. Let what you say be simply 'Yes' or 'No'; anything more than this comes from evil (Mt.5:34-37, ESV).

But above all, my brothers, do not swear, either by heaven or by earth or by any other oath, but let your "yes" be yes and your "no" be no, so that you may not fall under condemnation (Jas.5:12, ESV).

256. *Profession, False (See Integrity; Self-Righteousness)*

257. *Promises, God's*

[God has] given to us exceedingly great and precious promises, that through these you may be partakers of the divine nature, having escaped the corruption *that is* in the world through lust (2 Pe.1:4, NKJV).

Such things were written in the Scriptures long ago to teach us. And the Scriptures give us hope and encouragement as we wait patiently for God's promises to be fulfilled (Ro.15:4, NLT).

For all of God's promises have been fulfilled in Christ with a resounding "Yes!" And through Christ, our "Amen" (which means "Yes") ascends to God for his glory (2 Co.1:20, NLT).

Having therefore these promises, dearly beloved, let us cleanse ourselves from all filthiness of the flesh and spirit, perfecting holiness in the fear of God (2 Co.7:1, KJV).

And this is the promise that he [has] promised us, *even* eternal life (1 Jn.2:25, KJV).

"Praise be to the LORD, who has given rest to his people Israel just as he promised. Not one word has failed of all the good promises he gave through his servant Moses (1 K.8:56, NIV).

258. *Prosperity (See Blessings, God's; Subject Desired)*

Let them shout for joy and be glad, Who favor my righteous cause; And let them say continually, "Let the LORD be magnified, Who has pleasure in the prosperity of His servant" (Ps.35:27, NKJV).

Blessed *is* the man Who walks not in the counsel of the ungodly, Nor stands in the path of sinners, Nor sits in the seat of the scornful; But his delight *is* in the law of the LORD, And in His law he meditates day and night. He shall be like a tree Planted by the rivers of water, That brings forth its fruit in its season, Whose leaf also shall not wither; And whatever he does shall prosper (Ps.1:1-3, NKJV).

The generous man will be prosperous, And he who waters will himself be watered (Pr.11:25, NASB).

Do not let this Book of the Law depart from your mouth; meditate on it day and night, so that you may be careful to do everything written in it. Then you will be prosperous and successful (Jos.1:8, NIV).

259. *Protection, God's (See Security)*

Yes, and the Lord will deliver me from every evil attack and will bring me safely into his heavenly Kingdom. All glory to God forever and ever! Amen (2 Ti.4:18, NLT).

The name of the LORD *is* a strong tower; The righteous run to it and are safe (Pr.18:10, NKJV).

Those who live in the shelter of the Most High will find rest in the shadow of the Almighty. This I declare about the LORD: He alone is my refuge, my place of safety; he is my God, and I trust him. For he will rescue you from every trap and protect you from deadly disease. He will cover you with his feathers. He will shelter you with his wings. His faithful promises are your armor and protection (Ps.91:1-4, NLT).

The LORD will protect you from all evil; He will keep your soul (Ps.121:7, NASB).

"Fear not, for I have redeemed you; I have called you by name, you are mine. When you pass through the waters, I will be with you; and through the rivers, they shall not overwhelm you; when you walk through fire you shall not be burned, and the flame shall not consume you (Is.43:1b-2, ESV).

260. *Providence, God's (See Sovereignty, God's)*

And we know that all things work together for good to them that love God, to them who are the called according to *his* purpose (Ro.8:28, KJV).

The steps of a *good* man are ordered by the LORD, And He delights in his way (Ps.37:23, NKJV).

A man's heart plans his way, But the LORD directs his steps (Pr.16:9, NKJV).

261. *Provision of Life's Necessities*

But my God shall supply all your need according to his riches in glory by Christ Jesus (Phil.4:19, KJV).

"So don't worry about these things, saying, 'What will we eat? What will we drink? What will we wear?' These things dominate the thoughts of unbelievers, but your heavenly Father already knows all your needs. Seek the Kingdom of God above all else, and live righteously, and he will give you everything you need (Mt.6:31-33, NLT).

The Lord *is* my shepherd; I shall not want (Ps.23:1, KJV).

He provides food for those who fear him; he remembers his covenant forever (Ps.111:5, ESV).

262. *Purpose of Life* *(See Providence; Sovereignty; Will of God, Finding)*

The LORD will fulfill [his purpose] for me; your love, O LORD, endures forever—do not abandon the works of your hands (Ps.138:8, NIV).

"You are My witnesses," declares the LORD, "And My servant whom I have chosen, so that you may know and believe Me and understand that I am He. Before Me there was no God formed, and there will be none after Me" (Is.43:10, NASB).

With this in mind, we constantly pray for you, that our God may count you worthy of his calling, and that by his power he may fulfill every good purpose of yours and every act prompted by your faith (2 Th.1:11, NIV).

Furthermore, because we are united with Christ, we have received an inheritance from God, for he chose us in advance, and he makes everything work out according to his plan (Ep.1:11, NLT).

I am come that they might have life, and that they might have *it* more abundantly (Jn.10:10b, KJV).

For I know the plans I have for you," declares the LORD, "plans to prosper you and not to harm you, plans to give you hope and a future (Je.29:11, NIV).

And we know that God causes everything to work together for the good of those who love God and are called according to his purpose for them. For God knew his people in advance, and he chose them to become like his Son, so that his Son would be the firstborn among many brothers and sisters (Ro.8:28-29, NLT).

For we are God's workmanship, created in Christ Jesus to do good works, which God prepared in advance for us to do (Ep.2:10, NIV).

263. *Purposelessness* *(See Hope; Life, Abundant; Purpose of Life)*

264. *Questionable Functions and Behavior* *(See Discernment; Wisdom)*

One man considers one day more sacred than another; another man considers every day alike. Each one should be fully convinced in his own mind. He who regards one day as special, does so to the Lord. He who eats meat, eats to the Lord, for he gives thanks to God; and he who abstains, does so to the Lord and gives thanks to God....Do not destroy the work of God for the sake of food. All food is clean, but it is wrong for a man to eat anything that causes someone else to stumble. It is better not to eat meat or drink wine or to do anything else that will cause your brother to fall. So whatever you believe about these things keep between yourself and God. Blessed is the man who does not condemn himself by what he approves. But the man who has doubts is condemned if he eats, because his eating is not from faith; and everything that does not come from faith is sin (Ro.14:5-6, 20-23, NIV).

"Everything is permissible"—but not everything is beneficial. "Everything is permissible"—but not everything is constructive. Nobody should seek his own good, but the good of others (1 Co.10:23-24, NIV).

265. *Ransom* *(See Redemption)*

266. *Rebellion* *(See Obedience)*

267. *Reconciliation* *(See Love for Others; Unity)*

Now all things *are* of God, who has reconciled us to Himself through Jesus Christ, and has given us the ministry of reconciliation, that is, that God was in Christ reconciling the world to Himself, not imputing their trespasses to them, and has committed to us the word of reconciliation (2 Co.5:18-19, NKJV).

For he himself is our peace, who has made the two one [Jew and Gentile] and has destroyed the barrier, the dividing wall of hostility, by abolishing in his flesh the law with its commandments and regulations. His purpose was to create in himself one new man out of the two, thus making peace, and in this one body to reconcile both of them to God through the cross, by which he put to death their hostility (Ep.2:14-16, NIV).

For God was pleased to have all his fullness dwell in him [Christ], and through him to reconcile to himself all things, whether things on earth or things in heaven, by making peace through his blood, shed on the cross (Col.1:19-20, NIV).

So if you are offering your gift at the altar and there remember that your brother has something against you, leave your gift there before the altar and go. First be reconciled to your brother, and then come and offer your gift (Mt.5:23-24, ESV).

"If another believer sins against you, go privately and point out the offense. If the other person listens and confesses it, you have won that person back. But if you are unsuccessful, take one or two others with you and go back again, so that everything you say may be confirmed by two or three witnesses. If the person still refuses to listen, take your case to the church. Then if he or she won't accept the church's decision, treat that person as a pagan or a corrupt tax collector (Mt.18:15-17, NLT).

268. *Redemption* *(See Forgiveness of Sins; Salvation)*

For He [God] rescued us from the domain of darkness, and transferred us to the kingdom of His beloved Son, in whom we have redemption, the forgiveness of sins (Col.1:13-14, NASB).

I have blotted out your transgressions like a cloud and your sins like mist; return to me, for I have redeemed you (Is.44:22, ESV).

With his own blood—not the blood of goats and calves—he entered the Most Holy Place once for all time and secured our redemption forever. Under the old system, the blood of goats and bulls and the ashes of a young cow could cleanse people's bodies from ceremonial impurity. Just think how much more the blood of Christ will purify our consciences from sinful deeds so that we can worship the living God. For by the power of the eternal Spirit, Christ offered himself to God as a perfect sacrifice for our sins (He.9:12-14, NLT).

[Christ] Who gave himself for us to redeem us from all lawlessness and to purify for himself a people for his own possession who are zealous for good works (Tit.2:14, ESV).

269. *Regeneration* *(See Nature, Believer's New; Salvation)*

270. *Rejoicing* *(See Joy; Praise)*

I have set the LORD always before me; because he is at my right hand, I shall not be shaken. Therefore my heart is glad, and my whole being rejoices; my flesh also dwells secure (Ps.16:8-9, ESV).

Rejoice in the Lord alway: *and* again I say, Rejoice (Ph.4:4, KJV).

271. *Repent – Repentance (See Forgiveness of Sins)*

If my people, which are called by my name, shall humble themselves, and pray, and seek my face, and turn from their wicked ways; then will I hear from heaven, and will forgive their sin, and will heal their land (2 Ch.7:14, KJV).

Let the wicked forsake his way, and the unrighteous man his thoughts: and let him return [to] the Lord, and he will have mercy upon him; and to our God, for he will abundantly pardon (Is.55:7, KJV).

Then Peter said to them, "Repent, and let every one of you be baptized in the name of Jesus Christ for the remission of sins; and you shall receive the gift of the Holy Spirit (Ac.2:38, NKJV).

He heals the brokenhearted [repentant] And binds up their wounds (Ps.147:3, NKJV).

"But if a wicked man turns away from all the sins he has committed and keeps all my decrees and does what is just and right, he will surely live; he will not die (Eze.18:21, NIV).

272. *Rescue (See Deliverance; Salvation)*

273. *Resentment (See Love for Others; Reconciliation)*

274. *Rest (See Peace)*

Come to Me, all *you* who labor and are heavy laden, and I will give you rest (Mt.11:28, NKJV).

Rest in the Lord and wait patiently for Him; Do not fret because of him who prospers in his way, Because of the man who carries out wicked schemes (Ps.37:7, NASB).

For God alone my soul waits in silence; from him comes my salvation. He only is my rock and my salvation, my fortress; I shall not be greatly shaken (Ps.62:1-2, ESV).

275. *Resurrection, Believer's*

Jesus said to her, "I am the resurrection and the life. He who believes in Me, though he may die, he shall live (Jn.11:25, NKJV).

In a moment, in the twinkling of an eye, at the last trump: for the trumpet shall sound, and the dead shall be raised incorruptible, and we shall be changed (1 Co. 15:52, KJV).

For the Lord Himself will descend from heaven with a shout, with the voice of an archangel, and with the trumpet of God. And the dead in Christ will rise first. Then we who are alive *and* remain shall be caught up together with them in the clouds to meet the Lord in the air. And thus we shall always be with the Lord (1 Th.4:16-17, NKJV).

276. *Return, Christ's* *(See Resurrection, Believer's)*

In My Father's house are many mansions; if *it were* not *so,* I would have told you. I go to prepare a place for you. And if I go and prepare a place for you, I will come again and receive you to Myself; that where I am, *there* you may be also (Jn.14:2-3, NKJV).

And while they looked steadfastly toward heaven as He went up, behold, two men stood by them in white apparel, who also said, "Men of Galilee, why do you stand gazing up into heaven? This *same* Jesus, who was taken up from you into heaven, will so come in like manner as you saw Him go into heaven" (Ac.1:10-11, NKJV).

You also must be ready, for the Son of Man is coming at an hour you do not expect" (Lu.12:40, ESV).

Teaching us that, denying ungodliness and worldly lusts, we should live soberly, righteously, and godly, in this present world; Looking for that blessed hope, and the glorious appearing of the great God and our Saviour Jesus Christ (Tit.2:12-13, KJV).

For the Lord Himself will descend from heaven with a shout, with the voice of an archangel, and with the trumpet of God. And the dead in Christ will rise first. Then we who are alive *and* remain shall be caught up together with them in the clouds to meet the Lord in the air. And thus we shall always be with the Lord (1 Th.4:16-17, NKJV).

"Behold, I am coming soon! My reward is with me, and I will give to everyone according to what he has done (Re.22:12, NIV).

277. *Reunion with Loved Ones* *(See Resurrection, Believer's)*

Then we which are alive *and* remain shall be caught up together with them in the clouds, to meet the Lord in the air: and so shall we ever be with the Lord (1 Th.4:17, KJV).

But why should I fast when he is dead? Can I bring him back again? I will go to him one day, but he cannot return to me" (2 Sa.12:23, NLT).

278. *Reverence, for God* *(See Fear of God)*

279. *Reward*

If anyone's work which he has built on [Christ] endures, he will receive a reward. If anyone's work is burned, he will suffer loss; but he himself will be saved, yet so as through fire (1 Co.3:14-15, NKJV).

Therefore, my beloved brethren, be steadfast, immovable, always abounding in the work of the Lord, knowing that your labor is not in vain in the Lord (1 Co.15:58, NKJV).

For we must all appear before the judgment seat of Christ, that each one may receive what is due him for the things done while in the body, whether good or bad (2 Co.5:10, NIV).

"Behold, I am coming soon! My reward is with me, and I will give to everyone according to what he has done (Re.22:12, NIV).

280. *Righteousness*

Blessed are those who hunger and thirst for righteousness, for they will be filled (Mt.5:6, NIV).

"But seek first His kingdom and His righteousness, and all these things will be added to you (Mt.6:33, NASB).

For the eyes of the Lord *are* over the righteous, and his ears *are open* unto their prayers: but the face of the Lord *is* against them that do evil (1 Pe.3:12, KJV).

Tell the righteous that it shall be well with them, for they shall eat the fruit of their deeds (Is.3:10, ESV; see Ps.5:12).

The fruit of righteousness will be peace; the effect of righteousness will be quietness and confidence forever (Is.32:17, NIV).

281. *Sad – Sadness* *(See Happiness; Hope; Joy; Praise; Sorrow)*

282. *Safety* *(See Protection; Security)*

283. *Salvation* *(See Deliverance; Nature, Believer's New)*

So they said, "Believe on the Lord Jesus Christ, and you will be saved, you and your household" (Ac.16:31, NKJV).

For "WHOEVER WILL CALL ON THE NAME OF THE LORD WILL BE SAVED" (Ro.10:13, NASB).

For this [a quiet and peaceable life] *is* good and acceptable in the sight of God our Saviour; Who will have all men to be saved, and to come unto the knowledge of the truth (1 Ti.2:3-4, KJV).

Not by works of righteousness which we have done, but according to his mercy he saved us, by the washing of regeneration [the new birth], and renewing of the Holy Ghost; Which he shed on us abundantly through Jesus Christ our Saviour (Tit.3:5-6, KJV).

For the Son of man is come to seek and to save that which was lost (Lu.19:10, KJV).

For God so loved the world, that he gave his only begotten Son, that whosoever [believes] in him should not perish, but have everlasting life (Jn.3:16, KJV).

For by grace are ye saved through faith; and that not of yourselves: *it is* the gift of God: Not of works, lest any man should boast (Ep.2:8-9, KJV).

That if you confess with your mouth the Lord Jesus and believe in your heart that God has raised Him from the dead, you will be saved (Ro.10:9, NKJV).

Whoever believes and is baptized will be saved, but whoever does not believe will be condemned (Mk.16:16, ESV).

284. *Sanctification* ***(See Holiness)***

285. *Satisfaction* ***(See Joy; Contentment; Life, Abundant; Purpose of Life)***

"Blessed are those who hunger and thirst for righteousness, for they shall be satisfied (Mt.5:6, ESV).

For He satisfies the longing soul, And fills the hungry soul with goodness (Ps.107:9, NKJV).

My people shall be satisfied with my goodness, declares the LORD" (Je. 31:14[b], ESV).

They are abundantly satisfied with the fullness of Your house, And You give them drink from the river of Your pleasures (Ps.36:8, NKJV).

As for me, I will see Your face in righteousness; I shall be satisfied when I awake in Your likeness (Ps.17:15, NKJV).

286. *Schedule, Heavy* *(See Peace; Perseverance; Rest; Reward)*

287. *Security* *(See Assurance; Protection, God's)*

I give them eternal life, and they shall never perish; no one can snatch them out of my hand (Jn.10:28, NIV).

So we may boldly say: *"The Lord is my helper; I will not fear. What can man do to me?"* (He.13:6, NKJV).

Who are kept by the power of God through faith for salvation ready to be revealed in the last time (1 Pe.1:5, NKJV).

Cast your cares on the LORD and he will sustain you; he will never let the righteous fall (Ps.55:22, NIV).

For I am persuaded, that neither death, nor life, nor angels, nor principalities, nor powers, nor things present, nor things to come, Nor height, nor depth, nor any other creature, shall be able to separate us from the love of God, which is in Christ Jesus our Lord (Ro.8:38-39, KJV).

Now to Him who is able to keep you from stumbling, And to present *you* faultless Before the presence of His glory with exceeding joy, To God our Savior, Who alone is wise, *Be* glory and majesty, Dominion and power, Both now and forever. Amen (Jude 24-25, NKJV).

288. *Seduction* *(See Immorality; Temptation; Victory)*

289. *Seek – Seeking God*

"Seek the LORD while he may be found; call upon him while he is near; let the wicked forsake his way, and the unrighteous man his thoughts; let him return to the LORD, that he may have compassion on him, and to our God, for he will abundantly pardon (Is.55:6-7, ESV).

You will seek me and find me, when you seek me with all your heart (Je.29:13, ESV).

But if from there you seek the LORD your God, you will find him if you look for him with all your heart and with all your soul (De.4:29, NIV; see He.11:6).

But seek first the kingdom of God and his righteousness, and all these things will be added to you (Mt.6:33, ESV).

The LORD looks down from heaven upon the children of men, To see if there are any who understand, who seek God (Ps.14:2, NKJV).

290. *Self-Centered – Self-Exaltation* *(See Pride; Self-Righteousness; Self-Sufficiency)*

291. *Self-Control (See Self-Denial)*

But the fruit of the Spirit is love, joy, peace, longsuffering, kindness, goodness, faithfulness, gentleness, self-control. Against such there is no law (Ga.5:22-23, NKJV).

For the grace of God that brings salvation has appeared to all men. It teaches us to say "No" to ungodliness and worldly passions, and to live self-controlled, upright and godly lives in this present age (Tit.2:11-12, NIV).

Therefore, preparing your minds for action, and being sober-minded, set your hope fully on the grace that will be brought to you at the revelation of Jesus Christ (1 Pe.1:13, ESV).

Be self-controlled and alert. Your enemy the devil prowls around like a roaring lion looking for someone to devour (1 Pe.5:8, NIV).

292. *Self-Denial (See Self-Control)*

And He was saying to *them* all, "If anyone wishes to come after Me, he must deny himself, and take up his cross daily and follow Me (Lu.9:23, NASB).

Therefore, brothers, we have an obligation—but it is not to the sinful nature, to live according to it. For if you live according to the sinful nature, you will die; but if by the Spirit you put to death the misdeeds of the body, you will live (Ro.8:12-13, NIV).

I have been crucified with Christ and I no longer live, but Christ lives in me. The life I live in the body, I live by faith in the Son of God, who loved me and gave himself for me (Ga.2:20, NIV).

And those *who are* Christ's have crucified the flesh with its passions and desires (Ga.5:24, NKJV).

293. *Self-Esteem (See Self-Worth)*

294. *Self, New (See Nature, Believer's New)*

295. *Self, Old (See Nature, Believer's New)*

296. *Self-Righteousness*

He also told this parable to some who trusted in themselves that they were righteous, and treated others with contempt: "Two men went up into the temple to pray, one a Pharisee and the other a tax collector. The Pharisee, standing by himself, prayed thus: 'God, I thank you that I am not like other men, extortioners, unjust, adulterers, or even like this tax collector. I fast twice a

week; I give tithes of all that I get.' But the tax collector, standing far off, would not even lift up his eyes to heaven, but beat his breast, saying, 'God, be merciful to me, a sinner!' I tell you, this man went down to his house justified, rather than the other. For everyone who exalts himself will be humbled, but the one who humbles himself will be exalted" (Lu.18:9-14, ESV; see Lu.16:15; 2 Co.10:17-18).

Most men will proclaim...his own goodness: but a faithful man who can find? (Pr.20:6, KJV).

There are those who are clean in their own eyes but are not washed of their filth (Pr.30:12, ESV).

You say, 'I am innocent; surely his anger has turned from me.' Behold, I will bring you to judgment for saying, 'I have not sinned' (Je.2:35, ESV).

All the ways of a man *are* clean in his own eyes; but the LORD [weighs] the spirits (Pr.16:2, KJV).

Every way of a man *is* right in his own eyes: but the LORD [examines] the hearts (Pr.21:2, KJV; see Ga.6:3; Jb.33:8-9).

For if a man think himself to be something, when he is nothing, he [deceives] himself (Ga.6:3, KJV).

But we are all like an unclean *thing,* And all our righteousnesses *are* like filthy rags; We all fade as a leaf, And our iniquities, like the wind, Have taken us away (Is.64:6, NKJV).

297. *Self-Sufficiency*

You have plowed iniquity; you have reaped injustice; you have eaten the fruit of lies. Because you have trusted in your own way and in the multitude of your warriors (Ho.10:13, ESV).

He who trusts in himself is a fool, but he who walks in wisdom is kept safe (Pr.28:26, NIV).

Therefore let anyone who thinks that he stands take heed lest he fall (1 Co.10:12, ESV).

And whosoever shall exalt himself shall be abased; and he that shall humble himself shall be exalted (Mt.23:12, KJV).

The pride of your heart has deceived you, you who live in the clefts of the rock, in your lofty dwelling, who say in your heart, "Who will bring me down to the ground?" Though you soar aloft like the eagle, though your nest is set among the stars, from there I will bring you down, declares the LORD (Obad.3-4, ESV).

298. *Self-Worth* *(See Purpose of Life)*

Are not two sparrows sold for a penny? And not one of them will fall to the ground apart from your Father. But

even the hairs of your head are all numbered. Fear not, therefore; you are of more value than many sparrows (Mt.10:29-31, ESV).

You shall love your neighbor as yourself (Mt.22:39b, ESV).

Know that the LORD, he is God! It is he who made us, and we are his; we are his people, and the sheep of his pasture (Ps.100:3, ESV).

299. *Selfishness (See Giving; Service)*

300. *Separation, Spiritual (See Holiness)*

"Therefore come out from them and be separate, says the Lord. Touch no unclean thing, and I will receive you." "I will be a Father to you, and you will be my sons and daughters, says the Lord Almighty" (2 Co.6:17-18, NIV).

And do not be conformed to this world, but be transformed by the renewing of your mind, that you may prove what *is* that good and acceptable and perfect will of God (Ro.12:2, NKJV).

301. *Service – Serving Others*

But whoever has this world's goods, and sees his brother in need, and shuts up his heart from him, how does the love of God abide in him? My little children, let us not love in word or in tongue, but in deed and in truth (1 Jn.3:17-18, NKJV).

Jesus replied, "A man was going down from Jerusalem to Jericho, and he fell among robbers, who stripped him and beat him and departed, leaving him half dead. Now by chance a priest was going down that road, and when he saw him he passed by on the other side. So likewise a Levite, when he came to the place and saw him, passed by on the other side. But a Samaritan, as he journeyed, came to where he was, and when he saw him, he had compassion. He went to him and bound up his wounds, pouring on oil and wine. Then he set him on his own animal and brought him to an inn and took care of him (Lu.10:30-34, ESV).

"No, this is the kind of fasting I want: Free those who are wrongly imprisoned; lighten the burden of those who work for you. Let the oppressed go free, and remove the chains that bind people. Share your food with the hungry, and give shelter to the homeless. Give clothes to those who need them, and do not hide from relatives who need your help (Is.58:6-7, NLT).

In all things I have shown you that by working hard in this way we must help the weak and remember the words

of the Lord Jesus, how he himself said, 'It is more blessed to give than to receive'" (Ac.20:35, ESV).

We then that are strong ought to bear the infirmities of the weak, and not to please ourselves (Ro.15:1, KJV; see Ro.12:20).

Bear one another's burdens, and so fulfill the law of Christ (Ga.6:2, ESV).

Remember those in prison as if you were their fellow prisoners, and those who are mistreated as if you yourselves were suffering (He.13:3, NIV).

Pure religion and undefiled before God and the Father is this, To visit the fatherless and widows in their affliction, *and* to keep [oneself] unspotted from the world (Jas.1:27, KJV).

For I was hungry and you gave me something to eat, I was thirsty and you gave me something to drink, I was a stranger and you invited me in, I needed clothes and you clothed me, I was sick and you looked after me, I was in prison and you came to visit me.' "Then the righteous will answer him, 'Lord, when did we see you hungry and feed you, or thirsty and give you something to drink?... "The King will reply, 'I tell you the truth, whatever you did for one of the least of these brothers of mine, you did for me' (Mt.25:35-37, 40, NIV).

302. *Sex (See Forgiveness of Sins; Immorality; Marriage)*

303. *Shame (See Guilt; Forgiveness)*

For the Scripture says, "Everyone who believes in him will not be put to shame" (Ro.10:11, ESV).

May I be blameless in keeping your decrees; then I will never be ashamed (Ps.119:80, NLT).

For this reason I also suffer these things; nevertheless I am not ashamed, for I know whom I have believed and am persuaded that He is able to keep what I have committed to Him until that Day (2 Ti.1:12, NKJV).

304. *Sickness (See Healing; Help, God, My)*

305. *Sin*

For all have sinned, and come short of the glory of God (Ro.3:23, KJV).

Therefore, to him who knows to do good and does not do *it,* to him it is sin (Jas.4:17, NKJV).

Whoever commits sin also commits lawlessness, and sin is lawlessness (1 Jn.3:4, NKJV).

Therefore, just as sin came into the world through one man, and death through sin, and so death spread to all men because all sinned—(Ro.5:12, ESV).

306. *Sin, Ransomed from (See Redemption)*

The next day John saw Jesus coming toward him and said, "Look, the Lamb of God, who takes away the sin of the world! (Jn.1:29, NIV).

Here is a trustworthy saying that deserves full acceptance: Christ Jesus came into the world to save sinners—of whom I am the worst (1 Ti.1:15, NIV).

307. *Sinful Nature (See Nature, Believer's New)*

308. *Slander (See Speech—Tongue)*

309. *Sleep/Sleeplessness (See Thoughts, Control of)*

In peace I will lie down and sleep, for you alone, O LORD, will keep me safe (Ps.4:8, NLT).

My son, let them not depart from your eyes—Keep sound wisdom and discretion.... When you lie down, you will not be afraid; Yes, you will lie down and your sleep will be sweet (Pr.3:21, 24, NKJV).

310. *Sorrow (See Depression; Helper, God My; Hope)*

Blessed *are* they that mourn: for they shall be comforted (Mt.5:4, KJV).

In the same way the Spirit also helps our weakness; for we do not know how to pray as we should, but the Spirit Himself intercedes for *us* with groanings too deep for words; and He who searches the hearts knows what the mind of the Spirit is, because He intercedes for the saints according to *the will of* God. And we know that God causes all things to work together for good to those who love God, to those who are called according to *His* purpose (Ro.8:26-28, NASB).

But we do not want you to be uninformed, brethren, about those who are asleep, so that you will not grieve as do the rest who have no hope. For if we believe that Jesus died and rose again, even so God will bring with Him those who have fallen asleep in Jesus. For this we say to you by the word of the Lord, that we who are alive and remain until the coming of the Lord, will not precede those who have fallen asleep. For the Lord Himself will descend from heaven with a shout, with the voice of *the* archangel and with the trumpet of God, and the dead in

Christ will rise first. Then we who are alive and remain will be caught up together with them in the clouds to meet the Lord in the air, and so we shall always be with the Lord. Therefore comfort one another with these words (1 Th.4:13-18, NASB).

And God will wipe away every tear from their eyes; there shall be no more death, nor sorrow, nor crying. There shall be no more pain, for the former things have passed away" (Re. 21:4, NKJV).

They that sow in tears shall reap in joy (Ps.126:5, KJV).

311. *Sowing and Reaping*

Even as I have seen, they that plow iniquity, and sow wickedness, reap the same (Jb.4:8, KJV).

Do not be deceived: God is not mocked, for whatever one sows, that will he also reap. For the one who sows to his own flesh will from the flesh reap corruption, but the one who sows to the Spirit will from the Spirit reap eternal life (Ga.6:7-8, ESV).

312. *Sovereignty, God's (See Providence, God's; Purpose of Life)*

Daniel answered and said: "Blessed be the name of God forever and ever, to whom belong wisdom and might. He changes times and seasons; he removes kings and sets up kings; he gives wisdom to the wise and knowledge to those who have understanding (Da.2:20-21, ESV).

His dominion is an everlasting dominion, and his kingdom endures from generation to generation; all the inhabitants of the earth are accounted as nothing, and he does according to his will among the host of heaven and among the inhabitants of the earth; and none can stay his hand or say to him, "What have you done?" (Da.4:34b-35, ESV).

Know therefore today, and lay it to your heart, that the LORD is God in heaven above and on the earth beneath; there is no other (De.4:39, ESV).

Both riches and honor come from you, and you rule over all. In your hand are power and might, and in your hand it is to make great and to give strength to all (1 Chr.29:12. ESV).

Whatever the LORD pleases, he does, in heaven and on earth, in the seas and all deeps (Ps.135:6, ESV).

Now unto the King eternal, immortal, invisible, the only wise God, *be* honour and glory for ever and ever. Amen (1 Ti.1:17, KJV).

313. *Speech* *(See Honesty; Lying; Profanity; Truthfulness)*

But speaking the truth in love, we are to grow up in all *aspects* into Him who is the head, *even* Christ (Ep.4:15, NASB).

Do not let any unwholesome talk come out of your mouths, but only what is helpful for building others up according to their needs, that it may benefit those who listen (Ep.4:29, NIV).

Remind them of these things, and charge them before God not to quarrel about words, which does no good, but only ruins the hearers (2 Ti.2:14, ESV).

For *"He who would love life And see good days, Let him refrain his tongue from evil, And his lips from speaking deceit* (1 Pe.3:10, NKJV).

A gentle answer turns away wrath, But a harsh word stirs up anger (Pr.15:1, NASB).

He who guards his mouth and his tongue, Guards his soul from troubles (Pr.21:23, NASB).

314. *Stability* *(See Power; Strength)*

I have set the LORD continually before me; Because He is at my right hand, I will not be shaken (Ps.16:8, NASB; see Ps.28:7).

Fear not, for I am with you; be not dismayed, for I am your God; I will strengthen you, I will help you, I will uphold you with my righteous right hand (Is.41:10, ESV).

Whoever walks in integrity walks securely, but he who makes his ways crooked will be found out (Pr.10:9, ESV).

The steps of a man are established by the LORD, And He delights in his way. When he falls, he will not be hurled headlong, Because the LORD is the One who holds his hand (Ps.37:23-24, NASB).

To him who is able to keep you from falling and to present you before his glorious presence without fault and with great joy—to the only God our Savior be glory, majesty, power and authority, through Jesus Christ our Lord, before all ages, now and forevermore! Amen (Jude 1:24-25, NIV).

315. *Steadfast* *(See Perseverance)*

316. *Stealing* *(See Repentance; Work)*

"You shall not steal (Ex.20:15, NASB).

And not to steal from them, but to show that they can be fully trusted, so that in every way they will make the teaching about God our Savior attractive (Tit.2:10, NIV).

317. *Strength (See Power; Stability)*

But those who wait on the LORD Shall renew *their* strength; They shall mount up with wings like eagles, They shall run and not be weary, They shall walk and not faint (Is.40:31, NKJV).

Seek the LORD and his strength, seek his face continually (1 Chr.16:11, KJV).

And He said to me, "My grace is sufficient for you, for My strength is made perfect in weakness." Therefore most gladly I will rather boast in my infirmities, that the power of Christ may rest upon me (2 Co.12:9, NKJV).

I can do all things through Christ who strengthens me (Ph.4:13, NKJV).

Fear not, for I am with you; be not dismayed, for I am your God; I will strengthen you, I will help you, I will uphold you with my righteous right hand (Is.41:10, ESV).

318. *Stress (See Worry)*

319. *Strife (See Love for Others; Reconciliation; Unity)*

It is an honor for a man to keep aloof from strife, but every fool will be quarreling (Pr.20:3, ESV).

Iron sharpens iron, and one man sharpens another (Pr.27:17, ESV).

Do nothing from rivalry or conceit, but in humility count others more significant than yourselves (Ph.2:3, ESV).

320. *Stumbling (See Protection; Stability; Strength)*

321. *Substance Abuse (See Addiction; Deliverance; Helper, God My; Power)*

322. *Success (See Achievement; Blessings; Prosperity; Work)*

323. *Suffering (See Healing; Helper, God My; Hope; Power)*

I consider that our present sufferings are not worth comparing with the glory that will be revealed in us (Ro.8:18, NIV).

After you have suffered for a little while, the God of all grace, who called you to His eternal glory in Christ, will Himself perfect, confirm, strengthen *and* establish you (1 Pe.5:10, NASB).

So then, those who suffer according to God's will should commit themselves to their faithful Creator and continue to do good (1 Pe.4:19, NIV).

For he has not despised or disdained the suffering of the afflicted one; he has not hidden his face from him but has listened to his cry for help (Ps.22:24, NIV).

For our light and momentary troubles are achieving for us an eternal glory that far outweighs them all (2 Co.4:17, NIV).

324. *Temperance* *(See Addiction; Self-Control)*

325. *Temptation* *(See Victory)*

No temptation has overtaken you but such as is common to man; and God is faithful, who will not allow you to be tempted beyond what you are able, but with the temptation will provide the way of escape also, so that you will be able to endure it (1 Co.10:13, NASB).

For because he himself has suffered when tempted, he is able to help those who are being tempted (He.2:18, ESV).

My son, if sinners entice you, do not consent (Pr.1:10, ESV).

Submit yourselves therefore to God. Resist the devil, and he will flee from you (Jas.4:7, KJV).

For we do not have a High Priest who cannot sympathize with our weaknesses, but was in all *points* tempted as *we are, yet* without sin. Let us therefore come boldly to the throne of grace, that we may obtain mercy and find grace to help in time of need (He.4:15-16, NKJV).

So then, those who suffer according to God's will should commit themselves to their faithful Creator and continue to do good (1 Pe.4:19, NIV).

Blessed is a man who perseveres under trial [temptation]; for once he has been approved, he will receive the crown of life which *the Lord* has promised to those who love Him. Let no one say when he is tempted, "I am being tempted by God"; for God cannot be tempted by evil, and He Himself does not tempt anyone. But each one is tempted when he is carried away and enticed by his own lust (Jas.1:12-14, NASB).

326. *Tension* *(See Worry)*

327. *Thanksgiving, Spirit of* *(See Praise)*

Therefore, since we are receiving a kingdom that cannot be shaken, let us be thankful, and so worship God acceptably with reverence and awe (He.12:28, NIV).

Giving thanks always for all things to God the Father in the name of our Lord Jesus Christ (Ep.5:20, NKJV).

In everything give thanks; for this is the will of God in Christ Jesus for you (1 Th.5:18, NKJV).

Let them give thanks to the LORD for his unfailing love and his wonderful deeds for men, for he satisfies the thirsty and fills the hungry with good things (Ps.107:8-9, NIV).

328. *Thoughts, Control of* *(See Meditation)*

I rise before dawn and cry for help; I have put my hope in your word. My eyes stay open through the watches of the night, that I may meditate on your promises (Ps.119:147-148, NIV).

So letting your sinful nature control your mind leads to death. But letting the Spirit control your mind leads to life and peace (Ro.8:6, NLT).

Finally, brothers, whatever is true, whatever is honorable, whatever is just, whatever is pure, whatever is lovely, whatever is commendable, if there is any excellence, if there is anything worthy of praise, think about these things (Ph.4:8, ESV).

You will keep *him* in perfect peace, *Whose* mind *is* stayed *on You,* Because he trusts in You (Is.26:3, NKJV).

We demolish arguments and every pretension that sets itself up against the knowledge of God, and we take captive every thought to make it obedient to Christ (2 Co.10:5, NIV).

329. *Tired—Weary* *(See Strength)*

He gives strength to the weary and increases the power of the weak (Is.40:29, NIV).

And let us not grow weary while doing good, for in due season we shall reap if we do not lose heart (Ga.6:9, NKJV).

330. *Tithe—Tithing* *(See Giving)*

331. *Tongue* *(See Speech)*

332. *Trials* (See Helper, God My; Trouble; Victory)

My brethren, count it all joy when you fall into various trials, knowing that the testing of your faith produces patience [endurance] (Jas.1:2-3, NKJV).

Blessed is the man who remains steadfast under trial, for when he has stood the test he will receive the crown of life, which God has promised to those who love him (Jas.1:12, ESV).

333. *Triumph* (See Victory)

334. *Trouble – Troubles* (See Helper, God My; Victory)

The righteous cry out, and the Lord hears, And delivers them out of all their troubles (Ps.34:17, NKJV).

My brethren, count it all joy when you fall into various trials, knowing that the testing of your faith produces patience (Jas.1:2-3, NKJV).

"From six troubles He will deliver you, Even in seven evil will not touch you (Jb.5:19, NASB).

When you pass through the waters, I *will be* with you; And through the rivers, they shall not overflow you. When you walk through the fire, you shall not be burned, Nor shall the flame scorch you (Is.43:2, NKJV).

335. *Trust* (See Confidence; Faith; Hope)

You keep him in perfect peace whose mind is stayed on you, because he trusts in you. Trust in the LORD forever, for the LORD GOD is an everlasting rock (Is.26:3-4, ESV).

For thus the LORD GOD, the Holy One of Israel, has said, "In repentance and rest you will be saved, In quietness and trust is your strength." But you were not willing (Is.30:15, NASB).

"Blessed is the man who trusts in the LORD And whose trust is the LORD. "For he will be like a tree planted by the water, That extends its roots by a stream And will not fear when the heat comes; But its leaves will be green, And it will not be anxious in a year of drought Nor cease to yield fruit (Je.17:7-8, NASB).

Trust in the LORD with all your heart, And lean not on your own understanding; In all your ways acknowledge Him, And He shall direct your paths (Pr.3:5-6, NKJV).

Trust in the LORD and do good; Dwell in the land and cultivate faithfulness. Delight yourself in the LORD; And He will give you the desires of your heart. Commit your way to the LORD, Trust also in Him, and He will do it (Ps.37:3-5, NASB).

336. *Truth*

The Lord is near to all who call on him, to all who call on him in truth (Ps.145:18, ESV).

Jesus said to him, "I am the way, and the truth, and the life. No one comes to the Father except through me (Jn.14:6, ESV; see Pr.16:13).

Buy truth, and do not sell it; buy wisdom, instruction, and understanding (Pr.23:23, ESV).

337. *Truthfulness (See Honesty; Integrity; Lying; Speech)*

But speaking the truth in love, we are to grow up in all *aspects* into Him who is the head, *even* Christ (Ep.4:15, NASB).

Therefore, putting away lying, *"Let each one of you speak truth with his neighbor,"* for we are members of one another (Ep.4:25, NKJV).

Truthful lips will be established forever, But a lying tongue is only for a moment (Pr.12:19, NASB).

338. *Unbelief (See Believe; Faith; Trust; Victory)*

339. *Unemployed (See Confidence; Helper, God My; Hope; Provision of Life's Necessities; Worry)*

340. *Unfaithful – Unfaithfulness (See Faithfulness, Believers; Perseverance)*

341. *Unhappy – Unhappiness (See Happiness; Hope; Joy; Praise)*

342. *Unity (See Reconciliation)*

Do nothing from rivalry or conceit, but in humility count others more significant than yourselves. Let each of you look not only to his own interests, but also to the interests of others (Ph.2:3-4, ESV).

Behold, how good and how pleasant it is For brothers to dwell together in unity! (Ps.133:1, NASB).

Only let your conduct be worthy of the gospel of Christ, so that whether I come and see you or am absent, I may hear of your affairs, that you stand fast in one spirit, with one mind striving together for the faith of the gospel (Ph.1:27, NKJV).

Finally, all of you, have unity of mind, sympathy, brotherly love, a tender heart, and a humble mind. Do not repay evil for evil or reviling for reviling, but on the contrary, bless, for to this you were called, that you may obtain a blessing (1 Pe.3:8-9, ESV).

I therefore, a prisoner for the Lord, urge you to walk in a manner worthy of the calling to which you have been called, with all humility and gentleness, with patience, bearing with one another in love, eager to maintain the unity of the Spirit in the bond of peace (Ep.4:1-3, ESV).

Finally, brothers, rejoice. Aim for restoration, comfort one another, agree with one another, live in peace; and the God of love and peace will be with you (2 Co. 13:11, ESV).

I appeal to you, brothers, in the name of our Lord Jesus Christ, that all of you agree with one another so that there may be no divisions among you and that you may be perfectly united in mind and thought (1 Co.1:10, NIV).

343. *Upset (See Helper, God My; Hope; Worry)*

344. *Useless – Uselessness (See Life, Abundant; Purpose of Life; Satisfaction; Will of God, Finding)*

345. *Victory*

"I have told you these things, so that in me you may have peace. In this world you will have trouble. But take heart! I have overcome the world" (Jn.16:33, NIV).

But thanks *be* to God, who gives us the victory through our Lord Jesus Christ (1 Co.15:57, NKJV).

For everyone who has been born of God overcomes the world. And this is the victory that has overcome the world— our faith. Who is it that overcomes the world except the one who believes that Jesus is the Son of God? (1 Jn.5:4-5, ESV).

There is no wisdom, no insight, no plan that can succeed against the LORD. The horse is made ready for the day of battle, but victory rests with the LORD (Pr.21:30-31, NIV).

But thanks be to God, who always leads us in triumphal procession in Christ and through us spreads everywhere the fragrance of the knowledge of him (2 Co.2:14, NIV).

Through you we push down our foes; through your name we tread down those who rise up against us (Ps.44:5, ESV).

Who shall separate us from the love of Christ? *shall* tribulation, or distress, or persecution, or famine, or nakedness, or peril, or sword?...Nay, in all these things we are more than conquerors through him that loved us. For

I am persuaded, that neither death, nor life, nor angels, nor principalities, nor powers, nor things present, nor things to come (Ro.8:35, 37-38, KJV).

Finally, be strong in the Lord and in the strength of his might. Put on the whole armor of God, that you may be able to stand against the schemes of the devil. For we do not wrestle against flesh and blood, but against the rulers, against the authorities, against the cosmic powers over this present darkness, against the spiritual forces of evil in the heavenly places. Therefore take up the whole armor of God, that you may be able to withstand in the evil day, and having done all, to stand firm (Ep.6:10-13, ESV).

346. *Wandering Away* *(See Backsliding; Protection, God's; Security)*

347. *Weakness* *(See Power; Strength)*

In the same way the Spirit also helps our weakness; for we do not know how to pray as we should, but the Spirit Himself intercedes for *us* with groanings too deep for words; and He who searches the hearts knows what the mind of the Spirit is, because He intercedes for the saints according to *the will of* God (Ro.8:26-27, NASB).

Each time he said, "My grace is all you need. My power works best in weakness." So now I am glad to boast about my weaknesses, so that the power of Christ can work through me. That's why I take pleasure in my weaknesses, and in the insults, hardships, persecutions, and troubles that I suffer for Christ. For when I am weak, then I am strong (2 Co.12:9-10, NLT).

348. *Weary* *(See Tired—Weary)*

349. *Widow—Widowers* *(See Comfort; Helper, God My)*

The blessing of him that was ready to perish came upon me: and I caused the widow's heart to sing for joy (Jb.29:13, KJV).

He executes justice for the fatherless and the widow, and loves the sojourner, giving him food and clothing (De.10:18, ESV).

But I will protect the orphans who remain among you. Your widows, too, can depend on me for help" (Je.49:11, NLT; see Ps.146:9).

350. *Will of God*

The world and its desires pass away, but the man who does the will of God lives forever (1 Jn.2:17, NIV).

And do not be conformed to this world, but be transformed by the renewing of your mind, so that you may prove what the will of God is, that which is good and acceptable and perfect (Ro.12:2, NASB).

For this is the will of God, your sanctification: that you abstain from sexual immorality; that each one of you know how to control his own body in holiness and honor (1 Th.4:3-4, ESV).

351. *Will of God, Finding (See Guidance; Perseverance; Purpose of Life; Service)*

If any of you lacks wisdom, he should ask God, who gives generously to all without finding fault, and it will be given to him (Jas.1:5, NIV).

"This book of the law shall not depart from your mouth, but you shall meditate on it day and night, so that you may be careful to do according to all that is written in it; for then you will make your way prosperous, and then you will have success (Jos.1:8, NASB).

Your word is a lamp to my feet and a light to my path (Ps.119:105, ESV).

Trust in the LORD with all your heart, And lean not on your own understanding; In all your ways acknowledge Him, And He shall direct your paths (Pr.3:5-6, NKJV).

When the Spirit of truth comes, he will guide you into all truth. He will not speak on his own but will tell you what he has heard. He will tell you about the future (Jn.16:13, NLT).

352. *Wisdom (See Discernment)*

If any of you lacks wisdom, he should ask God, who gives generously to all without finding fault, and it will be given to him (Jas.1:5, NIV).

But the wisdom that comes from heaven is first of all pure; then peace-loving, considerate, submissive, full of mercy and good fruit, impartial and sincere (Jas.3:17, NIV).

The fear of the LORD is the beginning of wisdom; all those who practice it have a good understanding. His praise endures forever! (Ps.111:10, ESV).

353. *Witnessing*

Therefore go and make disciples of all nations, baptizing them in the name of the Father and of the Son and of the Holy Spirit, and teaching them to obey everything I have commanded you. And surely I am with you always, to the very end of the age" (Mt.28:19-20, NIV).

But you shall receive power when the Holy Spirit has come upon you; and you shall be witnesses to Me in Jerusalem, and in all Judea and Samaria, and to the end of the earth" (Ac.1:8, NKJV).

You have heard me teach things that have been confirmed by many reliable witnesses. Now teach these truths to other trustworthy people who will be able to pass them on to others (2 Ti.2:2, NLT).

But in your hearts set apart Christ as Lord. Always be prepared to give an answer to everyone who asks you to give the reason for the hope that you have. But do this with gentleness and respect (1 Pe.3:15, NIV).

Him we preach, warning every man and teaching every man in all wisdom, that we may present every man perfect in Christ Jesus (Col.1:28, NKJV).

And this gospel of the kingdom will be preached in all the world as a witness to all the nations, and then the end will come (Mt.24:14, NKJV).

Those who sow in tears shall reap with shouts of joy! He who goes out weeping, bearing the seed for sowing, shall come home with shouts of joy, bringing his sheaves with him (Ps.126:5-6, ESV).

354. *Word of God*

But He answered and said, "It is written, *'Man shall not live by bread alone, but by every word that proceeds from the mouth of God.'* " (Mt.4:4, NKJV).

For whatever things were written before were written for our learning, that we through the patience and comfort of the Scriptures might have hope (Ro.15:4, NKJV).

Do your best to present yourself to God as one approved, a worker who has no need to be ashamed, rightly handling the word of truth (2 Ti.2:15, ESV).

I have stored up your word in my heart, that I might not sin against you (Ps.119:11, ESV).

Your word is a lamp to my feet and a light to my path (Ps.119:105 ESV).

All Scripture *is* given by inspiration of God, and *is* profitable for doctrine, for reproof, for correction, for instruction in righteousness, that the man of God may be

complete, thoroughly equipped for every good work (2 Ti.3:16-17, NKJV).

The grass withers, the flower fades, But the word of our God stands forever (Is.40:8, NASB).

355. *Work* *(See Diligence; Lazy)*

Let him who stole steal no longer, but rather let him labor, working with *his* hands what is good, that he may have something to give him who has need (Ep.4:28, NKJV).

That you also aspire to lead a quiet life, to mind your own business, and to work with your own hands, as we commanded you, that you may walk properly toward those who are outside [the body of believers], and *that* you may lack nothing (1 Th.4:11-12, NKJV).

Whatever you do, work at it with all your heart, as working for the Lord, not for men, since you know that you will receive an inheritance from the Lord as a reward. It is the Lord Christ you are serving (Col.3:23-24, NIV).

Therefore, my beloved brethren, be steadfast, immovable, always abounding in the work of the Lord, knowing that your labor is not in vain in the Lord (1 Co.15:58, NKJV).

Slaves, in all things obey those who are your masters on earth, not with external service, as those who *merely* please men, but with sincerity of heart, fearing the Lord (Col.3:22, NASB).

Masters, treat your slaves justly and fairly, knowing that you also have a Master in heaven (Col.4:1, ESV).

For even when we were with you, we used to give you this order: if anyone is not willing to work, then he is not to eat, either. For we hear that some among you are leading an undisciplined life, doing no work at all, but acting like busybodies. Now such persons we command and exhort in the Lord Jesus Christ to work in quiet fashion and eat their own bread (2 Th.3:10-12, NASB).

356. *Worldly – Worldliness* *(See Holiness; Nature, Believer's New; Separation, Spiritual)*

357. *Worry* *(See Assurance; Confidence; Faith; Helper, God My; Peace)*

Don't worry about anything, but in everything, through prayer and petition with thanksgiving, let your requests be made known to God. And the peace of God, which surpasses every thought, will guard your hearts and your minds in Christ Jesus (Ph.4:6-7, HCSB).

"But seek first His kingdom and His righteousness, and all these things will be added to you. "So do not worry about tomorrow; for tomorrow will care for itself. Each day has enough trouble of its own (Mt.6:33-34, NASB).

You will keep *him* in perfect peace, *Whose* mind *is* stayed *on You,* Because he trusts in You (Is.26:3, NKJV).

He who dwells in the secret place of the Most High Shall abide under the shadow of the Almighty. I will say of the Lord, "*He is* my refuge and my fortress; My God, in Him I will trust" (Ps.91:1-2, NKJV).

358. *Worship, Daily* *(See Church; Meditation; Prayer)*

359. *Worthless – Worthlessness* *(See Life, Abundant; Purpose of Life; Satisfaction; Self-Worth; Will of God, Finding)*

SUBJECT INDEX

R

S

T

U

Scripture Index

Ephesians *page*

Philippians *page*

Colossians *page*

1 Thessalonians *page*

2 Thessalonians *page*

1 Timothy *page*

2 Timothy *page*

ACKNOWLEDGMENTS

Every believer is precious to the Lord and deeply loved. And every believer touches the lives of those who come in contact with him or her. The writing ministries of the following servants have touched this work, and we are grateful that God brought their writings our way. We hereby acknowledge their ministry to us, being fully aware that there are many others down through the years whose writings have touched our lives and who deserve mention, but whose names have faded from our memory. May our wonderful Lord continue to bless the ministries of these dear servants—and the ministries of us all—as we diligently seek to grow in the Lord and to reach the world for Christ.

Barclay, William. *Daily Study Bible Series.* Philadelphia, PA: Westminster Press, Began in 1953.

Cruden's Complete Concordance of the Old & New Testament. Philadelphia, PA: The John C. Winston Co., 1930.

Goodrick, Edward W. and John R. Kohlenberger, III. *The NIV Exhaustive Concordance.* Grand Rapids, MI: Zondervan Publishing House, 1990.

Greene, Oliver. *The Epistles of Paul the Apostle to Timothy & Titus.* Greenville, SC: The Gospel Hour, Inc., 1964.

Henry, Matthew. *Commentary on the Whole Bible.* Old Tappan, NJ: Fleming H. Revell Co.

New American Commentary. General Editor. E. Roy Clendenen. Nashville, TN: Broadman & Holman Publishers.

Robertson, A.T. *Word Pictures in the New Testament.* Nashville, TN: Broadman Press, 1930.

Rogers, Adrian. *Ten Secrets for a Successful Family.* Wheaton, IL: Crossway Books, 1996.

Strong, James. *Strong's Exhaustive Concordance of the Bible.* Nashville, TN: Thomas Nelson, Inc., 1990.

The Expositor's Bible Commentary. Grand Rapids, MI: Zondervan Publishing House.

The Pulpit Commentary, Edited by H.D.M. Spence & Joseph S. Exell. Grand Rapids, MI: Eerdmans Publishing Co., 1950.

Tyndale Old & New Testament Commentaries. Grand Rapids, MI, Eerdmans Publishing Co.

Wiersbe, Warren W. *Be Series.* Colorado Springs, CO: Victor Books.

PURPOSE STATEMENT

LEADERSHIP MINISTRIES WORLDWIDE

exists to equip ministers, teachers, and laymen in their understanding, preaching and teaching of God's Word by publishing and distributing worldwide *The Preacher's Outline & Sermon Bible®* and related **Outline Bible Resources**, to reach & disciple men, women, boys and girls for Jesus Christ.

MISSION STATEMENT

1. To make the Bible so understandable – its truth so clear and plain – that men and women everywhere, whether teacher or student, preacher or hearer, can grasp its message and receive Jesus Christ as Savior, and...

2. To place the Bible in the hands of all who will preach and teach God's Holy Word, verse by verse, precept by precept, regardless of the individual's ability to purchase it.

Outline Bible Resources have been given to LMW for printing and especially distribution worldwide at/below cost, by those who remain anonymous. One fact, however, is as true today as it was in the time of Christ:

THE GOSPEL IS FREE, BUT THE COST OF TAKING IT IS NOT

LMW depends on the generous gifts of believers with a heart for Him and a love for the lost. They help pay for the printing, translating, and distributing of **Outline Bible Resources** into the hands of God's servants worldwide, who will present the Gospel message with clarity, authority, and understanding beyond their own.

LMW was incorporated in the state of Tennessee in July 1992 and received IRS 501 (c)(3) nonprofit status in March 1994. LMW is an international, nondenominational mission organization. All proceeds from USA sales, along with donations from donor partners, go directly to underwrite our translation and distribution projects of **Outline Bible Resources** to preachers, church and lay leaders, and Bible students around the world.

Made in the USA
Middletown, DE
24 May 2024

54794673R00303